10.95
804

The English Elegy

THE ENGLISH ELEGY

Studies in the Genre
from Spenser to Yeats

Peter M. Sacks

The Johns Hopkins University Press
Baltimore and London

B.R. WELSHIMER MEMORIAL LIBRARY
MILLIGAN COLLEGE, TENN. 37682 /

PR
509
.E4
S23
1985

This book has been brought to publication with the
generous assistance of the Andrew W. Mellon Foundation.

© 1985 The Johns Hopkins University Press
All rights reserved
Printed in the United States of America

Originally published, 1985
Johns Hopkins Paperbacks edition, 1987

The Johns Hopkins University Press, 701 West 40th Street,
Baltimore, Maryland 21211
The Johns Hopkins Press Ltd., London

Library of Congress Cataloging-in-Publication Data

Sacks, Peter M.
  The English elegy.

  Bibliography: p.
  Includes index.
  1. Elegiac poetry, English—History and criticism.
1. Title.
PR509.E4S23   1985   821'.04'09   84-23381
ISBN 0-8018-3254-3 (alk. paper)
ISBN 0-8018-3471-6 (paperback)

For My Parents

97122

97122

Mosse le penne poi e ventilonne,
Qui *lugent* affermando esser beati,
Ch'avran di consolar l'anime donne.

. . . then moved his plumes,
And fanning us, affirmed that those, who mourn,
Are blessed, for that comfort shall be theirs.

Purgatorio XIX 49–51,
trans. Henry Francis Cary

Contents

Preface

> Where art so firmly occupies the cen-
> tre of existence as to make man one of
> its manifestations instead of recogniz-
> ing him above all as its basis . . . then
> all sane reflection is at an end.
>   Benjamin,
>   *The Origin of German Tragic Drama*

Perhaps the most striking aspect of Wordsworth's account of a poet was his insistence on the poet's "disposition to be affected more than other men by absent things as if they were present."[1] Wordsworth knew that the poetic imagination operates most powerfully within the spaces of absence or dislocation; and not surprisingly, his most emphatic claim for the substantiality of poetic language ("words, not only as symbols of the passion, but as *things*, active and efficient, which are of themselves part of the passion") was made in a note to "The Thorn," a poem in which if words become things, they do so by becoming "part of the passion" of deprivation.[2] In this poem, as often in Wordsworth's work, poetic language resembles the contradictory thorn itself, a snagging, troublesome marker that gives presence to a strongly felt absence.

Although recognition of the paradoxical "presence" in language of absent things has been renewed with unprecedented force in recent years, this renewal has been marked by a disconcerting tendency to deprive literature of much of that combination of strength and pathos so characteristically stressed by Wordsworth. For recent critics have not only undermined assumptions about the presentational powers of language, they have diminished the subjective pathos that attends those absences which the use of language may seek to redress or appease.[3]

That is to say, several current critical approaches have not only challenged the compensatory nature of literature by exposing the fabrications of its rhetoric; they have also tended to evaporate the pathos of disjunction and loss by regarding these not humanistically, in relation to language, but scientifically, as inherent features of the structure of signification itself. By *beginning* with the assumption that an essential lack is already inscribed within language, and hence within its user, this view risks abandoning a true sense of the experience of loss, or at least tends to slight the dialectical relationship between language and the grieving mind.

So, too, while it is important to examine skeptically the rhetorical construction of a "voice" or of an authorial "presence," and while it is necessary to recognize how thoroughly any self is affected or governed by language, one should beware of how easily the problem of subjectivity may be elided if its entire assimilation to the status of language is taken for granted. So thoroughly have we been told to regard the self as scarcely different from yet another textual structure that we have retained little sense either of what that "scarcely different" might mean or of the pain and resistance that go into the making of that structure.

This sketch may be a caricature; yet it delineates some features of the trend signaled by the warning quoted in the epigraph to this preface, a trend that has gathered momentum enough to lend eerie credibility to the much-echoed prophecy that man will disappear as soon as his knowledge discovers new forms of arrangement.[4] It is in response to this climate of thought that several subsidiary intentions of the following study have been formed. I am trying neither to remystify language nor to sentimentalize subjectivity, but I do hope to use this study of the elegy as a perspective from which to reexamine the connections between language and the pathos of human consciousness.

Of all genres, the elegy especially requires and provides such a perspective, for it is characterized by an unusually powerful intertwining of emotion and rhetoric, of loss and figuration. By regarding this intertwining as both an event and a structure and by asking how the figures and conventions of elegy emerge from and react upon the actual project of mourning, I shall necessarily be approaching the poem as indeed "the cry of its occasion, / Part of the res itself."[5] If this sounds naive, it should be stressed that I am trying to lend substance not so much to the figures of language as to the workings of the mind that uses them.

As we shall see, much of the elegist's task lies in his reluctant resubmission to the constraints of language. The elegy, therefore, gives us the chance to view man in tension with, rather than inertly constituted by, the language that so conditions him. Furthermore, since the elegists to be studied here actively revise the received conventions of their genre, this, too, lets us observe the vigorous interaction between the individual author and his inherited codes.

Besides asking the predominant question, How does man respond to loss and to his own mortality? I am, therefore, interested in asking the following, necessarily implicated questions. If the self may be regarded as a textual structure, how does it come to be that way? and what of its struggle within and against that condition? If in every case "a word is elegy to what it signifies," what then of an elegist's painful renegotiation with the substitutive and artificial nature of his own words?[6]

A note on procedure: After the introductory chapter, which develops an interpretive (rather than the traditionally descriptive) approach to the genre, I concentrate, as the book's subtitle suggests, on studies of individual works. It was the poems, after all—their emotional force, their beauty and complexity—that initially drew me to this investigation. My attempt is to understand and value them as fully as possible while also lending concretion and specificity to the generalized and often schematic suggestions of the introduction. The principal readings are, therefore, close, trying to appreciate both the particular and the generic nature of each work. Among these chapters, the third may appear anomalous, since it addresses revenge tragedies rather than elegies. However, the issues studied in that chapter—the relation between grief and anger, the revenger's refusal to accept the mediations of language or the law, the questions of inheritance and of a mourner's sexuality—shed light not only on the plays but on the elegy itself as a genre.

Finally, lest certain readers expect a wide survey of many elegies from each period, I should warn that what follows is not designed primarily as such a study. There is a strongly developmental dimension; and the individual works are, with some exceptions, treated in chronological order. But many elegies along the way have not been mentioned. I hope that they may be approached more satisfactorily in the light of the following studies.

Acknowledgments

A version of chapter III appeared in *ELH* 49, no. 1 (Spring, 1982), and part of chapter VI appeared in *Studies in Romanticism* 23, no. 3 (Fall, 1984). I wish to thank the editors of these journals for permission to reprint this material.

Permission to quote from the following sources is also gratefully acknowledged: Thomas Hardy, *The Collected Poems of Thomas Hardy* (New York: Macmillan, 1925); Geoffrey Hill, "In Memory of Jane Fraser," from *For the Unfallen* (London: Andre Deutsch, 1959) and "Veni Coronaberis" from *Tenebrae* (London: Andre Deutsch, 1978); and W. B. Yeats, "Tom O'Roughley" and "In Memory of Major Robert Gregory," reprinted with permission of Macmillan Publishing Company, from *The Poems of W. B. Yeats*, ed. Richard J. Finneran (New York: Macmillan, 1983) © 1919 by Macmillan Publishing Company, renewed 1947 by Bertha Georgie Yeats.

I wish to thank the following readers of early sections of this book: Margaret Ferguson, Stanley Fish, Harold Bloom, J. Hillis Miller, and Ronald Paulson. I would also like to thank Joanne Allen and Jane Warth for their editorial assistance, and Michael Moon for his help in preparing the index. Finally, my largest debt is to my wife, Barbara Kassel, for her encouragement and help during the writing of the manuscript.

I

Interpreting the Genre:
The Elegy and the
Work of Mourning

> Is the story in vain, how once, in the
> mourning for Linos, venturing earliest
> music pierced barren numbness, and
> how, in the horrified space [which] an
> almost deified youth suddenly quitted
> for ever, emptiness first felt the
> vibration that now charms us and
> comforts and helps?
>
> Rilke, *Duino Elegies*

Most studies of the elegy tend to describe rather than interpret the genre's conventions. In this introductory chapter, I attempt such an interpretation, asking how the traditional forms and figures of elegy relate to the experience of loss and the search for consolation. I wish to view this relationship between the language of elegy and the experience of loss as an event or action: rather than finding absence or loss to be somehow already "there" in the language, I am exploring how an elegist's language emerges from, and reacts upon, an originating sense of loss. Each elegy is to be regarded, therefore, as a *work*, both in the commonly accepted meaning of a product and in the more dynamic sense of the working through of an impulse or experience—the sense that underlies Freud's phrase "the work of mourning."[1]

To stress the dramatic and not just the structural relation between loss and figuration, I begin by noticing how mythopoetic accounts of the origin of certain features of poetry and music, particularly those associated with elegy, converge on the event of loss. I interpret these accounts briefly, for they have much to tell us about the elegy itself. Following this, to emphasize the ways in which the elegy should be seen as a working through of experience and as a symbolic action, I compare the genre with various nonliterary responses to loss. For the elegy, as a poem of mourning and consolation, has its roots in a dense matrix of rites and ceremonies, in the light of which many elegiac conventions should be recognized as being not only aesthetically interesting forms but also the literary versions of specific social and psychological practices.

Among the conventions to be interpreted in this way are the use of pastoral contextualization, the myth of the vegetation deity (particularly the sexual elements of such myths, and their relation to the sexuality of the mourner), the use of repetition and refrains, the reiterated questions, the outbreak of vengeful anger or cursing, the procession of mourners, the movement from grief to consolation, and the traditional images of resurrection. We also need to interpret the eclogic division within or between mourning voices, the question of contests, rewards, and inheritance, and the unusual degree of self-consciousness regarding the actual performance of the work at hand. One aspect of this last feature is the elegist's need to draw attention, consolingly, to his own surviving powers. More painful and more crucial, however, is the elegist's reluctant submission to language itself. One of the least well observed elements of the genre is this enforced accommodation between the mourning self on the one hand and the very words of grief and fictions of consolation on the other.

According to many accounts, the origins of architecture, sculpture, and even dance are essentially funerary. So, too, traditional narratives point to *loss* as the mother of the following, more specifically poetic, inventions: Orpheus's introduction of song, in mourning for the dead Linus, the blinded, love-torn Daphnis's invention of pastoral poetry; Apollo's frustrating derivation of the laurel, sign of poethood. The list could be longer, but it should at least include the invention of that most elegiac of instruments, the pipe or flute, by Pan, the patron god of pastoral and of elegy.

The term *elegy* itself derives from the Greek elegiac couplets, traditionally accompanied by the flute, or more precisely, by the oboelike doublepipe called *aulos*.[2] The elegiac verses of alternating dactylic hexameters and pentameters could contain a fairly broad range of topics, including exhortatory martial epigrams, political philosophy, commemorative lines, or amatory complaints. But behind this array of topics there may have lain an earlier, more exclusive association of the flute song's elegiacs with the expression of grief. As Margaret Alexiou has written:

> It is possible that Echembrotos, the Peloponnesian poet who was famous for his mournful *elegoi* accompanied by the *aulos*, was only one of a school of Dorian elegists, who used the form for a kind of lament; and it was this same Echembrotos whose music to the *aulos* was disqualified at the Delphic festival in 578 B.C. on the grounds that its mournful character was unsuitable. . . . Was it under some kind of pressure from the religious reforms of the sixth century that the mournful *elegos* was discontinued by the lyric poets, surviving only as a literary term?[3]

Latin adaptations of the elegiac form continued the fairly miscellaneous approach to content, but with an increasingly intense focus on the amatory complaint. Similarly, the English versions of the defining form admitted a variety of subject matter to so-called elegies. But the definition that gradually gathered currency, particularly after the sixteenth century, was that of a poem of mortal loss and consolation.[4] In this way, the genre returned to its ancient association with the flute song of grief. With Spenser, and more explicitly with Milton, we return to Echembrotos and the Dorian elegists whose *aulos* reeds precede the mournful pipe players of Theocritus and Virgil.

The *aulos* was related to the Phoenician *giggras*, flutes played at the funeral rites for Adonis, and descended from an Egyptian wind instrument associated with mourning and with its divine inventor, Osiris, god of the dead.[5] The Greeks themselves mythologized the invention of the wind instrument, clinching its association with loss and consolation in the legend of Pan and Syrinx, a legend whose particular sorrow invests the role of Pan and of pipes in pastoral and elegiac poetry as chronologically diverse as that of Theocritus, Spenser, Pope, Arnold, or Yeats. Even the contemporary poem "Syrinx," by James Merrill, continues the recognition of Pan as "the great god Pain."[6] One wonders why the legend maintains its power. The answer may be sought by reviewing the story as told by one of its most influential narrators, Ovid.

We recall the carefully contrived narrative link in the *Metamorphoses* between the Pan-Syrinx story and the analogous, earlier episode of Apollo and Daphne. After Daphne has been transformed into laurel, she is mourned and celebrated by a confluence of rivers. One river god is missing: Inachus, who is himself mourning the loss of his daughter, Io. Io, too, is bewailing her transformation into a milk-white cow guarded by Argos. To lull Argos and restore Io to herself and to her father, Mercury tells Argos various stories, including that of Pan's invention of the pipes. The reader thus comes upon this story in a complex network of metamorphoses and mournings linked back to the loss of Daphne.

The story of Apollo and Daphne itself exemplifies the dramatic relation between loss and figuration. Having insulted Cupid, Apollo is smitten with an unrequited passion for Daphne. [7] He pursues her to the riverbanks of her father, Peneus, whom she begs for deliverance. As Apollo grasps her, Daphne becomes the laurel tree—only her gleaming beauty (*nitor*) remaining unchanged. But this apparently organic metamorphosis, by which the tree substitutes for the nymph, is only part of the story. Apollo's embrace of the actual tree will not in itself give comfort, nor will it be accepted: "But even the wood shrank from his kisses" (*refugit tamen oscula lignum*) (1.556). [8]

Only when Apollo turns to the projected founding of a sign, the laurel wreath, does he appear to accept his loss, by having invented some consoling substitute for Daphne:

"... at, quoniam coniunx mea non potes esse,
arbor eris certe" dixit "mea! semper habebunt
te coma, te citharae, te nostrae, laure, pharetrae:
tu ducibus Latiis aderis, ..."

(1.557–60)

[Since thou canst not be my bride, thou shalt at least be my tree. My hair, my lyre, my quiver shall always be entwined with thee, O laurel. With thee shall Roman generals wreathe their heads, ...]

Even as he reiterates the desperate *te ... te ... te*, Apollo is having to *refer* to the nymph, or to the whole tree, by focusing on a detached part of that tree, the fragmentary sign alone which he can attach to his lyre, his quiver, or his hair, and which he already projects as a sign in the future absence of either nymph or tree. This second alteration, requiring an unnatural severing of the tree and an artificial entwining of its cut leaves, seems not only to suggest a move from organic nature to the item of an unnatural, societal code but also to enforce and confirm that Apollo's consoling sign can never enjoy a purely organic relation to the object that it signifies, or for which it substitutes.[9]

Instead of becoming the object of a sexual conquest, Daphne is thus eventually transformed into something very much like a consolation prize—a prize that becomes *the* prize and sign of poethood. What Apollo or the poet pursues turns into a sign not only of his lost love but also of his very pursuit—a consoling sign that carries in itself the reminder of the loss on which it has been founded. As a sign, the eventual relation between the wreath on the one hand and Daphne, or poethood, on the other is at once arbitrary and disjunctive. But Ovid's narrative invites us to watch the emergence of this arbitrariness and disjunctiveness as an event and to reintegrate the sign with the passionate story of its derivation. If there is a necessary distance between the wreath and what it signifies, that distance is the measure of Apollo's loss. Daphne's "turning" into a tree matches Apollo's "turning" from the object of his love to a sign of her. It is this substitutive turn or act of troping that any mourner must perform.

In view of the developing schema by which interruption and loss is followed by a figurative or aesthetic compensation, it is hard not to notice that the very *narration* of the similar Syrinx episode follows this design. Mercury's narrative actually breaks off just as Pan begins his equally interrupted plea to Syrinx. Since Argos has just fallen asleep, there is no need for Mercury to continue, and the story would be lost were its narration not displaced from the supposedly immediate teller to the explicitly mediating craftsman, Ovid. By an almost elegiac strategy, Ovid thus completes, as part of a more avowedly aesthetic object, the narrative that had been severed in the "actual" world.[10]

The Pan-Syrinx episode is similar to that of Apollo and Daphne:

. . . fugisse per avia nympham,
donec harenosi placidum Ladonis ad amnem
venerit; hic illam cursum inpedientibus undis
ut se mutarent liquidas orasse sorores,
Panaque cum prensam sibi iam Syringa putaret,
corpore pro nymphae calamos tenuisse palustres,
dumque ibi suspirat, motos in harundine ventos
effecisse sonum tenuem similemque querenti.
arte nova vocisque deum dulcedine captum
"hoc mihi concilium tecum" dixisse "manebit,"

> atque ita disparibus calamis conpagine cerae
> inter se iunctis nomen tenuisse puellae.

(1.701–12)

[. . . the nymph, spurning his prayers, fled through the pathless wastes until she came to Ladon's stream flowing peacefully along his sandy banks; how here, when the water checked her further flight, she besought her sisters of the stream to change her form; and how Pan, when now he thought he had caught Syrinx, instead of her held naught but marsh reeds in his arms; and while he sighed in disappointment, the soft air stirring in the reeds gave forth a low and complaining sound. Touched by this wonder and charmed by the sweet tones, the god exclaimed: "This union, at least, shall I have with thee." And so the pipes, made of unequal reeds fitted together by a joining of wax, took and kept the name of the maiden.]

As was true for Apollo, Pan's pursued object changes to a form in the natural world, a form that, like the laurel tree, must be further altered to yield a consoling sign or instrument. Once again, that subsequent alteration, moving from nature to artifice, requires both a cutting off and a refashioning of the cut fragment. Both episodes portray a turning away from erotic pursuits and attachments to substitutive, artificial figures of consolation. Unlike many other grievers in the *Metamomorphoses*, such as Cycnus, Pyramus and Thisbe, Egeria, Niobe, and even Orpheus—all of whom fail to invent or accept an adequate figure for what they have lost and all of whom are consequently altered or destroyed—Apollo and Pan are successful mourners. (The fact that they are, after all, gods may tell us something of Ovid's pessimism regarding the difficulty of their task.) For unlike the others, they accept their loss and can retain their identities by what we may call a healthy work of mourning, a work that, as Freud points out, requires a withdrawal of affection from the lost object and a subsequent reattachment of affection to some substitute for that object. Ovid presents a condensed version of this process, a metamorphosis in which the lost object seems to enter or become inscribed in the substitute, in this case the found sign or art. Of course only the object *as lost*, and not the object itself, enters into the substitutive sign, and the latter is accepted only by a turning away from the actual identity of what was lost. Consolation thus depends on a trope that remains at an essential remove from what it replaces. As Freud wrote to Binswanger regarding the question of substitution in the case of mourning, "No matter what fills the gap, even if it be filled completely, it nevertheless remains something else."[11]

Ovid's psychological acuity captures this paradox at its most vexing. Not only does he present the precise moment at which the original loses itself to the substitute but he reveals the very point beyond which the sexual impulse is both continued and deflected. For a moment, Apollo and Pan embrace, respectively, the laurel and the reeds, according them the passion meant for the nymphs. Yet even in this moment, they recognize that they are embracing "something else," and that recognition is confirmed and reinforced by their subsequent inventions. Not only have the forms of their desired objects changed but the form of their desires must, in this moment of recognition and acceptance, change as well. As we shall see, one of the most profound issues to beset any mourner and elegist is his surviving yet painfully altered sexuality. Although it is crucial for the mourner to assert a continued sexual impulse, that assertion must be qualified, even repressively transformed or rendered metaphorical, by the awareness of loss and mortality. Indeed, our consoling images are most often figures for an immortal but metaphorized sexual force.

In the story of Pan's invention of the pipes, we have a clear example of how the sexual impulse is continued yet displaced onto a symbol of itself, and onto an instrument for assuaging the sorrow of that displacement. Granted, the pipe or the flute is appropriate to mourning, for it joins a sighing breath to hollowness. At the same time, its phallic nature is obvious, and it is far from arbitrary that the goatlike Pan, associated with Priapus, should be the one to invent this woeful, reedlike instrument; or that he, together with the flute's blend of plaintiveness and oblique sexuality, should be so integral to the elegy.[12]

The movement from loss to consolation thus requires a deflection of desire, with the creation of a trope both for the lost object and for the original character of the desire itself. The laurel and flute must symbolize not only Daphne and Syrinx but also the thwarted sexual impulse of the pursuers. As the texts suggest, that thwarting resembles a castration, since in each case it is in the father's territory that the pursuer is forced to check his desires and since Apollo's sign and Pan's new instrument are the pieces of their transformed loves and of their own transformed sexual powers, broken or cut, wreathed or sealed. Each is left grasping the sign of what he lacks, an elegiac token that one can recognize in the cut flowers and the (sometimes broken or resigned) pipes of Alexandrian and Elizabethan elegists, or in Milton's painful plucking and shattering of berries and leaves, no less than in the mounds of broken lilacs in Whitman's elegy for Lincoln. These tokens do, of course, have several other layers of meaning; but this castrative aspect should not be slighted, for it lies at the core of the work of mourning.

It is becoming clear that there is a significant similarity between the process of mourning and the oedipal resolution. As I shall argue, the work of mourning appears to recapitulate elements of the earlier resolution. The full extent of this will emerge gradually in the course of this study, but certain features should be noted now. Each procedure or resolution is essentially defensive, requiring a detachment of affection from a prior object followed by a reattachment of the affection elsewhere. At the core of each procedure is the renunciatory experience of loss and the acceptance, not just of a substitute, but of the very means and practice of substitution. In each case such an acceptance is the price of survival; and in each case a successful resolution is not merely deprivatory, but offers a form of compensatory reward. The elegist's reward, especially, resembles or augments that of the child—both often involve inherited legacies and consoling identifications with symbolic, even immortal, figures of power.

Furthermore, since we noted that a paternal intervention forced Pan and Apollo not only away from erotic pursuits but toward an adoption of signs or aesthetic instruments, it is worth recognizing how thoroughly an important elaboration of Freud's Oedipus scenario stresses precisely this submission of the child to society's "symbolic order" of signs. According to Lacan, it is the figure of the father, representing the symbolic order, that formally intervenes between the child and the child's first object of attachment. The child's imaginary, dyadic relationship with its prior "love-object" is thus interrupted and mediated by a signifying system, which acts as a third term, much as the laurel sign or the pipes come between the gods and the nymphs. In the elegy, the poet's preceding relationship with the deceased (often associated with the mother, or Nature, or a naively regarded Muse) is conventionally disrupted and forced into a triadic structure including the third term, death (frequently associated with the father, or Time, or the more harshly perceived necessity of linguistic mediation itself).

The dead, like the forbidden object of a primary desire, must be separated from the poet, partly by a veil of words.

From this perspective the oedipal resolution actually governs the child's "entry" into language, an entry that the work of mourning and the elegy replay. (While it has other determinants, the "begin again" formula of so many elegies is only one indication of this reenforced entry into a preexisting order of signs or conventions.) Of course, the oedipal moment as Lacan presents it does not mark the child's first use of words! Rather it retraces and modifies earlier occasions when the self or its objects were displaced by signifiers of various kinds. Such occasions, notably the mirror stage and the *fort-da* episode, represent rehearsals for the formal alienation and symbolic castration of the child during the oedipal resolution. Since these superimposed occasions reveal themselves in the elegy, it is worth discriminating them now. I am by no means attempting comprehensive accounts of these stages, choosing instead to emphasize those aspects with greatest bearing on the elegy.[13] I should also mention that I regard these stages not as strictly empirical, *precisely* dateable events but rather as explanatory models or typified narrative constructs, nonetheless based as they are on sets of observations.

During the mirror stage, an infant between the ages of six months and eighteen months locates an idealized image of himself either in mirror images or in the forms of others—in each case imagining himself to possess the integrity and functional completeness of what remains nevertheless a merely specular self. The actual and as yet primarily unformed and incompetent self is thus alienated and displaced by a coherent image of an idealized self, an imaginary "rough-cast" of the ego. The child's relation to this mirror image is dyadic, remaining within a condition of primary narcissism but now revealing a preliminary split in, or we might say *for*, the constitution of the self. In other words, the child still attaches his affections to himself, although this "self" is now an image; and the child still fails to discriminate a world genuinely other than himself. This latter failure is not, however, quite the same as the infant's earlier state of original, supposedly undifferentiated union with the mother, for it now involves a split both within the self and between the self and an outside image. By force of fantasy, these splits are simply not yet adequately registered or enforced.

If the child were to remain at this level, he would obviously fail to

9

establish a stable, socialized sense of himself or the outside world. But the groundwork clearly has been laid for subsequent and more thorough suppressions of an inchoate self in favor of a formalized identity, one based not so much on the images of private fantasy as on the intervening signs and positional codes of society. So, too, this phase foreshadows the elegist's consoling construction of a fictional identity not only for the dead but for himself as well.

It is worth bearing these elements of the mirror stage in mind, for we shall see how often a mourner is forced back to this primitive form of narcissism. Outgrowing the mirror stage, the individual will form attachments outside the self and will develop a self-image that is conditioned by and aware of an outside world. He will achieve a more sophisticated and somewhat more realistic form of narcissism. But the present menace of death may shatter his own perhaps more sophisticatedly narcissistic illusions of security; and the deprivation of someone whose presence had supported the survivor's self-image may join the threat of death to drive the mourner back to the earlier form of narcissism.

This regression may also be caused by the withdrawal of affection from the dead, followed by an inability to reattach that affection, or, more strictly speaking, libido, elsewhere than upon the mourner's self. This is what Freud described as the secondary narcissism at the core of melancholia. One of the major tasks of the work of mourning and of the elegy is to repair the mourner's damaged narcissism—but without allowing that repair to have permanent recourse either to the melancholy form of secondary narcissism or to the fantasies of the primitive narcissism associated with the mirror stage. "Adonais" and *In Memoriam* are the most obvious examples of elegies that cannot be fully understood without observing how they perform this complex reparation.

With the *fort-da* episode, we more obviously pursue the child's entry into language. An understanding of this episode is especially important to interpreting the elegy, and some of its elements will be discussed later. [14] For the moment, we may recall Freud's description of the behavior of his eighteen-month-old grandson, who appeared to "master" the absences of his mother by the *fort-da* game. We know that children may master words before the age of eighteen months, but the *fort-da* game has captured the imagination of theorists like Freud and

Lacan because it seems to demonstrate the child's acceptance of certain rules of experience and of language. [15]

Whenever the child's mother left the room, he controlled his anger and grief by repeatedly casting away and then retrieving a wooden reel, to the accompaniment of the syllables *fort* and *da*. Freud saw the reel as a surrogate for the mother, and he interpreted the syllables to mean approximately "gone" (away) and "there" or "here" (in the sense of regained presence). Freud regarded this game of "disappearance and return" as "related to the child's great cultural achievement—the instinctual renunciation (that is, the renunciation of instinctual satisfaction) which he had made in allowing his mother to go away without protesting. He compensated himself for this, as it were, by himself staging the disappearance and return of the objects within his reach."[16] By a primitive form of mourning, the child not only comes to terms with the otherness and absence of his first love-object; he also learns to *represent absence*, and to make the absent present, by means of a substitutive figure accompanied by an elementary language.

The alienating displacement of the inchoate self during the mirror stage is thus reinforced by this instance of instinctual renunciation and by this substitutive use of reel and syllables. The child is manipulating signifiers which are at an obvious remove from the actual mother they signify. So, too, the differential structure of language, here overlapping with the difference between presence and absence, is evident in the child's play with the two opposing syllables. In these respects, the child appears to have advanced his entry into language. Once again, the groundwork has been laid for his subsequent and more thorough submission to the laws of renunciation and symbolic codes.

While the *fort-da* game displays the child's acquiescence to a separation from his mother, the castrative element of that acquiescence does not occur until the oedipal stage, approximately two to three years later. [17] Here, for the first time, the threatening figure of the father intervenes to enforce a separation that hitherto may have seemed only temporary or circumstantial. Now the child's instinctual renunciation requires a symbolic self-castration, designed to ward off the father's threat of actual castration. Henceforth the child's sexual satisfactions and choices of love-objects will necessarily take the forms of substitutes for his original desire. He will have to recognize that his sexual power is strictly limited: he cannot *be* the physical object capable of satisfying the desires of his mother, nor can he sexually return to his earlier state of union with his origins. Instead, he now comes to *possess* a castrated, figurative version of such an object or power—the phallus. As we shall see, this psychological process is extremely close to the procedure of the elegy, and to the mythology that underlies the genre.

At this point we should pause over the question of gender. The terms of the argument thus far appear to have been particularly applied and applicable to the male child, just as the figures of authority and of compensatory but figurative sexual power appear to be exclusively masculine. And yet our discussion, particularly in its bearing on the work of mourning, does apply with similar force to both genders. The female child, too, is prevented from remaining in unmediated closeness to the mother. Her first sexual impulses—whether toward the mother or toward the father—are checked and redirected toward the choice of a substitute. Her enforced self-suppression, her acceptance of the rule of substitution, and her adoption of a positional identity governed by a symbolic code are not sufficiently different from those of the male to invalidate our discussion's relevance to both genders. For both, one may speak of a castrative renunciation of primary desire, and one may point to the subsequent exercise of a displaced version of such desire. The phallus is more obviously associated with the male; and its predominance in the symbolic code is no doubt partly the product of a discriminatory male culture. But for our purposes it is important to regard it as being, for *both* sexes, what Juliet Mitchell describes as an "expression of the wish for what is absent, for reunion (initially with the mother)."[18]

Recognizing that the phallus is "a ghost," I would therefore keep in mind Jacqueline Rose's warning:

> When Lacan is reproached with phallocentrism at the level of his theory, what is most often missed is that the subject's entry into the symbolic order is equally an exposure of the value of the phallus itself . . . and that the status of the phallus is a fraud (this is, for Lacan, the meaning of castration). . . . Thus the phallus stands for that moment when prohibition must function, in the sense of whom may be assigned to whom in the triangle made up of mother, father and child, but at that same moment it signals to the subject that 'having' only functions at the price of a loss and 'being' as an effect of division. Only if this is dropped from the account can

the phallus be taken to represent an unproblematic assertion of male privilege. [19]

It would be a mistake, therefore, to see the phallic signifier itself as the source of an original alienation that, in the case of women, it no doubt aggravates and reduplicates. One may redress an imbalance by substituting a female figure for that of the phallus; but this would not entirely dissolve the woman's enforced distance (like that of the man) from her first object of desire; and while it would reduce the distance between male sexual emblems and female sexual power, it would not abolish the remaining distance between the preferred female emblem and the actual source or power from which it is disjunctively derived. The figure of the fertility goddess, or of a female fertility token, bears as metaphorical a relation to an individual woman's sexual impulse or powers as does the figure of Dionysus or Adonis or the phallus to those of a man. And if we were to substitute such a female figure for those in the subsequent discussion—a discussion largely reflecting the nature of the elegy thus far—our argument would keep much of its general force.

Only very recently, in the wake of the reconceived position of women in the society and culture at large, has a particular elegy positively reinstated the female fertility goddess and her emblems. In the Epilogue, I shall study how Amy Clampitt's "A Procession at Candlemas" rescues such figures from their virtual exclusion by masculine figures throughout the history of the genre. But for the moment we might anticipate that even this revisionary poem submits the goddess to the kind of chastening observed in the case of male figures.

Longstanding sexual discrimination has impinged on women's experience of mortal loss; and the difficulty in identifying with predominantly male symbols of consolation greatly complicates the woman's work of mourning. But we should not lose sight of how such symbols also relate to a sheer lack—man's or woman's—and how the genetic power that they represent could in many respects be of either gender. While I wish to draw attention to the hitherto largely unasked question of how differently men and women mourn, for the purposes of this study it is the substantial overlap in men's and women's mourning that should be stressed. Until as recently as Clampitt's poem, elegies written by women, such as Anne Bradstreet's or Emily Brontë's, have tended primarily to confirm this common ground.

13

Pursuing our sense of the child's entry into language, we should recognize that a further achievement occurs during the oedipal stage. Not only does the child manipulate signifiers, as in the *fort-da* game; he now takes up his own identity in relation to a symbolic code. Accepting the displaced and mediated relation forced on him by the authoritative third term, the father figure, he stabilizes an "I," a symbolic self that is now locked into a socialized *position*. The substitution of word for thing has thus been followed by the substitution of this conventionally prescribed signifier (this "I" within a harshly differential code) in place of a more thoroughly suppressed instinctual self. By virtue of this deeper act of "splitting," the child has taken up a position within the symbolic order. Once again anticipating the elegy, we recognize that by a work of divisive self-surpassal, or self-suppression, the child has created a "symbolic substitute for his own self."[20]

An understanding of such splittings and self-suppressions, and of the acceptance of positionality, hierarchy, and symbolic exchange, sheds light not only on the elegy, but also on several as yet inadequately understood conventions of the pastoral eclogue, to which we may turn in passing. The pastoral eclogue, after all, traditionally stood at the point of entry to a poetic career, hence in some ways replaying an entry into language. And even a cursory look at the eclogues of Theocritus, for example, particularly the first and eighth, shows how carefully such poems move toward the kinds of achievement mentioned above. Schematically speaking, many eclogues are obsessed with establishing who sits where (thus figuring positionality), who is more powerful or skilful, who relates and defers to what predecessor, who owns what property, who goes first, who wins or inherits, and what is exchanged (the principle of exchange itself being one of the cardinal establishments of the oedipal stage and of the complete entry into language). Very often the relation between two singers comes to be mediated by a third party, usually a judge. So, too, there is the frequent concern with the very character of language and artifice, a concern with what marks off language from nature, despite the many wishful comparisons between them. Eclogues are often about the very entry from nature to culture, and they are rife with the kinds of contests, renunciations, and displacements that we have been witnessing above. Not fortuitously, then, from Theocritus to Yeats the eclogue and the elegy have been closely related—a relation we will study further when addressing other eclogic aspects of the elegy itself.

The oedipal resolution also governs the creation of a superego; and here, too, we find an important relation to the work of mourning and the elegy. At the most obvious level, we recall Freud's suggestion that the superego is made up of the "illustrious dead," a sort of cultural reservoir, or rather cemetery, in which one may also inter one's renounced love-objects and in which the ruling monument is the internalized figure of the father. Since the father, as Freud suspected in *Totem and Taboo*, and as Lacan has stressed, intervenes and governs precisely as a *figure*, a totemic metaphor or name—the *Nom du Père*—any actual father thus has himself been displaced by a substitutive image with which the child seeks to identify. This displacement of the actual father by an idealized totemic figure involves an act very much like the child's castrative creation or adoption of the phallus, and we shall see how consistently such a totemic figure relates to the principal tropes of consolation.

While the argument seems once again to have skewed into exclusively male domain, and while Freud was notoriously discriminatory in his attitude toward the woman's achievement of a superego, I would claim that the woman's mourning *does* equally recapitulate not only her loss of the mother but also her internalization and identification with the idealized parental figure. And while that figure may be primarily female, it may in itself be sufficiently repressive or supervisory to serve as superego, or it may very well include traits of the renounced and controlling father figure, in triadic relation to which it has been established. The following lines from Emily Brontë's "Remembrance" sum up much of the argument thus far. Here the mourner repeats her separation from the mother but also adopts the role of the mother, a role not altogether unlike that of the intervening father figure in its stern prevention of an illegitimate and regressive desire:

> Then did I check the tears of useless passion—
> Weaned my young soul from yearning after thine;
> Sternly denied its burning wish to hasten
> Down to that tomb already more than mine.[21]

We said earlier that in both the oedipal resolution and the work of mourning an acceptance of mediation or substitution was the price of survival. We need to reinforce this claim and to suggest how the renunciation of the primary sexual impulse relates to the defense against death. In the oedipal stage, the father figure formally prevents the child's regressive desire to remain in a state of undifferentiated union with the mother, or in the fantasia of the mirror stage. Since this primary desire is for the extinction of desire itself, and for a state preceding or abolishing genuine individuation, it is closely allied to the death wish; and it is surely this wish that the father's authority is in part designed to forestall. (We recall Hamlet's wish "that the Everlasting had not fix'd / His canon 'gainst self-slaughter!") It is interesting that Freud thought it "possible to regard the fear of death, like the fear of conscience, as a development of the fear of castration."[22]

Yet another perspective reinforces our understanding of how a form of sexual renunciation relates to a defense against mortality. For it is through their genetic, reproductive power, associated as it is with sexual instinct, that men and women become aware of being mortal links in a potentially immortal chain. And it is just this procreative force that therefore seems to separate itself from them, to outlive and to mock their individual mortality. Lacan has written of "the pure life instinct that is to say immortal life, or irrepressible life . . . simplified, indestructible life. It is precisely what is subtracted from the living being by virtue of the fact that it is submitted to the cycle of sexed reproduction."[23] Similarly, but from a more exclusively masculine perspective, Freud wrote, "The ejection of the sexual substance in the sexual act corresponds in a sense to the separation of soma and germ plasm" (for Freud, this latter was "immortal"). [24]

It is not surprising, therefore, that man's defense against his consciousness of mortality involves a movement against his sexual instinct. In fact, as late as the time of Aristotle, the Greeks identified the seminal fluid, which they took to be cerebrospinal in substance, with the immortal life-stuff, the psyche, or as Weismann and Freud called it, the "immortal germ-plasm." Consequently, castration was thought to defend the individual against mortality by conserving his psyche. We shall return to this idea in our discussion of the vegetation deities and of the already mentioned construction of the castrated figure for an immortalized but purely symbolic sexual power.

The work of mourning, too, is largely designed to defend the individual against death. As Brontë's lines, together with those of many elegists, confirm, it is not simply a matter of reconstructing one's barriers against an external menace. Once again, a forced renunciation prevents a regressive attachment to a prior love-object, a potential fixation on the part of the griever, whose desire in such cases for literal identification with the dead is another force very much like that of the death wish. Melancholia usually involves a lasting return to the kind of regressive narcissism noticed before, often including an identification between the ego and the dead such that the melancholic tends toward self-destruction.[25] The healthy mourner, on the other hand, submits to a displacement of his prior attachments and to a disruption of his potential regression to dyadic fantasies, allowing his desires to be governed instead by a rule like that of the father's law of substitution. Only by repeating the child's acquiescence in this way can the mourner truly survive.

In both the oedipal resolution and the work of mourning, therefore, a father figure's castrative authority keeps us in life. His Law, the society's code, with its network of detours and substitutions, bars us from the fulfillment of a premature death *and* provides us with figures for what outlasts individual mortality.

We seem to have been on a long digression, straying far from the original discussion of Apollo and Pan. And yet we have only been elaborating the nature and implications of their stories in relation to the work of mourning and the oedipal resolution. In fact, it is as if Ovid has been waiting for us, or inviting us along this course of interpretation, for he directly follows the stories of Apollo and Pan with that of Phaeton, thereby rounding off the entire cluster of issues with this confrontation between a father and a son whose refusal of the oedipal detour brings about not merely his death but the most extensive display of grief in the entire poem.[26]

Reading this triptych, itself reinforced throughout the *Metamorphoses*, one recognizes that primary desire never attains its literal objective except in death, or in a deathlike loss of identity. The only object that such a desire can possess in life will be a sign or substitute for what it cannot have. In the cases of Pan and Apollo, desire and its object ironically unite only as metamorphs or metaphors of themselves. Indeed, we now may regard the very pursuits of Daphne and Syrinx as having been substitutive in the first place, and we understand why the nymphs themselves should have been so liable to subsequent transformation. Each substitution seems to repeat a prior change, just as each loss recapitulates a prior loss and each turn to consolation repeats an earlier deflection of desire. Our experiences of loss fold upon themselves in gathers, creating the highly stratified "occasion" that each elegy "begin[s] again" or enters "yet once more":

> And let us, Polydore, though now our voices
> Have got the mannish crack, sing him to th' ground,
> As once to our mother; use like note and words,
> Save that Euriphile must be Fidele. [27]

In an example that crystallizes much of our discussion, Shakespeare's Guiderius and Arviragus (under the disguising names Polydore and Cadwal) thus mourn the supposedly dead Fidele in the same language in which they once mourned their mother, Euriphile. It is the nature of this same language, the specific forms of an elegy's "note and words," to which we must now turn.

The Conventions

Since we have been stressing the ways in which the mourner or elegist must submit to the mediating fabric of language, a tissue of substitutions that may cover a preceding lack, few readers would need to be reminded how the word *text* refers back to a woven fabric rather than to an instrinsically more solid substance. Nor would they need to recall Freud's rather fanciful version of the invention of writing as an instance of hair-braiding. But it *is* worth noting the significant frequency with which the elegy has employed crucial images of weaving, of creating a fabric in the place of a void. We have already noted Apollo's laurel wreath and Pan's cut and bound reeds. The boy on the carved bowl in Theocritus's "First Idyl" plaits a cage of asphodel; the elegist in Virgil's "Eclogue X" weaves a basket while he sings; the mourning Camus in "Lycidas" wears a carefully embroidered hem "inwrought with figures dim"; Tennyson, in section 66 of *In Memoriam*, compares himself to a blind old man winding the curls of children's hair, or playing with threads; and summing up many examples, the figure of "peace after death" in Stevens's elegy for Henry Church is described as

> An immaculate personage in nothingness,
> With the whole spirit sparkling in its cloth,
>
> Generations of the imagination piled
> In the manner of its stitchings, of its thread.
> In the weaving round the wonder of its need. [28]

To speak of weaving a consolation recalls the actual weaving of burial clothes and shroud, and this emphasizes how mourning is an action, a process of work. In the remainder of this chapter, we shall study ways in which certain conventions of the elegy, related as they are to a variety of ritualistic social and psychological actions, reflect and carry on such work.

Probably the greatest influence on the form of the elegy has been the rituals associated with the death and rebirth of vegetation gods; and features of this influence are to be found even in those elegies that are not strictly pastoral. An obvious influence of such rites is the residually ceremonial structure of the elegy. The form has a measured pace and direction and develops the effect not only of an event but of a performance. The performance is in fact foregrounded by the genre's staging devices, a convention that draws attention to the mourner or cast of mourners.

This ceremonious self-dramatization and its framing devices can become fairly sophisticated, as in "Lycidas" or "Adonais" or as in the uses of irony in modern elegies. But even in its simplest forms—the dirge of Bion for Adonis or the elegiac eclogues of Theocritus and Moschus—one recognizes how this aspect serves not only to increase our sense of performance but also to assert and enhance the active responses of the living. The emphasis on the drama, or "doing," of the elegy is thus part of the crucial self-privileging of the survivors, as well as a way of keeping them in motion, ensuring a sense of progress and egress, of traversing some distance. For a stationary poet that distance may be figurative and purely psychological; but it is crucial to any successful mourning.

Indeed, few elegies or acts of mourning succeed without seeming to place the dead, and death itself, at some cleared distance from the living. Hence, in part, the sense of distance marked by the processions in elegies or by such related items as the catalogued offering of flowers. These offerings, apart from their figurative meanings and their function of obeisance, also add to the temporal or spatial respite within the rites, or within the poem itself; and the flowers, like the poetic language to which they are so often compared, serve not only as offerings or as gestures for respite but also as demarcations separating the living from the dead. The original function of a funeral hearse was, in fact, to serve as the coffin's cover or frame—a structure on which such demarcative offerings could be affixed. "Bouquets" of elegies were pinned or thrown on the hearse of Sir Philip Sidney, for example; and numerous succeeding elegies have found ways to "strew the laureate hearse," if only figuratively, with flowers or rather fictions designed "to interpose a little ease." In less idealizing terms, even a poet as recent as James Wright has pointed to the archaic, demarcative strategy still at work in our elegiac devotions by describing epitaphs as "deliberate scrawls to guard us from the dead."[29]

As for the content and direction of its ritual movement, the elegy follows the ancient rites in the basic passage through grief or darkness to consolation and renewal. Strangely enough, the Greek terms for these two phases of the ceremonies have made their way, not into literary criticism, but into science: as the cathode, or way (hodos) down (cata), and the anode, or way up. On the one hand these phases mimed the death and return of the vegetation god, while on the other they came to represent an initiate's descent to and ascent from a crisis of mysterious revelation.

The vegetation god, whose death and rebirth governed the phases of the rites (which would often occur in ceremonies set months apart), was a figure or personification serving several functions. On the one hand, such a figure reduces multiplicity to apparent unity, allowing the devotees or survivors to focus and, by simplification, to intensify their grief or gratitude regarding an otherwise manifold and ungraspable world of nature. What is more important, however, the creation of a human or human-divine rather than a merely elemental or vegetative figure for nature reveals much of the underlying motive for appearing to mourn nature's seasonal "death" in the first place. Why, after all, should man so bitterly lament the passing of a season that he knows will return unless it is his own unreturning nature that he mourns? And why should he represent nature by a human form unless he wants in this instance not only to mourn his own image but also to identify that image with nature's powers of regeneration? The trope is designed not so much to humanize nature, although this is partly the case, as to naturalize man.

The figure of the god has a further effect: it appears to reverse man's submission to nature or its changing seasons. Instead of grieving over the inhuman operation of nature or time, a setting and process on which he is unavoidably dependent, man creates a fiction whereby nature and its changes, the occasions of his grief, appear to depend on him. The withering vegetation is now no more the *cause* of human grief but rather the mourner or even the effect of a human-divine loss—the death of such figures as Adonis, Thammuz, Persephone, or Dionysus. Thus the so-called pathetic fallacy of nature's lament, one of the prominent elegiac conventions so frequently criticized for artifice and contrivance, actually has a naturalistic basis in the notation of seasonal change.

We may understand this reversal more fully by returning briefly to the child's *fort-da* game. The game's rhythm of loss and retrieval corresponds roughly to the two phases of the archaic rituals. But more importantly, a similar psychological reversal of dependence is achieved. Freud supposed that the child not only masters the disappearance of the mother but psychologically comes to *cause* it in representational form, by discarding the surrogate figure of the reel. Similarly, by the sacrifice or mimed death of the personification of nature, man "causes" nature's death, or at least brings on her deathlike mourning. As in the case of the child, man reverses his passive relation to the mother or matrix, perhaps even avenging himself against her and his situation.

From this point of view, the elegy's elaborate observations of nature's decline are not the fallacious products of man's self-pity but rather the expression of his attempted mastery of and vengeance against nature, or more precisely change. This may seem overstated, and indeed there are other powerful determinants of this convention, but the motives of mastery and revenge are surely present. They rise to the surface most explicitly in the many elegies in which man either exhorts nature to lament or even *curses* it: "Let all things be changed, and let the pine tree bear pears, since Daphnis dies, and let the stag drag down the dogs, and let the screech owl from the mountains contend with nightingales. . . ."[30]

If pursued, this attention to elegiac cursing would lead to a further discussion of the relation between grief and vengeful anger, a discussion reserved for the third chapter, on revenge tragedies, and for the studies of several elegies in particular. But while we are on the subject of anger and cursing, we should examine the related convention of elegiac questioning.

Since the first question with which Thyrsis opened his lament for Daphnis, in Theocritus's "First Idyl," the convention of questions, sometimes private and gnomic but more often in a sharply interrogative mode, addressed to a particular auditor, has echoed through-out the history of the elegy. Why should this be so? As with the other conventions, the determinants are multiple, and their specific applications will appear in later chapters. But some generalized answers can be made now.

One of the dangers besetting a mourner is the imprisonment of his affective energies, the locking up within himself of impulses previously directed toward or attached to the deceased. Just as the ancient vegetation rites sought to unlock the frozen or withered energies of nature, so, too, the mourner must prevent a congealing of his own impulses. One obvious function of elegiac questioning is to set free the energy locked in grief or rage and to organize its movement in the form of a question that is not merely an expression of ignorance but a voicing of protest.

More significantly, when the question is addressed to someone else, the mourner succeeds in shifting his focus from the lost object or from himself and turns outward to the world. If tinged with anger, as they often are, such questions actually carry that anger away from its possible attachment to the self—an attachment that, if unbroken, would enmesh the survivor in melancholia. By elegiac questions which often impugn others, the mourner may stave off that self-directed anger. He may thereby also deflect the closely related element of mourning—guilt—which if unalleviated would drag him toward melancholy.[31] The so frequent, formulaic Where were you? may thus mask the more dangerous Where was I? And the repetitive, incantatory nature of so much of this questioning emphasizes the possibly exorcistic or expiatory element of the ritual.

A further function of the elegiac question is to create the illusion that some force or agent might have prevented the death. Originally, such agents would have been the protective nymphs or gods, the parent deities, or, as in "Lycidas," "the Muse herself." Of course, there never effectively have been such guardians against mortality. But the question's creation of such a fictive addressee fosters the illusion that such a guardian was temporarily absent rather than permanently non-existent. Now the question Where were you? tropes not only such questions as Where are you (the deceased)? and Where was I? but also Why do you (the supposed guardians) not exist? Among the questions behind the ceremonious screen of questions, therefore, also lies the naked Why will no-one or nothing save us from death?[32]

Elegiac questioning, like the *fort-da* game and like the ritual origins of the genre, is marked by a significant use of repetition. Before returning to explore the figure of the vegetation deity, we should try to interpret why the elegy itself should be so conventionally repetitive. Such repetition takes several forms, and once again there are many determinants at work.

Often, elegies are presented as being repetitions in themselves. For example, even the lament within Theocritus's "First Idyl," the poem commonly regarded as initiating the genre, has, we are told, been sung by Thyrsis on earlier occasions. And Thyrsis's song contains within itself a refrain whose most frequent variant is "Begin, Muses, *begin again* the pastoral song" (my emphasis). We observed earlier how each loss recapitulates a prior loss. And we spoke of the elegy's re-enactment of an "entry" into a preexisting language and code. These are only partial reasons for the repetitious character of so many elegies and for the way so many seem to "begin again" or to commence with a "yet once more."

Repetition creates a sense of continuity, of an unbroken pattern such as one may oppose to the extreme discontinuity of death. Time itself is thereby structured to appear as a familiar, filled-in medium rather than as an open-ended source of possible catastrophe. Repetition is, moreover, one of the psychological responses to trauma. The psyche repeats the shocking event, much as the elegy recounts and reiterates the fact of death: "I weep for Adonis; lovely Adonis is dead. Dead is lovely Adonis; the Loves join in weeping."[33] By such repetitions, the mind seeks retroactively to create the kind of protective barrier that, had it been present at the actual event, might have prevented or softened the disruptive shock that initially caused the trauma.[34]

At the same time, the repetition of words and refrains and the creation of a certain rhythm of lament have the effect of controlling the expression of grief while also keeping that expression in motion. It is as if the grief might be gradually conjured forth and exorcised. This returns us to the idea of ceremony, and to the idea that repetition may itself be used to create the sense of ceremony. Certainly, by confessing its repetitive nature at large, the elegy takes comfort from its self-insertion into a longstanding convention of grief. And by repeating the form of the vegetation rites, for example, an individual elegy may borrow the ritual *context* of consolation. The particular lament is assimilated to a comforting commonality of grief, and the object of sorrow becomes identified with the oft-sung deity who returns each year.

Thus Moschus adopts the formulaic song for Adonis and applies it to his lament for Bion; and more than twenty centuries later, Shelley returns to the same form (and the same repetitions) in his elegy for Keats. The unique death is absorbed into a natural cycle of repeated occasions, and the very expression of mourning is naturalized as though it too were but a seasonal event. The end of Bion's lament for Adonis finally seeks to restrain the grieving Aphrodite by reminding her that this is an annual ceremony of mourning, that Time has not been arrested by this death, and that she, as a survivor, must move on in time: "Cease thy lamentations this day, Cytherea; refrain from beating thy breast. Thou must weep for him again; thou must bewail him again in another year."[35] One thinks ahead to Whitman's "When Lilacs Last in the Dooryard Bloom'd": "I mourn'd, and yet shall mourn with ever-returning spring."

But there are still more determinants for the repetitions found in elegies. One such cause is the highly important phase of mourning in which the griever must be convinced of the actual fact of loss. The powerful impulse to refuse such knowledge may, if uncorrected, lead to the condition of melancholy. According to Freud, "Melancholy is in some way related to an unconscious loss of a love-object, in contra-distinction to mourning, in which there is nothing unconscious about the loss."[36] In order for this resistance to be broken, the mind must be repeatedly confronted with the fact until the recognition has been achieved. Only once the loss is recognized can the griever continue the work of mourning by withdrawing his attachment from the dead. Examples of such uses of repetition are found in many elegies. Bion's lines quoted above are an obvious case, and he pursues them with Cytherea's lament ("'Alas for Cytherea; lovely Adonis is dead'") which in turn is repeated by Echo ("And Echo returned the cry, 'Lovely Adonis is dead'") and then again by the refrain, which repeats the opening line of the poem. Ronsard employs the same Echo motif ("Echo is not silent, but within her rocks redoubling her feigned voice, through pity for me is repeating my lament"), as does Bryskett in his elegy for Sidney.[37]

The echo particularly suits this recognitional function of repeti-tion, for it makes the voicing of loss seem to come from beyond the self, from the objective world of fact. Also, the echo would seem to work as a kind of trial, in which the mourner brings his loss into language, testing how it feels to speak *and hear* of it in words. Our earlier discussion of the mourner's replayed entry into language reinforces our sense of how the echo might represent the elegist's particular sensitivity to the fact that the language he uses is and is not his own. Here again we touch on the eclogic nature of elegies, and we anticipate the numerous moments in which elegists seem to submit, by quotation or translation, to the somehow echoing language of dead poets. [38]

Other obvious examples of the repetitive testing or proving of reality are Spenser's lines in the "November" eclogue ("For dead shee is, that myrth thee made of yore. / Dido my deare alas is dead, / Dead and lyeth wrapt in lead") and the line that this prefigures in "Lycidas" ("For Lycidas is dead, dead ere his prime"). [39] In her study of ancient Greek ritual laments, Margaret Alexiou shows how reiterated statements of death were an integral part of such laments, and she instances how "in Sophokles' *Trachiniai*, the news of Deianeira's death is not told as a simple statement of fact, but revealed gradually, point by point, in a prolonged series of statement and counter-statement, question and answer." [40] Perhaps more interesting, however, are the cases in which the crucial preliminary work of recognition and the repetitions it demands become not merely a verbal litany but an actual narrative structure, as in "The Book of the Duchess" and "Daphnaida." In each of these poems, a state of melancholy leads to a recognition that emerges from an act of narrative repetition.

One final interpretation of the elegiac convention of repetition must be suggested. This applies principally to the custom of repeating the name of the dead, a custom extending once again from the ancient vegetation cults. Alexiou writes: "And one element of the primitive lament which was never forgotten or ignored, even in the most sophisticated literary compositions, was the refrain calling the dying man or god by name. This invocation was frequently expressed by the verb *anakaleishtha* (to call upon, invoke). . . . Its function was to raise the spirit of the dead from the grave." [41] Alexiou goes on to reveal how the verb for the refrain was adapted to denote "the stone on which Demeter is said to have sat when she invoked Persephone. The ritual enactment of this *anáklisis* was continued by the women of Megara until Pausanias's day." It is interesting that the word *anáklisis*, literally "a leaning upon," has entered English usage as a psychoanalytic term denoting the choice of an attachment made on the basis of its resemblance to a previous, usually parental, attachment. We may almost call the repetition of the lost love-object's name a form of verbal "propping." The survivor leans upon the name, which takes on, by dint of repetition, a kind of substantiality, allowing it not only to refer to but almost to replace the dead. This virtual reification by means of repetition is described by Wordsworth in the note to "The Thorn" mentioned above:

> During such efforts there will be a craving in the mind, and as long as it is unsatisfied the speaker will cling to the same words, or words of the same character. There are also various other reasons why repetition and apparent tautology are frequently beauties of the highest kind. Among the chief of these reasons is the interest which the mind attaches to words, not only as symbols of the passion, but as *things*, active and efficient, which are of themselves part of the passion. [42]

Wordsworth's disclosure and employment of the primitive use of repetition as a *figure of thought* is characteristic of his intention to recapture the radical nature of poetry. The anaclitic use of this figure of thought, involving the name of the dead, may still be found in elegies as recent as those reiterative laments by Berryman for Delmore Schwartz:

> Delmore, Delmore,
> . . . .
> Delmore, Delmore,
> . . . .
> His throat ached, and he could sing no more.
> All ears are closed
> across the heights where Delmore and Gertrude sprang
> so long ago, in the goodness of which it was composed.
> Delmore, Delmore![43]

It is as though the history of the genre were, at least in this particular element, bent back to touch its origin; at those moments, we almost see Demeter on her stone.

With the mention of Demeter and her invocation of Persephone we should return to the figure of the vegetation deity to notice several as yet unmentioned aspects of its function. The vegetation god is, after all, the predecessor of almost every elegized subject and provides a fundamental trope by which mortals create their images of immortality. This is not a new field, having been studied by many scholars since the time of Frazer. Nevertheless, we can gain fresh insight by combining elements of our earlier psychoanalytic discussion with a concern for this specific tradition of elegiac mythology, thus developing interpretations that are, at most, latent beneath the figures and conventions that we otherwise take for granted. Among others, the following questions, for example, should be raised: Why is it that the death of the vegetation god is also a sexual martyrdom? How does this relate to the affirmation of immortality? What are the bases for our conventional images of return or resurrection? And finally, How have successive cultures adapted the function of the vegetation god to the needs of quite different societies and settings?

Persephone is raped or abducted by Death. Adonis is killed by a tusk wound in the groin. Atthis castrates himself and dies. Orpheus is torn apart and decapitated by women. Daphnis dies after being blinded by a jealous Aphrodite. The list could be extended, but already it is clear that these deities suffer a peculiarly sexual death. Our earlier discussion of mourning and symbolic castration is again relevant; but we need to focus now on related issues associated more specifically with the forebears and subsequent protagonists of the elegy.

The immortality suggested by nature's self-regenerative power rests on a principle of recurrent fertility. The personification of this principle attests to the comparable capacity in mankind—what we spoke of earlier as the so-called immortal germ plasm. Since individual humans are no more than mortal vehicles of this regenerative power, the particular human figure can represent the principle of sexuality only by appearing to undergo a succession of extinctions and rebirths. The vegetation deity, and especially his or her sexual power, must be made to disappear and return. Hence the specifically sexual or castrative aspects of the deaths.

An additional answer emerges when one recognizes that the vegetation deity, by merging with the matrix, fulfills the primary desire for a return to a state preceding individuation. As is made explicit in the relation of Adonis to Venus, or of Dionysus to Semele, or even in the filial bond preceding the abduction of Persephone from Demeter, this return is coterminous with an undeflected primary desire. It is therefore unavoidable that these representatives of undeterred desire should suffer particularly castrative fates. In a sense, they are punished for fulfilling their and our desire, and their periodic castrations and deaths are the price by which we purchase our figure for what survives. [44]

From either perspective, then, the figure for surviving sexuality, and hence for that aspect of humanity most comparable to Nature's immortality, requires a castrative moment for its construction. To put it simply, the figure for sexual power is only properly representative when separate from any particular body or, as in statues of Priapus, when the body is almost assimilated to the figure. Now however much the contents of this process of figuration may have been altered or supplied with different meanings, our dominant mode of consolation still depends on detaching from the deceased (or assimilating them to) a special potency or virtue that we regard as eternal. Within such alterations of meaning, however spiritualized, it is worth noting the persistence of the figure for fertility. Indeed, as we shall see, many of the tropes by which we signify immortality depend in large part on this figure, and upon the images originally associated with it. The nature of the power signified differs according to the survivors, for it depends upon the matrix of their needs. But whether such a matrix is that of nature itself, or that of spiritual belief, of fame, of justice, or of social order, the elegy works to create a figure by which that matrix can be refertilized. Perhaps needless to add, throughout the history of the elegy, from the time of Bion beyond that of Mallarmé, the matrices have always been inseparable from the implicit or often explicit matrix of language. Like the soil, the words of the tribe must be purified and resown.

How, then, has the essentially physical imagery associated with the function of the vegetation deity informed subsequent tropes for immortality? Just as the vegetation rites based a figure for perennial renewal upon the principle of fertility, as already mentioned, a Greek belief located part of the immortal attribute of mankind in a supposed cerebrospinal fluid. As R. B. Onians, Jacques Choron, and others have shown, this is where the psyche was alleged to reside, rather as Descartes "located" the soul in the pineal gland, or, more closely, as Weismann and Freud associated immortality with the germ plasm. [45] Gradually, however, as was true for the notions of emotional impulses and mental faculties, the concept of the soul was detached from its earlier, physical associations. [46]

And yet, the associations persisted in the *imagery* for the soul, which, for all its subsequent spurning of the body, has never been able to shake its dependence on images of physical properties, particularly those associated with fertility. Echoing ancient vegetation cults of *kalligenia,* or "fair birth," Christianity, for example, describes conversion as a "new birth," the fruit of an impregnation by the spirit of God. The ecstasy of Bernini's *Santa Teresa* returns us to the more explicitly sexual encounters of such predecessors as Danae, Leda, Io, or Europa with the supreme deity. One has only to reflect on the continued practice of the Eucharist, or even the custom of *eating* images of physical renewal during Easter, to realize the similarity between these contemporary rites and their originals. To take the wafer and the wine is to repeat, with a different interpretation, the rites of three millenia ago. Clearly, the significations of the figures have changed more than the figures themselves. It is this combination of change and permanence that must be analyzed.

In many of the earliest rites a youth, personifying the deity, would be dismembered, and his flesh and blood taken as nourishment by the community and by the soil. The figure for fertility would thus be literally ingested, a ritual counterpart to Freud's myth of the sons' ingestion of the dead father in a totem feast that Freud names the "first festival." Freud's myth also involves the reverence for an immortal figure representing the dead father, a figure that represents a power not only of fertility but also of sexual regulation. Just as Greek couples would go, at marriage, to invoke the blessings of the dead, so members of a tribe would refer and defer to the totem in their sexual choices. The totem thus became the symbolic tool for societal reproduction, not merely the emblem of sexual power itself. In this extension, one already sees how the figure may enlarge or alter its field of operation. Indeed, we have already explored some of this field in our discussion of how the figure of the father upholds the symbolic register.

The earliest rites probably provided a sense of merely germinal or genetic continuity, and they scarcely developed concepts of the soul or of spiritual immortality. These later concepts, on the other hand, developed partly out of reinterpretations of the early rites and figures. A consensus of scholars has supported Erwin Rohde's attribution of such revisions to the cults that descended southward into Greece from Thrace between the eighth and sixth centuries B.C. [47] Among the more important of these, particularly in relation to the elegy, was the cult of Dionysus. In its simple form, this cult involved ecstatic dancing (usually to flutes) and intoxication, together with the slaughter and consumption of an animal or human victim. But the individual participant passed beyond the mere ingestion of a symbol for the god to a frenzied *identification* with the god. The individual became a *Bakchoe*. This capacity for identification may have provided the wellspring for dramatic acting. Beyond this, however, it allowed mortal human beings to conceive of themselves as sharing an aspect of divinity.

It was Orphic and Pythagorean adaptation of the Dionysian cults that most fully advanced a concept of the immortal soul. This reform took place in a sophisticated, urban society rather than among rural communities, and it replaced the Bacchic frenzy with a contemplative and self-purificatory set of rites whereby the individual cultivated the aspect of himself most akin to the divinity. As is well known, this inward, mystical, and in a sense Protestant revision was a formative influence on both the beliefs and the dialogically self-purifying philosophical methods of Plato. So, too, these revisions profoundly affected the most widespread mystery cults of the Golden Age, the panhellenic Eleusinian mysteries. Largely by virtue of this new influence, the Eleusinian mysteries moved further away from their original connection to the Thesmophoria, the autumn sowing rites associated with Demeter and Persephone, and gravitated instead, though with the same deities, toward a ceremony prefiguring the death and rebirth of the *soul*. The recurrence of vegetation in this world was now made to signify the resurrection of the soul in the next, and the *sacra* handled by initiates functioned no longer merely as fertility charms but rather as mystical tokens endowing a guarantee of good fortune in the future life. "Blessed is the man who has beheld these holy acts; but he that is uninitiated and has no share in the holy ceremonies shall not enjoy a like fate after his death, in the gloomy darkness of Hades."[48]

The *sacra* of such mystery cults nevertheless still recalled fertility emblems, and the Orphic theory of the soul's divine heritage made use of a modified legend regarding the phallic figure of Dionysus. Dionysus, son of Zeus, had been dismembered and devoured by the Titans, who in turn were destroyed by Zeus. Born from the soot of the Titans' remains, mankind inherited an element of ingested divinity. It was this element (replenished by ceremonial consumption of Dionysus, often in the form of a bull) that the devotee nursed like a spiritual "heart" within himself. After a life dedicated to refining the sacred legacy from its Titanic dross, the true initiate could greet the ushers of the dead with such words as those inscribed upon an Orphic tablet: "I am the son of earth and starry heaven, and by birth I come from God: ye know this well yourselves."[49]

Of course, the other ritually stressed feature of the legend is the supposition that one organ of Dionysus, the "heart," escaped the Titans and was carried out by Athene, who concealed it in a fruit-laden basket. The survival of this organ allegedly enabled the second birth of Dionysus (whence his name, "twice-born"), this time from Zeus's union with the mortal Semele. In the rites commemorating this survival or rebirth, the "heart," usually a carved piece of fig wood, would be carried away in a special basket and "revived" by a group of women. (A similar and, indeed, perhaps prior version of this ritual and its image was the cult celebrating Athene herself—Zeus's other pro-geny. In this case, an image of olive wood was the object of devotion, no doubt here representing a specifically feminine power. It is this cult that Amy Clampitt rescues in her already mentioned revision of the genre.)

The heart in the basket thus also represented the discovered infant god, Dionysus-Zagreus, also called *Liknites* ("of the basket"). One thinks of the discovery of the infant Moses in the basket, or of Christ in his manger among farm animals. Indeed, one of the miracles of Saint Francis is his supposed momentary bringing to life of the figurine of a child in a cradle. Closer at hand, however, one hears Ezra Pound's lines from the elegiac "Hugh Selwyn Mauberley": "Christ follows Dionysus, / Phallic and ambrosial / Made way for macerations"; or Yeats's recapture of the primitive resonance of early ritual:

I saw a staring virgin stand
Where holy Dionysus died,
And tear the heart out of his side,
And lay the heart upon her hand
And bear that beating heart away;
And then did all the Muses sing
Of Magnus Annus at the spring,
As though God's death were but a play.[50]

The presence of the singing Muses in Yeats's lines recalls one of the first allegorizations to which the figure of the surviving organ or power of the deity has been submitted. For apart from its adoption by those believers who took it to signify the immortal spirit, the deity or its special attribute could be made to signify the immortal power of poetry. Rather than representing a restored world of nature, the group of women became Muses, constituting a poetic matrix to be refertilized by the potency of song. This allegorization is obvious in the case of Orpheus, whose severed organ is represented as a singing head, the "gory visage" of continuing song. So, too, the role of the young god Linus was transmuted from that of a springtime deity associated with new lambs (as Christ would be) to that of the inventor of song. Accordingly, his supposed fate changed from that of being devoured by wild dogs to that of being slain by a jealous rival musician, his father Apollo. Again, the mourners become not merely a group of women trying to allay famine but rather the Muses themselves.[51]

In this way we come back to Theocritus's "First Idyl," containing a lament for another vegetation deity elevated to poethood. Daphnis's castrative defeat lends a peculiar significance, as well as poignancy, to the relinquishment of his pipe, as he dies, to Pan: "Come, King, and bear away this honey-breathing pipe of hardened wax, a fair instrument, well curved to the lip; for I am now being dragged down to Hades by Love."[52]

From the original vegetation deity, dismembered to yield a figure for eternal fertility, we have thus moved to the unfortunate lover-poet yielding up the figuratively erotic instrument of his art. We recall the tale of Pan himself and look ahead from Daphnis to so many of his successors, who, in elegies by Moschus, Virgil, Spenser, and Milton, share this especially tangled sexual and poetic fate. It is fascinating to recognize how the entanglement matches the psychological nexus noted earlier in the necessarily castrative assertions of consolation. If the mourned *subject* of the elegy is made to yield a pipe, a reborn flower, or even a stellar influence, the elegist's *own* transaction of loss and gain must, as we have seen, also work toward a trope for sexual power.

Hence a remarkable convergence upon the originally sexual figure of consolation, and all its allegorical variants. It is at the locus, so to speak, of this figure that the elegist erects or inherits his legacy from the dead. Indeed, the figure *is* his legacy. And once we have recognized the *disguises* that such a figure and its attendant imagery may assume, as well as the other virtues or potencies that they may signify, we can read a little more deeply into the underlying thrust of such consolations as those in "Lycidas," "Adonais," or even in such apparently innocent elegies as those of Wordsworth for his brother John.

We have in fact now accumulated several perspectives from which to interpret the conventional elegiac images of consolation. We have, for example, already discussed the role of flowers both in terms of their ceremonial and interpositional function and in terms of their association with the vegetation deity. Further, we can recognize not only how the relation between cut and returning flowers reflects that between castration and the emblem of immortality but also how both these relations in turn reflect the very process of consolatory figuration. When Wordsworth fixes on the flower in a concluding section of the "Elegiac Verses" for his brother he uses a language that confirms a now familiar elegiac procedure. The poem moves, in short, from a failed urge to summon the powers of a bird's flight (the power that might have saved John) to the consolatory description of a flower that, though "meek," nevertheless "grows upon its native bed . . . cleaving to the ground . . . / With multitude of purple eyes, / Spangling a cushion green like moss."[53] It is this flower, figured beyond death, that Wordsworth hopes to see "in its pride" once he has "crossed the mountain." And it is after this surge of vigorous language that Wordsworth can speak of the power of his verse, as well as of letting a "monumental Stone / Stand—sacred as a shrine."

Thwarted in his desire to claim an unconditioned power that would forestall death, Wordsworth has had to accept the qualification of his desire; and it is only on the other side of the mountain, or indeed of death, that he can posit a consoling figure—one derived, as so often in Wordsworth's work, from a scarcely transformed sexual impulse toward the mother earth.[54] Ironically and yet necessarily, the establishment of the flower "in its pride" can only be posited in the unnatural world after death, once the mountain has been crossed. (Of course part of the function of the flower image is to mask the disjunction between this world and the next.) Finally, the clustered images of flowers, eyes, and spangles definitely do recall Milton's use of them in "Lycidas" and we are now perhaps more alert to the reason why such a cluster might, after two centuries, retain its hold on a poet so apparently scornful of conventional figures.

A similar reading is often required for a deeper appreciation of the images of *light* so crucial to elegies. As with the images of flowers,

WELSHIMER MEMORIAL LIBRARY
MILLIGAN COLLEGE, TENN. 37682

there are several levels of meaning, and similar currents run beneath the obvious significance of this figure for an energy that conquers darkness and outlasts human mortality. As in the Phaeton legend, the sun can serve as the symbol for the power of the father. But interestingly enough, as Mircea Eliade has shown, the sky god himself is often perceived as a castrated deity, or as an old god deposed by a youthful usurper. [55] Eliade attributes such perceptions to a belief in the enforced cessation of an otherwise prolonged intercourse between the sky and the earth. In other words, the sky god was emasculated and relegated to a remote height—a height thus ironically achieved by this very relegation. The figure of the sun thus functions like that of the phallus; and to lay claim figuratively (in contrast to Phaeton's literal attempt) to a solar or stellar light may thus be understood as another aspect of the mourner's characteristic resolution. Such a claim involves an attempted assumption of one's symbolic legacy and an attempt to assert a figure that, like the other consoling tropes of elegy, offers the most paradoxical blend of absence and presence, of weakness and strength.

Like that of the fertility god, the figure of the sun and the associated figures of light and of fire have undergone a history of resignification throughout the development of the elegy. In one of the earliest descriptions of mourning, that of Achilles after the death of Patroclus, wrath arouses Achilles from grief, and at that moment "Around his Brows a golden Cloud she [Pallas] spread / A Stream of Glory flam'd above his Head."[56] So intense was this light that it compared with beacon fires blazing forth at sunset, an artificial light emerging like a substitute for the sun. The subsequent variations of this fundamental image are too many to rehearse here, but we shall be pointing with much greater specificity to its survival in Milton's or Shelley's consolatory claims, no less than in the attenuated retrospective glimmerings of Hardy's elegies for his first wife. And whether the sun or the light signifies Achilles' angrily renewed martial strength (the light here associated, interestingly, with the female figure of Athene), or Milton's resurrective vision, or Hardy's memory, beneath this figure there plays a heritage of powerful contradictions associated with the original positing of any imagery of light on the far side of darkness, or of presence in the space of an absence. [57]

Turning from the arch-figures of consolation, we should consider one last set of conventions, involving the use of division between or within mourning voices. Margaret Alexiou discusses this use with regard to ancient Greek laments, showing how the practice influenced the Greek *threnos*, a formal chant performed by professional mourners, in conjunction with the *goos*, the less formal wailing of the bereaved. An antiphony would result, the voices of the bereaved coming to chime with the refrains of the paid singers. In the *Iliad* we read:

A melancholy Choir attend around
With plaintive Sighs, and Musick's solemn Sound:
Alternately they sing, alternate flow
Th'obedient Tears, melodious in their Woe. [58]

The lament continues, structured by a series of solo plaints, each joined at its end by the chorus of mourners. Similarly, in the *Odyssey* the shade of Agamemnon tells of the Muses' antiphonal singing at the funeral of Achilles.

The divided voice structure of the lament entered drama as the *kommos*, defined by Aristotle as a "tragic lament in dialogue form between chorus and actors," while the lyric form apparently most suited for the antiphonal lament was the eclogue. [59] But even in elegies that are not strictly eclogues the ancient practice continues: in Bion's dirge for Adonis, "the Loves join in weeping" as the refrain sets up a choral antiphony to the speaker's lament, which itself includes a further voice, that of the grieving Aphrodite. And even in elegies that call themselves "monodies," such as "Lycidas," the voice of the elegist seems to work through several moments of extreme divisiveness or multiplicity. [60]

How should we interpret this conventional fracturing or separation of voices? Three partial suggestions were made earlier. The first relates to the "splitting" and self-suppression that accompanied the self's first experiences of loss and substitution, its discovery of signs both for lost objects and for the self. The second is associated with the dramatizing strategy by which mourners not only lend ceremony to their rites but also intensify and indicate their own "work" as survivors. Thus the lament would have to include the semblance of another voice as stage director, introducing and spotlighting apparently other voices or choruses.

A third determinant lies in what we saw to be the confrontational structure required for the very recognition of loss. We recall how through a kind of repetitive dialogue the bereaved is forced to accept a reality that he might otherwise refuse. Allied to this is the general function of controlling or criticizing the mourner. As Sidney wrote, in one of the early English definitions of the "lamenting Elegiac," the elegy "surely is to be praised, either for compassionate accompanying just causes of lamentation, or for rightly pointing out how weak be the passions of woefulness."[61] As early as Theocritus's "First Idyl," the griever is addressed by voices urging him to temper his sorrow and to rejoin the community of the living, and the tradition is continued with variations through almost all the major elegies. In "Lycidas," the voices of address, internalized and dreamlike though they may be, are successors to an entire line of admonishing or sympathizing voices in the elegies of Theocritus, Petrarch, Boccaccio, and others.

A separation of voices thus reflects and carries forward the necessarily dialectical movement of the work of mourning, not merely in the process of recognition but for the entire project of withdrawal and reattachment of affections. If the mourner must break off and replace his attachments, the self that survives in this way has, in a sense, begun again, putting its former position behind it. An obvious instance of how the eclogue form may be used to provide this kind of division and progression is Virgil's "Eclogue V," in which the consoling voice of Menalcas soars beyond the disconsolate plaint of Mopsus. One finds a similar dynamic interplay of voices in the elegies of Petrarch, Sannazaro, and Spenser; but it is more subtly present in the self-surpassing turn of "Lycidas," or "Adonais," or in the Neoclassical elegies of Jonson and Dryden, where personal voice is distanced or assimilated to the apparent impersonality of inherited language.

The eclogue form has the further characteristic of lending itself to the presentation of a *contest*, and this, too, is closely related to mourning rites. The ancient funeral games here become transmuted to a poetry contest, but the original function survives. On one level, it provides a kind of distraction, a channeling of the energy of grief into a highly controlled and skilled exertion. The winner, too, becomes an attractive object onto which the mourners can temporarily transfer their attachments. What is more important, the winners exemplify and seem to immortalize the qualities of the deceased, or at least those virtues deemed important for the community's survival. The games thus take on the aspects of a contest for inheritance; we see this especially clearly in the elegiac eclogues where, beneath an apparently innocent singing match, a poet asserts his position as true heir to a poetic legacy.

Originally, as we have seen in the vegetation rites and in their spiritualized successors, the act of mourning quite simply *included* the act of inheritance, for the participant ingested the god or its symbol. (To take the wafer and wine is still an act of repeated inheritance.) The connection between mourning and inheritance has remained a close one throughout history. Most interesting for any reader of the elegy is the fact that in Greece the right to mourn was from earliest times legally connected to the right to inherit. There were, predictably enough, contests, even at the gravesite, over who should most legitimately mourn. The issue is central to *The Oresteia*, written at a time when inheritance laws in Greece were changing, and we shall return to it more fully in discussing *Hamlet*. But for the moment it is worth indicating its presence within the otherwise neutral-seeming elements of an aesthetic convention. Few elegies can be fully read without an appreciation of their frequently combative struggles for inheritance.

Furthermore, the ancient law prevented anyone from inheriting *unless* he mourned. Alexiou quotes Isaios: "Is it not a most unholy thing if a man, without having done any of the customary rites due to the dead, yet expects to take the inheritance of the dead man's property?"[62] It is clear that since the time of Moschus's lament for Bion, many elegies pivot around the issue of poetic inheritance. In this case, the heir apparent must demonstrate a greater strength or proximity to the dead than any rival may claim; but he must also wrest his inheritance *from* the dead. More than a mere ingestion, some act of alteration or surpassal must be made, some device whereby the legacy may be seen to have entered a new successor. Auden's lines for Yeats, recalling, as we are now in a position to see, one of the most primitive images of inheritance, are especially true for elegists:

> The words of the dead
> Are modified in the guts of the living.[63]

In its earliest conflictual structures, as also in successive adaptations of the eclogue form, the elegy clarifies and dramatizes this emergence of the true heir.

II

Spenser: *The Shepheardes Calender* and "Astrophel"

It is tempting to turn now to the Greek and Latin elegies, and to their early Renaissance successors, to see the conventions in the relative clarity of their beginnings and to watch how the genre lends itself to the tempers of different cultures and to the needs of different poets. But to work through the elegies of Theocritus, Bion, Moschus, and Virgil and on through those of Petrarch, Boccaccio, Sannazaro, Castiglione, Marot, and Ronsard would require a long digression. Rather, I begin with Spenser, hoping to show how his works modify yet carry the tradition through the complex crosscurrents of the English Renaissance.

My approach to Spenser follows two principal lines of inquiry. The first briefly studies sections of *The Shepheardes Calender* to emphasize the relation between mourning and that characteristic Renaissance concern, the question of poetic inheritance. The second focuses on how Spenser's wariness of the artifice of fiction per se, a no less typically Renaissance concern, complicated his attitude toward the traditional elegy. "Astrophel" should be seen as having followed a series of experiments in which Spenser carefully explored various poetic expressions of loss, searching throughout for a consolation that would satisfy not only his needs as a mourner but also his unusual sophistication as a maker of fictions. While the second theme is studied mainly in relation to "Astrophel," its terms envelop the entire inquiry and must be mentioned at the outset.

"Astrophel" was, after all, written several years later than even Spenser thought appropriate. It was not published until 1595, nine years after Sidney's death, while as early as 1591, in his dedication of "The Ruines of Time" to Sidney's sister, Mary, Countess of Pembroke, Spenser had accused himself of ungrateful delay "for that I have not shewed anie thankefull remembrance towards him or any of them; but suffer their names to sleep in silence and forgetfulnesse."[1] Why the delay? It cannot be that Spenser's preoccupation with *The Faerie Queene* prevented him from writing the elegy, for he was able to write "The Ruines of Time," along with a sheaf of other "complaints" published in 1591. Knowing what we do of the elegist's complex problem of poetic inheritance and of self-comparison to the dead, it is conceivable that Spenser had to wait until he had become the poet of *The Faerie Queene* before he could elegize the poet of the *Arcadia*. It has been suggested that Spenser was simply reluctant to have his particular response swamped by the outpouring of a nation's grief. Even so, nine years seems more than adequate a delay on those grounds. There may be other biographical reasons, one of which we shall see to be Spenser's unquestionable ambivalence toward Sidney's final pursuit. But whatever such reasons may be, I do not think that they exclude the possibility of regarding the nature of his earlier elegies themselves as a further clue to the delay.

Several features of *The Shepheardes Calender,* "Daphnaida," and "The Ruines of Time" must have given Spenser pause when he turned to mourn Sidney in "Astrophel." The obvious problem is the dominance of inert states of melancholy to the exclusion of vigorous engagements in mourning. But added to this is the more general question of the pronounced artificiality of the poems: their enclosures within the fictional realms of pastoral or of quasi-visionary encounter and their dependence on obvious and rather creaky fictions, such as the heavily framed lament or the medieval paraphernalia of woe—personifications of Sorrow, "grieslie ghosts" and "fyrie furies," together with such clichés as "yclad in clay" or "wrapt in lead."

As already mentioned, Spenser had an unusually acute sensitivity to the question of artifice itself, a deep ambivalence toward the figurative nature of language. His works are sewn through with moments in which language not only draws attention to its own fabricated nature but by extension questions the very ideals or principles (such as monarchy, justice, courtesy) in whose construction it plays so crucial a role. Furthermore, Spenser's careful attitude toward figuration must have been especially keen in the "presence" of Sidney. For Sidney's own poetry is marked by a profound sense both of the artificiality of literature's imaginary beings or landscapes and of the devastating way in which ideals of love and pastoral simplicity, of chivalry and virtue, can be exposed as illusory phantoms. This skepticism in turn aggravated Sidney's harsh awareness of the difficulty of finding true consolation. Elegiac passages in the *Arcadia* have a tendency to move toward an increasingly self-conscious sense of imprisoning sorrow, often turning against the very medium of lament as if that, too, were conspiring against the griever: "And stoppe mine eares, lest I grow mad with Musicke."[2]

Moreover, who but Sidney had so thoroughly exposed, in however celebratory a manner, the fictive nature of poetry? As he declared in *A Defence of Poetry*, "It is not rhyming and versing that maketh a poet . . . but it is that feigning notable images of virtues, vices, or what else."[3] Like an echo, the words *feign, image, figure,* and *counterfeit* repeat themselves throughout the essay, as Sidney emphasizes how far ideal poetic constructions are removed from the flawed nature of the given world. The reader is usually swept along by this reiterated privileging of imagined poesie over impaired reality; but if for a moment the emphasis on the fictional "another nature" were to strengthen his skepticism more than his belief, he might feel stranded between a degraded world of nature and history on the one hand and an unreal world of phantoms on the other. Indeed, Sidney's frustrations with his own career suggest that he was finally more eager to engage the fallen world directly in action than to feign improved versions of it in the enclosures of his verse. It may be well to elevate the "feigned Cyrus in Xenophon" above the "true Cyrus in Justin" (an elevation that Spenser partially recalls in his letter to Raleigh regarding *The Faerie Queene*), or the "feigned Aeneas in Virgil" above the "right Aeneas in Dares Phrygius"; but how consoling is the existence of an admittedly artificial Cyrus to someone who is constrained or rusticated by an actual tyrant? And how easily can a poet who mourns a thirty-two-year-old victim of a battle at Zutphen in the Low Countries turn for consolation to an ideal realm he knows to be inhabited by "forms such as never were in Nature"?

The Shepheardes Calender

Before analyzing Spenser's resolution of this problem, in "Astrophel," it is worth turning for a sense of contrast and development to his earlier elegiac works. I suggested that in order to write "Astrophel" Spenser had in some way to move beyond these works, with their prevalence of dispirited melancholy, their heavy framing devices, and their rather passive dependence on received modes of figuration. At a narrative level, the most obvious feature of the poems is that the principal griever in each (Colin Clout, the city of Verulam, Arthur Gorges) is left entirely disconsolate at the end. In each case, the uneasy and baffled narrator is quite unable to comfort the griever. In "The Ruines of Time," the lament of the city of Verulam is followed by her disappearance, which leaves the narrator faint, wordless, and "frosen" with horror. He withdraws rather abruptly into a hermetic series of emblematic visions deriving from van der Noodt's *A Theatre*, a work that Spenser had helped to translate from a French version twenty years before. "Daphnaida," too, ends with the cheerless separation of griever from narrator, a separation in which the bereaved and melancholy Alcyon (Gorges) rejects all proffered consolation and wanders off "With staggring pace and dismall lookes dismay, / As if that death he in the face had seene" (*Works*, 534). Heavily modeled on Chaucer's *Book of the Duchess*, the poem is a recognition topos, in the sense of a mourner's recognition, discussed above. But instead of gaining some control over the griever, the narrator in Spenser's poem merely relegates him to the "darke night," and the poem ends with a line of disengagement and ignorance ("But what of him became I cannot weene"). [4]

It is on *The Shepheardes Calender* that I wish to pause, partly to observe its elegiac passages but also to explore the relation between mourning and the quest for poetic inheritance. Despite their variety, the poem's several threads overlap in the almost unremittingly mournful figure of Colin Clout, who, while bemoaning the indifference of his beloved, the corruption of the church, and the demise of the very line of English poetry that he would inherit, casts doubts on the potency both of his verse and of his manhood. This twofold doubt, whose objects are both symbolized by the pipe, is especially critical for a young poet struggling to come into a poetic inheritance. [5] A great and perhaps underrated cause of Colin's sorrow is his frustrated inability to assume, in his own estimation, the mantle of his chosen forebear, and the predicament infiltrates the *Calender* more pervasively than one may immediately recognize. [6] While readers have demonstrated at formal levels Spenser's deliberate adaptation of a legacy of various verse traditions, I know of none who has shown how fully the problem of inheritance is actually *thematized* in the poem. [7]

The connection between Colin and Spenser, while never exact, and while deliberately distanced, is sufficiently close in this regard to deserve mention. The *Calender* was Spenser's first true bid for poethood, a bid opposed to the current prevalence of Europeanized literary taste in England. A young poet interested in reviving the supposedly rougher, more archaic English tradition might feel not a little diffidence regarding his ability to command a wide acclaim. Add to this Spenser's difficult position on the margins of the shifting circles of favor at court, and one recognizes further grounds for self-doubt in one who set out suddenly from relative obscurity to restore the line of Chaucer, with himself as heir.

E. K.'s letter to Gabriel Harvey introduces the *Calender* as most definitely a project of attempted inheritance and one that had to be fought against the forces of neglect and even usurpation. The prince of poets felt bitterly that his domain, the English language, had been usurped, and, as E. K. wrote, he "laboured to restore, as to their rightfull heritage such good and naturall English words, as have ben long time out of use and almost cleane disherited" (*Works*, 417). Yet this was only part of what Spenser sought by way of legacy. The entire *Calender* is in fact an extraordinarily self-conscious attempt by Spenser to place himself at, or rather *as*, the confluence of two traditions. On the one hand he would revive the native strain flowing from the undefiled wellhead, Chaucer; while on the other, as E. K. again notes, he would follow Theocritus, Virgil, Mantuan, Petrarch, and the line of great European poets, seeking to imitate the trajectories of their careers as well as certain elements of their verse. In the very act of rechristening Chaucer Tityrus, the name Virgil had chosen for his pastoral persona, Spenser blends traditions and manufactures an ideal forebear. And it is this compound figure of Tityrus who dominates the quest for inheritance as it surfaces in the *Calender*.

A frequently overlooked moment in the "May" eclogue not only supports and illuminates our interest in the question of inheritance but also points ahead to "Lycidas." For just as Milton will engineer an astonishingly effective and consoling redefinition of *fame*, shifting its meaning from that of the secular Renaissance term to that of a spiritualized Protestantism, so Spenser works a similar redefinition of the word *inheritance*. He in turn is echoing Moschus, who in his elegy for Bion distinguished between legacies: "I am heir to that Dorian Muse which thou didst teach to thy pupils and with which thou didst endow me, leaving thy wealth to others, but to me the heritage of song."[8] In

"May" we hear Piers attacking the worldly clergy and urging shepherds—meaning ministers—to reject the kind of material inheritance
of "welth" and to prefer instead the true, spiritual inheritance such as
shepherds originally received from Pan, here meaning Christ. As any
reader of the *Calender* knows, the identity of Spenser's Pan is remarkably fluid—one of the instances of a conventional figure threatening
to unravel beneath the load of conflicting interpretations (the pagan
god, Christ, Henry VIII, and even Satan, as E.K. tells us certain
thinkers mistakenly assume). By Pan's legacy we may, therefore, at
least assume a poetic as well as a religious inheritance. Translated into
poetic equivalents, the distinction between "welth" and Pan's true
legacy may be the difference between a more crudely self-serving *and*
more rewarded poetry on the one hand and a more inward, reclusive,
and potentially unnoticed poetry on the other. It is partly this distinction and his own particular choice that Spenser is trying to clarify and
advance in the correlative language of a religious critique.

The issue is deepened by the fable that Piers goes on to relate. At
the simplest allegorical level, the story of a gullible kid who is tricked
and killed by a cunning fox embodies Piers's warning against a selfish
clergy who exploit naifs. But the kid is also an heir, the sole heir, in
fact, of a deceased father. As we have learned to expect, descriptions
of inheritance often retain in their imagery a residue of the originally
sexual and vegetational nature of their subject. Hence the mother
expresses her hope

> To see thee succeede in thy fathers steade,
> And florish in flowres of lusty head.
> For even so thy father his head upheld,
> And so his hauty hornes did he weld.
>
> (*Works*, 438, lines 203–6)

It is this inheritance, together with his life, that the kid loses by
yielding not merely to a corrupt fox but to the temptations of narcissism, with whose instrument (the mirror) the pedlar finally beguiles
his prey. At a symbolic level the story throws light on the plight of
that other self-centered faltering heir, Colin Clout, while at a more
general level the nexus between inheritance and narcissism goes deeply into the nature of mourning and elegy.

The issue is more dramatically joined in the next eclogue, "June,"
when Colin turns directly to elegize Tityrus. The context is Hob-

binol's attempt to lift Colin's depression by reviving his ambition as a poet. It is an encounter like those within traditional elegies, in which the griever is visited by a comforter or admonisher. Colin rejects Hobbinol's advice as well as his compliments, complaining that the Muses are beyond his orbit, particularly since his patron god, Pan, has been defeated by Apollo. Now "pyping low in shade of lowly grove, / I play to please my selfe, all be it ill." And yet, when he turns to mourn for Tityrus, a few lines later, his desire curiously enough revives, as though he glimpses the power he might have if he could inherit that deified predecessor's force.

> The God of shepheards *Tityrus* is dead,
> Who taught me homely, as I can, to make.
> . . . .
> Nowe dead he is, and lyeth wrapt in lead,
> (O why should death on hym such outrage showe?)
> And all hys passing skil with him is fledde,
> The fame whereof doth dayly greater growe.
> But if on me some little drops would flow,
> Of that the spring was in his learned hedde,
> I soone would learne these woods, to wayle my woe,
> And teache the trees, their trickling teares to shedde.
>
> (*Works*, 442, lines 81–96)

Here quickening against the leaden inertia of death is the image of inheritance, a rather pagan version, presented as drops that would flow from the spring of Tityrus's head to Colin. Again we recognize the primitive origins of this imagery and notice how thoroughly Spenser follows out the associations still at work within the figure. For, could Colin inherit some of the potent drops from that great head, he would absorb the power to move the trees to tears. We do not have to recall how the tears of Isis continued the vitalizing juices of her dead Osiris, nor do we need to recall Freud's association of tears with semen, to be aware of the metaphorically sexual element of the transfer imagined here, as the trees absorb and in turn secrete the transmitted liquid influence of Tityrus. Colin's power to affect the trees clinches these associations by its reminiscence of Orpheus and the vegetation gods before him.

By an inheritance, therefore, of the dead god's power, the poet would come upon his own defense against mortality. The energy of this defense, although deflected into poetic power, is still close to its origins in sexual desire, as the following lines make even more clear. For Colin's plaints would next "pierce [Rosalind's] heart with poynt of worthy wight." The mourner's power to pierce and to breed pity will be invoked again in the opening lines of "Astrophel"; but for the moment, that power is still beyond Colin ("since I am not as I wish I were"). He may move Hobbinol to tears, but he does not have the strength he seeks, and the emblem for the eclogue, *Gia speme spenta*, reflects his turn toward despair.

With further foreshadowings of "Lycidas," "July" turns explicitly to attack the corrupting ambitions of self-interested clergymen.[9] Less directly, the eclogue continues to explore opposing attitudes toward inheritance. The arrogant Morrell regards the hilltops as the appropriate region for followers of Pan, and for any who seek to express their affinity with the titanic sun. For Morrell, that affinity should not be mediated, and it is quite consistent with this attitude that he seeks to negate the Fall and its exclusion of herdsmen from "delight." Thomalin, on the other hand, claims that the true heir of the dead shepherds and saints earns his legacy through deliberate humility and through maintaining a deferent, even evasive attitude toward the sun. For him, some "coverture" is needed to mediate the "cruell scortching heate," and delight is to be deferred in favor of duty.

"July" is not an elegy, but as we shall see in several elegies to come, Thomalin's submissive attitude is a crucial element of any successful mourning. In its isolation, however, Thomalin's resigned self-abasement is too extreme. In fact, this eclogue reveals an unresolved ambivalence regarding the question of ambition or inheritance. The issue is polarized between two inadequate antagonists, the overreaching Morrell and the underreaching Thomalin. The necessary *blend* of self-aggrandizement and self-effacement, a blend that we shall find in "Lycidas" and other successful elegies, is not yet composed by these two isolated positions. If Thomalin is the moral victor of the eclogue, his pallid modesty and his closing reference to the injured Algrin, who "lyes in lingring payne," offer little advance beyond the disconsolation of "June."

Colin's inability to assume a satisfactory manner of grieving is one of the very themes of "January." The immediate cause of Colin's wintry plight there is neither the season itself, which merely reflects his woe, nor yet his unrequited love as much as it is his sorrowful expressions themselves:

> All so my lustfull leafe is drye and sere,
> My timely buds with wayling all are wasted:
> The blossome, which my braunch of youth did beare,
> With breathed sighes is blowne away, and blasted
> And from mine eyes the drizling teares descend,
> As on your boughes the ysicles depend.
>
> (*Works*, 422, lines 37–42)

In these lines, the wailing and the sighing are the immediate enemies of Colin's "lustfull" energies. Instead of flowing freely, his tears congeal and freeze, and Colin's complaint moves indeed toward a rejection of his pipe and of the sexual and poetic powers that it could represent:

> Wherefore my pype, albee rude *Pan* thou please,
> Yet for thou pleasest not, where most I would:
> And thou unlucky Muse, that wontst to ease
> My musing mynd, yet canst not, when thou should:
> Both pype and Muse, shall sore the while abye.
> So broke his oaten pype, and downe dyd lye.
>
> (*Works*, 422, lines 67–72)

By refusing to exercise even the displaced sexuality of consolatory piping, Colin opts, as he does in "June," to lie low. His consequent withdrawal, rejecting Pan and the entire elegiac procedure of discovering or inventing a substitute for his lost love-object, moves him away from mourning toward the paradoxical blend of narcissism and self-contempt that we associate with melancholy.

Although Colin drops temporarily out of the poem, his indirect presence is strongly felt, and the exploration of his problem continues only somewhat less overtly in the following eclogues. "February" picks up the theme of congealment, as well as the ancient imagery for melancholy, thereby adding emotional depth to Colin's premature entry into old age. More interesting still is Thenot's story, itself transmitted from Tityrus: a cautionary tale about a youth who rashly has his old shelterer, the oak, hacked down. Certainly, the story is an allegory designed in part to criticize the Earl of Oxford's arrogance toward Leicester, seventeen years his senior. But when one reads the description of the sacred and enchanted oak, "often halowed with holy water dewe," one can hardly help recognizing that this ancient and mysterious tree functions also as a totem. The youth's aggression against this father-totem suggests a bid for premature inheritance. And it is against this bid that Thenot's text works. [10] Once again, as in "June," the question of self-advancement and of attempted inheritance is turned against the young aspirant. Like Colin, the briar is left "disconsolate," and "upright he can stand no more."

As the *Calender* develops, the gloom deepens, with "March" obliquely and "April" directly referring to Colin's plight. "May," as we have seen, broaches the question of inheritance and includes the negative example of the kid. "June" shows Colin in despair, while in "August" Cuddie signs a dark lament by Colin, who thus resumes his ghostly identity offstage. The lament itself seeks to attune its "deadly cryes" to the "signe of dreery death." "October" carries the mood and the ideas yet further, and one sees Colin's pessimism infecting Cuddie, just as his sorrow had enveloped Hobbinol. Cuddie questions the efficacy or durability of verse ("Sike words bene wynd and wasten soone in vayne") and complains that the patrons and the subjects of heroic poetry are now "yclad in clay" or "liggen wrapt in leade." Piers nevertheless insists on the elevating inspiration of love, but his claim is undercut by Cuddie's instance of Colin, whose love is precisely what debars him from "mounting high." Piers does not have the strength to reject Colin as an inadequate exemplar, a moping melancholic, and the eclogue is left somehow in Cuddie's hands.

In a similar movement to that of Colin in "June," Cuddie concludes "October" by approaching and then declining from a momentary stirring of ambition and desire. As Colin had invoked the pure drops of Tityrus's influence, so Cuddie conjures the power of Bacchus's wine. Again, the influence is figured as an invigorating liquid, a power that would enable the lowly Cuddie to "reare the Muse on stately stage, / And teache her tread aloft." But as in "June," the aspirant is found lacking, and with a detumescent cooling of his "corage" (a word whose connotations Shakespeare's sonnets explore more boldly), Cuddie sinks back to the charm of "slender pipes."

Piers's inability to offer a sufficiently forceful counter to Cuddie or Colin is symptomatic of the entire *Calender*. Despite his moment of grandeur as elegist of Dido in "November," Colin lapses even further into the wintry melancholia of "December," a lament that orients him inescapably toward death. If Spenser is above this melancholy withdrawal, it is curious how reticent he is about asserting his superiority.

47

Nowhere within the poem is there an adequate answer to Colin, and nothing retards the momentum of his despair. Were "December" and "November" reversed, there would at least be a perceptible upturn, but Spenser chooses instead to follow the elegy by Colin's final isolation and decline. This in turn has the effect of making us read the elegy as a circumscribed set piece, somehow remote from Colin's personal fate.[11]

A superficial reading might, however, suggest that there *is* a definite closeness between "November" and Colin's decline in "December." The elegy's valorization of death as a release of the soul, coupled with Colin's expressed desire to follow Dido, might then be supposed to pave the way to Colin's acceptance of death's approach in "December." But this reading would fail to recognize the crucial difference between the two eclogues. "November" draws its strength from its Virgilian leap to a supernatural realm. The "December" eclogue, on the other hand, is totally devoid not only of any supernatural reference but also of any *affirmative* aspiration on the part of Colin toward the death he had seemed to value in the elegy. On the contrary, "December" resolutely traps Colin in an exclusively natural world, dragging him and even his former poems into a physical degeneration such as that of rotting nature. The imagery has a kind of demented botanical consistency as Colin exhaustively catalogues his bare boughs, rotted fruit, withered flowers, and desiccated roots. Nowhere is there a suggestion that this is the celebrant of the winged soul of Dido. Nowhere is there even the hint that this natural death might be of the order of a vegetation god's periodic descent.

A closer look at "November" tends to confirm the suspicion regarding its relative remoteness. The first remarkable aspect is that its subject, the death of Dido, is introduced, not as the cause of grief, but as a convenient subject with which to match a prior sorrow. Refusing Thenot's request for a joyous song, Colin claims that his mood and the time of year incline to sadder themes. Only then does Thenot, who a minute ago was ready for "merimake," offer the topic of Dido's death, a kind of correlative to Colin's woe. Colin becomes, in other words, something of a professional mourner (indeed Thenot entreats him "to bewayle my wofull tene"), at a personal remove from his actual subject. And even though he enlists his own sorrows, one does not quite get over this initial impression of remoteness.

The set-piece effect is increased by the highly stilted and theatrical beginning of the elegy proper.

> Up then *Melpomene* thou mournefulst Muse of nyne,
> Such cause of mourning never hadst afore:
> Up grieslie ghostes and up my rufull ryme,
> Matter of myrth now shalt thou have no more.
>
> (Works, 461, lines 53–56)

E.K.'s note to this should not be missed: "Up griesly gosts) The manner of Tragicall Poetes, to call for helpe of Furies and damned ghostes: so is Hecuba of Euripides, and Tantalus brought in of Seneca. And the rest of the rest" (*Works*, 463). Spenser has followed a train of figures too long for even E.K. to catalogue. And if there is a note of weariness or boredom in that wonderful phrase "and the rest of the rest," it is not inexcusable in the face of this rather stale summons to the ancient machinery of grief. Nor do the dogged alliteration and labored syntax much refresh the weary figures:

> For dead shee is, that myrth thee made of yore.
> *Dido* my deare alas is dead,
> Dead and lyeth wrapt in lead:
> O heavie herse.
>
> (Works, 461, lines 57–60)

Is it so unfair to look forward to Shakespeare's parody of the formulae at large?

> But stay! O spite!
> But mark, poor knight,
> What dreadful dole is here!
> Eyes, do you see?
> How can it be?
> O dainty duck! O dear! . . .
>
> Approach, ye Furies fell!
> O Fates, come, come;
> Cut thread and thrum,
> Quail, crush, conclude, and quell. [12]

It would certainly be unfair and inaccurate not to recognize that the elegy becomes far less mechanical as it continues. But even so, there is little in the first half of the poem that we might not have read in Spenser's immediate model, Marot's elegy for Louise of Savoy. Only in its eleventh stanza does the elegy assume a freer motion to match its sudden widening of reference: "O trustlesse state of earthly things, and slipper hope / Of mortal men, that swincke and sweat for naught." Suddenly, in these Chaucerian lines, Colin impresses us as commanding something of a view, as being on enough of an elevation to generalize. The words are not strikingly original, it is true, but they do suggest an access of power. Appropriately enough, this stanza concludes the descending, sorrowful movement of the poem and forms a bridge to the consolation. The following diction is still clogged and conventional, but the reversal is triumphant: "But maugre death, and dreaded sisters deadly spight, . . . She hath the bonds broke of eternall night" (Works, 462, lines 163–65).

Here Spenser unquestionably overgoes Marot, even though he follows the French poet in placing Dido in Elysium. Whereas Louise is passively absorbed into Elysium ("Elle est aux champs Elisiens receue"), Dido's soul exerts its own dramatic breakthrough.[13] Spenser's Neo-Platonism shows itself more strongly here than in Piers's abortive appeal to love. Its very freshness is apparent in Spenser's difficult choice of a language for the soul, for he tries to describe it in terms neither exclusively pagan nor merely Christian. Dido becomes a blend of goddess and saint, a "blessed" drinker of nectar.

This problem of how to name the transfigured Dido raises a question that Spenser does not elaborate here but will explore more fully in "Astrophel." If Dido has "her soule unbodied of the burdenous corpse," what shape has she assumed? What figure is she now? In other words, how will Spenser figure her? For along with her body she has abandoned whatever "might be in earthlie mould." Spenser's punning use of *mould* is of course designed to blend the idea of shape with that of decaying dross, so that we are left with the idea of Dido's soul not so much having become transfigured as having departed beyond any recognizable figure whatsoever. If she is now without mould, how is she to appear? Spenser faces the problem discussed in a text whose influence on him here is clear, noted as it is in the gloss: Plato's *Phaedo*. Although Socrates declares that the soul "departs to that place which is, like itself, invisible, divine, immortal," he goes on to limn that place's properties, relying, as he admits, on inadequate figures of speech.

How then can one give visible shape without reimporting the mould of figuration? Spenser does not press the dilemma here, allowing Colin to hasten instead toward the enthusiastic envisioning of Dido's soul: "I see thee blessed soule, I see." Only the gloss keeps the question open, by praising the very *pretense* of Colin's figure of sight: "I see) A lively *Icon*, or *representation as if* he saw her in heaven present" (*Works*, 463, my emphasis). The poem continues with a depiction of Elysium, and we presumably fall under the sway of belief. But the seed of the problem is there.

Perhaps the most interesting feature of the gloss is this disconcerting skepticism regarding almost every figure in the poem.[14] By skepticism I mean the insistence on the figure as figure, thereby checking the reader from any simple completion of reference. We are told that the eclogues are a labor of concealment; that the names are pseudonyms shadowing hidden identities; that such figures as Pan, Niobe, Atlas, Endymion, Titan, and the Fates are all dependent on the "feigning" of poets and are all susceptible to an array of interpretations. The gloss is like an odd mirror containing the poem's reflection of its fictions. This curious, potentially undermining relation is crucial to almost all Spenser's work. In *The Faerie Queene* it is present in the poem's constant admissions of the use of shadows and reflections and within the poem's own narrative explorations of the ineradicable connection between figure and falsity. In "Astrophel" it is intrinsic to the unfolding of the poem itself, being geared to the very dialectic of mourning.

"Astrophel"

The most obvious change as one moves from Spenser's earlier elegiac works to "Astrophel" is that the poet seems to have crossed into an apparently less unreal world. The pastoral garb is more loosely worn, and the poem is not as enclosed as the *Calender*, with its cycle of months and its entire cast of shepherds. Nor is it located within the realm of quasi-visionary encounters such as in "The Ruines of Time" or "Daphnaida." The mourning voice is that of the poet himself, and he seems to speak from within our world:

> Shepheards that wont on pipes of oaten reed,
> Oft times to plaine your loves concealed smart:
> And with your piteous layes have learnd to breed

Compassion in a countrey lasses hart.
Hearken ye gentle shepheards to my song,
And place my dolefull plaint your plaints emong.

To you alone I sing this mournfull verse,
The mournfulst verse that ever man heard tell:
To you whose softened hearts it may empierse,
With dolours dart for death of Astrophel.

$$\text{(Works, 547, lines 1–10)}^{15}$$

This is clearly an assured bid for inclusion in the company of poets. Unlike the isolated Colin Clout addressing Pan, Spenser is now speaking directly to his fellow poets, commanding their audience. Some of these poets are the other elegists whose poems are published here with Spenser's. In fact, Spenser has maneuvered these poets, all of whose elegies preceded his in time, into a position of posteriority and dependency. [16] It is he now who leads the mourning, introducing their poems after his.

Also within this introduction we recognize the familiar motif of piercing and breeding. The poem's power to impregnate suggests the surviving poet's ongoing, if displaced, sexual energy, his assertion of a thrusting force that one already feels must carry him beyond the weaker introversions of melancholy. This force is complicated by its aggressiveness. The figurative resemblance between the poet's piercing power and the power that killed Astrophel suggests that a part of the elegy's motive, however troped, lies in an impulse to wound almost as death wounds. It is as though some of the violence of death's power enters man's anger against that power. But this anger is as much a rage against man's own susceptibility to death, hence a rage against the self. And it is not surprising to hear that rage take on the characteristics of death itself. In the introductory chapter, I explored some of the psychological background of this tendency to self-injury, and we shall see its elaboration in later works. The purpose of raising the subject in discussing "Astrophel" is not merely to delve beneath that otherwise apparently fortuitous similarity between the piercing power of the elegist and that of death (compare the related anger and destructive power of the elegist in the opening of "Lycidas"). It is also to make some sense of the surprisingly vicious fury of Astrophel's foreign campaign:

Eftsoones all heedlesse of his dearest hale,
Full greedily into the heard he thrust:
To slaughter them, and worke their finall bale,
Least that his toyle should of their troups be brust.
Wide wounds emongst them many one he made,
Now with his sharp borespear, now with his blade.

His care was all how he them all might kill,
That none might scape (so partiall unto none).

(103–10)

The distaste that many readers feel for this passage stems, I think, from a failure to read beyond its surface, and even beyond the allegorization of Sidney's battle against the Spanish. It is true that after the evocation, earlier in the poem, of the perfect "gentle" shepherd, this may seem an incongruously harsh picture, but there are several ways to understand its significance. Most important of these is to consider what the poem tells us of Astrophel's disdain for the world. His unhappiness is in fact presented as his only "fayling," and we are shown how it relates to his unassuageable devotion to the ethereal Stella. So exclusively is Stella presented as a star that this figure entirely occludes any human referent. It is this very occluding or excluding quality that marks the attitude of her adorer. As star she is immortal, attracting Astrophel away from the mortal world. It is in relation to this dislocative *contemptus mundi* that Astrophel's violence takes on some of its meaning, for it is thus seen as a channeling of what we may suppose to be the wrath enfolded within his contempt. Astrophel's heedlessness toward the world is directed no less against his own nature ("All heedlesse of his dearest hale"). Just as suggested, he takes on a role not unlike that of Death itself, whence the description of his thorough and impartial slaughter.

Added to the impulse behind this depiction of Astrophel's rage against mortality is of course Spenser's own fury against death, both as mortality and as event. The violent lines therefore bear the weight of his own anger and sorrow. There is, however, a further element at work here: Spenser's hostility or at least ambivalence toward Astrophel's lethal pursuit. At an obvious level, Spenser finds it difficult to approve the very choice that led to Sidney's death. His criticism is pointed in the language of "Did prick him forth with proud desire of praise" and in the query "What needeth peril to be sought abroad?" More interesting yet is the way Spenser displays how Astrophel becomes reduced to the very savagery that kills him. Spenser captures the way violence recoils on the self, and by a momentary ambiguity he blurs the identities of the hunter and the beast:

> So as he rag'd emongst that beastly rout,
> A cruell beast of most accursed brood
> Upon him turnd (despeyre makes cowards stout)

> (115–17)

The case of Spenser's critique assumes added interest when one recalls that Astrophel's choice is equated by Spenser with a rejection of language. For Astrophel was not content with a merely verbal wooing or praising of Stella, and chose instead the unmediated and here almost suicidal pursuit of violent action. Spenser's ambivalence poises on one of those reversals so typical of this poem: "Ne her with ydle words alone he wowed, / And verses vaine (yet verses are not vaine)" (67–68). Do we hear the note of an inner debate within whose dialectic the voice of Sidney had come to play its associated part? Does Spenser's parenthesis answer that side of the poet that shares Sidney's skepticism? The issue goes to the core of "Astrophel," for as suggested earlier, the poem achieves its work of mourning precisely by resolving this question of the adequacy of language and its figures of consolation.

To sketch it most simply, this resolution comes about by the thorough way in which the second part of the poem, "The Lay of Clorinda," questions and moves beyond the consolation figured in the earlier part. [17] The withdrawal from or rather rejection of the figure of the Astrophel flower, and the substitution for it of a further, more advanced consolatory figure (the soul as celestial infant) performs a process similar in form to the work of mourning itself—the undoing of a prior position or attachment and the substitution for it of a fresh attachment. The problematic intervening phase, involving as it does a temporary return of affect and interest upon the self, is also present in the poem. The remainder of this chapter will elaborate upon this schema.

The first part of the poem moves from the introductory self-presentation of the elegist to a picture of the young Astrophel. The

conventional enumeration of the qualities of the deceased goes back
to the earliest attempts to perpetuate the powers or virtues of the
dead in the bodies, and later in the minds, of the living. But as we
read Spenser's evocation of the young Astrophel, we are reminded of
another motive for this kind of repetition: the retrospective creation
of a defense against shock. This is especially evident in the way
Spenser seeds the early part of the poem with warning signals, miniature reversals that prepare us for the catastrophic reversal to come.
The characteristic form of these reversals is the turning of a word or
line against itself: "Both wise and hardie (too hardie alas)" (72); "Besides in hunting, such felicities, / Or rather infelicitie he found" (79–
80). This creates a cushion of expectation, but it also instills a ver-
tiginous instability, as though within language, as in life, there were
this sudden tendency for reversal or cancellation, the sudden opening of a chasm. Hardiness threatens to collapse upon its own excess,
felicity hovers over infelicity, the word lies on its shadow or
negation.

The account of Astrophel complicates itself, as his life did, with the
turn to Stella. And as we have seen in our view of that love's associations and implications, this leads in turn to the narrative of his death.
A sense of causality and plot, even of fatality, thus emerges, and as one
rereads, details of this plotting declare themselves. An example of the
careful timing of such details is the implicit comparison of Astrophel
to Orpheus, "And many a nymph . . . both crystall wells and shadie
groves forsooke, / To heare the charmes of his enchanting skill" (43–
46), which comes just before the reorienting of the poem toward the
otherworldly Stella. By associating Astrophel with Orpheus, the poet
casts a little more premonitory shade upon his shepherd, moving him
a step further toward his doom, and toward his fictional assimilation
to that other vegetation god, Adonis.

We have already observed the account of battle following this, and
we come thence to the wounded Astrophel, pouring forth "huge
streames of blood" upon the "cold deare earth." The image of the
vegetation god giving his warm blood to the cold earth is obvious, but
Spenser delays any suggestion of the fertilizing consequences of this
martyrdom. Such consequences will come only with the metamorphosis of victim to flower later in the first part of the poem, and
even that consolatory figure will prove short-lived. As we shall see,
the delay is deliberate, for it allows Spenser to show to what extent the

pastoral world, together with its resources for cure or comfort, has been disrupted.

For the moment, Spenser turns to the conventional questions addressed to those who might have prevented the death. We have already discussed such conventional elegiac questioning, and it is unnecessary to repeat all its determinants and effects here. [18] One aspect does, however, stand out in Spenser's use of the convention—the fact that his addressees are not the traditional gods or nymphs of preceding elegies but rather Astrophel's "shepheard peares" and companions. While this departure may indicate Spenser's unease with the inherited fictions, it also reinforces our suspicion that much elegiac questioning is designed to avert an angry or guilty self-questioning. The distance between Spenser and Astrophel's peers is, after all, relatively slight. And recalling Spenser's unease regarding his long-delayed elegy, the words *unpitied* and *unplayned* lend a specific edge to this aspect of his questioning.

But Spenser is also drawing attention to the way in which Sidney's pursuits as a soldier cut him off from those of his peers who were devoted to poetry. This focus points toward the question, and the complaint, regarding the difficult relation between poetry, particularly pastoral poetry, and historical events—an issue that the poem now turns to address.

In the passage describing the foreign shepherds' discovery of the wounded Astrophel, Spenser surely suggests that even if Sidney's friends had been there, they might not have saved him. The shepherds have been following the hunt. This alerts us to the polarity of shepherds and hunters, a polarity as old as the Adonis myth itself and one that Spenser uses to focus the unhappy relation between pastoral and history, between a realm of fiction and one of action and death. The crucial point is that the pastoral world can neither cure itself nor defend itself against the violence of history.

As Astrophel bleeds to death—"They stopt his wound (too late to stop it was)" (145)—the pastoral world has certainly been "launched" by the "cruell beast" of history. The implications for pastoral elegy are especially dire, and they go to the heart of Spenser's clear-eyed and original relation to his tradition. For how can a conventional pastoral elegy find comfort for a death inflicted by a world whose realities have so clearly ravaged the realm of pastoral itself? Spenser's answer will require his revision of the tradition, including the myth of Adonis. But that revision comes much later in the poem.

Like Adonis, Astrophel is mourned by his Venus figure, Stella. But something very odd happens in this second representation of Stella. What we see is no less than the utter disintegration of the figure of the star into that of a grieving woman. She who was "the fairest star in skie" is suddenly tearing her "yellow locks," rending the roses in her "red cheeks," and despoiling the treasury of her "fair brest." The figure of a woman now occludes that of the star, thus continuing to undermine any dubious or facile substitution of figures like that of the star for human individuals. While thus undoing the tropes of conventional elegy, Spenser pursues a decidedly Ovidian account of inadequate mourning. Like the models by which it is influenced, Spenser's account combines psychological acuity with metamorphic figurations. As Stella weeps over her beloved, she "deformes" her face "like him to bee." Instead of withdrawing from the dead, Stella makes the common psychological response of identification, a response which, as Ovid and Spenser knew, may involve a lethal deformation of the self. Stella dies "untimely" and flies off like a turtledove to join her mate. Even though that "untimely" may be read as an expression of the poet's sorrow, it tends to confirm our suspicion that Stella is not designed to serve as an example of successful mourning.

It is against this negative example that the mourning of Clorinda will be dramatically counterpoised. In this progressive, oppositional structure, Spenser is again ensuring that the development of his poem enacts the work of mourning. Stella represents the part of the self that adopts an untenable position beyond which the mourning self must move. She is like Alcyon or the city of Verulam in this respect, but in "Astrophel" Spenser is able to move beyond them to a positive inventor of consolations. And it is precisely this surpassing movement that is so crucial to effective mourning.

The surpassal consists in more than merely replacing Stella by Clorinda. More significantly, it has to do with how Clorinda rejects and surpasses the attempted consolation that initially followed the deaths of Astrophel and Stella. The gods, we are told, pitied the dead lovers and transformed them into a single flower, henceforth given the name of Astrophel. The figuration here is not a little contrived, working as it does to include both lovers in a single emblem which changes from red to blue, which carries the star insignia of Stella, and which darts forth beams of light from the dew that represents her tears! Added to this are the variety of names by which the plant is called—Penthia (from the Greek word meaning "tearful sorrow"),

Starlight, and Astrophel. Clearly, there is an extreme self-consciousness about the positing of this figure. Nor is one's belief in its
substantiality reinforced by the bewildering series of disfigurations
that have preceded it. Stella the star, we recall, became the grieving
woman who became a turtledove that then gave way to a flower that in
turn resembles the original star.

This instability of the figure is intensified by the poem's departure
from what might have been its guiding myth or framework of figuration, the myth of Adonis as transmitted by Bion, Ovid, and Ronsard.
Such departures will become even more obvious as the poem continues, but already we notice that Stella is at a far remove from the
Venus figure who would normally be grieving over the dying Adonis.
We have seen Stella subjected to fluctuations of form and identity, and
she finally dies, unlike her immortal model.

At the same time, the movement beyond the figure of Venus,
associated as she is with the mother as lover, performs the mourner's
essential detachment from such a figure—his recapitulation, in the act
of mourning, of the disjoining from his original attachments. "Lycidas" and "Adonais" will offer clear repetitions of this, and we shall study
the movement more closely in those poems. For the moment, we may
notice how thoroughly Spenser has thus far revised his myth, reducing Venus to this metamorphic Stella, who survives only as a highly
contrived and decorative flower. The mourner's movement beyond
the Venus figure would thus seem to go hand in hand with the skeptical attack on inadequate fictions. And it is at this critical point that
Spenser closes the first part of the poem, introducing the subsequent
mourners who come to bewail the double death. By an almost eclogic
succession, he turns from Stella to Clorinda's more adequate voice of
mourning.

The switch toward a new mourner, opening up a distance from the
unfortunate Stella and from the figures discussed above, begins with a
section corresponding to the intermediate phase of mourning mentioned earlier, in which there is a detachment of affections and interest
from the lost love-object and a temporary return of these upon the
self. From this stage the mourner works outward once more, trying to
find or invent a new object of attachment. It is, therefore, fascinating
to note how thoroughly Spenser's poem works *through* this very process. Clorinda's lay begins with an intense withdrawal from the external world and a return inward to the self:

Or where shall I enfold my inward paine,
That my enriven heart may find reliefe?
Shall I unto the heavenly powres it show?
Or unto earthly men that dwell below?

To heavens? ah they alas the authors were,
And workers of my unremedied wo:
. . . .
To men? ah they alas like wretched bee,
And subject to the heavens ordinance:
. . . .
Then to my selfe will I my sorrow mourne,
Sith none alive like sorrowfull remaines:
And to my selfe my plaints shall back retourne,
To pay their usury with doubled paines.

$$(3-22)^{19}$$

In these lines we notice, too, that Clorinda has undone the fiction
of divine benevolence posited earlier by the pitying gods' transformation of the lovers into a flower. As she continues her lament, she
undoes the consolatory flower figure itself: she grieves for Astrophel
as a flower that has been cruelly and "untimely cropt." Twice she says
that death has totally "defaced" the flower, thereby defacing by association the supposedly immortalizing figure as well. This undoing is,
however, far more rigorous, as Clorinda actually turns to analyze and
then reject the earlier figure:

What is become of him whose flowre here left
Is but the shadow of his likenesse gone.
  Scarse like the shadow of that which he was,
  Nought like, but that he like a shade did pas.

$$(C\ 57-60)$$

The flower is therefore discarded as quite incapable of figuring
Astrophel. It is "the shadow of his likenesse gone," in other words, an
image merely of his vanished appearance. Even the resemblance is
inadequate ("Scarse like . . . Nought like"), except that its very shad-
owiness gives it a claim to comparison. For Astrophel resembled a
shadow only in his ephemerality. So it is not the content of the figure
(the flower) but rather its status *as figure* or shadow that gives it title to
an admittedly far from consoling resemblance. Not only has the figure
thus been exposed for what it is but the very tenor of its function has
been scorned and discarded.

This is an extraordinary example of Spenser's revisionary power over his received myth. What we previously called a departure, Venus's death, is here followed by a radical rejection of the mythical transformation of the god into a flower. An unmistakable feature of this rejection is the similarity of its condemnatory language to the language of Plato's attack on the poets: "but the shadow of his like-nesse." But more important is the Platonic bias against the merely physical body of likeness of which that flower figure was a shadow. With this double degradation of both the figure and the merely phys-ical existence of Astrophel, the poem moves to its final invention, the consolatory figure of the heavenly infant. It is to this new-found or rather newly created object that the mourner can now transfer her feelings and thereby complete the work of mourning.

As one might expect from what we have already seen of this Neo-Platonic revision of the Adonis myth, the new consolation is also determined by Spenser's philosopher. For by way of a near-Socratic *but*, Clorinda moves immediately from the inferior world of shadows and likenesses of embodied life to the pure world of the liberated soul:

> But that immortall spirit, which was deckt
> With all the dowries of celestiall grace:
> By soveraine choyce from th'hevenly quires select,
> And lineally deriv'd from Angels race,
>   O what is now of it become, aread.
>   Ay me, can so divine a thing be dead?
>
> Ah no: it is not dead, ne can it die,
> But lives for aie, in blisfull Paradise:
> Where like a new-borne babe it soft doth lie.

(C 61–69)

As one moves from the discarded Adonis myth to these lines, one is traversing the history of religious philosophy sketched in Chapter I. We saw how the primitive vegetation deities such as Adonis were spiritualized by the Orphic sects, who substituted ideas of the resur-rection of the soul for the mere notion of a returning principle of fertility and who made use of the infant deity figure to represent the newborn soul in the next world pleading its claim of divine lineage: "I am the son of earth and starry heaven, and by birth I come from God: ye know this well yourselves." These Orphic beliefs in turn influenced Plato, who associated the figure of the infant with his notion of the soul in full possession of all it will lose in earthly life. Spenser's Neo-Platonic use of this consoling figure of the soul as infant—hitherto unseen in elegies for persons other than children—originates its own tradition, influencing such elegists as Wordsworth, Shelley, and Yeats.

Although it is not quite as explicit here as in later elegies, we should note the particular current of sexuality that plays such a powerful and inescapable role in elegy, as in the work of mourning. In the previous chapter, I suggested that the mourner must, in deference to death, sacrifice not only the lost object but also his own primary sexual desire. The sacrifice, not unlike a symbolic self-castration, is necessary not only as a defense against death but also as the means of erecting the *figure* for what survives—a figure that, however spiritualized, retains its connection with the phallic power of the vegetation god. The consolation in elegy will, therefore, include the mourner's assertion of an ongoing but displaced and troped sexuality. Like a maturing child, he must discover a substitute love-object; he must invent or inherit a figure for his own potency and for his own association with images of return or resurrection.

To sketch this in "Astrophel" (for we shall see it more dramatically in "Lycidas"), Astrophel suffers a mortal, castrative wound, and the flowers that image him are themselves either plucked or "untimely cropt." This cropping of Astrophel is in turn matched by the mourners' own castrative gestures as they break their garlands and break the bitter alder from the boughs. In addition, we have already noted how the poem reduces and effectively discards the Venus figure of the eternal, loving mother. The movement beyond Venus-Stella toward the sister, Clorinda, strongly suggests a deliberate purging or chastening of the maternal or erotic connection. It is in relation to this movement, together with the many castrative gestures, that the final consolation asserts its recovery of a figurative sexual power.

The image of the infant not only represents an originally phallic power, as it did in the reborn Dionysian infant figure, the fig-wood phallus in the basket, and in the derivative figure of the Christ child in the manger. It also surely reflects the metaphorical sexual power of the poet who has engendered it. The elegist has thus moved from the cropt flower and broken garlands of loss to the resurgent "making" of this newborn infant. We are returned to the poem's introductory mention of the elegist's power to pierce and breed, while the image of the child itself returns us to the opening line of the elegy proper ("A gentle shepheard born in Arcady"). Spenser has thus feigned a spiraling return, from the infant born in Arcady to the child that the poet has figured forth in Paradise.

Despite this achievement, Spenser is inexorably still within the realm of figures. But as the consolatory figure is spelled out, we see how carefully Spenser treads. The soul is "like" an infant, and what the infant sees is, unlike the parallel situation in the more naive "November" elegy, expressly invisible to us ("which no eye can see"). The child itself sees these "immortall beauties" only in dream. Hence Spenser does not sacrifice his poem's hard-won sophistication as regards the unavoidable presence of figuration. He allows Clorinda to mourn effectively, without trapping her in the blindness of false claims. Her status as a critic of figures is unimpaired. Spenser has thus performed the work of mourning and moved from discarded to reinvented figures; but he has done so in a manner that, by bringing that very critique and reinvention into the poem, could satisfy his skepticism regarding the nature of fictions and might well have satisfied even Sidney himself.

The poem continues with a brief surge in celebration of celestial love before wisely subsiding with a recognition of limits and a shift of focus back to the mourner, who, no longer isolated, speaks from within a community: "But live thou there still happie, happie spirit, / And give us leave thee here thus to lament" (C 91–92). A healthy division of the "there" from "here" assures us that in contrast to the case of Stella, no dangerous identifications are being made. And finally, with clear self-knowledge regarding the true motives of man's mourning ("mourning in others, our owne miseries"), the poem comes to its close.

Spenser's achievement in "Astrophel" has, therefore, been won against and yet through his extreme awareness of his dependence on fictions. In the last book of *The Faerie Queene*, however, and in the works of several of his contemporaries, one finds an increasing absence of consolation, coupled with a yet darker distrust of language. Nashe's lines from "Summers Last Will and Testament" reflect more than a momentary or idiosyncratic skepticism:

Hels executioner
Hath no eares for to heare
What vaine art can reply. [20]

For poets like Nashe, it had become increasingly difficult to prove how, in the face of death or injustice, "verses are not vaine."

In the following chapter, I shall explore how the work of mourning breaks down when the attitude toward figuration becomes too pessimistic. When no consoling substitution is available even in language, the griever will be unable to avoid responses such as melancholy or revenge, both of which bear directly on the present study. With reference to *The Spanish Tragedy*, *Titus Andronicus*, and *Hamlet*, I hope to show how the revenger, like the melancholic, is something of an elegist *manqué*. The course of his inability to find adequate solace in the mediations of language or law involves a trial of those mediations themselves and is, therefore, of interest to any student either of elegy or of the relation between grief, anger, and language in general.

III

Where Words Prevail Not: Grief, Revenge, and Language in Kyd and Shakespeare

> Where words prevail not,
> violence prevails.
> > *The Spanish Tragedy* 2.1.110
>
> The mere word's a slave
> Debosh'd on every tomb, on
> every grave
> A lying trophy, and as oft is dumb
> Where dust and damn'd oblivion is
> the tomb
> Of honor'd bones indeed. What
> should be said?
> > *All's Well That Ends Well* 2.3.137–41

Toward the end of the sixteenth century, the question of "what should be said" in the face of suffering and death had become particularly vexing. Since supposedly immutable principles of divine, human, and natural order were increasingly suspected of being no more than man's figural impositions on an essentially intractable reality, the traditional means of consolation were robbed of their protective charm.

Many poems of the time testify to this predicament. But it is in such plays as *The Spanish Tragedy*, *Titus Andronicus*, and *Hamlet* that one finds the most moving dramatization of the dilemmas that ensue when man's need for consolation or redress is obstructed by his loss of faith in the power of art's reply. With "art" we may here associate not only such fictions as those of pastoral elegy but also the no less artificial, and linguistic, mediations of justice and the law. These plays reveal that no work of mourning can be successfully completed without positive recourse to various forms of mediation; and while they offer penetrating views of melancholics and revengers, they invite us to study these failed mourners not as pure phenomena but rather in their inescapable and unhappy relation to such artful fabrics as those of language and the law.

Since revengers are, in a sense, elegists *manqués* and since many revenge tragedies refer to the perversion of a consoling pastoral world, it is worth preceding a study of the plays by noting the contemporary decline of the traditional pastoral elegy. So, too, revengers are unsuccessful plaintiffs, and we should also look briefly at some of the current problems besetting the principle of justice, particularly with regard to revenge.

Admittedly, elegies have always questioned the adequacy of their own utterance. But Spenser's antiphonal hovering over "verses vaine (yet verses are not vaine)" is far more radical than Moschus's "If I too had such power with the pipe, / I should myself sing before Pluteus."[1] For Moschus doubted only his ability to match the song of Bion, whereas Spenser apparently doubts the efficacy of song itself. In "Astrophel" the comforting pastoral matrix, and hence the very locus of elegy, is shown to be so vulnerable to the violence of history that Spenser can only salvage the image of pastoral by a forceful critique and a bold Neo-Platonic revision of its fictions.

Few of Spenser's contemporaries and followers, however, could match his odd blend of faith on the one hand and skeptical poetic sophistication on the other, and the pastoral form was increasingly rejected as a fictional resource for consolation. Ellen Lambert has shown, for example, how the elegies of Drayton employed pastoral motifs as mere decor, while those of Basse and Browne explicitly rejected the old conventions. As Basse declared with the leaden solemnity that so often marked the current elegist's lack of power:

> Not (like as when some triviall discontents
> First taught my raw and luckless youth to rue)
> Do I to Flockes, now, utter my laments,
> Nor choose a tree, or streame, to mourn unto:
> My weightier Sorrow now (Dear Sir) presents
> These hir afflicted features to your view.[2]

We may recall Guiderius's mockery of his brother's elegiac strewings in *Cymbeline*: "Prithee have done, / And do not play in wench-like words with that / Which is so serious" (4.2.230–32). In each case, the question returns, What should be said? For it seems that the mythos of the vegetation deity, with its attendant imagery of resurrection, has shrunk like the merest flower, much as Spenser's Clorinda had insisted. In Ben Jonson's beautiful lyric "Slow, Slow, Fresh Fount," a voice, singing of Narcissus, laments that "Nature's pride is now a withered daffodil." The very sign, therefore, of consolatory transformation and renewal has been superseded by a withered version of itself. And the singer, after all, is Echo.

As Ruth Wallerstein has well demonstrated, the solacing powers of pastoral continued to diminish as the political and religious uncertainties of the age deepened, and by 1637, "Lycidas" alone among the more than thirty poems for Edward King was written as a pastoral elegy.[3] Not surprisingly, the dominant motifs of the entire collection were those of the felt inadequacy of language, coupled with a hesitant groping for an obscured principle of justice.

For not only the fictions of *pastoral* had lost their power to console. A similar onset of skepticism had undermined trust in the divinely guaranteed nature of *justice*, leaving in its wake not merely the sense of an exclusively mundane and fallible system of human law but a suspicion that the "justice" that had now departed to heaven had perhaps never been more than a fiction, dependent for its "presence" on such figures as the personification *Astraea*. Ovid had depicted the forlorn ascent of *Astraea*, last of the divinities to forsake the fallen world, and by the end of the sixteenth century, there was a widespread return to Ovid's scenario. In *The Spanish Tragedy, The Faerie Queene,* and *Titus Andronicus* one finds only three of the many complaints that "justice is exiled from the earth."[4]

Part of the reason for this loss of faith in the existence or operation of justice was the entire climate of unhingement between sacred principles and secular practices. By the mid-sixteenth century in England, Parliament had taken responsibility for many judgments that previously had been left to the absolute monarch, thus introducing a sense of justice as a matter of interpretation and human vote rather than of heaven-sent verdicts.[5] So, too, the judiciary itself had become far more bureaucratic, with a proliferation of courts and jurors, a kind of swell of mediations that delayed and made increasingly opaque the actual administration of justice. (Hamlet's catalogue of torments, we recall, includes "the law's delay.") It must have been well-nigh impossible to preserve a sense of the divine nature of justice while being sent from court to court in a procedure that in many cases might last for well over a year.

This loss of faith in legal justice, together with the doubts as to the existence of a divine justice, even in the next world, had a severe effect on any mourner seeking consolation, especially for an "unjust" death. From the frantic complaints of Videna in *Gorboduc* (1561), questioning the abeyance of "Jove's just judgment," to Milton's turn to a powerfully reposited "all-judging Jove" in "Lycidas," the relation between justice and consolation is close and troubled, and some of the most vivid literary presentations of grief and, in particular, of unsuccessful mourning are those that also address the problem of an absent or imperfect principle of justice.

Obviously a crucial element of consolation is the belief that the deceased died for a just reason and will somehow receive his just reward in the next world. But there is a further connection between justice and mourning—one which relates more to the just administration of revenge in *this* world. As both anthropologists and readers of the ancient classics have noted, an act of retribution commonly attends a funeral in tribal or ancient societies. In *The Elementary Forms of the Religious Life*, Emile Durkheim writes in survey of tribal funerary practices.

> It should be pointed out . . . how it [the vendetta] is connected with the rites of mourning, whose end it announces . . . .
>
> If every death is attributed to some magic charm, and for this reason it is believed that the dead man ought to be avenged, it is because men must find a victim at any price, upon whom the collective pain and anger may be discharged. [6]

Durkheim goes on to show how the anger and self-mortification of the survivors are turned upon the victims of a frequently inexact revenge. Indeed, retribution is sought regardless of whether the deceased had been murdered. Thus seen, revenge is a crucial marshaling of anger, but more significantly, it is an action in which the survivor assumes *for himself* the power that has bereaved him. It is perhaps in this sense that Bacon wrote, "Revenge conquers Death." The violence suffered is returned, paid back; the griever has shifted the burden of loss and anger to another bearer, thus, by some strangely arithmetical tally, canceling out his sense of violation and passivity.

Since the end of the fourteenth century, however, the individual had had to yield this act of revenge to the agents of the state. [7] His anger would have to find indirect satisfaction in the official execution of the law. When, therefore, the principle and operation of justice were found wanting, the revenger would be faced not only with the original burden of his anger but with an intensely privatized version of that anger. He would find himself suddenly outside the law, hence outside society and frequently, as we shall see, outside the public institution of language. With his language itself tending toward the impossible and self-defeating condition of privacy, the issue of his madness would be close at hand, and this, together with his role as passionate definer and critic of the boundaries of public domain, made him an intriguingly dramatic figure for an audience so nervously self-conscious about the altering relation between the individual and his society.

Vengeful anger may, of course, be displaced in other media than that of legal retribution. As a variety of elegies—from Theocritus's "First Idyl" to "Lycidas" and "Adonais"—show, vindictive wrath may be mediated by literary language. But when doubt is cast upon language and its figures, when its function as a medium is diminished, it is natural to find unbound anger flowing back toward less mediated expression. In regressing toward violence, therefore, the revenger has invariably found himself at odds not only with the law but also with a language that seems to have grown equally opaque, reduced, as Hamlet says, to "words, words, words"; or to mere papers, as Hieronimo furiously tries to *show* by tearing up legal petitions with his teeth. Almost every revenge tragedy, therefore, includes a trial and violation of language. And it is worth noting the frequency with which acts of vengeance are performed in ways that apparently make use of a theatrical or verbal mediation only to disrupt it.

The Spanish Tragedy

The Spanish Tragedy begins with a shuffle of judgment in the next world, implying that even there justice may be a problem. The threefold judge pronounces conflicting opinions as to whether the ghost of Andrea should be committed to the afterworld of lovers or that of soldiers. In a referral to another court, so typical of the late Elizabethan age, Andrea's case is presented to Pluto, who in turn allows Proserpine to summon Revenge. Revenge leads Andrea through the gates of horn ("Where dreams have passage in the silent night") to view the ensuing action on earth. The suggestion is that the entire play to come is but a dead man's dream.

We move to the court of Spain to hear the king rejoicing over his victory against Portugal: "Then blessed be heaven and guider of the heavens, / From whose fair influence such justice flows" (1.2.9–10). His words echoing the traditional view of justice will be ironized throughout the play, as the heavenly source of influence is shown to be in fact a diamond-hard wall, impervious to the words or needs of man. As though to introduce the problem, the king is immediately embroiled in a scene of judgment where he must decide between the claims of Horatio and Lorenzo, rival captors of the Portuguese prince Balthazar, who has slain Andrea. His words, "Then, by my judgment, thus your strife shall end," will also be ironized by the following conflict.

It is probably unnecessary to rehearse the plot except to note a persistent slighting of language at crucial moments of its development. Bellimperia, in love now with Horatio, rejects Balthazar's suit: "These are but words of course." And her brother, Lorenzo, in league with Balthazar, bribes Pedringano "not with fair words, but store of golden coin" to assist in the murder of Horatio. Lorenzo has, after all, decided that "where words prevail not, violence prevails."

The murder of Horatio is a vicious rupture and perversion of a miniature pastoral world. "The court were dangerous, that place is safe," says Bellimperia referring to "the pleasant bow'r the field" of Horatio's father as a rendezvous. Yet it is in this allegedly idyllic spot, "made for pleasure, not for death," that Horatio is hung up in the trees and stabbed to death: "'What, will you murder me?' / 'Ay, thus and thus: these are the fruits of love.'" This perverse substitution of death for fruit is echoed much later by one of Hieronimo's laments for his son:

This was the tree; I set it of a kernel: . . .
. . . .
It grew a gallows, and did bear our son
It bore thy fruit and mine—O wicked, wicked plant!

(3.12.64–72)

And the motif culminates in the extraordinary scene in which Isabella, insane with grief, destroys the remnants of this pastoral world.

Isabella's rampage is a literal *enactment* of the elegiac verbal curse against nature, or of the pathetic fallacy that asserts nature's suffering. For Isabella has none of the elegist's necessary trust in words. She has heard and said enough:

> Tell me no more!
> Since neither piety nor pity moves
> The king to justice or compassion,
> I will revenge myself upon this place
> Where thus they murder'd my beloved son.
> [She cuts down the arbor.]
>
> (4.2.1–5)

We notice the "thus" of the revenger: she destroys the trees "in the same way as" the murderer had killed her son.

> Down with them Isabella; rent them up,
> And burn the roots from whence the rest is sprung.
> I will not leave a root, a stalk, a tree,
> A bough, a branch, a blossom, nor a leaf,
> No, not an herb within this garden-plot—:
> Accursed complot of my misery.
> Fruitless for ever may this garden be.
>
> (4.2.10–16)

Isabella's literalization of the language of elegy, her inability to rest content with the mere words, will of course be matched by her husband's similar refusal to allow the trope of theater to remain mere trope. Her destruction of the pastoral setting is followed by her own suicide, another actual performance of the kind of "breast-wounding" or "piercing" that we encounter only figuratively in elegies.

It is, however, Hieronimo who most claims our attention. For it is he who most suffers from a sense of the inadequacy of language and from an attendant loss of faith in justice:

> O sacred heav'ns! if this unhallow'd deed . . .
> . . . .
> Shall unreveal'd and unrevenged pass,
> How should we term your dealings to be just,
> If you unjustly deal with those that in your justice trust?
>
> (3.2.5–11)

> Yet still tormented is my tortur'd soul
> With broken sighs and restless passions,
> That winged mount; and, hov'ring in the air,
> Beat at the windows of the brightest heavens,
> Soliciting for justice and revenge:
> But they are plac'd in those empyreal heights,
> Where, countermur'd with walls of diamond,
> I find the place impregnable; and they
> Resist my woes, and give my words no way.
>
> (3.7.10–19)

Here, then, for Hieronimo, is the essential failure of language as intermediary agent of justice or compensation. The human court is equally impregnable, leaving Hieronimo to circle desperately, calling for "Justice, O, Justice to Hieronimo . . . Justice, O, justice, justice, gentle king." By its very repetition, almost an obverse of the elegiac *anáklisis*, the word is apparently losing value, becoming a mere sound.

In a crucial scene, Hieronimo receives the petition of an old man seeking redress for the murder of a son. Declaring that "on this earth justice will not be found," Hieronimo proposes a quest in which the old man will act as his Orphic courier:

> I'll down to hell, and in this passion
> Knock at the dismal gates of Pluto's court,
> . . . .
> Yet lest the triple-headed porter should
> Deny my passage to the slimy strand,
> The Thracian poet thou shalt counterfeit:
> Come on, old father, be my Orpheus,
> And if thou canst no notes upon the harp,
> Then sound the burden of thy sore heart's-grief,
> Till we do gain that Proserpine may grant
> Revenge on them that murdered my son.
> Then will I rent and tear them, thus and thus,
> Shiv'ring their limbs in pieces with my teeth.
> [He tears the papers.]
>
> (3.13.108–22)

Since Moschus's elegy for Bion, the figure of Orpheus has been close to the consciousness of most elegists; but that closeness is by no means unequivocal. On the one hand Orpheus is an attractive figure for the elegist, having the power to enchant not only the natural world but also the guardians of the threshold to the world of death. On the other hand he is an unsuccessful mourner, as Ovid emphasizes, a negative model for the elegist. For Orpheus insists on rescuing his *actual* wife rather than a figure or substitute for her. His looking back and her subsequent return to the underworld are proof that she herself can never be revived. And it is Orpheus's failure to reattach his affections elsewhere that brings about his martyrdom. The resentful women tear him apart precisely because of his refusal to turn away from or to trope the dead.

Like Orpheus, Hieronimo will die for his refusal to accept what might be considered the mediated forms of consolation, either in language or in law. His final transgression will be to literalize the actions of what is supposed to be a play within the play and thereby to kill *in fact* the victims whose "killing" he might only have *represented* in theater. In the light of this association of Hieronimo with Orpheus, we understand more fully why it is that he is finally led in the next world to the fields "where Orpheus plays." For the moment, however, we are left with the image of Hieronimo, in his role as chief justice of Spain, *literally* ripping apart what represents the fabric of language and the law, in fact avenging himself against it with the same "thus and thus" equation that his wife makes in the arbor.

Before concluding with the play within the play, it is worth noting how the "painter scene" affords yet another example of the ways in which Hieronimo constantly defines the limits of *any* intermediary signs or representations. He demands a painted narration of his loss, but does so in a way that would completely overtax the painter's medium:

> "Canst paint a doleful cry?"
> "Seemingly, sir."
> "Nay it should cry. . . ."
>
> (3.12.127–29)

The rejection of illusion per se is thus paired with the demand for an unavailable language or cry. And the merely painted cry, like that of Lucrece's painted Hecuba, serves only to mock the mournful viewer's own lack of effective utterance. Nor is this all. "Stretch thine art," Hieronimo insists, commissioning a representation of noises, speeches, and successive events, which are designed finally to abolish the difference between the viewer and his painted image, having on the former the therapeutic effect that is to be depicted in the latter:

> Make me curse, make me rave, make me cry, make me
>   mad,
> make me well again, make me curse hell, invocate heaven,
> and in the end leave me in a trance—and so forth
>
> (3.12.161–63)

With an ironic sense of the impossibility of these demands, the painter asks, "And is this the end?" to which Hieronimo, in one of the great moments of the play, admits that there can be no rest for him within any kind of medium: "O no, there is no end: the end / Is death and madness" (3.12.165–66).

At Hieronimo's insistence, the play within the play is enacted in various languages, as though to emphasize his sense of the opacity of *any* language and to "breed confusion," a kind of impossibility of interpretation such that action itself will seem to have the only meaning. After the killings, he disabuses the audience by explaining how the mediate has in fact been made immediate: "Haply you think—but bootless are your thoughts— / That this is fabulously counterfeit" (4.4.75–76). Significantly, Hieronimo concludes his entire war against language, expressing the "rupture of [his] part," by biting out his tongue. And as if this were not yet sufficient proof of how consistently his violence has been assaulting language itself, he makes signs for a knife to mend his pen but uses the knife instead to stab the duke of Castile and at last to kill himself.

One cannot forget that Kyd has framed his play by the suggestion of its being Andrea's dream and by the fact that it is viewed by Andrea and Revenge as audience, like ourselves. Kyd thus implies that although imperceptible to the benighted Hieronimo, there *is* contact between the diamantine heavens and the fallen world. Hieronimo's words do penetrate above, and the principle of Revenge does watch over events. But this is paradoxical, for there would have been no revenge had not Hieronimo felt its absence and had he not felt compelled to take justice into his own hands. However much one may invoke theories about the so-called scourge-of-God attitude, Hieronimo is plagued by his very *separation* from authority. Indeed, by having Hieronimo become insanely violent, killing even the innocent duke, Kyd suggests that the instruments of revenge are themselves always imperfect and that there may be some flaw in the actual embodiment or vehicle of this now dubious principle we see personified as leaning over the play.

Critics have argued that Kyd is deliberately portraying the aberrations of a man who loses faith in justice and abandons spiritual hope. [8] But the hapless, mournfully secular nature of the action and language of the play nevertheless goes a long way toward shaking our belief that there *is* another, "higher" level than merely that which is shared by the dramatist and spectator. Indeed, when we recall that Revenge is the usher of Andrea's dream, we see these two inhabitants of that "upper" realm as little more than versions of the playwright and his audience. And as we turn to *Titus Andronicus*, we find that the personification of Revenge, supposedly arriving from some extramundane world, is presented only as a fraudulent imposter—the villainous Tamora in fancy dress. In fact it is Shakespeare's destruction of personification and of the transcendent realm to which it may refer that is a primary ingredient of that play's unmitigated darkness.

Titus Andronicus

Before commenting on *Titus Andronicus*, I would like to note briefly how its near contemporary, "The Rape of Lucrece," may be read as a similar study of grief and of the relation of language to those two responses to loss, melancholy and revenge, both of which refuse to be consoled by figures or mediations of any kind. In one of the best examples of the interconnection between language and law as possible but rejected means of compensation, the violated Lucrece cries,

> "Out, idle words, servants to shallow fools,
> Unprofitable sounds, weak arbitrators!
> Busy yourselves in skill-contending schools,
> Debate where leisure serves with dull debaters;
> To trembling clients be you mediators.
> 　　For me, I force not argument a straw,
> 　　Since that my case is past the help of law."
>
> 　　　　　　　　　　　　　　　　　　(1016–22)

In a movement similar to that of Hieronimo, she turns "for means to mourn some newer way" to the possible solace of a painting. But she, too, rejects the limitations of the formal medium, complaining that the painted Hecuba, like Lucrece herself, has no recourse to language: "and therefore Lucrece swears [the painter] did her wrong, / To give her so much grief, and not a tongue" (1462–63). Just as Hieronimo beat the painter off the stage, so Lucrece finally attacks a section of the painting with her nails.

When her husband, Collatinus, returns to find her "clad in mourning black," Lucrece tells of her suffering and enjoins on him an oath of revenge against Tarquin. She herself can find no true appeasement in revenge, for, as is true of the melancholic response to loss, the griever's pain has become intermixed with an overpowering guilt and anger against the self. The revenger, while his career resembles that of the melancholic, involving a similar rejection of the fabric of language and law, finally differs by virtue of the opposite *direction* of his anger. True enough, the revenger is often marked by self-hatred, but his anger does at last turn outward against some victim. Whereas the extreme destination of melancholic self-anger is a form of suicide, the endpoint of vengeful anger is murder. These two modes are directly counterpointed by Shakespeare in the persons of Lucrece and Collatinus. (Of course, Collatinus does not actually murder Tarquin. In this case, banishment is the equivalent act of retribution.)

Collatinus's first response, like Lucrece's melancholy, does turn against the self, moving him toward the kind of identification with the dead that we saw in Spenser's Stella. "He falls and bathes the pale fear in his face, / And counterfeits to die with her a space" (1775–76). What saves him is "manly shame," the kind of ancient self-regard that E. R. Dodds has so illuminatingly distinguished from the more inward-turning attitude of guilt.[9] Collatinus's anger will not, therefore, attach to the self and moves outward instead against Tarquin. But first, as is typical of both the revenger and the melancholic, his grief is shown to be explicitly at odds with language.

The deep vexation of his inward soul
Hath serv'd a dumb arrest upon his tongue,
Who mad that sorrow should his use control,
Or keep him from heart-easing words so long,
Begins to talk, but through his lips do throng
    Weak words, so thick come in his poor heart's aid,
    That no man could distinguish what he said.

(1779–85)

75

It is interesting to notice how the two responses, melancholy and revenge, dominate a world in which matrices for consolation are apparently lost. Lucrece has no use for law; no pastoral fictions are available; nor, finally, is there any suggestion of an adequate religious or mythological context in which to find redress. The very brief description of Lucrece's death signals this: "Her contrite sighs unto the clouds bequeathed / Her winged sprite" (1727–28). Not only is the narrator's description quite outside the mourning Collatinus's consciousness but the description itself is terse and unconsoling. Her "sprite," which might be no more than her breath, is emitted into the mere clouds, with no suggestion of some realm beyond those shifting barriers.

With such works as *The Spanish Tragedy,* "The Rape of Lucrece," *Titus Andronicus,* and *Hamlet,* we are clearly in the fallen world that Walter Benjamin has so brilliantly described as the context for the *Trauerspiel,* or lamentation play, a form of Baroque drama that he opposes to tragedy and that he characterizes by its obsession with unconsoled mourning, its "overstrained transcendental impulse," and its almost unremittingly melancholy toiling with and against an allegorical rhetoric that is felt to be drastically divided from its referents. [10] *Titus Andronicus,* in particular, comes as close, perhaps, as any English play to the *Trauerspiel.* It is a play that has been rejected by many critics for precisely the same reasons that Benjamin's chosen genre was criticized: a strained conventionality, an artificial and heavily emblematic style, and above all, a revoltingly grotesque series of horrors that seem to have little function but to ironize man's inadequate expressions of pain and loss.

Titus Andronicus opens with a problem of inheritance, the kind of problem that we have come to recognize as closely connected to the issue of mourning. I have already suggested how inheritance and mourning overlap in a nexus that is not only legal but also psychological. The achievements of consolation and succession, particularly in cases of leadership or poethood, require the survival and transmission of a symbol for power, whether of fertility, rule, or creativity. That symbol, like the totem, originally represents the sexual power of the father, or of the vegetation deity, but in a curious relation to castration. For the totem is only erected after the death of the father, as a symbol that must be separable from him. In deference to this symbol, the sons divert their sexual choices to substitutes for their primary desire, a substitution similar in structure to that required in the work of mourning. Paradoxically, then, while there is no successful mourning without the creation of a figure for the surviving power of the dead, that power nevertheless works as a source of prohibition and regulation. It allows survivors to exercise the inherited power, but in a controlled way. If they fail either to mourn or to acquiesce in the mourninglike regulation of their own desires, they subvert the very authority that they should inherit. And conversely, if there is some obstacle to the process of inheritance or to the construction of a legacy, we may often note an attendant problem not only in the area of mourning but also in the regulation and exercise of the survivor's sexuality.

This cluster of issues will be most noticeable in *Hamlet*. But it is present in *Titus Andronicus* and indeed in *Gorboduc*, which looks ahead to both plays. We remember how *Gorboduc* begins with a foundering of justice precisely on a fraternal dispute over inheritance. The introductory dumb show with its breaking of sticks in fact symbolizes this fragmentation of the totem: the father has undermined his sway by a premature delegation of power. In the absence of a totemic power, the brothers struggle to inherit both the kingdom and the mother.

> When greedy lust in royal seat to reign
>   Hath reft all care of gods and eke of men,
>
> . . . .
>
> Behold how mischief wide herself displays,
>   And with the brother's hand the brother slays.
>
> (4.2.266–70)[11]

Titus Andronicus, too, begins not only with brothers fighting for the succession but also with the kind of sexual confrontations that again suggest a struggle in the wake of a vanished totemic power. Hence, too, an explanation for the extraordinary profusion of castration scenarios in the play. For, together with the totem and the right to inherit, the authority for castration is itself in dispute. Saturninus (whose name suggests the son of the castrated god) and Bassianus, sons of the late emperor, are rival heirs, but it is to the aging general and father figure, Titus, that the tribunes appeal for leadership, asking him "to set a head on headless Rome." Titus declines in these words:

> A better head her glorious body fits
> Than his that shakes for age and feebleness.
> . . . .
> Give me a staff of honor for mine age,
> But not a sceptre to control the world.
> Upright he held it, lords, that held it last.

(1.1.187–200)

Titus nominates Saturninus, as first-born, to assume the totemic, sunlike role of "ripening justice," and Saturninus immediately asserts his power of sexual choice by taking to wife Lavinia, daughter of Titus. Bassianus defies the pronouncement, carrying off Lavinia as his alleged fiancée. In the fray Titus, as though trying to throw his weight behind totemic authority, kills one of his own sons, who, siding with Bassianus, blocked Titus's pursuit of the stolen woman. The quasi-oedipal conflict is, however, rendered pointless by Saturninus's acceptance of his brother's claim, thereby, significantly enough, acceding to this contempt for inherited sway. Saturninus himself marries Tamora, the captive queen of the Goths, who lusts after nothing (except the villainous Aaron) so much as revenge on the Andronici. For in an act of inexact sacrificial revenge, Titus had "hewn the limbs" of her eldest son—the first of many such castrative hewings in the play. Titus's rejection of her pleas was, too, the first of many instances in which language is mocked by violence.

As though to underscore the issues, Tamora's surviving sons now repeat the struggle for sexual primacy. And once again, no assertion of supremacy or authority is achieved, for the melancholy villain, Aaron, confessedly dominated by the castrated god Saturn, allows *both* brothers to exploit their lust for Lavinia. He counsels them to "strike her home by force if not by words" and by raping her in the forest to "serve [their] lust, *shadowed* from heaven's eye." The obscured eye is of course both the sun and the totemic symbol of rule, "Titan's rays."

The rape scene, like the murder of Horatio in *The Spanish Tragedy*, is another grotesque violation of the pastoral world. Once again, the possible matrix of consolation is itself debauched, and Titus's celebration—"the fields are fragrant, and the woods are green"—is grossly ironized by the rape of his daughter and the murder of his son-in-law. In another instance of "stopped" speech, Lavinia's pleas are refused ("I will not hear her speak . . . I know not what it means"). She is raped and, in a fate worse than that of her prototype, Philomel, deprived not

78

only of her tongue but also of her hands. Here the limb-hewing motif deliberately joins that of the attack on the power of language, either spoken or written.

> So now go tell, and if thy tongue can speak,
> Who 'twas that cut thy tongue and ravish'd thee.
> . . . .
> Write down thy mind, bewray thy meaning so,
> And if thy stumps will let thee play the scribe.
>
> (2.4.1–4)

Lavinia's uncle, Marcus, finds her "lopp'd and hew'd," her "body bare / Of her two branches." And instead of speech, only "a crimson river of warm blood" issues from her mouth. In a long complaint, Marcus bewails the impossibility of consolation or revenge, thereby casting doubt on the efficacy of mourning ("we will mourn with thee; / O, could our mourning ease thy misery!"). He compares Lavinia to Philomel and, by an oblique simile, to that almost ever-present "Thracian poet," Orpheus. But here there is none of the Ovidian consolation, the miracle by which a girl became a nightingale or whereby a head and lyre, caught by the river Hebrus, continued to issue forth music. Instead of being saved by some metamorphic fluidity of compensation, Lavinia becomes a frozen emblem of loss. The irremediable nature of her suffering, together with her dismemberment, give her a statuesque, immutable pathos—almost the stillness of an allegorical figure.

Walter Benjamin has shown how such petrified, emblematic motifs of inconsolability characterize the lamentation play, which tries to achieve neither tragic revelation nor consolatory grace but rather an image of hopeless, yet dogged, endurance. In Benjamin's view, it is as though the lamentation play were a landscape in which each character is a stranded fragment or ruin (compare Titus: "O, here I lift this one hand up to heaven, / And bow this feeble ruin to the earth" [3.1.206–7]). Indeed, Lavinia's muteness only increases the resemblance, and, as we shall see, other characters come to share her oddly static, gestural attitude of grief.

Titus's two sons have been framed for the murder of Bassianus, and now it is Titus who must suffer the impotence of language, as his pleas go unheard: "O noble father, you lament in vain . . . My gracious lord, no tribune hears you speak" (3.1.27–32). Once again, the focus of complaint is on the inability of language to afford a certain kind of transparency or efficacy, as though the passage from word to referent, or from speaker to auditor, were always being blockaded or, worse, interrupted. As Titus replies,

> . . . yet plead I must,
> And bootless unto them.
> Therefore I tell my sorrows to the stones,
> Who, though they cannot answer my distress,
> Yet in some sort they are better than the tribunes,
> For that they will not intercept my tale.
>
> (3.1.35–40)

Titus's impotence is itself horribly mocked and emphasized by a scheme designed precisely to ridicule the very process of compensation. He is told that his sons will be freed in return for one of his hands. The castration motif returns as a sign of powerlessness and is in fact multiplied by the cruel "reward" for Titus's offering. Instead of his sons, only their heads are brought in by a messenger, whose speech stresses that grief itself has become an object of contempt: "Thy grief their sports! thy resolution mock'd!" (3.1.239). This is a particularly devastating moment, for it suggests that even the primitive, self-castrative submission to the dynamic of sacrifice and reward, of ascesis and compensation, so crucial to the work of mourning has lost its economy. Here loss is only exchanged for further losses. The very notion of substitution is made to seem absurd. Instead of the power of death being reduced by invention or revenge, it is as though that power were actually multiplied. As Titus realizes, "sorrow flouted at is double death" (3.1.245).

At this point the play reaches its most static, emblematic moment—a kind of spatialization that Benjamin describes as marking a *hopelessly* fallen world in which time itself no longer bears the promise of eventual remedy. The statuary quality noted earlier is increased as Marcus adds himself to the inventory of mutilation or paralysis:

> . . . see thy two sons' heads,
> Thy warlike hand, thy mangled daughter here,
> Thy other banish'd son with this dear sight
> Struck pale and bloodless, and thy brother, I,
> Even like a stony image, cold and numb.
>
> (3.1.254–58).

Only the wrath of vengefulness can unfreeze these postures, and Titus moves into the position of Hieronimo, pursuing a justice that has been exiled from the earth ("*Terras Astraea reliquit* . . . she's gone, she's fled"). In what is almost a literalization of Hieronimo's attempt to pierce Heaven, Titus directs message-bearing arrows up into the skies and eventually turns instead to a descent like that of Hieronimo: "I'll dive into the burning lake below / And pull her [Revenge] out of Acheron by the heels" (4.3.44–45).

Ironically enough, it is Tamora herself who provides Titus with the means to revenge. Planning to deceive him, she proffers her services as the supposed personification of Revenge. But like a true distruster of all figures and mediations, Titus penetrates the fraud, once again reinforcing this play's abolition of all extraterrestrial principles and their personifications. Like Hieronimo using the play within the play only to break through its theatricality, Titus pretends to accept the disguises, while in fact he is planning to kill the actual players. He lays hold of Tamora's sons, the supposed personifications of Rapine and Murder, and with yet another instance of the stopped-speech motif ("Stop their mouths, let them not speak to me"), he has them slaughtered, ground up, and fed in a grotesque pasty to their mother. Not only is this a reversal of procedure, according to which offspring mourn by metaphorically ingesting their parents, but the metaphorical version gives way to the untroped horror of actual cannibalism.

The play ends with a flurry of killings, and Titus's son Lucius returns from exile at the head of an army of vengeful Goths. He is hailed as the new ruler and the healer of Rome's wounds. It is fascinating to note that the image of inherited power, in which Lucius is compared to "our ancestor" Aeneas, is precisely that of *speech*. It is as though the symbolic organ of renewal were now the very tongue that we have seen mutilated or so frequently stopped throughout the play: "Speak, Rome's dear friend, as erst our ancestor, / When with his solemn tongue he did discourse" (5.3.80–81).

But the theme of speechlessness and inconsolability is perhaps too strong for reversal in this closing scene. Lucius cuts short his speech, declaring that his "scars can witness, dumb although they are, / That my report is just and full of truth" (5.3.114–15). Titus's grandson weeps and says, "My tears will choke me, if I ope my mouth." And the final lines conclude this entire drama of unsuccessful and inadequate mourning with yet one more rejection of the traditional ceremonies, a kind of macabre leftover or remainder of "non-mourning," perhaps the essential note of the play:

> As for that ravenous tiger Tamora,
> No funeral rite, nor man in mourning weed,
> No mournful bell shall ring her burial,
> But throw her forth to beasts and birds to prey.

(5.3.195–98)[12]

Hamlet

In the wake of such a brutal and yet somehow inevitable rejection of the ceremonies and language of consolation, it is difficult to imagine how the fabric may be repaired. *Titus Andronicus* has shown the predominance of revenge or melancholia in a world without faith or justice, a world in which the words of sufferers seemed doomed, like Titus's arrows, to fall back as to a ground of mute inconsolability. It is to *Hamlet* that we look for a continued examination of the problem and for a resolution that, moving as it does away from the attitudes of revenge and melancholy toward one that is closer to elegy, requires a renewal of faith and a restored confidence in language.

Hamlet's first speech is, after all, a rejection of the conventional expressions of grief. We are still close to the tone of the plays above:

> 'Tis not alone my inky cloak, [good] mother,
> Nor customary suits of solemn black,
> Nor windy suspiration of forc'd breath,
> No, nor the fruitful river in the eye,
> Nor the dejected haviour of the visage,
> Together with all forms, moods, [shapes] of grief,
> That can [denote] me truly. These indeed seem,
> For they are actions that a man might play,
> But I have that within which passes show,
> These but the trappings and the suits of woe.

(1.2.77–86)

Once again, we face a mourner who is impatient with mere mediations. His repudiation of "all forms, moods, shapes of grief" is precisely that of the melancholic who can find no figure or emblem to signify the incommensurable inwardness of his condition. Like the figure in Dürer's *Melancholia I*, Hamlet is as though surrounded by discarded iconography, in his case the "trappings" of woe. It is surprising that T. S. Eliot did not recognize that there can never be a perfect objective correlative for melancholia: its signs can only signify their distance from a state that defies correlation. In fact the attitude of melancholy, with its preponderance of narcissism, would be threatened were an adequate external figure to be found.

Hamlet is, of course, not only a mourner, but one whose mourning has been thwarted by the abortive nature of his father's funeral rites and by the usurpation of his inheritance. As we know, the right to inherit was traditionally linked to the right to mourn. Here Claudius has usurped both rights. Having curtailed the funeral, he tries to dissuade Hamlet from a prolonged grieving. It is important to recognize, therefore, that Hamlet, by drawing attention to his private right to mourn, is subversively contesting the inheritance. This, rather than any early suspicions of Hamlet's knowledge of the crime, is what accounts for Claudius's initial unease.

Unable to mourn, Hamlet will neither accept nor invent a substitute for the lost object of his love. That object is complex and stratified, since, as we know, any loss recapitulates the primary experience of loss, namely, the separation that fractures an infant's unified world. In having to turn from his dead father, Hamlet is called upon to recapitulate the loss of his mother, or of the unified matrix that she had once represented. The torment of that necessity is intolerable now that he is actually losing her again, to Claudius, a travesty of his father. And it is particularly intolerable because Hamlet has just lost the very figure of paternal authority in whose name and under whose aegis such a renunciation might be made. What Hamlet had once suffered in the name of a genuine totemic figure he is now asked to repeat in the name of a mockery of that figure. With such elements in mind, we may complement the narrower view that describes Hamlet's fixation on his mother as merely oedipal. That fixation must be seen as a susceptibility that may beset many mourners, and one that Hamlet's peculiar circumstances have exaggerated in a tragically overdetermined way.

Given our sense of Hamlet's reluctance to perform the substitutive work of mourning, we may expect him to yearn for the primary object of desire, an object associated with the extinction of desire itself and with the return to a state preceding individuation.[13] Indeed, the opening words of his first soliloquy express a version of this suicidal, undeviating wish for a final regression:

> O that this too too sallied flesh would melt,
> Thaw, and resolve itself into a dew!
> Or that the Everlasting had not fix'd
> His canon 'gainst [self-]slaughter!

> (1.2.129–32)

Hamlet yearns by actual deliquescence to become literally what a mourner should wish to associate himself with figuratively—a purified or distilled force that involves individual death but also has the power to survive extinction. In this case, dew may connote spiritual purity, but it retains its earlier relation to the immortal seminal potency on which almost all images for the spirit subsequently have been based.[14]

His regressive desire barred, however, Hamlet moves directly to an expression of melancholy: "How weary, stale, flat, and unprofitable, / Seem to me all the uses of this world!" As he had rejected "all" forms of grief, so he despises all available "uses." This total withdrawal of affection from everything outside the self, intensified as it becomes in later speeches ("this goodly frame, the earth, seems to me a sterile promontory . . . / Man delights not me—no, nor woman neither") is a prominent symptom of melancholy in Freud's definition, according to which "the distinguishing mental features of melancholia are a profoundly painful dejection, abrogation of interest in the outside world, loss of the capacity to love, inhibition of all activity, and a lowering of the self-regarding feelings to a degree that finds utterance in self-reproaches and self-revilings, and culminates in a delusional expectation of punishment."[15] As the play develops, Hamlet exhibits each of these symptoms: his contempt for the world, his rejection of Ophelia, his inhibition of activity, his self-reviling ("O, what a rogue and peasant slave am I"), as well as his sense of punishment ("but Heaven hath pleas'd it so, / To punish me with this"). Along with all of these is the melancholic's or the revenger's antagonism toward language, and it is on this that I should like to dwell briefly.

Hamlet's melancholia is, of course, only one of the various responses to loss that this play presents. After each death, the ceremony of mourning is truncated: King Hamlet's funeral cut short by a marriage celebration, Polonius receiving an "obscure funeral . . . No noble rite nor formal ostentation," or Ophelia's burial with "maimed rites." It is not surprising, therefore, to discover that Hamlet, Ophelia, and Laertes all display a particularly unhappy relation to language and to the forms of grief.

Ophelia's expressions of grief evoke the shattered world of pastoral elegy, its debris falling from her as she wanders lunatic through the court of Elsinore. Nothing in her fractured words or gestures calls up the kind of consolatory strength that would be needed here. For in this realm of corruption, the delicacy and significance of herbs and flowers fall by the way, elegizing, if anything, the world that might have given them meaning. Here, the figures of consolation have become the signs of madness. Once again, as we saw in *The Spanish Tragedy* and *Titus Andronicus*, the pastoral world exists only to be violated. King Hamlet was, after all, poisoned in his orchard, and to his son the world itself has become "an unweeded garden / That grows to seed." Finally, Ophelia's death scene only emphasizes the powerlessness of her expressions, for it is her very singing that seems to render her "incapable of her own distress." She is pulled from her melodious lay to muddy death.

Laertes, on the other hand, is the furious revenger, whose Senecan rant and unfair play evidence Shakespeare's design not only to question the traditional practice of revenge but also to distance Hamlet from that accepted role. Whereas Hamlet, much as he detests language and reflection, is unable to pass beyond words to action, Laertes is frantically ready to prove his grief in deeds not words, as Claudius challenges him to do: "what would you undertake / To show yourself in deed your father's son / More than in words?" (4.7.124–26). Relative to this antiverbal impatience, Hamlet's imprisonment within language begins to take on positive value. Indeed, the play comes to plead increasingly on behalf of language.

To Laertes' readiness "to cut [Hamlet's] throat i' th' church" Claudius responds, "No place, indeed, should murther sanctuarize." It is against this explicitly irreligious depravity that Hamlet's reluctance as a revenger, together with his increasingly fatalistic attitude, begins to take on a religious cast. This contrast between the two men and between their attitudes toward language, revenge, and religion may remind us of the contrastive structure within an elegiac eclogue. Their opposition is especially dramatized by the scene in which Laertes and

Hamlet contest the right to mourn Ophelia, a kind of grotesque funeral game that carries through to their final duel.

We have spoken of Hamlet's melancholy, and from our reading of *The Spanish Tragedy* and *Titus Andronicus* we are familiar with certain elements of his predicament. Justice is unavailable ("The oppressor's wrong . . . the law's delay"); the forms of grief are felt to be not only inadequate but an actual sham; and language, grown opaque (as "words, words, words"), is loathed for its inefficacy and for its tendency to prostitution: "This is most brave, / That I . . . Must like a whore unpack my heart with words" (2.2.582–85).

Unlike Hieronimo or Titus, however, Hamlet does not initiate an actual plan of revenge. It is true that he does engineer a play that, like Hieronimo's play, is designed to effect more than a merely figurative action. But Hamlet's play, which is no less disrupted by reality, has for its intended effect an act of interpretation, a diagnosis of Claudius's conscience. Shakespeare's revision of the revenger's play within the play does more than indicate the degree to which the events of previous plays have become events of consciousness in *Hamlet*. By focusing on a crisis of conscience, the play within the play moves the entire drama further toward a moral and religious framework. And at the same time, its entire effect is to suggest the power of avowedly fictional representations. Hamlet is perhaps gaining some confidence in performances that occur, as he says, "tropically."

It is interesting, therefore, to note how in the following scene with his mother, Hamlet has assumed new confidence and strength in language. He will "speak [daggers] to her, but use none," and later she will admit that "These words like daggers enter in my ears." By his passionately rhetorical language and by his use of pictorial representations ("the counterfeit presentment of two brothers"), he forces his mother to her version of Claudius's crisis of conscience: "O Hamlet speak no more! / Thou turn'st my [eyes into my very] soul (3.4.88–89). The force of Hamlet's verbal assault on Gertrude is clearly to be preferred both in means and effect to the rash stabbing of Polonius, with which it is contrasted in this very scene. Finally, Hamlet defends his sanity by referring precisely to his discursive control: "It is not madness, / That I have utt'red. Bring me to the test, / And [I] the matter will reword . . ." (3.4.141–43).

Increasingly, therefore, Hamlet is coming to recognize the efficacy of the mediating shows and forms that he had rejected at the opening of the play. Another instance is Hamlet's speech to Horatio, in which he narrates his alteration of Rosencrantz and Guildenstern's commission:

> . . . [I] wrote it fair.
> I once did hold it, as our statists do,
> A baseness to write fair, and labor'd much
> How to forget that learning, but, sir, now
> It did me yeman's service. Wilt thou know
> Th' effect of what I wrote?
>
> (5.2.32–37)

Hamlet's changing relation to language is part of a general shift of attitude, even with regard to the nature of his project or to death itself. He learns, for example, to integrate what had earlier been his opposed perspectives on individual and general mortality. His intimate confrontation with individual death in the form of Yorick's skull ("Here hung those lips that I have kiss'd") prompts not so much a self-centered complaint as a generalizing philosophical view of human mortality, precisely the view of Nature's "common theme" that he had so fiercely rejected at the beginning of the play. The second aspect of this change is Hamlet's related sense of a "divinity that shapes our ends." Moving away from his earlier resemblance to Hieronimo, who had so painfully to shape his own destruction, Hamlet acquiesces finally to a received design. His reflection on mortality itself assumes something of a providential cast as he muses on the dust of Alexander. And it is beneath the wider skies, so to speak, of this less personal view of destiny that Hamlet arrives at his final stance:

> . . . we defy augury. There is special providence
> in the fall of a sparrow. If it be [now], 'tis not
> to come; if it be not to come, it will be now; if
> it be not now, yet it [will] come—the readiness
> is all. Since no man, of aught he leaves, knows what
> is't to leave betimes, let be.
>
> (5.2.219–23)

Here, then, and in the events that follow, Hamlet's passivity is at last redeemed, as though destiny comes down to enfold his immobility, or rather to catch him up in the web of a final plot. As Claudius says, "he shall not choose but fall." When Hamlet eventually kills Claudius, one feels that here, indeed, is the minister of a more than personal force. As Walter Benjamin writes somewhat exaggeratedly, "His life, the exemplary object of his mourning, points, before its extinction, to the Christian providence in whose bosom his mournful images are transformed into a blessed existence."[16]

The play's resolution against the ethic of an individual *pursuit* of revenge is supported by the fact that Fortinbras, who had expressly renounced revenge against the Danes, eventually inherits what he had refrained from reclaiming by force. And the manner in which Hamlet confers this inheritance indicates a final confidence in the authority and power of his speech: "he has my dying voice."

Even more interesting is the arch that is spanned between the injunctions of the two dying Hamlets. King Hamlet's speech to his son and the son's speech to Horatio are phrased so similarly as to invite a recognition of their differing contents:

> *Ghost:* If thou didst ever thy dear father love . . .
>
> . . . .
>
> Revenge his foul and most unnatural murther.
>
> (1.5.23–25)

> *Hamlet:* If thou didst ever hold me in thy heart,
>   Absent thee from felicity awhile,
>   And in this harsh world draw thy breath in pain
>   To tell my story.
>
> (5.2.346–49)

The distance traversed is nothing less than that from vengeful to elegiac pursuits, from action to language. And with the request, or rather bequest, of storytelling, the play refers back to itself, as though suggesting that its entire unfolding could already have been a version of that "story." The story would, after all, seem to commence with Horatio's epilogue-prologue:

>   . . . give order that these bodies
>   High on a stage be placed to the view,
>   And let me speak to [th'] yet unknowing world
>   How these things came about. So shall you hear
>   Of carnal, bloody, and unnatural acts,
>   Of accidental judgments, casual slaughters,
>   Of deaths put on by cunning and [forc'd] cause,
>   And in this upshot, purposes mistook

Fall'n on th' inventors' heads: all this can I
Truly deliver.

(5.2.377–85)

It is as though the play were thus a prologue to its own reenactment—
or, rather, renarration, being recast this time in words alone.

This conversion from action to language, confirming what we have
recognized as one of the play's significant tendencies, precisely reverses the movement of *The Spanish Tragedy* and goes beyond the
struggling but abortive counterassertion of verbal powers at the end of
Titus Andronicus. Furthermore, the conversion itself is foregrounded by
Horatio's suddenly acquired tone of authority. If Fortinbras has inherited the scepter, clearly Horatio has inherited a legacy of verbal
power, which now calls forth a respectful obedience from its political
counterpart: "Let us haste to hear it," Fortinbras responds, "And call
the noblest to the audience" (5.2.386–87).

Finally, whereas the objects of grief in the earlier revenge tragedies
and throughout most of *Hamlet* seemed to baffle rather than inspire a
language of solace, Hamlet's death evokes not only a majestic public
obituary but also a personal benediction that inhabits the consoling
realm of elegy even as it refers specifically to the active and redemptive power of song: "Goodnight, sweet prince, / And flights of
angels sing thee to thy rest!" (5.2.359–60). Admittedly, the stage is
littered with corpses, and the atmosphere is one of gloom and waste.
But the way in which a voice of mourning has emerged from self-
contemptuous soliloquy or gnomic self-concealment into a position of
centrality and publicity, as well as into the stance of benedictory
farewell, does much to repair the sense that something of value may
be said, and heard, at such a time.

As we look from *Hamlet* to "Lycidas," we find another work in which
a mourner struggles to emerge from a sense both of injustice and of the
unsatisfactory nature of conventional "forms, moods, shapes of grief,"
toward a position that seems to restore the fabric of belief and to
renew the power of a mourner's words.

IV

Milton: "Lycidas"

In reading "Lycidas," one might well begin by recognizing how many different yet mutually reinforcing "works" the poem performs. Admittedly, a great many circumstances converged on the genesis of the poem; but it was Milton's extraordinarily ambitious imagination that so thoroughly amplified the complexity of his occasion. At least two characteristics of Milton's temperament, apart from his ambition, fitted him for seizing the occasion in this way: his combative spirit, in which the desire to write was never more strongly aroused than by some obstacle or challenge; and his closely related fascination with loss, where, again, his desire and imagination seemed to stir most powerfully against deprivation or constraint. Indeed, Milton's motto might have been "So much the rather. . . ." I shall speak of this more concretely during what follows, but for the moment we may agree that another way of inquiring into the occasion of "Lycidas" is to ask what adversaries in addition to death—what circumstances, powers, even traditions—Milton chose to range himself against, and to surpass.

We have already remarked on the decline of the pastoral elegy during the three decades preceding "Lycidas," a decline confirmed by the fact that Milton was conspicuously alone among more than a score of elegists in his choice of what by 1637 was regarded as an unconvincing, even trivial, form for a poem of mourning. Milton was no doubt excited by the opportunity to reconquer the ground lost by the genre and to carry the tradition onward to unprecedented greatness. Here occurs one of the convergences that so distinguish the creation of this poem. For Milton himself was at this time straining to herald his future career as an epic poet by mastering and surpassing the pastoral mode. The historical needs of the declining genre thus interlocked with the personal needs of a rising poet.

This interlocking is, however, far more profound, for Milton's ambition was not merely to write a consummate pastoral poem but to secure immortality. In the often-cited letter to Diodati, written in September, two months before "Lycidas," Milton wrote, "You ask what I am thinking of? So may the good Deity help me, of immortality!"[1] Now what could agitate that desire for immortality more urgently than death itself, which in the year of King's death had already carried off not only Ben Jonson, the reigning poet, in whose wake men spoke of poetry's demise, and not only numerous victims of the plague (some even in Milton's village of Horton), but also, in April, Sara Milton, mother of the poet? And what could appease that same desire for immortality more fully than a work that was itself not merely a promise of approaching fame but a poem designed precisely to create a figure for what surpasses death?

None of Milton's earlier elegies are strictly pastoral, and it was not until King's death that Milton had a subject truly suited to that form. An obvious suitability is the fact that Milton and King both had been "nursed upon the self same hill" of Cambridge. This allowed the pastoral fiction of a shared locale and common pursuits. The convention of mourning a fellow shepherd was now legitimate, and what is more important, Milton's relative closeness to King (compared to his remote relation to previously elegized figures) provoked the poet's defense against his *own* mortality more strongly than had hitherto been the case.

Furthermore, King died at an age (25 years) that lent itself to an association with the martyred vegetation deities, an association augmented by King's having been both a poet and a clergyman, two roles well suited to the allegorical conventions of the genre. Here was a set of circumstances that permitted Milton to attempt an elegy, which, unlike his earlier exercises, could be measured against a definable and hence surpassable series of works. Joining company with Theocritus, Virgil, Sannazaro, and Spenser, Milton was now where he felt most at home and most inspired: in the arena with and against the tradition he had so carefully absorbed.

By reflecting on the abrupt death of a young clergyman (who had in fact died en route to his first parish, in Ireland), Milton also saw his chance to exploit fully the pastoral elegy's potential for theological criticism or political satire. This tradition was not new, having had strong practitioners in Mantuan and Spenser, to name only two of whom Milton was aware. But no elegy had ever mounted an attack so magisterially swingeing and so menacingly prophetic as the speech of

Saint Peter in "Lycidas." Here again, we face a convergence of personal and historical forces in Milton's poem.

What, then, was the historical context in which Milton mourned the death of a young member of an oppressed minority of good clergymen? While most critics have noted Milton's antagonism toward Roman Catholicism, and more especially toward the tyranny and corruption of the high Anglican clergy, few have examined the situation as closely as they might.

During the years preceding 1637 the courts of James I and Charles I had severely increased their repression of Puritanism. Archbishop Laud, Primate of England since 1633, had extended the power of the High Commission Court and had added that vigorous instrument of nationwide surveillance and suppression, the Metropolitan Visitation. At the same time, the church exercised absolute rights of censorship, preventing or punishing the publication of any seditious works. To clinch his reactionary campaign, Laud prescribed certain elements of ceremony in all services and proscribed the Puritan practice of sermons or lectures, hence denying Milton a potential source of income, leaving him "church-outed by the prelates" ("and shove away the worthy bidden guest").

It was partly in reaction to this dramatic extension of church tyranny that the nation began to reassert liberty of conscience and expression; and a reader of "Lycidas" should be aware that 1637 was indeed the first year of the so-called revolutionary epoch. In this year, Scotland rebelled against the *Book of Common Prayer*, Hampden's ship-money case drove in a wedge against authority, and in June, in the presence of vast numbers of outraged sympathizers in the palace yard at Westminster, the Puritans Prynne, Bastwick, and Burton were cut and branded for sedition.

These men had written and circulated an outspoken attack entitled *A Breviate of the Prelates intollerable usurpations, both upon the Kings Prerogative Royall, and the Subjects Liberties.* In this work they decried the abrogation of the rule of law and the perversion of the entire fabric of justice by churchmen who had "crept up above all." They denounced the wolfish clergy for preying upon instead of nourishing their congregations, and they prophesied the vengeance of God upon the nation. The language and the stance prefigure part of Milton's poem, and the fate of the three men must have harshly sealed their influence on the poet.

Milton may actually have been in London in late June on one of the periodic visits he is known to have made from Horton. Even were he not among the crowds at Westminster, he would certainly have heard of the events and of the eloquent orations made from the pillory, since a sympathetic *Relation* of the entire procedure, together with a report of the speeches, was rapidly circulated. What is significant for us is the *manner* in which the victims and their supporters perceived the event. For the *Relation* is marked by a combination of denunciatory, vengeful anger, together with a sense of martyrdom, ceremony, and grace.

The account speaks of the three "Servants of Jesus Christ . . . having their way strawed with sweet hearbes from the house out of which they came to the Pillory, with all the honour that could be done unto them."[2] They might have been the subjects of an elegy or of a funeral procession. And their own language on the pillory has a ring that we hear again in Milton's poem written only five months later. Here is Dr. Bastwick, moments before his ears were hacked off: "If the Presses were as open to us, as formerly they have beene, we would shatter his Kingdome about his eares." And here is Prynne after he had been cut and branded: "The more I am beate down, the more am I lift up."[3] These phrases happen to coincide with words and figures in "Lycidas,"[4] but beyond them, the entire drama, with its currents of wrath and resilience and its fervid revolutionary appeal to a retribution and consolation that derive from beyond this world, is part of what we must recognize as Milton's chosen occasion.

King's death was an accident—there was no one to blame. And yet Milton, no doubt realizing that he needed some actual target for his anger, chose to rage against the conspiracy of those "perfidious" forces that strike down the good while leaving the wicked in triumph. It is this channeling of wrath outward to revenge that contributes so fully to his resolution of the question of justice, and to his completion of the work of mourning. Our appreciation of this should be especially keen after the study of revenge tragedies above, and we shall recognize how Milton stages a displaced, verbal revenge, while also managing to conjure a transcendent context in which such vengeance is sanctified.

We have not yet quite exhausted the complex nature of the occasion. Another set of problems was provoked by King's having died so young and so abruptly, just as he was literally making his passage from years of diligent preparation to what may have been years of fruition.

Milton's preparation for his own work and for his future claim to immortality was even now just coming to an end after several years of ascetic self-discipline. In a letter to Diodati, Milton spoke of his undistracted labors: "Whereas my genius is such that no delay, no rest, no care or thought almost of anything, holds me aside until I reach the end I am making for, and round off, as it were, some great period of my studies."[5] The very rhythm and balance of his phrasing suggest the dogged purposiveness of his drive, while the goal is expressed in a conventional figure of sublimation. As he writes in his next letter, "And what am I doing? Growing my wings and meditating flight; but as yet our Pegasus raises himself on very tender pinions. Let us be lowly wise."[6]

It is clear, therefore, that before writing "Lycidas," Milton had already made a rather decisive deflection of desire, channeling it not into such enjoyments as the blithe Diodati suggested but rather into projects of a more spiritual elevation. Not a little energy must have been bound to this pursuit, and the effect of King's sudden death was, therefore, to cut the entire knot of Milton's intended transaction. He would now have to question and renegotiate the supposed exchange by which renunciation buys its own reward and self-sacrifice defends against mortality.[7] At the same time, he would have to retain control of the energy itself, which must have threatened to come unbound as the justification for its constraint was so abruptly threatened. As we have seen, these are tasks crucial to the work of mourning. By confronting them at their most pressing, Milton forced his poem to its particular intensity.

> Yet once more, O ye Laurels, and once more
> Ye Myrtles brown, with Ivy never sere,
> I come to pluck your Berries harsh and crude,
> And with forc'd fingers rude,
> Shatter your leaves before the mellowing year.
> Bitter constraint, and sad occasion dear,
> Compels me to disturb your season due:
>
> (1–7)

I have already said much about the elegiac "Yet once more," so I will not repeat the earlier account of the various functions of repetition. In Milton's case, the statement has an obvious literal as well as rhetorical meaning in that he is writing yet another elegy within his own career, as well as within the career, so to speak, of pastoral elegy itself. (It is typical of Milton to associate the careers in this way.) One may be sure, therefore, that the repetition itself deliberately repeats such usages in Theocritus, Virgil, Sannazaro, and others, this being but the first of many indications that Milton is not only adding to but re-capitulating the tradition. As one reads on, one realizes how fully the assembly of allusions and echoes in this poem allows the poet to gather up the genre as though to carry it forward in his own poem. [8]

The mention of laurels, myrtle, and ivy is another obvious use of the conventional symbols, and Milton's phrasing, too, recalls a specif-ic line from Virgil's "Eclogue II": "Et vos, o lauri, carpam, et te, proxima myrte." But in these lines Milton already extends what he inherits. At least two elements should be dwelt on briefly: (1) he contrives both to quicken the original meaning of the old symbols and at the same time to widen their reference; and (2) he begins immedi-ately to exploit the rhetorical power of the vocative mood, which so distinguishes this poem.

Laurels, myrtle, and ivy are of course ancient tokens of poethood, but by using them as figures for poetic offerings, Milton adds his personal urgency regarding the question of his own ripeness as a poet. Related figures had marked his anxiety previously in sonnet 7: "But my late spring no bud or blossoms show'th . . . inward ripeness doth much less appear." It is a common device, but Milton's real achieve-ment is to associate the prematurity of the unmellowed King's death with the possibly premature verse of the elegist, thereby confronting the possibility that he himself and his career may be as mortally vulnerable as King.

Furthermore, by subjecting the figures to a curious literalization, Milton allows a reemergence of latent symbolic meanings. We are shown not the immutable, conventional tokens but leaves and berries, which may be shattered or plucked—the action is jarringly physical, as though the figurative status of these plants were itself breaking in the poet's hands. We recall Spenser's similar literalization of the Astro-phel flower, his rejection of its traditionally consoling symbolism, allowing the flower to be "untimely cropt." And it is interesting to note that Milton's original version of these lines in the Trinity Manuscript reads "and crop your young" in place of the later "shatter your leaves." Milton's effect is similar to Spenser's, for it, too, literally breaks the traditional figures of compensation in order to prepare a substitution of more spiritualized "plants." He shatters the brittle signs of a merely earthly fame in order to make way for the higher variant that "lives and spreads aloft" in heaven.

The harsh, emphatically physical violation of the plants evokes a further meaning, one whose implications are underscored by the language of reluctance and compulsion ("Forc'd fingers," "constraint," "compels me"). As previously suggested, the work of mourning involves a castrative moment of submission to death and to a necessary deflection of desire. The way in which the poet here is being forced to a bitter shattering and plucking of leaves and of berries "harsh and crude" is not unlike the compulsion to an act of symbolic castration, which the subsequent images of the decapitated Orpheus and the abhorred shears confirm. And it is against the cluster of this and other related imagery that the consolation of a resurgent yet displaced and spiritualized sexual energy will have to triumph.

In addition to his revision of the familiar plant symbols, I mentioned Milton's intense use of the vocative mood, which extends throughout the poem; and it is important to see how the energy of the poem is braced from the outset by being directed to some kind of addressee. The poem is thus tautened by a sinew of address, a compelling tone of engagement. The near-magical manner in which Milton keeps changing fictive addressees is also crucial to the development of the poem, for the long passage from the personified laurels to the Genius of the shore may be read as an intensifying exercise in making up or evoking a presence where there is none—a fundamentally elegiac enterprise. So, too, the repeated vocative mood not only palliates the solitude of the bereaved but grips the reader as though he, too, were being continually addressed.

> For *Lycidas* is dead, dead ere his prime,
> Young *Lycidas*, and hath not left his peer:
> Who would not sing for *Lycidas*? he knew
> Himself to sing, and build the lofty rhyme.
> He must not float upon his wat'ry bier
> Unwept, and welter to the parching wind,
> Without the meed of some melodious tear.

> (8–14)

I referred earlier to the repetitive calling of the dead by name. Certainly the ceremonial practice of invocation and the psychological *anáklisis*, or propping, are at work here, but in a flexible and unobtrusive way. The mourner calls, but his call is worked into his discourse, and once again Milton reveals his nuance and control, his way of allowing the conventions to function even as he subordinates them to his personal manner.

The opposed images in lines 11–14 initiate the contrast between entire clusters of images throughout the poem. While individual elements of this contrast have been noted by several critics, the "cluster" aspect, the close relation between apparently different kinds of images, has not been stressed. [9] This is largely due to the neglect of the more original meanings of such figures and of their relation to the energy and consciousness of the griever. For example, the purposeful, ultimately consoling elevation of the "lofty rhyme" opposes the random and desolate horizontality of a "wat'ry bier," a contrast repeated in several versions and culminating in that between the guarded mount and the risen soul on the one hand and the whelming tide and far-flung corpse on the other. But what is the relation of this contrast to that between a consoling, invigorating liquid and a barren, parching wind, or between reward and an almost punitive neglect?

What does a cluster such as that of elevation, poetry, liquid, and reward imply? We have spoken of consolation as the achievement of a deflected sexual assertion, of a trope for a procreative force that outlasts individual mortality. The erection of tombs or stelae or indeed of a survivor's verse may be seen, therefore, as understandably associated with images of an invigorating liquid. The dew that Colin Clout sought to inherit from the dead Tityrus was such a liquid—an originally sexual power allegorized as poetic creativity. In "Lycidas" the imagery of a saving and surviving liquid, the figure for ongoing desire and creativity, hence of successful mourning, is even included in mythological form in the Arethusa-Alpheus legend (also present in Virgil's "Eclogue X"), as well as in the form of the swift Hebrus who bears the gory visage of continuing song to the Lesbian shore. These are the liquids that, unlike the barren diffusion of the sea, retain a direction and a continuing force, associated as they must be with the melodious tear and the lofty rhyme. It is in no way surprising, therefore, that Milton immediately associates his inspiration with the sacred well.

> Begin then, Sisters of the sacred well,
> That from beneath the seat of *Jove* doth spring,
> Begin, and somewhat loudly sweep the string.

Hence with denial vain, and coy excuse,
So may some gentle Muse
With lucky words favor my destin'd Urn,
And as he passes turn,
And bid fair peace be to my sable shroud.

(15–22)

Significantly, the sacred well "springs" (reinforcing the suggestion of lofty rhyme and of an originally seminal power) from Jove's seat, as though this were somehow *his* liquid power. The line alludes not only to the opening of Hesiod's *Theogony*:

With the Heliconian Muses let us start
Our song: they hold the great and godly mount
Of Helicon, and on their delicate feet
They dance around the darkly bubbling spring
And round the altar of the mighty Zeus. [10]

It also alludes to the barely Christianized version in Revelation 22: "And he showed me a pure river of water of life, clear as crystal, proceeding out of the throne of God and of the Lamb."[11] Almost like Alpheus, this liquid will surface again at the end of the poem in images of those "other streams" and that "Nectar pure."

Furthermore, the presence of the Sister Muses deepens our recognition that the poet is asserting a residually sexual poetic power, particularly as he urges, "Hence with denial vain, and coy excuse," as though this were indeed an erotic relationship. We notice how the vocative has shifted to an imperative mood, a clue to Milton's desire to control the personages of his poem. Nor is this imperiousness a matter of chance as he addresses the Muses. The very echo in "somewhat loudly" of Virgil's *paulo maiora* alerts us to the fact that Milton has his eye on Virgil's "Eclogue IV," with its move from pastoral to prophetic utterance.

After this summons, the poet suddenly confesses much of his motivation, his desire for a defense against his own obliteration, in short, for immortality, a power that, after death, may yet compel a later poet to turn to him in homage and benediction. Milton seems to wrestle with the timing of this statement. The urgency of his need is, I think, at odds with his tact. What results is an uneasy compromise: on the one hand the undeniably abrupt admission, as though the expressed intention could not be restrained a moment longer; on the other the clever ambiguity of the "so may," which tempers the boldness of purpose (*so* meaning "in order that") by the more neutral possibility of a mere analogy (*so* meaning "just as").

The expression of personal motive and anxiety increases the urgent intimacy of the poem, carrying us forward into the prolonged identification of the mourner with his lost friend and predisposing us to recognize the degree of self-mourning that gathers in the following lines. The past and its landscape, together with the figure of the dead shepherd, are, after all, versions of a lost self.

> For we were nurst upon the self-same hill,
> Fed the same flock, by fountain, shade, and rill.
>   Together both, ere the high Lawns appear'd
> Under the opening eyelids of the morn,
> We drove afield, and both together heard
> What time the Gray-fly winds her sultry horn,
> Batt'ning our flocks with the fresh dews of night,
> Oft till the Star that rose, at Ev'ning, bright
> Toward Heav'n's descent had slop'd his westering wheel.
> Meanwhile the Rural ditties were not mute,
> Temper'd to th'Oaten Flute;
> Rough *Satyrs* danc'd, and *Fauns* with clov'n heel
> From the glad sound would not be absent long,
> And old *Damaetas* lov'd to hear our song.
>
>   (23–36)

Only a few features of these lines need be remarked here. The figure of nursing suggests the benevolent, nourishing mother, the loss of whom I have claimed to be an inescapably recapitulated element of any mourning. By attachment to the mother I mean attachment to a unity that seems to precede a sense of individuation and of separate mortality. Figures for this matrix could be the flowery lap of Nature or the Muse. In this poem, written a mere seven months after Milton had lost his own mother, that grief is overwhelmingly important, as we shall see. In keeping with the evocation of life in the presence of the mother, time and place are described as strangely seamless, both encompassed by an unbroken circle of natural routine, a kind of rhythmic browsing. The poem's larger temporality (a day's song) will enlarge and repeat this particular figure of the diurnal round, healing, in fact, the "heavy change" which suddenly comes to rob the inset, recollected pastoral of its perfection.

97122

The high lawns repeat the motif of elevation, which is brought into significant association now with eyes and morning, both figuring the virile, watchful sun, a symbol of paternal power and of totemic immortality. Here the young sons set off *before* that power has fully risen. They are still close to a nursing nature, as yet evading, one might say, the father's fully opened eyes, the pure eyes of all-judging Jove which the poet will come to know more intimately through loss. [12]

While the songs of this idyllic day are equally unmarked by loss or even by a more than momentary absence, Milton does contrive to insinuate the idea of loss, as the double negatives allow the possibility of deprivation to surface in consciousness: "were not mute . . . would not be absent long." The effect is reminiscent of Spenser's almost subliminal warnings in "Astrophel": "Both wise and hardie (too hardie alas!) . . . He vanquisht all, and vanquisht was of none," signals preparing and cushioning the mind against a sudden loss. Milton's narrative timing, like Spenser's and like that of many elegists in the tradition, is carefully designed to situate the recollected idyll after the mere statement of loss but before the fuller narration and elaboration of that loss. The reader is, therefore, somehow both prepared for loss and yet forced to reexperience its reality. The mourned subject is made to die again. [13]

Even were the idyll not explicitly framed by loss, it has an unmistakable air of unreality, a vulnerable, fictive quality, as though the recollection were a wish-fulfilling dream. Hence the curiously self-englobed temporality, a perfect wheel of time made to revolve within the larger narrative. Hence, too, the way in which the idyll concludes with an unobtrusive clue to its own fictionality. For while the conventional pastoral fiction (shepherds for poets, the hill for Cambridge) can be reduced to its literal referents, the mention of satyrs and fauns introduces a further, less reducible level of fictionality; and from here the entire idyll seems to be retrospectively illuminated by the brightened light of unreality. It is a subtle version of the poet's later, more explicit admissions of fond dream or false surmise, and it is difficult to imagine a more superb and gentle manner of both indulging and yet distancing one's recollections of the past and of the dead. [14]

The idyll concludes with a mention of Damaetas's approval, and it is fitting that this period of innocent nursing, of small rural ditties, and of proximity to nature, should be unthreatened by any truly powerful figure of authority. Unlike that of all-judging Jove, Damaetas's approval is not contingent upon sacrifice or loss. Yet old Damaetas does, however mildly, prefigure the later judge. And our understanding of the genre and of the work of mourning makes us appreciate why a mention of this figure terminates the recollected idyll. So, too, we are less unprepared to follow this first mention of an older figure of authority by what might otherwise, despite the fictionality of the idyll, appear to be a surprisingly abrupt turn to the confrontation of disastrous loss.

> But O the heavy change, now thou art gone,
> Now thou art gone, and never must return!
> Thee Shepherd, thee the Woods, and desert Caves,
> With wild Thyme and the gadding Vine o'ergrown,
> And all their echoes mourn.
> The Willows and the Hazel Copses green
> Shall now no more be seen,
> Fanning their joyous Leaves to thy soft lays.
> As killing as the Canker to the Rose,
> Or Taint-worm to the weanling Herds that graze,
> Or Frost to Flowers, that their gay wardrobe wear,
> When first the White-thorn blows;
> Such, *Lycidas*, thy loss to Shepherd's ear.
>
> (37–49)

Here is the harshly elaborated loss of that ideal, recollected world, whose images of freshness and nurture have given way to those of insidious disease and of a specifically premature ruin. While Milton's use of the pathetic fallacy is conventional, he nevertheless modulates the passage away from fallacy into extended simile, thereby adding a measure of sophistication (he *declares* the figurative nature of such comparisons) and control (he uses the similes to *define* the precise nature of the loss). In fact, as though it were moving toward a single destination, the entire passage accumulates and converges upon a center of loss, the shepherd's ear. This emphatic focus deserves more interpretation than it has received, and some elements of our theoretical approach may be of help.

It is not enough to say merely that the ear has been deprived of what it used to hear. That is *not* the exact nature of its loss. Rather, as the tenor of the similes urgently suggests, the ear is itself an object of ruin: as Canker (cankerworm, a caterpillar that destroys leaves) kills the rose, as Taint-worm invades the weanling herds, and as frost destroys the flowers, so this loss assaults the ear. The worm imagery is especially well chosen, the worm's motion being so perfectly menacing to the labyrinth of the ear.[15]

We may, therefore, regard the loss as not only *to* but *of* the shepherd's ear. At a simple level we can point, as anthropologists and psychologists might, to the practice whereby a mourner isolates a part of his body as the locus of pain—the synecdoche allowing him to localize an otherwise diffuse hurt. But beyond this is the crucial practice of symbolic self-injury or castration in relation to the work of mourning. Just as the child performs a voluntary symbolic castration to avoid death or what he fears as actual castration, and just as the vegetation deity suffers a particularly castrative martyrdom so that the phallic principle of fertility may be renewed, so, too, the griever wounds his own sexuality, deflecting his desire, in order to erect a consoling figure for an ongoing, if displaced, generative power. We have already seen how an act of shattering and plucking will eventually, by the power of Jove, yield the immortal plant of heavenly praise. Similarly, the wounded and trembling ear will yet be touched and more than repaired by the ministry of Apollo. The ear that loses its capacity to hear the songs to which it was attached is granted the power to hear strains of a "higher mood." We recall the refrain of Saint John: "He that hath an ear let him hear what the spirit saith." The movement is from a physical to a spiritual organ. It is what happens visually in *Paradise Lost*, where the poet's blindness to the external world yields a higher, inner vision: "So much the rather thou Celestial Light / Shine inward." In each case, a castrative loss or curbing yields a higher, almost always immortalizing strength.[16]

> Where were ye Nymphs when the remorseless deep
> Clos'd o'er the head of your lov'd *Lycidas*?
> For neither were ye playing on the steep,
> Where your old *Bards*, the famous *Druids*, lie,
> Nor on the shaggy top of *Mona* high,
> Nor yet where *Deva* spreads her wizard stream:
> Ay me, I fondly dream!
> Had ye been there—for what could that have done?
> What could the Muse herself that *Orpheus* bore,
> The Muse herself, for her enchanting son
> Whom Universal nature did lament,

When by the rout that made the hideous roar,
His gory visage down the stream was sent,
Down the swift *Hebrus* to the *Lesbian* shore?

(50–63)

We may recall how such conventional questioning is in large part designed not only to avert potential self-accusation but also to *create* the fictive addressees, substituting the pretence of temporary absence for the suspicion of nonexistence or permanent neglect. At least three features of Milton's personal use of the conventions deserve notice. First, Milton revises Virgil's own revision of Theocritus. In his "First Idyl," Theocritus had Thyrsis ask where in Sicily (i.e., his own recollected locale) the nymphs had been. Virgil's "Eclogue X," however, shifts the scenario to Arcadia, a realm quite remote from himself or Gallus. Milton follows Theocritus in using his own national locale— Bardsey, Anglesey, and the river Dee. The effect is an added immediacy, as well as the vigor of an achieved rather than received transfiguration of geography.

Second, the imagined locations of the nymphs share aspects of the positive, consoling images in lines 11–14 noted above. They are associated either with elevations ("the steep . . . the top of Mona high") or with a special, purposeful liquid force ("Where Deva spreads her wizard stream"). Yet now these haunts are empty and remote. Their associated images of protection and strength are brought into question.

The third and more significant feature of this address is Milton's characteristic, self-critical rejection of an indulged fiction. As usual, Milton curbs in order to surpass himself—an essentially elegiac maneuver. The wish fulfillment is renounced "in deference to reality," and the loss is more fully confronted. Here the realization is that of the Muses' inefficacy, and it precipitates the most complicated crisis in the poem.

The poet has to mourn the loss of Lycidas *and* his own loss of belief in the Muses' protection, in particular that of Calliope, the mother of Orpheus. [17] This loss is made especially catastrophic by being cast in terms that recapitulate Orpheus's violent death. We are thus brought to that crux in mourning: a recapitulated loss of the mother, together with a scenario of castration. "Lycidas" confronts this with such unparalleled force in part because Milton always seems to renovate conventional images and myths. But it is difficult in this case to exclude additional, biographical factors—Milton's obsessive sense of his own career (his relation to the Muse) and the death, five months previously, of his mother. A full discussion of the issues involved here carries us at least into the immediately following section of the poem.

>   Alas! What boots it with uncessant care
> To tend the homely slighted shepherd's trade,
> And strictly meditate the thankless Muse?
> Were it not better done as others use,
> To sport with *Amaryllis* in the shade,
> Or with the tangles of *Neaera's* hair?
> *Fame* is the spur that the clear spirit doth raise
> (That last infirmity of Noble mind)
> To scorn delights, and live laborious days;
> But the fair Guerdon when we hope to find,
> And think to burst out into sudden blaze,
> Comes the blind *Fury* with th'abhorred shears,
> And slits the thin-spun life. "But not the praise,"
> *Phoebus* repli'd, and touch'd my trembling ears;
> "*Fame* is no plant that grows on mortal soil,
> Nor in the glistering foil
> Set off to th'world, nor in broad rumor lies,
> But lives and spreads aloft by those pure eyes
> And perfect witness of all-judging *Jove*;
> As he pronounces lastly on each deed,
> Of so much fame in Heav'n expect thy meed."

(64–84)

The cruel cutting short of a career arouses the poet to question his own defense against mortality and to redefine the possible regard, if any, for his own ascetic pursuits. In discussing the occasion of this poem, I noted that one of the tasks facing Milton was that of controlling the energy that is suddenly released once the object or rationale of its binding attachment is threatened. Not surprisingly, therefore, Milton questions the value of his asceticism, wondering whether an unsublimated eroticism is not worth indulging after all. Presumably the justification for strictly meditating the Muse was a promise of fame, and a special relation to that motherly figure, the Muse. By curbing desire, diverting it into poetic ambition, he could retain the close relationship. Or so he might have thought had he not abruptly discovered that the Muse may not be interested, may be quite thankless, and may, after all, show an alarming ability to give way to a kind of anti-Muse, one who mocks at and even causes martyrdom— an Atropos malevolently wielding the shears. By dwelling with horror on the decapitation of Orpheus, Milton not only reenacts the harsh event but does so with a bitter momentary ignorance of what it may achieve. It seems to be a lose-lose situation, one that may remind us of Titus sacrificing his hand for the severed heads of his sons. The economy of sacrifice and reward has collapsed. Or is it that the notion of reward must be revised, a revision somehow earned more fully, after all, by this very submission?

Immediately following this cry of outrage, therefore, the poem turns to what the harsh fate *does* in fact secure: not an earthly fame, which is made to seem an insufficiently displaced or sublimated object of desire, but rather a more spiritualized version—the divine approval granted by an otherworldly judge. We have seen the attendant imagery of reward prepared earlier, in the figures of shattered foliage and of the shepherd's blighted ear. The damage to these is now repaired as they, too, make way for more spiritual versions and functions.

There is, however, a residual cautioning in Apollo's gesture, as any reader of Virgil's "Eclogue VI" will recall: in Virgil's poem the gesture signified Apollo's rebuke to the poet's premature ambition. In "Lycidas" the criticism takes the form of a more extended chastisement, preparing us, surely, for a Christian reading of this entire episode. From that perspective, achieved more clearly later in the poem, the fate of Orpheus represents the chastening of man's soul in submission to a divine father. Paul's epistle to the Hebrews spells out the Christian version of the oedipal transaction:

> . . . My son, despise not thou the chastening of the Lord, nor faint when thou art rebuked of him:
> For whom the Lord loveth he chasteneth, and scourgeth every son whom he receiveth.
> If ye endure chastening, God dealeth with you as with sons; for what son is he whom the father chasteneth not?
> . . . .
> Furthermore we have had fathers of our flesh which corrected *us*, and we gave *them* reverence: shall we not much rather be in subjection unto the Father of spirits, and live?
>
> (Heb. 12.5–9)

105

Milton's focus on the authority of the father is marked in the dramatic movement from female to male figures, a movement that is itself part of the work of mourning: the separation from the primary object of desire associated with the mother and an identification with the father and his symbols of power. Hence the movement away from the sisters, the nymphs, and Calliope toward Apollo and Jove, with particular attention to the powerful, even seminal, influence of Jove's eyes. Eyes are the emblems of virility and of a father's gaze. Here, the spiritual version of that virility still has the power to raise aloft, and its totemic prestige is firmly linked to a judging power.

With these ideas in mind, we are now in a position to return to Milton's biography, where we discover not only that Sara Milton died in April 1637 but that this death left the poet with a father who happened at this very time to be as powerful a figure of judgment as Milton could possibly have faced. Since 1634, Milton had in fact struggled with his father's distrust of a poetic career. He had devoted himself primarily to the study of Church history and was at least partly trying to accommodate his father's directive, namely, to engage the clerical issues of the time in sermon and debate. Certainly, he was biding his time, preparing for epic pursuits, but the fact remains that "Lycidas" was probably the first poem Milton wrote following his final revision of *Comus*. The poem therefore had to bear a heavy burden of proof if Milton were to convince his father that poetry could in fact engage serious concerns. Milton writes a poem not only affected by the loss of his mother but also designed for the eyes of his father. [18]

There is still the unanswered question of why, on a clear summer's day, a ship mysteriously foundered and sank in the Irish sea, carrying to his death a twenty-five-year-old clergyman and poet.

> O Fountain *Arethuse,* and thou honor'd flood,
> Smooth-sliding *Mincius,* crown'd with vocal reeds,
> That strain I heard was of a higher mood:
> But now my Oat proceeds,
> And listens to the Herald of the Sea
> That came in *Neptune's* plea.
> He ask'd the Waves, and ask'd the Felon winds,
> What hard mishap hath doom'd this gentle swain?
> And question'd every gust of rugged wings
> That blows from off each beaked Promontory.

They knew not of his story,
And sage *Hippotades* their answer brings,
That not a blast was from his dungeon stray'd,
The air was calm, and on the level brine,
Sleek *Panope* with all her sisters play'd.

(85–99)

The poet modulates back to the more strictly pastoral mode symbolized by Arethusa and Mincius, doing so in a way that deliberately
calls attention to the manner in which he has surpassed this mode.
The stage-managing device is thus inseparable from a continuing act
of self-commentary.

Triton learns from Hippotades (Aeolus) that neither had there been
any disturbance nor had the waves and winds so much as heard of
Lycidas's fate. While maintaining the opposition between male constraint (his dungeon) and feminine pleasure (the sport of Panope), the
lines present further, disquieting separations, not only between man
and nature but between man and the mythological presences he may
once have cherished. The poem is indeed moving, in a typically
Miltonic manner, to a Christian distancing or revaluation of Classical
myth. There is no sympathy here between the nymphs and a drowning man. Worse yet, they play while he sinks. It is precisely this blend
of remoteness and suspected triviality that characterizes the "merely"
pastoral world that Milton is even now so thoroughly undertaking to
surpass. The play of Panope thus becomes associated with the dance
of fauns and satyrs to the rural ditties, glad sounds that we now seem
to have heard so long ago.

As if to increase this remoteness, the following three lines move to
a blend of harsh diction with religious rhetoric:

It was that fatal and perfidious Bark
Built in th'eclipse, and rigg'd with curses dark,
That sunk so low that sacred head of thine.

(100–102)

The Orphic figure is already undergoing the kind of Christianizing
that we studied in chapter I. Perhaps it was with a view to this that
Milton carefully revised the Orpheus episode in such a way as to delay
until now the Christian revision: for example, he began with "goarie
scalpe," then altered it to "divine head," then "divine visage," but then,
significantly, went back to "gory visage," deleting mention of the

107

divinity.[19] So, too, the rout of savage maenads is now replaced by a suggested agent of Sin, associated with perfidiousness and with the eclipse. The eclipse evokes both the crucifixion (hence moving the subject yet further from a pagan to a Christian martyrdom) and the original Fall. We recall how in *Paradise Lost* the first sign of Eve's sin is precisely an eclipse.

The catastrophe thus begins to find its place more securely within a Christian context of sin, Fall, and redemption, as the later sections of the poem will elaborate.

> Next *Camus*, reverend Sire, went footing slow,
> His Mantle hairy, and his Bonnet sedge,
> Inwrought with figures dim, and on the edge
> Like to that sanguine flower inscrib'd with woe.
> "Ah! Who hath reft" (quoth he) "my dearest pledge?"
>
> (103–7)

Camus, personification of the river Cam and of Cambridge University, recalls the mild figure of old Damaetas. But Camus has an added dignity: he is a "reverend Sire," his "footing slow" is different from the light steps that accompanied Damaetas's well-loved songs, and his attire enhances his majestic sadness. We have already studied how the imagery of weaving and embroidery is so frequently associated with the work of mourning; I shall therefore merely note its careful contrivance in these lines. Apart from their customary connotations, and their allusion to prior elegiac weavings, the lines seem to achieve a close yet unobtrusive metaphorical blending of the natural and the human worlds: the garments and embroidery are also the actual margins of the stream, where, amid dim reeds and sedge, one may discern apparent figures, brighter growths inscribed into the fabric like Apollo's words of grief, *ai, ai*, inscribed upon the hyacinth. It is as though the differing worlds can overlap only by metaphor and artifice occasioned by loss. Camus himself seems to pace at the borders of the pastoral world, a world now ineradicably embroidered with mortality. His single utterance is that questioning cry of deprivation, which can be answered only from another realm, in a "dread voice."[20]

> Last came, and last did go,
> The Pilot of the *Galilean* lake.
> Two massy Keys he bore of metals twain
> (The Golden opes, the Iron shuts amain).

He shook his Mitred locks, and stern bespake:
"How well could I have spar'd for thee, young swain,
Enough of such as for their bellies' sake,
Creep and intrude and climb into the fold?
Of other care they little reck'ning make,
Than how to scramble at the shearers' feast,
And shove away the worthy bidden guest;
Blind mouths! that scarce themselves know how to hold
A Sheep-hook, or have learn'd aught else the least
That to the faithful Herdman's art belongs!
What recks it them? What need they? They are sped;
And when they list, their lean and flashy songs
Grate on their scrannel Pipes of wretched straw.
The hungry Sheep look up, and are not fed,
But swoln with wind, and the rank mist they draw,
Rot inwardly, and foul contagion spread:
Besides what the grim Wolf with privy paw
Daily devours apace, and nothing said;
But that two-handed engine at the door
Stands ready to smite once, and smite no more."

(108–31)

For the physical appearance of Saint Peter we are given only two items, but they are rich in significance. The keys have been amply glossed, but our understanding of the sexual economies of loss and consolation, together with our sense of more primitive totemic representations of authority and resurrection, should alert us to a wider range of connotation than is customarily evoked.

So, too, the "Mitred locks" deserve a fuller interpretation. The figure of the abhorred shears had certainly emphasized the castrative nature of loss, and the emphasis will be repeated by Saint Peter's mention of the shearers' feast. Hair is a traditional symbol of sexual power, and Saint Peter's locks represent an immortal version of that power. We notice that the locks are not merely worn but shaken like an instrument, and their power is sanctified by the totemic headdress that they support. The association between locks of hair and a resurrected vitality will be reinforced by the figure of the rising sun tricking his beams and flaming in the forehead of the morning sky and ultimately by that of Lycidas, whose oozy locks are laved in heaven with nectar pure. It is with a sense, then, of Saint Peter's particular totemic attributes that we hear his speech.

What is the real significance and function of Saint Peter's opening words? I do not think that the purpose of his "How well could I have spar'd thee . . . Enough of such" has been adequately noted. He is making an equation, and it is important in the light of what follows to recognize this as the essential equation of the revenger. One Lycidas is worth enough of such, and it is against that number—that tally—that the entire speech unrolls like a single act of vengeance. Here is the controlled release of rage that we have seen to be so crucial to the work of mourning. Once again, it involves the locating of a target for a wrath that must be turned outward; the shifting of the burden of pain; the reversal from the passive suffering of hurt to the active causing of it; and above all, the assumption of the power to hurt, a power that we have studied in its relation to the totemic force associated with a metaphoric sexual immortality. This may well account for the penumbra of mystery and awe surrounding the two-handed engine. Its strangeness and apartness is surely an aspect of its power as a totemic instrument, and as such, it must be associated with the two keys and with the miter, which we know to be tall, conical, and two-peaked.[21]

So much of the poet's energy pours into Saint Peter's tirade that it is difficult and artificial to separate its elements. We can at least point to the following: the accumulated frustration of the questions, Where were ye? What hard mishap? Who hath reft?; the energy bound to years of laborious preparation and self-denial (here, whatever energy could not quite be rededicated to the pursuit of divine praise could be marshaled into a legitimized rage); the anger against those who had prevented Milton from the possibility of church lecturing; the bitter fury against those who had punished Burton, Bastwick, and Prynne; the anger against a mother or Muse who deserted the son she should have protected; the anger at having to mourn, at having one's rude fingers forced to their shattering work; the anger, finally, of any ambitious poet against his own thus far (to him, and to his father) inadequate work. The last-named element finds it way, I think, into the contempt for those who "grate on their scrannel pipes of wretched straw."

Before leaving this speech, we may admire Milton's resolution of the revenger's problematic sense of separation from the agents or source of justice. We have seen Titus and Hieronimo petitioning the gods in vain and receiving only neglect or scorn from the human courts. For them, language loses its efficacy; their grief itself is mocked. Milton heals the breach by the radical device of summoning Saint Peter in person—a summons enabled only by Milton's extremely Protestant internalization of divinity. That is to say, whereas Titus and Hieronimo regard divine power as impossibly remote and external, withdrawn somewhere beyond a diamantine wall, Milton regards it as potentially within the self. So much so that he can give it voice. Milton's words become Saint Peter's. They give him presence. In a sense, they create him. If we balk at supposing that Saint Peter is somehow within Milton, we have no choice but to conclude that Milton is somehow within the saint.

> Return *Alpheus*, the dread voice is past
> That shrunk thy streams; Return *Sicilian* Muse,
> And call the Vales, and bid them hither cast
> Their Bells and Flowrets of a thousand hues.
> Ye valleys low where the mild whispers use
> Of shades and wanton winds and gushing brooks,
> On whose fresh lap the swart Star sparely looks,
> Throw hither all your quaint enamell'd eyes,
> That on the green turf suck the honied showers,
> And purple all the ground with vernal flowers.
> Bring the rathe Primrose that forsaken dies,
> The tufted Crow-toe, and pale Jessamine,
> The white Pink, and the Pansy freakt with jet,
> The glowing Violet,
> The Musk-rose, and the well-attir'd Woodbine,
> With Cowslips wan that hang the pensive head,
> And every flower that sad embroidery wears:
> Bid *Amaranthus* all his beauty shed,
> And Daffadillies fill their cups with tears
> To strew the Laureate Hearse where *Lycid* lies.
> For so to interpose a little ease,
> Let our frail thoughts dally with false surmise.

(132–53)

When well expressed, wrath itself is sweet, like honey; and Milton, as he turned from the diatribe of Peter to the sweet yield of the valleys, must have felt something of what Homer and Plato meant. [22] Milton coaches Alpheus to renew the current of his desire. As we know, Alpheus, the stream, is a figure for an already once-deflected

111

passion: the youth underwent a transformation in order to continue his pursuit. The stream is a figure, in other words, for the mourner's sexuality, and for its necessary willingness to accept not only a detour but a sacrificial change. And despite the great beauty and apparent relaxation in this so-called interlude, the work of sacrifice is minutely continued.

It is important to view the present offering in contrast to the bitter plucking of the poem's start. Now, the anger has been purged, and the rewards (the undying flowers of praise) have been established. The process can be repeated in a sweeter, more decorative manner, even while the clues of sacrifice are unmistakable: the offering of "quaint enamell'd eyes" (the "white Pink," incidentally, also connotes a little eye, *pink* meaning "eyelet"); the hanging, pensive heads (not only of cowslips but of pansies too); the flowers chosen as emblems of frustrated or forlorn young love ("the rathe Primrose that forsaken dies"); or flowers like the "tufted Crow-toe" (*orcus mascula*) or the amaranth, here explicitly urged to shed his beauty (the amaranth is, literally, the unfading flower, the never-quenched life flame. Its tiny red spires revive in water long after plucking—perfect emblems for a sacrificed but resurrected power). [23]

While essential to the poem's development and to its high level of self-awareness, the recognition of "false surmise" reflects not only on the fictive presence of the dead in "Lycidas" but on the figurative action that underlies any such ceremonial offering, any such imagining that the dead person—someone addressed as *he* or *thou* rather than *it*—is actually in the mourner's presence. In this sense, the interposing tribute is any elegy, any invention of farewell addressed to one who has already gone. And in the turbulent lines that follow, however much one feels a certain harsh confrontation with the unadorned ugliness of death, the fiction of address is being maintained, even as the exact locating of that address is forcibly bewildered.

> Ay me! Whilst thee the shores and sounding Seas
> Wash far away, where'er thy bones are hurl'd,
> Whether beyond the stormy *Hebrides*,
> Where thou perhaps under the whelming tide
> Visit'st the bottom of the monstrous world;
> Or whether thou to our moist vows denied,
> Sleep'st by the fable of *Bellerus* old,
> Where the great vision of the guarded Mount

Looks toward *Namancos* and *Bayona's* hold;
Look homeward Angel now, and melt with ruth:
And, O ye *Dolphins*, waft the hapless youth.

$$(154-64)$$

The movement away from the fictive hearse to the great diffusion of the rolling sea definitely accelerates the withdrawal of attachment from the dead. And the distance opened up by those *whethers* and *ors* prepares, as it should, for the necessary reattachment of love to a substitute. That substitute is, as we know, a transfigured version of the lost Lycidas, and it is fascinating to note how Milton actually combines the movement of detachment with a subtle premonition of the apotheosis to come. For the diffusion of place hints, in however painful a voice, at the kind of omnipresence of a deity. The hint is strengthened by the orotund language ("the bottom of the monstrous world") and by the possible suggestion of Christ's visit to harrow hell. It is furthered by reference to Bellerus, Saint Michael, and the legendary figure of Palaemon.

Palaemon was the drowned youth whom dolphins carried to the shore. A temple was erected in homage to him as the guardian of sailors, a role to be accorded Lycidas. Bellerus is the fabled giant who will arise from his slumbers as though from death. And Saint Michael is not only the patron of mariners (hence again prefiguring the "Genius of the shore") but also the agent of Justice, wielding a sword that should remind us of the two-handed engine of divine vengeance. Tradition has it that men of faith could see the apparition of Michael on the mountain at Land's End. There Milton places him, on his fortified elevation guarding against the Spanish strongholds across the sea. The image of consolidated defense surely reflects on the poet's own increasingly assured defense, his conviction that a concentrated power (be it his lofty rhyme, his praise aloft, or even the power of his reinforced repression, his rededication to an ascetic quest) will stand erect against less high desires and against death itself.[24] It is because these lines so brilliantly effect that distancing of the lost object, the relic of the actual Lycidas, *and* so fully prefigure the new object of attachment, the resurrected Lycidas, that the poem can now finally move to the lines that follow.

Weep no more, woeful Shepherds weep no more,
For *Lycidas* your sorrow is not dead,

Sunk though he be beneath the wat'ry floor,
So sinks the day-star in the Ocean bed,
And yet anon repairs his drooping head,
And tricks his beams, and with new-spangled Ore,
Flames in the forehead of the morning sky:
So *Lycidas*, sunk low, but mounted high,
Through the dear might of him that walk'd the waves,
Where other groves, and other streams along,
With *Nectar* pure his oozy Locks he laves,
And hears the unexpressive nuptial Song,
In the blest Kingdoms meek of joy and love.
There entertain him all the Saints above,
In solemn troops, and sweet Societies
That sing, and singing in their glory move,
And wipe the tears for ever from his eyes.
Now *Lycidas*, the Shepherds weep no more;
Henceforth thou art the Genius of the shore,
In thy large recompense, and shalt be good
To all that wander in that perilous flood.

(165–85)

Here, then, is the act of substitution, without which no work of mourning is complete, the reattachment to a new object of love, in this case a troped, indeed apotheosized, version of the physical Lycidas who had sunk "beneath the wat'ry floor." The turn to the mounted Lycidas thus necessarily reflects a spiritualization of the poet's own attachment, a refined reassertion of desire evident in the accompanying imagery (the emphasis on mounting, on repairing a drooping head, on laving the oozy locks, and finally on the nuptial song in the kingdom of joy and love). We discern not merely the mourner's reinvestment of desire but the conclusion of the archaic funeral rites for the vegetation god—the retrieval or establishment of an emblem of renewed fertility and the celebration of a reunion that regenerates the natural world. Here, of course, in a Christianized version we have the elevation of the soul (still imaged, however, by the sun) and its entry into a spiritually raised, rather than physically renewed, natural world, a world now of other streams and groves, where the nuptial song celebrates the marriage of the Lamb, or of the human spirit, to God. The pastoral world is reinscribed in heaven.

As for the figure of the sun, apart from its totemic power and its history as a crucial elegiac trope, it has been carefully contextualized

in "Lycidas," situated in relation to so many other images and prefigurations that it now gathers up a vast range of meaning in its final,
triumphant rise. It recalls the opening eyelids of the morn; it fulfills
the aborted sudden blaze of fame; it sheds the eclipse; it raises all
those fallen, pensive, sunk, or severed heads.

Yet it is intriguing to notice how the poet, even while he exploits
this figure of the sun as a simile for the rising soul, manages to
supersede it by the Christian force that according to Milton makes
that simile possible. Lycidas rises like the sun but does so through the
dear might of Christ. We are invited to see how this power, as a force
that can *cause* a sunlike rise, exceeds that of the sun. We may even be
reminded that in a Christian cosmos God is the creator or cause of the
sun itself. This set of ideas is important to the coda of the poem, and it
is stressed further by the motif of an enabling or *positing* power man-
ifested in the poet's *fiat*: "Henceforth thou art the Genius of the shore."
The accent is very nearly that of command. Is the poet himself now
playing a Christ-like role?

> Thus sang the uncouth Swain to th'Oaks and rills,
> While the still morn went out with Sandals gray;
> He touch't the tender stops of various Quills,
> With eager thought warbling his *Doric* lay:
> And now the Sun had stretch't out all the hills,
> And now was dropt into the Western bay;
> At last he rose, and twitch't his Mantle blue:
> Tomorrow to fresh Woods, and Pastures new.
>
> (186–93)

The mourner's act of self-distancing and self-surpassing, so essential to mourning, is here taken one step further. Even the successful
mourner is suddenly superseded, in a way that reminds us of the place
of this poem in the context of Milton's developing career. He has
written his consummate pastoral, and has achieved within it instances
and proofs of epic power. Not only is this coda written in *ottava rima*,
the form for Italian epic, but it reads precisely like those moments in
epic poetry when the narrator follows the speech of a protagonist with
"Thus sang. . . ." It is as though Milton, in ending and describing his
elegy, has already entered an epic.

The line "He touch't the tender stops of various Quills" is surely
meant to counterpoint, in a gentle fashion, the forced fingers rudely

shattering the leaves. And "touch't the tender stops" ought, too, to recall "touch't my trembling ears," thereby suggesting a development that the poet has now made, an assimilation of the Apollonian, epic touch within the Doric "warble." Once again we admire the mourner's absorption of the gestures of authority, which culminates in the assimilation of the elegist to the guiding figure and power of the poem, the sun. Assimilation and yet, as always, surpassal.

First, there is the power deriving from an accelerated description of the sun's motion, as though the poet's act of description were hurrying the sun, somehow even causing tenses to collapse into the timeless now of eternity, or indeed of poetry: "And now the Sun . . . And now was dropt." Following this is the master stroke of replacing the sun by the elegist, sliding from one to the other via a deliberately ambiguous pronoun, *he*. That ambiguity is even prepared for by the attribution to the elegist of a "Mantle blue," somehow part of the same attire as the "Sandals gray;" and by the brilliant succession "And now was dropt . . . At last he rose." The physical Lycidas had sunk; his spirit has mounted high. The sun sinks; the poet rises. [25]

The "Mantle blue" calls for a few comments. It is perhaps only the coventry blue cloak of a shepherd. But how to distinguish it now from the blue sky surrounding the sun? What is more interesting, it is a consoling revision of the "mantle black" that surrounded a disconsolate Colin Clout at the end of "January." It is the last and perhaps most pointed of Milton's allusions to the tradition he has overgone. [26]

The way in which the elegist preempts the rising of the sun reflects back on Christ's power to effect a spiritual sunlike rise for man. But Milton has calmly assumed that power himself: *he* makes the uncouth swain rise, and he himself has risen, as though he were another sun. We find it hard to avoid the recognition that it is, after all, the poet who has Christ raise Lycidas. The frame of fictionality encompasses even that supreme action; which brings us to the disquieting region of conjecture, so important to Milton, of whether Christianity may be no more than a superior product (superior to Classical mythology, for example) of man's imagination. What we have already seen to be the poem's repeated questioning of its own fictions cannot entirely be escaped. (The accelerated temporality of the sun's motion is no more real than the rhythmic circle of the idyll. And the sun, in order to behave as a symbol for resurrection, has to *appear* to have a nocturnal demise, another of man's fictions. And how is he who walked the waves so different from Palaemon? Is he more real? or is he simply more powerful?)[27]

Near the end of Revelation, a text we see alluded to and even quoted in "Lycidas," there is a verse that reads:

> And the city had no need of the sun, neither of
> the moon, to shine in it; for the glory of God
> did lighten it, and the Lamb is the light thereof.
>
> (21:23)

John's highly rhetorical imaging of God as the light of the new Jerusalem depends on substituting God for the original solar figure. But "Lycidas," moving as it does from submissive gestures of compulsion and loss to an internalizing counter-usurpation of totemic power, has substituted the figure of the elegist for both the sun and God. As we see the rising poet imaginatively projecting, as no sun can, the landscape of the future, we may think ahead to Ruskin's statement regarding "invention spiritual":

> Man is the sun of the world; more than the real sun.
> The fire of his . . . heart is the only light
> and heat worth gauge or measure. Where he is,
> are the tropics; where he is not, the ice-world.[28]

V

Jonson, Dryden,
and Gray

After 1637, almost two centuries elapsed before "Adonais" (1821) successfully took up the legacy of "Lycidas," "Astrophel," and the traditional pastoral elegy. During the interim, conventional practitioners abounded, but no one deliberately dared to reinfuse the pastoral conventions with the kind of personal passion and revisionary invention that alone could assure them a more than decorative survival.

As we have seen, Milton himself had had to resurrect a form that, by 1637, had already fallen into decline. He had returned to the genre with solitary ambition, and his had been a solitary success. His example proved too difficult and too remote to influence even his admirers, and the fortunes of the pastoral elegy ebbed more drastically after "Lycidas" than in the decades preceding it. In 1649 the elegies collected for Hastings had not a single pastoral among them. Not from Herrick, Marvell, Denham, nor Dryden. And later attempts to revive the inherited form seemed only to bury it further beneath the dead weight of academic imitation. Oldham's elegy for Rochester, Dryden's "On the Death of Amyntas," Pope's "Winter," Thomson's "Damon"—these and others of their kind shared the general powerlessness of the pastoral elegy throughout this period. [1]

This does not mean that there were no convincing elegies between Milton's and Shelley's. It simply means that such intervening successes were not strictly *pastoral* elegies. They obeyed other norms and worked out other resolutions. In this chapter, I shall try to describe some of the distinctive features of these poems. While noting their difference from purely pastoral modes, nonetheless I hope to show how they share certain elements that characterize the elegy at large.

As Ruth Wallerstein has shown, elegists during the seventeenth century turned from pastoral conventions either toward an exploitation of metaphysical wit, elaborate conceits, and strong lines or toward the more tight-lipped poise of rational stoicism.[2] In either case, a context of social turmoil, a preoccupation with religious and philosophical debate, and a waning confidence in the expressive or referential value of fictions combined to render apparently trivial such figures as the lamenting shepherd and his flute.

Throughout most of the eighteenth century, too, this prejudice against the pastoral elegy persisted. We see it in John Dennis's pronouncement that "no sort of imagery can ever be the language of grief. If a man complains in simile, I either laugh or sleep."[3] And we find it elaborated in Johnson's stringent critique of "Lycidas." Along the way, there are parodies by Prior, Gay, and Swift, and there is the contemptuous but amusing reduction by Tickel:

> Indeed most of the occasional Pastorals we have, are built upon one and the same plan. A shepherd asks his fellow, why he is so pale? if his favourite sheep hath strayed, if his pipe be broken, or Phyllis unkind? He answers, None of these misfortunes have befallen him, but one much greater, for Damon (or sometimes the god Pan) is dead. This immediately causes the other to make complaints, and call upon the lofty pines and silver streams to join in the lamentation. While he goes on, his friend interrupts him, and tells him that Damon lives, and shows him a track of light in the skies to conferm it; then invites him to chesnuts and cheese. Upon this scheme most of the noble families in Great-Britain have been comforted; nor can I meet with any right honourable shepherd that doth not die and live again, after the manner of the aforesaid Damon.[4]

Turning to the alternatives, we find the metaphysical wielders of hard conceits and strong lines exemplified at best by Donne and at worst by Cleveland. While the latter's elegy for Edward King (its best line being "I am no poet here") should have served Johnson's quarrel with insincerity, even Donne's brilliant and passionately argumentative style was too idiosyncratic, too programmatically religious, to win many able followers in an increasingly secular and decorous age.

It is to the other, more restrained mode that we must look for elements that characterize many of the finest elegies of the seventeenth and eighteenth centuries. In doing so, we shall be examining what may be broadly recognized as the Neoclassical elegy. The poems under study will be Jonson's "On My First Son," Dryden's "To the Memory of Mr. Oldham," and Gray's "Elegy Written in a Country Churchyard."[5]

Ben Jonson

On My First Son

Farewell, thou child of my right hand, and joy;
    My sin was too much hope of thee, loved boy.
Seven years thou wert lent to me, and I thee pay,
    Exacted by thy fate, on the just day.
O, could I lose all father now! For why
    Will man lament the state he should envy?
To have so soon 'scaped world's and flesh's rage,
    And, if no other misery, yet age?
Rest in soft peace, and asked, say here doth lie
    Ben Jonson his best piece of poetry,
For whose sake, henceforth, all his vows be such
    As what he loves may never like too much. [6]

Tight-reined as it is, Jonson's epigram for his son is already looser and more emotional in form than the two elegiac epigrams that precede it, those for his daughter and for Margaret Ratcliffe. The former is almost entirely in end-stopped tetrameter couplets, while the latter, also in tetrameters, is further bound to the masthead of its acrostic form. In his poem for his son, Jonson not only lengthens his expression of loss into pentameter lines but breaks these up with shifting and dramatic caesurae. So, too, he unleashes three enjambments to augment the nuanced tension between formal and emotional pressures.

The first lines exemplify how some of these subtle irregularities give form to Jonson's emotion while also complicating our response to his seemingly straightforward speech. What is the effect of the couplet's identically delayed caesurae if not to give the last foot in each line ("and joy," "loved boy") a fragile and tragic detachability? Benjamin is thus presented as a vulnerably exposed and indeed severed extension of Jonson's "line." Also, if one listens carefully, the last words in each line sound almost like echoes, although they repeat no particular sound within their lines. They have the sad aftersound of echoes, the sound of something cut off but lingering. And the echo of their rhyme one with another seals the effect.

Our sense of Benjamin as an extension of the poet's line is no doubt prompted by Jonson's explicit translation of the name, "child of my right hand," with its attendant connotations of dexterous, fortunate, even blessed. A similar play will of course mark the concluding lines' reference once again to Jonson's procreative relation to his son as to his "poetry." We shall explore this eventually consoling condensation later. For the moment, we should notice that the epigrammatic restraint, with its apparently sober rejection of florid diction or elaborate images, does not rule out a careful manipulation of figurative language, however much this may seem to be legitimized by literal translation.

Other rhetorical uses are normalized by convention. For example, the first word of the poem, *Farewell*, together with the quickly repeated pronouns *thou* and *thee* with their echoing extensions, *joy* and *boy*, reveals a heavy reliance on the elegiac feigning of address and on the ritual of repetitive invocation. In each case, as elsewhere throughout the poem, Jonson seems to legitimize or normalize his fictions, to render them unobtrusive, and thus to absorb or contain the nonetheless vigorous work of mourning which they help him to perform.

In the second line, Jonson stoically criticizes his own excess, "My sin was too much hope of thee, loved boy." The word *sin* binds the stoicism to Christianity and suggests several possible meanings. Has Jonson idolized his son to the exclusion of God? Has he wrongly assumed that Benjamin was protected by parental desire even to the point of being invulnerable to God's will? Or is it simply that Jonson has cherished his son more hopefully than one should cherish any mortal creature?[7]

While all of the above possibilities are valid, the important question is, Why so strong a word as *sin*? Certainly, the word summons a context of error and punishment, in which loss, as penance, is at least made comprehensible. Furthermore, the context offers a narrative model of consolation, in which sin and penance yield to redemption—a Christianized version of the old myth of descent, purification, and renewal. As we shall see, Jonson does in fact employ a version of this paradigm. Apart from this, however, the strength of the self-rebuke, its self-punitive quality, is one we should recognize from our readings of other elegies and from our understanding of the work of mourning. For this turn against the self is part of the attempt to curtail one's residual attachment to the dead, to curb, even apparently to renege, one's affection for them. By reference to sin, Jonson enlists the help of the highest authority for this painful task.

We may speculate further on a possible measure of Jonson's psychological rather than Christian guilt. This would mean considering the effect of losing one's first son, of being deprived of this most palpable evidence of one's procreative strength as a man. It would mean asking whether Jonson may have felt, however irrationally, that he had not fulfilled a father's role—even that his absence from London at the time of Benjamin's death had been culpable.

And yet, however comprehensively we understand Jonson's sense of sin and the function it performs, we cannot rule out a possible protest in the very extravagance of the word. The severity of self-condemnation would thus serve to allow a certain bitter recoil in which the charge of sin accuses or impugns the fairness of the very prosecution. Several elements of the poem bear out this complexity. Even the phrasing of the second line begins the tenacious undersong. If Jonson had written "Loved boy, my sin was too much hope of thee," the statement of error would have superseded the "loved boy," who, in Jonson's line, has the opposite power of superseding the accusation. However short, that carefully offset foot almost counterpoises what precedes it. And Jonson's deliberate spondee not only adds to its counterweight but forces us especially to register the irregularly stressed *loved*. The boy, still loved in the moment of this address, returns to haunt the line, and we begin to measure the tension of a still imperfect renunciation.

This complexity or counterpressure is even more evident in the second couplet: "Seven years thou wert lent to me, and I thee pay, / Exacted by thy fate, on the just day." Once again, the poet argues on behalf of the powers that have bereaved him. The motif of penitence ("I thee pay") elaborates that of sin and moves the poem further along its narrative course. But the language of religion has been secularized and subdued to that of commerce. The matter-of-fact rhetoric represents an attempt not only to rationalize the loss and to assimilate it to a mundane sphere of transaction but also to deny its very nature as loss. The idea of possession is replaced by that of loan, which has the further effect of "justifying" the actual year of the boy's death.

And yet, as before, Jonson's grief resists. The third line, ostensibly *about* meeting the obligations of number, ripples and strains against the iambic pentameter norm. Jonson has forced twelve syllables into a narrower, essentially decasyllabic room. And like the last foot in each of the first two lines, the extra syllables suggest a residue of unassimilable grief. "Exacted" only further stresses the poet's resistance. By the time we read "just day," our sense of submission is somewhat ironic, and certainly incomplete.

It is therefore with relief that we read the exclamation of the fifth line. Having lost his son, Jonson would lose precisely that residue of affection that we have been noticing, that disconcertingly tenacious relation to the boy. The force of the cry is irresistible, coming as it does after two lines whose very form and content speak of nothing but constraint. In addition to its open and assonantal ease of movement, the phrase's yearning for utter loss is especially expansive relative to the preceding calculus of exchange. The very notion of loan and repayment, of careful accounts, is obliterated by the call for sheer loss. And just as the language of religion had been partially eclipsed by that of commerce, so, too, this latter language, together with its framework for rationalizing loss, has had to yield to that of unappeased lament.

Thus it is that Jonson has to turn now to confront the issue of lamentation. As he does so, he shifts ground, setting forth the traditional stoical valorization of death. The preceding lines, with their expression of present pain and constraint, certainly contribute to the persuasiveness of Jonson's argument, and his presentation is extremely powerful. The vantage of the philosopher with its vista of humankind in general ("why will man lament") provides a respite from the intimacy of personal grief. And the denunciation of life allows the release of anger, which we have found essential to the mourner's progress. If we listen to the line "To have so soon 'scaped world's and flesh's rage," with its sibilant, almost snarling alliteration and its harsh crushes of obstructive sound, we may recall Spenser's "So as he rag'd amongst that beastly rout" or Milton's "Grate on their scrannel pipes of wretched straw." Whether it is displaced to the rage of Sidney, of Saint Peter, or of the flesh, in each case we are unquestionably hearing the elegist's wrath. And in each case the vengeful aspect of that wrath is of the essence.

As we have noted elsewhere, the expression of anger, rather than of sheer lament, often frees the elegist to conjure images of peace. Like Milton calling on the vales, Jonson now turns quietly to offer a benediction: "Rest in soft peace." The classical conventionality suggests how well Jonson is maintaining his stoical poise, while the epithet *soft* has a telling effect: added to the *Requiescat in pace,* *soft* makes us think of the actual earth it may have described, and hence of the substitution whereby the very earth has yielded to peace.

But having assigned his son to an enviable quietus, how is Jonson to resolve his own fate as a survivor? What follows is just such a resolution:

> . . . and asked, say here doth lie
> Ben Jonson his best piece of poetry,
> For whose sake, henceforth, all his vows be such
> As what he loves may never like too much.

The speech is, of course, ascribed to Benjamin, and I shall discuss the ascription after exploring just two elements of what the lines say. The first element is the reference to Jonson's "best piece of poetry." The second is the question of the poet's future vows.

As is well known, Jonson plays on the etymology of *poetry,* just as he had earlier translated the name of Benjamin. Both cases involve extensions of reference away from the boy toward the father's powers of making. Now although one obvious interpretation of this is that Jonson sadly values his son more highly than any of his literary creations, nonetheless one cannot underestimate the consolatory aspect of the specific figure, and of the turn of attention that it involves. We have come to see how this movement, together with the focus on a form of generative power, particularly that of the survivor, is a familiar and essential ingredient of consolation. What Jonson does here is not only to remind us of the trope in *poetry* but to repeat the original act of figuration that gave rise to the literary meaning of the word. By replacing the literal statement "my best piece of procreative making" with "my best piece of poetry," Jonson maintains the sense of his physical power even while he translates that power into another sphere of activity whose products, such as this very epigram, this very "piece of poetry," are deathless.

Jonson's consolatory troping of sexual power—submitting it to a displaced but enduring figurative version—together with his almost eclogic way of pointing to his poem, reveals the deep bond to pastoral elegy, and we may wonder at the deft condensation with which Jonson's poem has achieved so much. In fact, if we examine Jonson's actual mode of rhetoric for this celebration of his "poetic" energies, we notice that both *Benjamin* and *poetry* function condensively as puns. And puns, as Freud has shown, involve precisely a "saving" (compression) and subsequent release of energy as the doubling of meaning is recognized and "discharged."[8] Jonson's rhetoric itself generates and releases a measure of the energy that it celebrates.

The second consoling element in these closing lines is the mention of forthcoming vows. It is true that there is a decided sorrow, even bitterness, in the intended limitation of these vows. And the difficult phrasing and wry ambiguity undercut much of the resolution, returning us to the kind of wrestling seen earlier in the poem. For the sake of this dead son, Jonson should never love as powerfully again, or never find an object of his love too pleasing. It is a painfully contorted formulation. Nevertheless, the orientation *is* to the future, to a renewal of surviving life, and love. And this renewal, particularly in its chastened form, with its return to the religious language of vows, has been earned by the progress of sin and penitence. As an elegist should, therefore, Jonson closes with a *henceforth*, while the vows remind us not only of his return to devotion but of his interest in continuing to perform certain acts of language. (*Vow* should be associated with *veu* [wish] and with *vox* [voice, vowel, utterance].)[9]

The last line of Jonson's poem translates the final line from one of Martial's elegiac epigrams; and while I cannot here discuss Jonson's general debt to Martial, I would like to keep this particular act of translation in mind, for it underscores Jonson's final turn to the consolation of poetry, a line of which is here shown in its translated survival sixteen hundred years after it was first written.[10] It is the classical realm of this survival that Jonson honors, even as he elevates his poem to its precincts.

Even more important and more consoling, is the fact that his dead son participates in this classical realm, by uttering the translation of Martial. Benjamin thus seems to speak not only as from within or beyond the grave but with the voice of the ancient author whose company he has joined. It is a beautifully Neoclassical consolation. For such as Jonson, where would heaven be if not among the likes of Martial?

Finally, there is something characteristically Neoclassical in the way Jonson's elegy ends in a voice that is and is not quite his own. We have seen how almost any elegy requires a progression of voice, a sequence by which the mourner supersedes his grieving self. But in the

Neoclassical era, with its high incidence of personae, it is interesting
to note how often the elegist actually concludes as though with *someone
else's* voice. Here, as Jonson ventriloquizes through the persona of his
son, who in turn becomes a persona or mouthpiece for Martial, we
remember that the word *persona* itself originally referred not merely to
masks but to the facial images of the dead. It is the voice of these
masks that Jonson inherits as he continues to animate them precisely
by his impersonation. And what finer destiny for the child of his right
hand than to be assimilated to that voice and mask which the poet has
in turn bequeathed to him—to become, after all, an eternally speaking "piece of poetry"?

Dryden

Dryden's poem for John Oldham represents a rejection of his earlier
exercise in the flamboyantly metaphysical, or "hydrographical,"
school of Cleveland; and this turn away from his elegy for Hastings
exemplifies a general shift of taste toward the Augustan norms which
Jonson had heralded at the beginning of the century.

To the Memory of Mr. Oldham

Farewel, too little and too lately known,
Whom I began to think and call my own;
For sure our Souls were near ally'd; and thine
Cast in the same Poetick mould with mine.
One common Note on either Lyre did strike,
And Knaves and Fools we both abhorr'd alike:
To the same Goal did both our Studies drive,
The last set out the soonest did arrive.
Thus *Nisus* fell upon the slippery place,
While his young Friend perform'd and won the Race.
O early ripe! to thy abundant store
What could advancing Age have added more?
It might (what Nature never gives the young)
Have taught the numbers of thy native Tongue.
But Satyr needs not those, and Wit will shine
Through the harsh cadence of a rugged line.
A noble Error, and but seldom made,
When Poets are by too much force betray'd.

Thy generous fruits, though gather'd ere their prime
Still shew'd a quickness; and maturing time
But mellows what we write to the dull sweets of Rime.
Once more, hail and farewel; farewel thou young,
But ah too short, *Marcellus* of our Tongue;
Thy Brows with Ivy, and with Laurels bound;
But Fate and gloomy Night encompass thee around.[11]

Like Jonson's epigram, Dryden's poem is cast in heroic couplets, and it shares the earlier poem's epitaphic blend of dignity, brevity, and restraint. Its three principle sections (lines 1–10, 11–20 and 21–25) all employ the fiction of address, and this repetition both tightens and underlines the neat ordonnance of the work. The opening lines, beginning with "Farewel" and including the stoical attention to degree ("too little," "too lately") as well as to the precariousness of possession, are especially reminiscent of Jonson. And as the elegy unfolds, we recognize a similarly Neoclassical preoccupation with the issues of poetry itself. In this case, the concerns are explicitly those Augustan topics of craft, decorum, elegance, and the classics.

The following reading of the poem dwells mainly on two subjects: Dryden's treatment and display of poetic technique and his use of allusion.

John Oldham, twenty years Dryden's junior, died in 1683 at the age of thirty-one. He had been a promising satirist with a flair for caustic and headstrong verse. As Dryden's "too lately known" admits, the two men had only become acquainted a relatively short time (two years) before Oldham's death. But Dryden's poem expresses an elevated spirit of comradeship, and much of the elegy's interest lies in his attempt to accommodate a clear-eyed sense of Oldham's poetic immaturity with a gracious and compassionate farewell.

Almost immediately, we note how Dryden emphasizes his attitude toward poetry itself as a source of highest value. In the cases of Oldham and himself, the very shape and definition of the soul is one accorded by the practice of poetry.[12] So, too, any discussion of Oldham's life and death is, according to Dryden's poem, best conducted with reference to his poetry. The entire question of a premature death, and the consideration of the precise loss involved, is therefore weighed in terms of poetic development and in terms of that typically Renaissance and Neoclassical concern, the shape of a career. Furthermore, it is scarcely surprising to find that whatever consolation the elegy may invent will also relate to a principally poetic context.

By conventional elegiac figures of vegetation, very possibly borrowed from Milton, Dryden associates Oldham with the figure of the young fertility god ("O early ripe! . . . Thy generous fruits"). *Generous* retains some of its original meaning, but the procreative power is definitely transferred to that of poetic creativity, and Dryden keeps his attention carefully focused on questions of poetic achievement.

Had he lived longer, Oldham might have attained the kind of finesse and smooth control that Dryden is even now self-consciously exercising. Dryden takes pains to demonstrate these attainments not only in the entire design of the poem but in the deliberate shows of formal mastery that mark certain lines. While seeming to defend Oldham's rough versification (". . . Wit will shine / Through the harsh cadence of a rugged line"), Dryden writes an enjambed series of rugged, irregular feet, through whose apparent harshness the momentum travels to its fulfilling cadence. So powerfully imitative is the rhythm of the line that it appears to render the cadence itself transparent to the light of wit.

A second example of this kind of self-conscious virtuosity is Dryden's description of poetic maturation: ". . . and maturing time / But mellows what we write to the dull sweets of Rime." Again, he seems to be deferring to Oldham's immature strength. The "But" and the "dull sweets" seem to suggest that Dryden holds these mellowings somewhat cheaply. This is important, for I think that the posture of deference is part of the successful mourner's complex blend of symbolic obeisance and self-approval in relation to the dead. The latter intention is surely there in the amplitude with which Dryden formally embodies the very qualities that he seems to slight. Enjambment, followed by an alexandrine, draws out the utterance into the continuous and lengthy period of maturation. This is precisely the kind of formal solace we crave after the abrupt discontinuity of "O early ripe!"

The play of alliteration and assonance in these lines is more detailed than I can here afford to note, but we should at least register how the consonants of *mellows* are among the most heavily alliterated, so that the lines themselves seem to resolve into one long utterance of the word: ". . . maturing time / But *mellows* *what* *we* write to the *dull* *sweets* of Rime." Within the alliterations are further plays, such as the reversal of "*mellows*" in "*sweets*," or, even more telling, the complex alliterative and assonantal modulation from "time" to "write" to "Rime," a progression in which rhyming becomes the resolution of writing and time. Even the harshness of the dental *t* is made to yield and ripen to the soft *m* we heard so often earlier in the line. Finally, rhyme itself has been prolonged and matured in this last word of the only rhymed triplet in the poem. Here, then, is the yield of maturity, the consolations offered by a surviving poet's form, which in itself seems to bring to fruition the early promise of a poet whose works had been abruptly "gather'd ere their prime."

To the consolations of formal virtuosity Dryden adds the consolatory effects of two perfect allusions. Appropriately enough for a poem of and about mellowness and craft, both allusions are from the *Aeneid*. The first is to the footrace in *Aeneid* 5.315 ff. The second is to Aeneas's sighting of Marcellus in the underworld in *Aeneid* 6.

The situation of the footrace itself is significant, for it is that of the funeral games for Aeneas's father, Anchises. With this allusion to Classical mourning practices, and in particular to those performed by Aeneas, Dryden thus brings to his poem and to his act of mourning the stature of Virgil's great exemplar of piety and decorum. Furthermore, as we know, contests have an especially important function, not only in their original form of funerary ritual but in the closely related form of singing matches or other scenarios of contest within many elegies. I have discussed the elegiac contest in its relation to such issues as the struggle for inheritance, the proof that certain powers survive, the foregrounding of an elegist's skill, and the dynamic of work and its compensatory reward. The richness of the topos should therefore be recollected even as we regard the more specific aspects of Dryden's purpose.

An immediate function of the allusion is to provide a reserved yet elevated statement of Dryden's friendship with Oldham. Earlier in the poem, he had established his affinity with the younger man, and there, too, he had mediated that expression by referring to shared poetic pursuits. Now, he again purifies the relationship of the merely personal, referring to it indirectly by way of Virgil's poetry. In each case, poetry itself provides a zone that lends both dignity and a measure of neutrality to an expression of personal feeling. Interestingly, whereas Dryden comes upon the allusion as though principally to clarify the nature of his "race" against Oldham, he is honoring the actual relationship by comparing it to that of the two men whom Virgil himself had chosen as the very exemplars of friendship.

In fact it is Nisus, the Dryden figure, whom Virgil singles out for fame in this regard: "Nisus, for friendship to the youth renowned." And it is Nisus who goes on to demonstrate the virtue of his friendship and to win a significant *consolation* prize.

The details of the race are familiar, but their complex contribution to Dryden's poem have never been entirely registered. Readers have certainly noted the dominant parallels: Nisus (Dryden) started ahead of Euryalus (Oldham) in the race (of life). Although closer to the goal (death), Nisus slipped, and Euryalus went on to win. Thus the allusion neatly captures the paradoxical reversal of expectation and consolingly converts Oldham's seeming defeat into a victory. But if we explore the event further, we recall that Euryalus won because the fallen Nisus had intervened on his behalf (Nisus deliberately tripped Salius, who had been running between him and Euryalus). While illustrating Nisus's selfless assistance to his friend, the detail invites us to recognize that it is, after all, the intervention of the elegist, with his fiction of the race, that allows the dead Oldham any such thing as a victory. The allusion thus reflects what Dryden is even now performing for his friend.

While we are on this point, we should remember that Nisus slipped in the blood of the oxen that had been sacrificed in the rites for Anchises. Virgil describes him as "besmeared with filth and holy gore," a description surely befitting a mourner if we think either of the primitive rites or of an elegist's related conjunction of self-abasement and self-consecration.

Finally, Virgil concluded the footrace episode with an elaborate scenario of judgment and reward, motifs that we recognize as crucial to the concern of almost every elegist. Again, the details are minutely appropriate, for Virgil concentrates especially on the ability of a fair judge, Aeneas, to remedy the blunders of Fortune ("'But . . . Fortune's errors give me leave to mend, / At least to pity my deserving friend'"). [13] The lines are astonishingly apt, and it is intriguing that it is Nisus, the Dryden figure, who formulates most clearly the concept of the consolation prize. He pleads on his own behalf, but the wider relevance to Dryden's purpose is obvious:

"If such rewards to vanquished men are due"
(He said), "and falling is to rise by you,
What prize may Nisus from your bounty claim,
Who merited the first rewards and fame?"[14]

When we see Nisus-Dryden the elegist rewarded with "an ample shield, / Of wondrous art," this bestowal upon him of an aesthetically wrought instrument of defense seems, as does every other detail that the allusion has evoked, to be almost uncannily appropriate.

This brings us to Dryden's concluding allusion:

> Once more, hail and farewel; farewel thou young,
> But ah too short, *Marcellus* of our Tongue;
> Thy Brows with Ivy, and with Laurels bound;
> But Fate and gloomy Night encompass thee around.

The first line is wonderfully poised, a renewed address with its own internal echo repeating, almost answering, "Farewel" across the caesural pause. "Once more, hail and farewel" seems to blend the conventional pastoral elegiac "yet once more" with the Roman *ave atque vale* of Catullus and others. The result combines reluctant, repetitional lingering with formal dignity.

Like the allusion to Euryalus, the allusion to Marcellus associates Oldham once again with a figure (in this case, two figures) in the *Aeneid* (6.1180–1247). And once again, Dryden has chosen a context associated with Aeneas's devotion to his dead father. Here we are actually in the underworld, where Anchises adumbrates the future of Rome. Dryden's allusion to Marcellus is complex, as it points both to the victorious general Marcus Claudius Marcellus and to the promising but short-lived nephew of Augustus. In Virgil, although these men are seen together, walking side by side, it is the very unfulfillment of the association that is mourned. In Dryden's poem, on the other hand, the final description of Oldham is carefully designed to integrate the figures of both the victor and the vanquished. This is done in two principal ways, as Arthur Hoffman has shown.[15] "*Marcellus* of our Tongue" suggests a conquering warrior in the field of language (a suitable metaphor for a pugnacious satirist who warred against knaves and fools). Admittedly, Dryden could also be thinking of Oldham as the young Marcellus cut off from a promised career of poetic exploits. But the reference to the crowning ivy and laurels maintains the victor's triumph and deliberately complicates Virgil's univocally dark description of the young man (*Sed nox atra caput tristi circumvolat umbra*). As has been noted, Dryden's final line is a near-literal translation of Virgil's verse.

Dryden's closing lines have a grandeur that itself is somewhat consoling, and the image of a laureled brow encompassed by the gloom is heroic. But perhaps the deepest consolation stems from the fact that Oldham has once again, as in the Euryalus allusion, been elevated to the status of a noble figure in the *Aeneid*. Just as an explicitly Christian elegy, such as Dryden's own poem for Anne Killigrew, would have elevated the elegized to a Christian heaven, so in this consummately Augustan poem the figure of the dead is elevated to the domain of the classics.

But the allusion demands still closer scrutiny. Surely much of its force is missed if one forgets that Virgil follows the *Sed nox atra* line with Anchises' powerfully expressive lament for Marcellus. The lament includes high praise, profound regret, and a ceremonious, elegiac sweetness ("Full canisters of fragrant lilies bring, / Mixed with the purple roses of the spring. / Let me with funeral flowers his body strew"). Consequently, if we read with anything approaching Dryden's comprehensive sense of his allusion, this entire display of grief will be brought to bear on the figure of Oldham, even as Dryden excludes its burden from his actual text. It is an astounding feat of tact and indirection. The expression of grief is there, but only by allusion.

Also, we miss much of Dryden's triumph if we do not note that just as the Oldham-Euryalus allusion had the attendant effect of likening Dryden himself to a figure in the *Aeneid*, so, again, the final allusion has a similar but even greater associative effect on the elegist. Oldham becomes Marcellus and is described, in Dryden's last line, by words originally spoken by Aeneas. For this moment, therefore, Dryden speaks with the voice of the Trojan hero: the elegist is lifted to the plane of the immortalized father of Rome.

But beyond even this, Dryden is speaking with the voice of Virgil, creator of Aeneas's speech. Or perhaps we should say that Dryden has contrived to have Virgil speak again through him. And as we listen to Dryden-Aeneas-Virgil addressing and describing his Oldham-Marcellus friend, we hear what is no less than a timeless farewell. Once again, as in Jonson's epigram, we witness an Augustan elegist's uncanny strategy of impersonation, a brilliant compound of self-glorification and self-effacement, of inheritance and submission. The elegist seems to merge with the mask of the revived dead: Virgil, Catullus, and, by extension, that all-inclusive ancestral mask, the inherited language of literature.

Gray

There is some question as to whether Gray's "Elegy Written in a Country Churchyard" in fact belongs to the kind of elegy I have been defining, namely, a poem of mourning occasioned by a specific death. Gray had originally entitled the poem "Stanzas Wrote in a Country Church Yard," and the later title was his friend William Mason's suggestion. Mason recognized the alternatingly rhymed iambic pentameter quatrains as the form used by such "elegists" as Hammond and Shenstone, poets who were reviving the license of a merely formal definition to write so-called elegies on subjects of love or philosophical reflection.

And yet, Gray's poem is, of course, a poem of mourning. Even if we unwisely discount the specificity of his residual grief for Richard West (who had died in 1742), the "Elegy" mourns a particular death over and above those of the obscure villagers. This individual death, albeit imaginary, is that of the poet himself. The preliminary description and meditation in the graveyard is, in part, a presentation of the sensibility of that poet and a definition of the terms by which he should be mourned. It is carefully modulated so as to climax with a plea on behalf of any dying person's desire for remembrance. And this is accordingly followed by a projection of the poet's death, a projection that includes a local swain's account of the poet's life and burial (stanzas 24–29), together with a presentation of the epitaph written by the poet himself (stanzas 30–32). [16] This entire two-part closing section (stanzas 24–32) has an effect that is reminiscent of the original eclogic forms of pastoral elegy, in which one expression of mourning or memorializing supersedes another.

This very issue of supersession lies at the heart of the poem. It reflects Gray's need to develop a language for the "voice of Nature" crying from the tomb. He has to create a language that seems to supersede both his own living speech and the speech of the swain. And so urgently does the poet need the assurance that his final, posthumous language (the epitaph) will continue to assert itself beyond his death that he contrives an action *within* the poem in which that epitaph seems actually to be read. [17] It is a superb accomplishment, all the more effective for the discretion of its managerial design.

As is well known, the figure of the poet in the opening scene derives from the Miltonic Penseroso, a melancholic solitary courting

133

prophetic vision. Gray's deliberate cultivation of this figure is of course part of the mid-eighteenth-century revaluation of melancholy, a movement pursued by such contemporaries as Shenstone and the Wartons. [18] But in view of what follows, the particularity of Gray's association with Milton will have to be stressed.

The introduction not only sets a scene but introduces several interrelated aspects of an attitude toward the dead, an attitude that the poet hopes will eventually be accorded to himself. The attitude includes piety, compassion, respect, and attentiveness—the kind of attentiveness we owe the mute. In fact, throughout, there is a fascinating preoccupation with the theme of muteness as opposed to sound, or eventually, of an epitaphic script as opposed to a living voice. The preoccupation is complex, since, as we may expect, Gray comes to favor the silence of his final script, despite his own desire for voice.

In the opening description there is, therefore, a specific attentiveness given to sounds that emerge from a predominating silence. Their emergence is usually one of near-redemptive exception, the ability to be "saved," quite literally, from the hold of "solemn stillness." In the context of a churchyard at nightfall, these are like the haunting sounds that escape or survive death—positive tokens, even models, we may suppose, for any elegist. But Gray seems already to be aware that any posthumous *human* language will be unvoiced, dependent on the quiet mediation of an epitaphic script. And he begins to woo not only our attention to, but also our respect for, quietude. Hence the contemptuous lines referring to varieties of useless sound:

> Nor you, ye proud, impute to these the fault,
>   If Memory o'er their tomb no trophies raise,
> Where through the long-drawn aisle and fretted vault
>   The pealing anthem swells the note of praise.
>
> Can storied urn or animated bust
>   Back to its mansion call the fleeting breath?
> Can Honor's voice provoke the silent dust,
>   Or Flattery soothe the dull, cold ear of Death?
>
>   (37–44)

The silent dust and cold ear are quite impervious to the provocations of voice or music. Hence, too, Gray elicits respect for "some mute, inglorious Milton," in a position of curious strength, now, relative to any vocalizer whom Death will silence. Having already suggested the unavoidable muteness of the dead, Gray uses that muteness as a perhaps illegitimate means to qualify the vocal strength even of such as Milton. In other words, by aligning himself with muteness as the only condition, if any, of a posthumous existence, Gray assuages his melancholy fear of being a mute inglorious Milton himself. [19]

Similarly, Gray marshals a defense of obscurity at large by juxtaposing it against examples of fatuous and cruel "greatness" and revealing it as the necessary condition of the dead. His praise seems to extend, therefore, to those who live in such a way—obscure and silent—as to suffer the least alteration by death. Hence, too, "they kept the noiseless tenor of their way."

But a countervailing protest is rising beneath the burden of this repression, and in the final stanzas of the introduction (20–23) Gray expresses his desire for a saving power of voice. Admittedly, he begins with images of various scripts, but the eloquent plea for remembrance mounts to the following climax:

> On some fond breast the parting soul relies,
>   Some pious drops the closing eye requires;
> E'en from the tomb the voice of Nature cries,
>   E'en in our ashes live their wonted fires.
>
> (89–92)

Here, then, recklessly overcoming the sober arguments for silence, is the urge for voice, albeit one displaced somewhat onto Nature. This is the most freely energetic moment in the poem. (Incidentally, no other stanza has verbs at the ends of as many as three lines.) But Gray has risen to the expression of a wish, not a truth. The first two lines are literally credible, for the supposed person is in the process of dying. But the last lines are different, and Gray cannot win us by sheer momentum. The sudden boldness of his figuration itself betrays him, striving as he is to believe that a vigorously crying voice or a fiery glow can outlast death.

With this crystallization of his desire for remembrance after death, the poet turns directly to the task of guaranteeing that remembrance. But predictably, the argument carries him away from the desire for vocal immortality and leads him instead to recognize his inevitable dependence on written words. Indeed, the transition is harsh, and as he turns to address himself ("For thee who, mindful of the unhonored

135

dead"), we switch abruptly from the cry of voice to an explicit reference to the very lines of this poem ("Dost in these lines their artless tale relate").

And yet, the sound of a voice, even if no longer strictly the poet's, *does* continue, in the person of the "hoary-headed swain," who tells some possible "kindred spirit" about the poet. Here is a possible strategy, a form of posthumous ventriloquism, Gray putting his words into the mouth of a survivor. But this does not suffice, for several reasons. A measure of intimacy is lost; no swain can do justice to this poet, particularly considering the latter's obscurity and isolation; the swain himself is mortal, and his spoken account must fall mute when his breath, too, is extinguished.

So it is that the poet turns finally to the only form of language that can assure him of its, and therefore of his, posthumous identity. Despite the swain's rather touching use of the word *lay*, the transition from the oral narration to the silent script of the epitaph could hardly be more emphatic: "Approach and read (for thou canst read) the lay, / Graved on the stone beneath yon aged thorn." The repetition of *read* and the almost cruel distance between the illiterate swain and the literate "spirit" are jolting. (The choice of the word *spirit* suggests that now, finally, the poet's language is about to find an undying reader.) One cannot miss the heavily and irregularly accented *Graved*, a pun suggesting the relation between epitaphic writing and burial. Relentlessly, the detailed placement of the "graved" stone "beneath yon aged thorn" implies that the language of the epitaph will itself be communicating from within its own entombment.

When the swain stops speaking, the poem seems to fall silent. The reader falls into an uncanny solitude. There is no longer a voice to interpose between himself and the epitaph. Indeed, the poem has been about the dying of a voice. The reader must cross, now, from the alleged utterance of the living to the engraved script of the dead. And there he must attend even more intently than the poet, earlier, among the minute sounds of the churchyard, had invited him to do.

Regarding the figure of the elegized poet, as presented both by the swain and by the epitaph, many of his attributes should be familiar to us. Gray has blended the traits of the Penseroso with those of Lycidas and his elegist (compare "Oft have we seen him at the peep of dawn / Brushing with hasty steps the dews away, / To meet the sun upon the upland lawn" with "Together both, ere the high Lawns appeared / Under the opening eyelids of the morn, / We drove afield. . ."), as well as with those of that self-mourning elegist, Colin Clout (compare "Now drooping, woeful-wan, like one forlorn, / Or crazed with care, or crossed in hopeless love" with "For pale and wanne he was, [alas the while,] / May seem he lovd, or els some care he tooke").

As we hear and then read of him, the poet himself thus seems to recede and merge into the generalized figures of elegy. Beyond them we recognize an archaic vegetation deity returning to the common mother ("Here rests his head upon the lap of earth, / A youth. . ."). It is from the distant repose of this carefully fictionalized existence, as much as from the bosom of his God, that the poet would not be disturbed, either by those who would disclose his merits or by those who would draw out his frailties. Despite his bid for remembrance, he has finally asked us to remember him as enshrined in a highly literary, even divine, obscurity.

VI

Shelley: "Adonais"

While William Collins's "Ode on the Death of Mr. Thomson" (1749) remains very much a poem of its century, it nevertheless brings us to the foyer of the Romantic elegy, providing a convenient point of comparison with Wordsworth's "Remembrance of Collins," composed forty years later. The poems share similar concerns and a common form, but their differences are worth investigating. Instead of offering detailed readings, I shall merely sketch a few comparisons before going on to study Shelley's "Adonais."

Ode on the Death of Mr. Thomson

1

In yonder Grave a DRUID lies
    Where slowly winds the stealing Wave!
The *Year's* best Sweets shall duteous rise
    To deck *it's* POET's sylvan Grave!

2

In yon deep Bed of whisp'ring Reeds
    His airy Harp shall now be laid,
That he, whose Heart in Sorrow bleeds
    May love thro' Life the soothing Shade.

3

Then Maids and Youths shall linger here,
    And while it's Sounds at distance swell,
Shall sadly seem in Pity's Ear
    To hear the WOODLAND PILGRIM's Knell.

4

REMEMBRANCE oft shall haunt the Shore
    When THAMES in Summer-wreaths is drest,
And oft suspend the dashing Oar
    To bid his gentle Spirit rest!

5

And oft as EASE and HEALTH retire
    To breezy Lawn, or Forest deep,
The Friend shall view yon whit'ning Spire,
    And 'mid the varied Landschape weep.

6

But Thou, who own'st that Earthy Bed,
    Ah! what will ev'ry Dirge avail?
Or Tears, which LOVE and PITY shed
    That mourn beneath the gliding Sail!

7

Yet lives there one, whose heedless Eye
    Shall scorn thy pale Shrine glimm'ring near?
With Him, Sweet Bard, may FANCY die,
    And JOY desert the blooming Year.

8

But thou, lorn STREAM, whose sullen Tide
    No sedge-crown'd SISTERS now attend,
Now waft me from the green Hill's Side
    Whose cold Turf hides the buried FRIEND!

9

And see, the Fairy Valleys fade,
    Dun *Night* has veil'd the solemn View!
—Yet once again, Dear parted SHADE
    Meek NATURE's CHILD again adieu!

10

The genial Meads assign'd to bless
    Thy Life, shall mourn thy early Doom,
Their Hinds, and Shepherd-Girls shall dress
    With simple Hands thy rural Tomb.

11

Long, long, thy Stone and Pointed Clay
    Shall melt the musing BRITON's Eyes,
O! VALES, and WILD WOODS, shall HE say
    In yonder Grave YOUR DRUID lies![1]

Collins's very title betrays some of the generic indeterminacy that
will characterize the coming age, for odelike qualities scarcely domi-

nate this elegiac poem. The formal resemblance to the quiet, Horatian ode is surely no greater than to a truncated, tetrameter version of the elegiacs of Gray, Hammond, and Shenstone; or, indeed, to the Shakespeare songs "Full fathom five . . ." and "Fear no more . . ." (the latter of which directly inspired Collins's "A Song from Shakespeare's *Cymbeline*"). In the dim light of the poem's resolution, the title seems to reveal something of Collins's characteristic establishment of a desired model or standard from which he can then measure his decline. In this case, the invocational or celebratory intentions of an ode yield to the elegiac accents of a mild farewell.[2]

The poem is haunting and beautiful, but it deserves study also for its particular reemployment of pastoral conventions. Admittedly, much of its effect comes from the very diffidence with which the generic figures are presented and, in effect, withdrawn or shrouded. But in Collins's poem, the traditional elements of pastoral elegy do seem to stir again in an actual locale, and they do find a delicate yet compelling relevance both to a poet's reflection on his own creative powers and to his brooding on the ability of those powers to withstand the hazards of time and mortal loss. These concerns are, as is usual in Collins, further entwined with a meditation on the disenchantment of the natural world and on the general decay of poetry itself.

Reading the Jonson and Dryden elegies prompts one to recognize several residually Neoclassical elements in Collins's poem: the formal and tonal restraint; the attempted suppression of personality, with an attendant focus on poetry itself; and the approximately epitaphic closure cast in a language that seems to quote and yet to supersede the elegist himself. Collins's diction and his use of conventional personifications are yet further instances of his general allegiance to certain Augustan norms.

But Collins's mourning has a gentle power which quietly outdistances these borrowings. The very term "DRUID" reveals his turning not to the classics but to his country's own original enchanters. In doing so, he was following Thomson's earlier example, and he was participating in a broader, mid-eighteenth-century revival of things Gothic and Druidic. Still, Collins's revivals were always deeply complicated, even tormented, and his characteristically tenuous mode of evocation gives this poem a distinctive subtlety and pathos. As we shall see, even the Druid attribution is a source both of comfort and of inescapable dismay.

One way to register the poem's complexity, as well as its incipient Romanticism, is to weigh the poet's own relation to the Druid. By calling Thomson a Druid, Collins elegiacally assimilates the dead poet to the kind of figure that he, Collins, reveres and yearns to be—a poet-priest whose powers conjure supernatural presences in natural regions. If this implies a consolation, it is undermined by Collins's fears that he himself will never exercise a Druid's power and that perhaps the only place for a Druid in contemporary Britain is, after all, a grave. [3]

As an obvious instance of this diffident blend, or rather contradiction, one puzzles over the uncertainty of the Druid's placement, oscillating as it does between a comforting diffusion and a bleaker specificity. By *diffusion* I mean perhaps *infusion* of the Druid into the landscape such that he animates and hallows it, as if he were a version of the vegetation deity become a *genius loci*. As long as his presence is thus somehow unlocatable and permeative, he remains alive, abroad. And as long as Collins can keep the Druid abroad, he will himself be exercising something of a Druid's power, thereby earning a crucial measure of consolation.

The opening words themselves introduce the odd mixture of diffusion and specificity. "In yonder grave" means in the actual confines of that grave, which is nevertheless vaguely distant, over yonder. The distance is not only spatial but, by virtue of the mild archaism, temporal and literary as well. If the Druid is in his grave, it is consolingly difficult to establish just where and when he may be. And if we expect greater precision from the second line, the effect is only one of further diffusion: "Where slowly winds the stealing Wave!" Once again, the vagueness is both spatial and temporal—there where the Thames slowly and continuously flows.

This interplay of precise grave and more vaguely indicated landscape is pursued throughout the poem. Thomson's Aeolian harp is laid in a bed of reeds, hence buried, yet also suspended so that its notes may float and "swell" into the distance. The Thames itself becomes imbued with Thomson's spirit, so that only by ceasing to disturb the water can a traveler "bid his gentle Spirit rest!" And the whitening spire is a clear, if fictional (Richmond church has never had a spire), marker, which nevertheless dominates a wide terrain.

At the same time, however, there is the bleak exactness of "that Earthy Bed," named at the moment when Collins doubts the efficacy of any remembrance. There follows mention of the "cold Turf" hiding the buried friend, and in the final stanza the actual tomb is depicted ("thy Stone and Pointed Clay"). The poem thus evolves a complicated sense of Thomson's pervasive presence but tends increasingly to confine that spirit-in-the-landscape to the confines of the tomb.

As one might expect, this shrinking of the Druid's presence is inseparable from the elegist's own weakening powers of evocation, his recognition that the Thames is no more graced by "sedge-crowned SISTERS" and that his view of "Fairy Valleys" has already been veiled by "Dun *Night*." (The similarity to "Ode to Evening" and "Ode on the Poetical Character" is unmistakable.) He asks the Thames to waft him away, as though he were now almost deceased himself, dying away from the very scene he might have hoped to animate. Is this not Collins drifting further from the shrouded regions of dead poets and of poetry itself, as though it is *this* departure that the poem finally mourns? Even the vengeful curse against the scorners of poetry is far too weak to carry Collins beyond his minor key, and the poem ends with images of grief having replaced those of genial blessing, with the tears of mere pity, not solace, melting in a Briton's eyes. The final mention of "YOUR DRUID" instead of "a DRUID" does imply some possessive affinity between the landscape and the dead poet. But the musing Briton who speaks the words seems to be rather excluded from the comfort of that close relation. It is, finally, a relation to be remembered. And it is Collins's image of Remembrance that most catches the imagination of *his* memorializer, Wordsworth.

Remembrance of Collins

Glide gently, thus for ever glide,
O Thames! that other bards may see,
As lovely visions by thy side
As now, fair river! come to me.
O glide, fair stream! for ever so,
Thy quiet soul on all bestowing,
Till all our minds for ever flow
As thy deep waters now are flowing.

Vain thought!—Yet be as now thou art,
That in thy waters may be seen
The image of a poet's heart,
How bright, how solemn, how serene!
Such as did once the Poet bless,

Who, murmuring here a later ditty,
Could find no refuge from distress
But in the milder grief of pity.

Now let us, as we float along,
For *him* suspend the dashing oar;
And pray that never child of song
May know that Poet's sorrows more.
How calm! how still! the only sound,
The dripping of the oar suspended!
—The evening darkness gathers round
By virtue's holiest powers attended. [4]

The title warns us that this is no elegy but rather a "remembrance," and
in fact these stanzas were originally the final three stanzas of a five-
stanza poem in *Lyrical Ballads* entitled simply "Lines Written While
Sailing in a Boat at Evening" (written in 1789). The first two stanzas of
that poem dwelt on the poet's wishful dream of unfading light, a
dream of continuity such as recurs in Wordsworth's major poems. The
three stanzas for Collins pursue the wish, but now, taking into account
mortal ruptures, Wordsworth rejects the "vain thought" of mere inces-
sancy and works toward a self-empowering gesture of memorial
homage.

Wordsworth pursues the naturalizing direction of Collins's poem,
dispensing altogether with personification, floral deckings, maids and
youths, even the Druid figure. The meditation is expressly personal,
privatized, and the Thames itself now becomes an image of a flowing
mind, or of the medium in which a later poet can envision the image of
a predecessor's heart. By this internalization alone we have entered a
later mode of poetry. And Wordsworth's confident powers of will and
imagination, rejecting Collins's "milder grief of pity" and establishing
an almost mesmeric symbol of reenchantment, carry us even further
into this new domain.

Wordsworth's quotation of Collins's phrase about the oar is a nice
gesture of respect both for Collins's poetic image and for his place in a
tradition that now stretches from Thomson to Collins to the nineteen-
year-old Wordsworth himself. But Wordsworth deliberately prays for
a better fate than that of Collins. And *his* suspension of the oar is a far
bolder device. Collins attributed the gesture to Remembrance personified, and he forlornly disqualified himself from the veiled, if once-

enchanted, landscape. Wordsworth, on the other hand, is confidently present, and his figure of the oar becomes an axis of continuing enchantment. Around this image of the poised memorial imagination, the darkness "gathers round / By virtue's holiest Powers attended." We may think back to the laureled head of young Marcellus, forming a similar center for the encompassing darkness of Hades. Or we may look forward to a jar in Tennessee that made the "slovenly wilderness / Surround that hill." Between the Neoclassical allusion to a Virgilian hero and the symbolist deportment of a bare gray jar is *Wordsworth's* image of centripetal power, quietly gathering its attendant virtues, persistently marking the mind's insertion into both landscape and time.[5]

I cannot here read Wordsworth's elegiac poetry at large—the Lucy poems, the many epitaphic pieces, the "Immortality Ode," the several poems for John, the graveyard section of *The Excursion,* and the frighteningly repressive "Laodamia." But the lines for Collins have interesting points of connection with Wordsworth's general elegiac strategy of inventing figures of persistence that gather to themselves protective accretions of power. Whether this power is of nature, darkness, or time, it is invariably associated with that of the self-protective mind. To cite only the most obvious example, Peele Castle becomes a symbol for Wordsworth himself, "Cased in the unfeeling armour of old time," braving the storms both of the ocean and of the grieving heart.

In what we recognize as a typically elegiac procedure, Wordsworth here rejects the fantasy, like that of the mirror stage, of a quasi-maternal natural continuity in which the erotically powerful "rugged Pile" seemed to be forever "sleeping on a glassy sea" of contentment "beneath a sky of bliss." Disrupting this fantasy, he bows, not just to the presence of death, but more crucially to the irrevocable loss of his own power as it yields to a previously unrecognized control:

So once it would have been—'tis so no more;
I have submitted to a new control:
A power is gone, which nothing can restore;
A deep distress hath humanized my Soul.

(*Works*, 453)

While this sacrifice occasions the first mention of the poet's soul, it also, as we have come to expect, represents the apparent socialization of the mourner (although this will be brought into doubt somewhat by the image of the tower). This socialization is at first expressed as humanization, but the poet goes on to express a commitment to the social world ("farewell the heart that lives alone, / . . . at distance from the Kind!") and to include the elegiac acceptance of a triadically determined positionality that we associate with this process of mourning: Wordsworth hails the painter George Beaumont, who enters the poem as a third figure, intervening between the poet and the poet's dead brother. Significantly, this intervention also involves the explicit recourse to the aesthetic mediation supplied by an actual work of art. And it is only by virtue of this work of art that Wordsworth erects his chastened, hence "sublime," self-image of defensive strength. Like the suspended oar, Wordsworth's tower has precisely the kind of phallic, totemic qualities that one expects in an elegy—it is the product of loss and submission, the symbol both of strength and of a suspended, deadened, yet resistant power.

Obviously, our understanding of Wordsworth's elegies would benefit from a far more careful and detailed application of our generic approach, but it is to Shelley's "Adonais" that I wish to turn—a poem that takes us back to the very mainstream, however revised, of the pastoral elegy.

It has become a commonplace that Romantic poets played havoc with the definitions of poetic genres, creating "visionary forms dramatic," autobiographical epics, "lyrical ballads," townscape sonnets, and other strange hybrids. Not surprisingly, Blake, Wordsworth, Coleridge, Keats, and Byron avoided the pastoral elegy, with its highly traditional set of conventions. "Adonais" would therefore seem to be something of an anomaly, and any reader must wonder how the intricacies of Romantic self-consciousness are nevertheless elaborated in this most archaic and most revolutionary of poems.

As is well known, Shelley described "Adonais" as "a highly wrought *piece of art*, perhaps better in point of composition than anything I have written."[6] The poem's carefully "wrought" texture has made it particularly susceptible to close readings. Yet these readings, of which Earl Wasserman's has been the most comprehensive, have left ungauged the deepest level of the poem's complex movement.[7] In some ways this is not surprising, for the objective of an elegy is, after all, to displace the urgent psychological currents of its work of mourning into the apparently more placid, aesthetically organized currents of language. Though elegies may weep, they must do so formally. They may not "break up their lines to weep" within that weeping. [8]

In what follows, I shall try to go beyond a description of the form of "Adonais" to suggest how the pattern of its language relates to psychological and philosophical currents running deep within the poem. My questions include the following: What and how does Shelley mourn? How does he revise the inherited fictions of elegy? What is his relation to Urania? How does his narcissism affect the work of mourning? What are the implications of the poem's extraordinary ending, and how does it relate to Shelley's ambivalence toward figurative language? Finally, how does this ambivalence, directed against the very fabric of the poem, relate specifically to the predicament of a mourner?

"Adonais" has two epigraphs. The first is a Greek couplet ascribed to Plato in the *Greek Anthology*. Following the common misattribution of the couplet to Plato the philosopher, Shelley translated the lines:

> Thou wert the morning star among the living,
>   Ere thy fair light had fled; —
> Now, having died, thou art as Hesperus, giving
>   New splendour to the dead. [9]

Besides drawing attention to the stellar imagery of consolation, Shelley's choice of the epigraph indicates his desire to believe in a poetry somehow compatible with Platonic thought. [10] The fact that Shelley misattributed the lines to the harsh judge of poetry underscores the problem, and it is interesting to see how thoroughly and with what personal urgency "Adonais" reveals the contradictory nature of Shelley's aspiration.

The second epigraph quotes the lines in Moschus's elegy for Bion, referring to the poet's having been poisoned by some insensitive scorner of verse. Shelley will return to this in stanza 36, elaborating his theory about Keats's death. While stressing the accusation's relevance to the poem, the epigraph foregrounds Shelley's debt to the Alexandrian elegy at large. [11] The debt is immediately apparent in the opening line, which reads almost as a translation of Bion's "Lament for Adonis":

> I weep for Adonais—he is dead!
> O, weep for Adonais! though our tears

Thaw not the frost which binds so dear a head!
And thou, sad Hour, selected from all years
To mourn our loss, rouse thy obscure compeers,
And teach them thine own sorrow, say: 'With me
Died Adonais; till the Future dares
Forget the Past, his fate and fame shall be
An echo and a light unto eternity!'

(Works, 432)

The first difference from Bion is, of course, the name Adonais, blending those of the vegetation deity, Adonis, and the Judaic Adonai. As historians of religion have shown, the originally physical significance of the fertility gods was allegorized and spiritualized by successive cults; and elegists, too, have continually revised the meaning of this most crucial figure of the genre. It is especially intriguing to note how Shelley has conserved the original figure within the new, for the poem itself unfolds the very *process* of resignification, moving from natural, sexual referents toward their spiritualized successors. Shelley's act of renaming neatly suggests his intention to use and yet alter the inherited elegiac tradition: to use its essential strategy of assimilating the deceased to a figure of immortality, while redefining the meaning of that figure.

A second difference declares itself at once: unlike Bion, Shelley turns immediately to question the efficacy of weeping. By so doing, he begins a long interrogation of conventional gestures and figures of mourning. This oddly skeptical employment of conventions marks this poem as a true heir of "Lycidas" and "Astrophel," whose obsessions with "false surmise" and "verses vaine" had driven them to carefully persuasive consolations. As our reference to the "Plato" epigraph hinted, and as the poem will in fact show, Shelley's struggle with his legacy and with his very medium itself is particularly vexed. We can perhaps see this in the unusual prematurity with which he initiates the self-questioning or self-qualifying mode. Spenser had at least gathered momentum before examining the vanity of verse. And although Milton did begin with a self-doubting admission of sour immaturity, he at least did not suspect the "meed of some melodious tear."

Shelley's struggle to begin his work of mourning is further apparent in his deliberate *delegation* of such work to various figures throughout the opening sections of the poem. In fact, it is not until quite far into the poem that Shelley moves beyond these delegate-mourners to

147

assume a more personal voice. The delegates have at least two functions: they are all inadequate mourners, allowing Shelley to criticize
them and to distance himself from various forms of unsuccessful grieving; and yet they keep his poem in motion, giving it the processional
character of traditional elegies, allowing it to achieve the self-purifying and self-surpassing ceremonies so important to the work of
mourning.

Already in the fourth line, therefore, Shelley turns to the first of
these delegates, calling on the Hour to grieve and asking her in turn to
transfer her sorrow to her compeers. The Hour's utterance reaches
forward to the traditional conclusion of elegy, with its eternizing
assertion. But this is felt to be proleptic, for the grief has somehow
been elided, and the consolation unearned. It is too quick, with the
kind of problematic sheerness of the opening line. We reread the
statement and register a complication: "With me / Died Adonais."
This Hour is past and dead. With its death died Adonais. Is it speaking
from within death, speaking with the odd death-in-life intonation of a
sepulchral inscription? And since this is a persona voice for Shelley,
does it not already suggest some troubling association between Keats's
death and Shelley's sense of having died with him? It is precisely this
double death that the poem must avoid—or at least postpone long
enough for Shelley to have immortalized himself and Keats. How else
will Adonais's fate and fame keep echoing and shining to eternity?

In the second stanza, Shelley moves further into the conventions of
pastoral elegy by querying the absence of the attendant deity:

> Where wert thou, mighty Mother, when he lay,
> When thy Son lay, pierced by the shaft which flies
> In darkness? Where was lorn Urania
> When Adonais died?

We have already interpreted this conventional questioning several
times, and it is therefore on the specificity of Shelley's version that we
should dwell. The figure of Urania is of immediate interest. Just as he
had compounded the sexual-spiritual identity of Adonais, so now
Shelley merges Venus (mother of earthly life and the incestuous lover
of Adonais) with her intellectual and spiritual self (Urania, Muse of
astronomy, "Heav'nly Muse" of Milton). More significantly, Shelley's
turn to the "mighty Mother" recalls Milton's anguished "What could
the Muse herself . . . for her enchanting son . . . ?"[12] We are at the

core of loss, the elegist's bereavement not only of his friend or fellow but of the maternal figure, the original loss of whom this new bereavement recapitulates. As was true for Milton, Shelley will have eventually to work free from his attachment to this unavailing figure of the mother-Muse, submitting both her and himself to the ironic and repressive force of death. Only in the harsh light of that repression may an abiding object of consolation be found.

Shelley calls on Urania to mourn, but his address, like that in the first lines of the poem, turns to criticize its own futility:

> Oh, weep for Adonais—he is dead!
> Wake, melancholy Mother, wake and weep!
> Yet wherefore? Quench within their burning bed
> Thy fiery tears, and let thy loud heart keep
> Like his, a mute and uncomplaining sleep;
> For he is gone, where all things wise and fair
> Descend;—oh, dream not that the amorous Deep
> Will yet restore him to the vital air;
> Death feeds on his mute voice, and laughs at our
> despair.

The echo of "Hyperion" is unmistakable, and Shelley had in fact been reading Keats's poem immediately before composing "Adonais." Here Shelley sounds like Thea, skeptical of her attempt to rouse the fallen Saturn:

> "Saturn, look up—though wherefore, poor old King?
> . . . .
> Saturn, sleep on—O thoughtless, why did I
> Thus violate thy slumbrous solitude?"[13]

Shelley, lacking Thea's sedate fatigue, moves quickly to a bitter ironizing of the grief, again somehow obstructing its release. It is an odd situation: Shelley attempting to awaken a sleeper to mourning while at the same time checking that very attempt. And if the yet ungrieving Urania is the "most musical of mourners," surely Shelley is still trying to rouse himself to fuller song. Shelley appeals to Urania as the mother of a line of poets—Homer, Dante, and Milton—and he calls on her to weep for her most recent loss. From this perspective, Shelley, like Thea, is trying to compel a certain recognition: while Thea would have Saturn recognize his own divinity, Shelley would have Urania recognize and admit the poet Keats to a grand genealogy, one

149

that would perhaps include himself, if she should recognize and respond to his cry.

At first, however, Shelley seems to make little impression on Urania. She is presented "with Veiled eyes," the first of many derogatory references to any form of interpositional texture or cloud. This very veiledness is somehow paradisal, a false Eden of blindness in which the deluded Muse fondly supposes her poets to be invulnerable. There is, too, a faint suggestion that a certain kind of poetry may itself share the blame for this delusional masking of mortality (". . . the fading melodies, / With which, like flowers that mock the corse beneath, / He had adorned and hid the coming bulk of Death"). Perhaps Shelley seeks a more clear-eyed poetry that unveils and takes account of the coming bulk. The traditional association of flowers with rhetoric alerts us to how disconcertingly Shelley is already moving against the very properties of poetic language, linking them here with precisely the natural, vegetative, and material realm that the poem so forcefully attacks and so desperately seeks to transcend.

Pursuing this critical association of flowers, material fabrics, and mortality, Shelley describes the physical death of Adonais. The details are significant, for Adonais is presented as a sexually unfulfilled and indeed broken flower ("Like a pale flower by some sad maiden cherished, / And fed with true-love tears, instead of dew"). In line with this castrative imagery of deprivation and submission, Shelley introduces the repressive, patriarchal figure of "kingly Death," in whose capital the shadow and the "mortal curtain" are forever drawn.

The presence of these gathering fabrics of shadow, veil, and curtain testifies to an elegist's acceptance not only of Death's castrative power, but also of the elegist's recapitulated entry into, and submission to, those very mediations of language that interpose between him and his object of loss or desire. The elegist's riposte to Death, his consoling counterassertion, however displaced, of desire and of the trope for a surviving power, must, therefore, come to terms with the enforced fabric of substitutions. This is where one of Shelley's most vexing problems comes to the fore. For while trying to rebut Death's power, Shelley also struggles to purge his counterassertive language of its inherent association, as language, with all the interposing fabrics—of Death's curtain, or of life's erotic but mortal physicality, or of the traces of this latter physicality in the material flowers, however spiritualized, of rhetoric.

For the moment, Death governs, and Shelley's repeated urgings of Urania fall on silence. This increases his isolation, as though he were circling on the outside of a center of power and on the edges of a grander stance of mourning. Certainly, he is still circling his own grief. Part of this circling, as already suggested, involves the delegation and criticism of mourners. The flocks of Keats's "ministers of Thought" are therefore shown to droop, incapable of renovation, "round the cold heart." One such angelic figure believes that the tear she sheds is Keats's own. Another's gesture of symbolic substitution is undone or at least exposed by the poet's analysis:

> Another in her wilful grief would break
> Her bow and winged reeds, as if to stem
> A greater loss with one which was more weak;

Yet another unavailingly seeks to revitalize the body with a caress that fades out like a meteor enwreathed in vapor.

All these ineffective mourners keep the poem in motion, even though they are distanced by the yet withdrawn poet. As they multiply in a profusion of allegorical figures, they appear to interpose further between the poet and his own emotion. This interposition, apart from Shelley's sense of their inadequacy as mourners, seems to lie behind his description of their "moving pomp" as a "pageantry of mist on an autumnal stream." They are useless forms of mourning, a decorative mist or texture that seems to absorb rather than provide energy. This, too, is why each stanza has a movement of subsidence, an attempted quickening that trails off in a dying ebb. Shelley's particularly skillful use here of the Spenserian stanza will be reversed in the last section of the poem, where the stanzas yield their potential for exploratory romance, for the progressive crossing of thresholds. There the alexandrines do not seal a falling cadence; rather, they mount beyond themselves. [14]

Shelley ends the first movement of the poem by extending the cast of mourners to include even the traditional figures of consolation, the regenerated Hyacinth and Narcissus. These flower-tropes themselves are now impotent, like the broken lily, Adonais ("wan they stand and sere . . . with dew all turned to tears . . ."), and as with Adonais, their seminal dew has yielded to salt. So, too, Shelley includes Spring herself in this general loss of vigor. Though beautiful, she is un-aroused, finding no reason to awake the sullen year. The gathering association between a failure of mourning and a lack of natural or even figurative regeneration seems fatal, but there is a surprising development within the seventeenth stanza:

> Thy spirit's sister, the lorn nightingale
> Mourns not her mate with such melodious pain;
> Not so the eagle, who like thee could scale
> Heaven, and could nourish in the sun's domain
> Her mighty youth with morning, doth complain,
> Soaring and screaming round her empty nest,
> As Albion wails for thee: the curse of Cain
> Light on his head who pierced thy innocent breast,
> And scared the angel soul that was its earthly guest!

By a remarkable turn in the seventh line, the elaborate comparison is suddenly followed by a curse, as though that curse had been gathering like another voice beneath the preceding language. Now, disjunctively, the curse breaks through, and it carries perhaps the first true ring of Shelley's voice. It cuts impatiently through the pageantry of mourners, disrupting the delicate melancholy of their poise.[15] And this is, after all, the first reference to Keats's alleged destroyer, the hostile reviewer in the *Quarterly Review*.

It is fair to say that Shelley's notion of the cause of Keats's death was a misinterpretation motivated by his own experience of malignment. In the first draft of his preface to "Adonais" he had written,

> Persecution, contumely, and calumny have been heaped
> upon me in profuse measure; and domestic conspiracy
> and legal oppression have violated in my person the
> most sacred rights of nature and humanity.
>
> (*Works*, 444)

This passage, which Shelley omitted on the advice of John Taaffe, confirms the identification and leaves us certain that the sudden direct utterance in the seventeenth stanza is a burst of anger by Shelley partly on his own behalf. At last, by moving closer to the self in this way, Shelley has released some of the energy for mourning, hitherto held in check.

Interestingly enough, the second movement of the poem begins immediately after this release of anger. Yet critics have only related the ensuing expression of woe to the juxtaposition of a still mourning poet over against a reviving world. This is not untrue, but surely that first note of personal grief—"Ah, woe is me"—is the result of the breakthrough at the end of the previous stanza. By expressing anger, Shelley has begun to undo the repression of his grief, and stanzas 17–20 contain repeated images of a distinctly erotic release:

> The amorous birds now pair in every brake,
> . . . .
> And the green lizard, and the golden snake,
> Like unimprisoned flames, out of their trance awake.
>
> . . . .
> Through wood and stream and field and Ocean
> A quickening life from the Earth's heart has burst
> . . . .
>
> All baser things pant with life's sacred thirst;
> Diffuse themselves; and spend in love's delight,
> The beauty and the joy of their renewed might.

The irony behind this release is that the elegist himself remains apparently unmoved. He is unable to endorse the erotic flow and channels it into Nature's, rather than his own, renovation. This is crucial, for like Spenser and Milton, and indeed like any true mourner, Shelley must submit the natural force of his desire to a repressive refinement. It is essential that these energies be released—but only so that they may be troped and spiritualized.

Hence Shelley focuses contrastingly on what he would like to see immortalized: not man's genetic power, but rather his intellectual faculty, "that which knows." And yet, this higher faculty is represented by imagery that reflects originally physical referents:

> . . . Shall that alone which knows
> Be as a sword consumed before the sheath
> By sightless lightning?—the intense atom glows
> A moment, then is quenched in a most cold repose.

The cognitive being is thus represented by a sword, or by an atom whose glow is surely related in kind to the "unimprisoned flames" of Nature and to the forces that spend themselves "in love's delight." Nevertheless, it is with such residually erotic and material images of elevation, penetration, and glowing radiance that Shelley will have to reach for consolation, trying to cut or burn through all material textures (present once again, here, in the form of the sheath).

Fearing the extinction of these purer powers, Shelley is now moved to a further expression of genuine grief, his second truly direct utterance. Now recognition of his own mortality brings on not anger but painful perplexity, the gnomic questioning that one associates with elegy:

> Alas! that all we loved of him should be,
> But for our grief, as if it had not been,
> And grief itself by mortal! Woe is me!
> Whence are we, and why are we? of what scene
> The actors or spectators?[16]

Shelley still cannot bear this burden alone, and again he transfers it to his chief alter mourner, Urania. The language becomes urgent, irresistible, and Urania wakes abruptly: "Swift as a Thought by the snake Memory stung, / From her ambrosial rest the fading Splendour sprung." She moves "like an autumnal Night" "out of her secret Paradise." This disparadising of Urania by a snake suggests that Shelley has finally been able to arouse her by curiously satanic means. It is a troubling suggestion, and it will return with Shelley's later self-images of sexual transgression ("Had gazed on Nature's naked loveliness, / Actaeon-like") and damnation ("branded . . . like Cain's"). Predictably, Shelley's success here brings on its own rebuke, as Urania moves directly into the dominion of that father figure Death, under whose aegis her extravagantly sexual mourning will be mocked and where the separation from her son will be most punitively enforced.

As Urania enters the death chamber, her intensity momentarily cows even Death and seems to send a "pale light" through the body of the poet. But hers is an intensity only of bereavement. She has nothing with which to oppose or menace Death, and he recovers his sway with a magisterially ironic gesture: "her distress / Roused Death: Death rose and smiled, and met her vain caress." Like the jealous father, Death exercises his prerogative, claiming the caress meant for the son. With this submission of the mother-son attachment to the male figure of Death, a crisis in the work of mourning is confronted. The primary experience of rupture is represented, here in the guise of a role reversal similar to that studied before in the primitive vegetation rites or in the child's *fort-da* game. The child's separation from its mother, or man's separation from a withering nature, is performed but psychologically reversed, so that the mother / nature becomes the victim or mourner. And with this presentation of Urania, Shelley reaches his most acute and no doubt exorcistic critique of inadequate modes of mourning. [17] The speech is Urania's:

> 'Stay yet awhile! speak to me once again;
> Kiss me, so long but as a kiss may live;
> And in my heartless breast and burning brain
> That word, that kiss, shall all thoughts else survive,
> With food of saddest memory kept alive,
> Now thou art dead, as if it were a part
> Of thee, my Adonais! I would give
> All that I am to be as thou now art!
> But I am chained to Time, and cannot thence depart!'

In "Mourning and Melancholia," Freud distinguishes between the normal response to loss, what he calls the work of mourning, and the abnormal condition of melancholia, in which the subject cannot move beyond an unhealthy, often inert, reaction to loss. [18] The work of mourning requires a gradual detachment from the lost object, followed by a transfer of the detached affections or libido onto a new love-object outside the self. The case of melancholia is complex, but as we saw before, it may occur either when the subject cannot renounce the lost object or when the detached and released libido regresses to an earlier form of narcissism by reattaching itself to the ego instead of to a new, external object. The various responses may be related to rhetorical tropes. It would seem that a detachment would involve a figure of disconnection, most simply irony (or a strongly substitutive metaphor), while a refusal to detach oneself would be associated with the more connective tropes of metonymy or synecdoche. In her melancholia, Urania cannot turn away from the dead poet. On the one hand she would take a last kiss-word from him to serve as a metonymic reminder of him. In fact, so tenacious is her attachment that it forces her to drive that metonymy to a synecdochic extreme ("a part of thee, my Adonais"). The lost object would thus be synecdochically internalized within Urania's "heartless breast and burning brain." On the other hand, yet again refusing to withdraw from Adonais, she would relinquish her own ego in order to be identified with the object of her attachment. She remains prostrate, unable to *do* either and yet unable to renounce the dead Adonais. [19]

Having used Urania in a way that has allowed him to objectify one form of potential melancholia and also to further his own necessary departure from this mother figure, Shelley turns, in the remainder of the poem, to work his way through other forms and stages that Freud unquestionably regarded as symptoms of a griever's melancholia. Freud writes:

> First there existed an object-choice, the libido had attached itself to a certain person; then, owing to a real injury or disappointment concerned with the loved person, this object-relationship was undermined. The result was not the normal one of withdrawal of the libido from this object and transference of it to a new one, but something different for which various conditions seem to be necessary. The object-cathexis proved to have little power of resistance, and was abandoned; but the free libido was withdrawn into the ego and not directed to another object. It did not find application there, however, in any one of several possible ways, but served simply to establish an *identification* of the ego with the abandoned object. Thus the shadow of the object fell upon the ego, so that the latter could henceforth be criticized by a special mental faculty like an object, like the forsaken object. In this way the loss of the object becomes transformed into a loss in the ego, and the conflict between the ego and the loved person transformed into a cleavage between the criticizing faculty of the ego and the ego as altered by the identification. [20]

To this Freud adds the logical suggestion that in such a case, the original object choice was narcissistic, this being indeed a part of "the disposition to succumb to melancholia." Now, as has been suggested, Shelley's original view of Keats's death *was* narcissistic, seeing Keats not only as a brother poet but also as a reflection of Shelley's own sense of martyrdom. Reacting to the death of Keats, Shelley withdrew from the dead youth, but reattaching his affections only to himself, he identified his ego with the abandoned object. Or rather, and this is crucial, he identified *a part* of his ego with the lost object. For the kind of splitting that Freud describes occurs within Shelley, setting a criticizing voice over against the weaker, vulnerable aspects of himself, seen now with frightening clarity in the light of their identification with the dead Keats. The splitting takes the form of an elaborate self-objectification. Not only does Shelley use the third-person *he* in referring to himself but he emphasizes the division by retaining, in close juxtaposition, the *I* that makes this reference.[21] Here is Shelley's portrait of himself among the procession of poet-mourners who pay homage to Adonais:

> XXXI
> Midst others of less note, came one frail Form,
> A phantom among men; companionless
> As the last cloud of an expiring storm
> Whose thunder is its knell; he, as I guess,
> Had gazed on Nature's naked loveliness,
> Actaeon-like, and now he fled astray
> With feeble steps o'er the world's wilderness,
> And his own thoughts, along that rugged way,
> Pursued, like raging hounds, their father and their prey.
>
> XXXII
> A pardlike Spirit beautiful and swift—
> A Love in desolation masked;—a Power
> Girt round with weakness;—it can scarce uplift
> The weight of the superincumbent hour;
> It is a dying lamp, a falling shower,
> A breaking billow;—even whilst we speak
> Is it not broken? On the withering flower
> The killing sun smiles brightly: on a cheek
> The life can burn in blood, even while the heart may
>   break.
>
> XXXIII
> His head was bound with pansies overblown,
> And faded violets, white, and pied, and blue;
> And a light spear topped with a cypress cone,
> Round whose rude shaft dark ivy-tresses grew
> Yet dripping with the forest's noonday dew,
> Vibrated, as the ever-beating heart
> Shook the weak hand that grasped it; of that crew
> He came the last, neglected and apart;
> A herd-abandoned deer struck by the hunter's dart.

The passage is complicated, in typically Shelleyan fashion, by a multiplication of images. Within the flux we make out versions of the vegetation deities, Actaeon and Dionysus (the [leo]pardlike spirit with the thyrsis wand). "Nature's naked loveliness" associates Diana with Aphrodite-Venus, hence with the mother-Urania. Actaeon's transgression is, therefore, precisely the error a mourner must forego, and it is interesting to note how Shelley is both identifying with and yet objectifying and distancing himself from just this error. Actaeon is punished by the enervation and eventual *sparagmos* that typifies castrative martyrdom.

The Dionysus identification is a more unsettling complex of weakness and assertion. More precisely, assertive strength struggles to issue from an enveloping wreckage. The latter is marked, once again, by sexual expense and fragmentation ("It is a dying lamp, a falling shower, / A breaking billow; —even whilst we speak / Is it not broken? On the withering flower / The killing sun shines brightly: . . .") Shelley is here even identified with Adonais, the broken lily. But there is the contrastive figure of Dionysus holding his vibrating and dewy cone-tipped spear. Juxtaposed with the preceding imagery of expense and devastation, this phallic thyrsis does seem to hold out the consoling promise of recovery, but it will remain for Shelley to reestablish its significance. For the moment, the promise is still "girt round with weakness," as Shelley switches back momentarily to the more Actaeon-like figure of the stricken deer.

Returning to our recognition of the self-divisive aspect of Shelley's work of mourning, it is clear that this self-presentation in terms of wounded, withered, and annihilated vegetation figures identifies the mortal part of Shelley's ego with the slain Adonais. And this melancholically narcissistic identification prepares the way for a different identification, one that continues yet transforms the poet's narcissism. For even as Shelley's ego has cleaved into critic and criticized, observer and victim, this division corresponds to a division perceived in the nature of Adonais: the immortal poetic genius, the "angel soul," as divided from the empirical man who had been its temporary home. And it is this former genius-soul with whom Shelley will come to identify his own purified, immortal self. In the remainder of the poem, therefore, Shelley completes the work of mourning by a powerful detachment from the natural man and the natural world and a subsequent reattachment to a transcendent ideal instead.

But first, Shelley has a second, more expansive outbreak against the object of his anger. This outbreak is well situated. On the one hand, it allows Shelley to discharge his wrath in a burst of energy that will fuel his subsequent ascent. On the other hand, his vitriolic contempt for the anonymous reviewer, Croker, conveniently supplies an extreme example of the lowest, wormlike or kitelike level of existence that Adonais is immediately shown to have transcended ("Nor let us weep that our delight is fled / Far from these carrion kites that scream below").

As I have already suggested, Shelley's transcendent ideal definitely draws on his narcissistic libido. Just as Shelley had distorted in his own image his version of Keats's death, so, too, his version of the immortal Keats is cast in his own ideal likeness. The process of narcissistic idealization has been analyzed in general by Heinz Kohut, one of the first theorists to explore the beneficial potential of narcissism. Kohut's essay "The Forms and Transformations of Narcissism" is particularly relevant here, for he stresses the important connection between narcissism and the acceptance of loss and death:

> More difficult still, however, than the acknowledgment of the imperma-
> nence of object cathexes is the unqualified intellectual and emotional
> acceptance of the fact that we ourselves are impermanent, that the self
> which is cathected with narcissistic libido is finite in time. I believe that
> this rare feat rests not simply on a victory of autonomous reason and
> supreme objectivity over the claims of narcissism but on the creation of a
> higher form of narcissism. 22

The "higher form of narcissism" involves the construction of an ego ideal, what Kohut calls the "grandiose self." For Shelley, this is the transcendent human, or more strictly, the poetic spirit. I think Kohut's addition to Freud's theory of narcissism (particularly in relation to melancholia) may thus apply closely to the case of Shelley as he works through to the end of "Adonais."

Kohut's view of the "higher narcissism" may itself be too idealistic, however. In the concluding section of this chapter I hope to suggest how fragile and how specular the "grandiose" self-image remains. We should here recall Lacan's portrayal of the mirror stage. As I suggested earlier, a mourner may lapse back to a form of this stage—another potential factor in narcissistic melancholia. Shelley's work of mourning does appear to revert to elements of the mirror stage; and "Adonais" (particularly following the self-portrait beginning in stanza 31) is marked by that phase's unstable opposition between the condition of fragmentation on the one hand and idealized images of coherence on the other.

Shelley's represented reversion to the mirror stage is, admittedly, controlled by an exorcistic self-objectification, one that shatters and discards its imagings in order to reconstitute a higher version of the self. But this higher version, despite its apparently triadic inclusion of Death, may not entirely escape the dangers of the earlier mirror stage. If the griever seeks literally to identify with the new image—to literalize what must remain specular and fictional and to make immediate what must remain a mediated resemblance—he risks a delusional entrapment in another dyadic fantasy. By stressing, with Lacan, the degree of alienation and fictionalizing in any narcissistic self-imaging, we may recognize the vulnerability of Kohut's "grandiose self," even as we see with particular urgency the problems besetting Shelley in the remainder of his poem.

We have still to ask what ingredients, in Shelley's case, compose the immortal ideal ego. Of what, exactly, does Shelley construct the alternative to his fragmented and rejected self imaged earlier as a broken billow or withered flower? Who is the immortal Adonais with whom Shelley's higher self may be identified? Continuing the dramatic, oppositional argument that began with his rejection of the reviewer, Shelley pursues this exaltation of the soul:

> Dust to the dust! but the pure spirit shall flow
> Back to the burning fountain whence it came,
> A portion of the Eternal, which must glow
> Through time and change, unquenchably the same,
> Whilst thy cold embers choke the sordid hearth of shame.

After its shattering demise in the "falling shower" of an explicitly sexual and mortal ruin, the earlier sexual imagery of fertile liquids and glowing fires here returns, but in a spiritualized version of itself, as the soul flows back to its origin and glows beyond extinction.

In order for this pure spirit to be an ideal self *for Shelley*, it must be more specifically defined. Most crucially, it must represent the poetic genius—not any generalized poetic genius, but the genius as Shelley defines it. This means that Shelley must modify the immortal Keats-Adonais so as to reflect and accommodate the immortal Shelley. Necessarily, this requires a distortion of Keats.

Shelley declares that the disembodied spirit of Keats flows back in purity to the "burning fountain whence it came." It is free "from the contagion of the world's slow stain." Now this in fact controverts

Keats's own view of the soul and of the mundane world. For Keats there is indeed a part of every human being, the "intelligence," which is a spark of the eternal. "I[n]telligences," he wrote to George and Georgiana Keats on 28 April 1819, "are atoms of perception—they know and they see and they are pure, in short they are God."[23] But whereas Shelley rejects the circumstantial world as contagious dross, Keats goes on to insist that an "intelligence" should be immersed "in the medium of a world like this" in order that it may advance to take on an "identity." Only this "identity" can be called a soul. For Keats, this attainment of a soul adequately stained by the world and by the heart constitutes salvation—a far different idea from that of Shelley's celebration of the return of a disembodied purity to its source.

A further misrepresentation of Keats in Shelley's adaptation of Adonais to his own ideal likeness is his implicit negation of Keats's espousal of empathy, unobtrusiveness, and negative capability. In their stead, Shelley associates Keats's poetic spirit with a shaping power more like that of egotistical sublimity:

> He is a presence to be felt and known
> In darkness and in light, from herb and stone,
> Spreading itself where'er that Power may move
> Which has withdrawn his being to its own;
> Which wields the world with never-wearied love,
> Sustains it from beneath, and kindles it above.

>   XLIII
> He is a portion of the loveliness
> Which once he made more lovely: he doth bear
> His part, while the one Spirit's plastic stress
> Sweeps through the dull dense world, compelling there,
> All new successions to the forms they wear;
> Torturing th'unwilling dross that checks its flight
> To its own likeness, as each mass may bear;
> And bursting in its beauty and its might
> From trees and beasts and men into the Heaven's light.

Within Shelley's declaration we also note his revisionary employment of the vegetation deity. That figure's original infusion into Mother Nature has now become a reunification, not with a matrix to be fertilized, but rather with the shaping power of a narcissistic demiurge.

Greater yet than his need to see not Keats but himself as the beckoning star was Shelley's need to ensure that his projected orbit was well clear of the "lone star" he had once called Wordsworth. This is perfectly consonant with Shelley's need to celebrate an alternative to loss and death, and the early sonnet in which he had described Wordsworth as a "lone star" had in fact begun with the lines, "Poet of Nature, thou has wept to know / That things depart which never may return" (*Works*, 526). [24] For Wordsworth, the disappearance of the visionary gleam was irrevocable, but it led to the compensatory colorations that the humanized mind's eye lends to what remains. Shelley sought to refuse the very need for such a consolation. The glory and the freshness were always here, within a poet's vision of the world. Or, if that glory seemed to have "fled," then the poet's spirit, rather than remaining in an impoverished world, however hued by sad maturity, should follow after the gleam, returning to its first radiance.

In order to controvert Wordsworth, Shelley has to use Wordsworth's language, and the last eighteen stanzas of "Adonais" contain many echoes of the "Immortality Ode." This is partly a matter of certain words (such as *embers, fountain, light, splendour, glory,* and *radiance*). But there are more concerted passages in which Shelley echoes Wordsworth only to depart from him:

> . . . . Thou young Dawn,
> Turn all thy dew to splendour, for from thee
> The spirit thou lamentest is not gone;
> Ye caverns and ye forests, cease to moan!
> Cease, ye faint flowers and fountains, and thou Air,
> Which like a mourning veil thy scarf hadst thrown
> O'er the abandoned Earth, now leave it bare
> Even to the joyous stars which smile on its despair!

What at first sounds like the final stanza of Wordsworth's ode veers off into an un-Wordsworthian and characteristically Shelleyan address to the Air. The address cuts specifically against Wordsworth's stanza, which, as we recall, goes on to appreciate "the clouds that gather round the setting sun." Wordsworth's resignation colors and hymns the very barriers that gather between him and the clear sky, and it is to the "meanest flower" here below that he finally turns in the last lines of his poem.

For Shelley, on the other hand, the earth is deliberately "abandoned," left to its despair (not unlike the desolate Urania), and no veiling scarf must intervene between it and the smiling (rather cruelly joyous) stars. By such antithetical counterpointing, both to the mundane world and to what he regarded as the defeated poetry of that world, Shelley in effect begins to approach the beckoning ideal poetic self toward which he makes his final trajectory:

> The soft sky smiles,—the low wind whispers near:
> 'Tis Adonais calls! oh, hasten thither,
> No more let Life divide what Death can join together.

LIV

> That Light whose smile kindles the Universe,
> That Beauty in which all things work and move,
> That Benediction which the eclipsing Curse
> Of birth can quench not, that sustaining Love
> Which through the web of being blindly wove
> By man and beast and earth and air and sea,
> Burns bright or dim, as each are mirrors of
> The fire for which all thirst; now beams on me,
> Consuming the last clouds of cold mortality.

LV

> The breath whose might I have invoked in song
> Descends on me; my spirit's bark is driven,
> Far from the shore, far from the trembling throng
> Whose sails were never to the tempest given;
> The massy earth and sphered skies are riven!
> I am borne darkly, fearfully, afar;
> Whilst, burning through the inmost veil of Heaven,
> The soul of Adonais, like a star,
> Beacons from the abode where the Eternal are.

This conclusion is profoundly disturbing, as many readers have found. Shelley, as we know, perished a year later, precisely by giving sail to the tempest (accounts relate that Shelley, who could not swim, refused to follow a passing crew's advice to strike his sail during the storm).[25] But even if we did not know this, "Adonais" surely concludes on a suicidal note, and we may wonder what measure of success to accord the poet's work of mourning. Has Shelley not somehow burst beyond the elegy as a genre? The problem is deep-seated, for in many ways Shelley's poem has, since its first epigraph, worked against the possibility, the very form and texture, of poetry itself. This conflict has great urgency, for as we saw in the cases of Hieronimo, Titus, and Hamlet, quarrels with literary or legal mediation are often inseparable from suicidal quarrels with life.

Several of these contradictions in "Adonais" have come to a head in the concluding stanzas of the poem. Shelley's ideal self, endowed with Light, Beauty, and Benediction, is nonetheless an image upheld in a mirroring relationship with the aspiring self. Here the latter is felt to be the reflection, while the ideal is seen as the original ("as each are mirrors of / The fire for which all thirst"). When Shelley moves to consummate his love for that ideal (that fire "now beams on me, / Consuming the last clouds of cold mortality"), we may think of Narcissus diving to the depths of what he had taken to be a substantial self. Shelley's course ("No more let Life divide what Death can join together") would necessarily rupture the specular *medium*, the dividing mirror, in which his very goal is imaged.

But if Shelley's figure of the star depends on an intervening medium, this suggests an unexpected connection between images of light and those of textured veils and clouds which the light would seem to oppose. The destruction of one must threaten the other. To make war on poetic language as an interpositional texture associated with a scarf, a veil, a pageantry of mist, a sheath, a dome of many-coloured glass, a web of being—all of which are to be trampled or torn—is to assault the very means by which the counterimage of a radiant star can be posited. 26

From this point of view, we may look back on Wordsworth's sunset clouds or Collins's veilings as the markers of a sad but saving wisdom. They indicate an elegist's sober sense, as at the end of Clorinda's lay in "Astrophel," of what divides the "there" of the deceased from the "here" of a survivor. Similarly, they reveal the elegist's self-knowledge regarding his unavoidable dependence on the fabric of his poem.

Indeed, if we review the entire history of the elegy, we recall countless images of weaving that characterize the genre. It is perhaps with relief that we turn from Shelley's antitextual flight to such figures as the basket-plaiting elegist in Virgil's "Eclogue X." Whether it be by way of Camus's garments "Inwrought with figures dim, and on the edge / Like to that sanguine flower inscrib'd with woe," or Milton's framing review of his own Doric lay, or Jonson's witty focus on his "best piece of poetry," or Gray's attention to his own engraved epitaph, or Stevens's "weaving round the wonder of . . . need," almost all elegists have found a way to suggest the very materiality of their poems. After all, that material not only allows the dead to be "robed," as Shelley himself could not help writing, "in dazzling immortality"; it also marks the saving distance between the dead and their survivors.

Shelley has successfully completed much of the work of mourning. He has renarrated and accepted the fact of death. He has ironized and surpassed inadequate modes of grief. He has expressed and purged his anger. He has submitted to a chastening power that deflects his own attachment to the dead and to the mother-Muse. By transforming his primary narcissism, he has created a consoling substitute for the mortal identities of both Keats and himself. And he has apparently accepted the fabric of language, not only to mediate his anger and desire, but also to represent the substitutive object of his affections. But having done all this, Shelley insists on what seems to be a literal rather than a figurative identification with the consolatory image. Refusing to accept that such an image exists only by virtue of his own material figurations, he threatens to "consume" the entire network of mediations so painfully woven in the poem. It is the very triumph of his mourning imagination, its apparently literal rather than literary thrust, that draws him on to what all mourners most need to avoid— their own drive beyond life and beyond the language whose detours and saving distances keep them alive.

Toward the end of "Lycidas," Milton wrote of the perilous flood. And it was to a protective "Genius of the shore" that he transformed Edward King. For Shelley, the perilous flood is shoreless, more vertical than horizontal. And the beacon does not so much protect as beckon. "Burning through the inmost Veil," the star would seem to carry Shelley beyond the possibilities of poetry, certainly beyond the assurance of pastures new. If we wondered how Shelley could have accepted this most conventional of forms, the pastoral elegy, we recognize now how thoroughly he has driven his version of the genre to the brink of its own ruin. Not surprisingly, "Adonais" marks an extremity that no later elegy would reach.

VII

Tennyson: *In Memoriam*

"Adonais" was first printed in Pisa on 13 July 1821, and copies were
sent to the Ollier brothers to distribute in London. It was not, however, until 1829, seven years after Shelley's own death, that the poem
was first printed in England. Two Cambridge undergraduates were
responsible for this act of homage and salvage. Despite his un-
popularity in England, Shelley impressed them and their intellectual
club, The Apostles, as having been one of the greatest poets of the
preceding decades, and the club was soon to defend this estimate in a
debate against the Oxford admirers of Wordsworth. One of the two
sponsors of the reprint was Richard Monckton Milnes, later to become Lord Houghton, Keats's first biographer and an influential
friend to many poets and writers of the century. The other was the
promising young scholar and critic Arthur Hallam, whose sudden
death four years later at the age of twenty-two would move his closest
friend, Tennyson, to work for seventeen years on one of the most
extraordinary elegies ever written.

Despite both Hallam's and Tennyson's reverence for Shelley, *In
Memoriam* is strikingly different from "Adonais." Tennyson lacked little
of Shelley's technical skill. Indeed, he could imitate the Romantic poet
so convincingly that during their debate at Oxford his fellow Apostles
were able to pass off some of his lines as being Shelley's own. But as we
have remarked, Shelley had driven the elegy to an extremity that few
succeeding poets, least of all a poet of the Victorian period, could
match.

There were many reasons why "Adonais" would have been a difficult
example for a *Victorian* elegist, in particular, to follow. The later poets
were more skeptical with regard not only to religious or philosophical
beliefs but also to the nature and products of the poetic imagination.
Shelley had doubted the means rather than the sources or objects of
poetic expression, whereas for the Victorians even the latter were
suspect. This far-reaching doubt subverted more than the poet's confi-

dence in his particular works or in his vocation. Unable to rely, as the
Romantics had, on idealist assurances that individual reason or imagination might participate in a realm beyond that of the merely empirical, the Victorian poet found it no less difficult to rely on notions
of an ideal self or soul, an entity to which the merely personal could be
subsumed.[1] When the self was regarded as something idiosyncratic—
in short, as personality—how was one to imagine some transpersonal
element of identity that would survive an individual's death? Whereas
"Adonais" celebrated the return of Keats's soul to the universal fountain
of its origins, Tennyson resists precisely this sacrifice of the narrowly
defined personality of Hallam:

> That each, who seems a separate whole,
>   Should move his rounds, and fusing all
>   The skirts of self again, should fall
> Remerging in the general Soul,
>
> Is faith as vague as all unsweet:[2]

How, then, was one to mourn? If the self and its attachments were
uniquely and hence irreplaceably personal, how could they be transformed or displaced? How could the deceased or the survivor be
submitted to that process of self-purification or to versions of that
universalizing myth of the martyred and reborn deity that we have
come to regard as so essential to the search for consolation? Amidst
the proliferating details and furnishings of Victorian funerary practices, behind the crepe and the highly personalized souvenirs, the
very mainspring of the work of mourning had weakened. As Matthew
Arnold complained, "The nobleness of grief is gone— / Ah, leave us
not the fret alone."[3]

In Memoriam presents many reflections of this general predicament,
exaggerated as it was by Tennyson's own temperament and by the
immense personal significance to him of Hallam's death. We have
already glanced, for example, at Tennyson's insistence on a highly
personalized sense of identity. Before exploring this and other thematic examples, we should look at the formal reflections of the problem.
There is, first of all, the poem's extreme length, close to three thou-
sand lines. Written during seventeen years, the poem narrates an
almost three-year-long mourning period, a period unprecedentedly
long for any elegy. The poem's length, moreover, represents no

smoothly unfolding process, no *strictly* unified development to which all parts are organically subordinated:

> The sections were written at many different places, and as the phases of our intercourse came to my memory and suggested them. I did not write them with any view of weaving them into a whole, or for publication, until I found that I had written so many. The different moods of sorrow as in a drama are dramatically given. . . .[4]

Refusing to submit the idiosyncracy of his grief to the shape of conventional ceremony, the poet is concerned rather to accentuate each moment and nuance, each erratic fluctuation of response. Elements of the elegiac conventions are certainly evident, as we shall see, and Tennyson did later rearrange his sections so that they might broadly conform to the general structure of an elegy. But these elements are thoroughly dispersed among details of personal narrative and reflection, which heavily overscore and often contradict the poem's general trend.

Perhaps more important than the poem's length or the way in which the highly personalized moments tend to fracture any strict generic coherence is the fact that *In Memoriam* is created precisely by an *accretion* of moments. Tennyson in fact works against the very dictates of mourning: he collects and elaborates rather than strips or refines; he accumulates rather than lets go. As Verlaine complained, "He had many reminiscences."[5] By their "drama," these "Fragments of an Elegy," as Tennyson once thought of entitling the poem, tend to interfere not only with the elegy's narrative progress but with the very movement of time itself.[6]

For it is against the unfolding of time that Tennyson struggles here, as elsewhere in his poetry. He is not merely trying to cling to the lost object of his love; he is also resisting the very passage of time that makes loss so irreversible. The accretions may therefore be seen as attempts to congeal the flow of time in order to preserve personalities or moments whose definitions are threatened by change. Arthur Hallam himself had spoken of the Victorian "poetic impulse" as "a check acting for conservation against a propulsion towards change."[7]

Reinforcing the slow, accretive structure of the poem is the actual form of its 133 sections. These sections are variously long accumulations of iambic tetrameter quatrains. The relative terseness of the line, together with an *abba* rhyme scheme, gives each stanza a self-encysted quality, an effect of being withheld from time, in a unit whose end echoes its beginning. Each stanza thus seems to cancel out its motion, to bury or seal itself in a past on which it seeks to confer a timeless presence. One is reminded of Henry James's acute remark: "When Tennyson wishes to represent movement, the phrase always seems to me to pause and slowly pivot upon itself, or at most to move backwards."[8]

Clearly, these formal features—the slow and lengthy accretiveness; the stress on disjointed, self-enclosed fragments; the resistance to time or narrative—reflect an attitude that we recognize as melancholia; and the poem certainly justifies Auden's observation that there was very little that Tennyson did not know about that condition.[9] Throughout, *In Memoriam* reveals the melancholic's self-love and self-doubt, his guilt and self-contempt, his insistence on personality and on the discrete particulars of experience, his distrust of mediation, especially that of his own language, and his reluctance to accept any remedy for grief. And yet *In Memoriam* does eventually represent a successful work of mourning, one whose most intriguing aspect is not Tennyson's skepticism—"the quality of his doubt"—but rather the unique if tortuous way in which he achieves consolation by *revising* rather than rejecting the constraints of his own melancholia. To assess that achievement, the reader must ask such questions as the following: How can Tennyson's resistance to time allow for the consoling belief in evolution? How does that allowance itself depend on precisely the kind of figurative language that the melancholy poet distrusts? And how is Tennyson's acceptance of such language an important part of his work of mourning? What inherited symbols and elements of ritual do survive in this poem, and how do they enable the elegist to perform his idiosyncratic version of the mourner's task?

The prologue to *In Memoriam* is itself a perplexing introduction, raising several issues beyond those that we have begun to note. By at once offering and discussing what follows, it resembles a dedication to a patron or reader, in this case the "Strong Son of God, immortal Love," whose existence is, however, immediately presented as a problematic object of belief rather than knowledge ("Believing where we cannot prove"). *In Memoriam* is famous for its noncognitive faith. But what has not been remarked is the fact that Tennyson's very manner of proposing this faith conforms to what we have come to regard as the elegiac process of self-chastisement. For as we shall see, Tennyson closely associates knowledge with an anarchic desire that brooks no detour, precisely the kind of desire that the elegist must quell or reform. The way in which Knowledge is rebuked in section 114, and replaced there by Wisdom or faith, is thus inseparable not only from the way in which the physical presence of Hallam is gradually supplanted by its more spiritual successor but also from the elegist's displacement of his own desires.

Returning to the prologue, we recognize that the entire poem to come is thus addressed to an auditor whose presence is both invisible and unprovable. Almost all elegies have shown variants of this strategy whereby the act of address invents the presence of an addressee. And we have seen how many elegies begin and continue in the mode of address. But seldom has the elegist so immediately and so explicitly drawn attention to the unverifiable nature of his audience. And seldom has the latter been more than an admissible fiction such as that of the nymphs, the Muses, or the spirit of the dead. Here, it is no less than the "Son of God."

The problem of addressing his poem to an unverifiable audience must have affected Tennyson more severely than any elegist. For him, there was not only the matter of having to posit a supreme being, or of having to write out of a painful, Victorian sense of private isolation from an unprecedentedly large and faceless reading public. For Tennyson, the very object of his grief, Arthur Hallam, had in fact been his invaluably attuned personal audience. It was Hallam who had written the brilliant and sympathetic review of Tennyson's early poems in 1831 and who had continued to appreciate and find publishers for his friend's work at a time when Tennyson felt most crushed by hostile critics. The influential Lockhart and Croker had abused the *Poems* of 1832, and even though Tennyson wrote some of his finest poems in 1833, he would not publish another volume until 1842. According to his son, Tennyson "was so far persuaded that the English people would never care for his poetry, that, had it not been for the intervention of his friends, he declared it not unlikely that after the death of Hallam he would not have continued to write."[10] That "silent" decade was certainly marked by sheer grief and solitude, but there is little doubt that a crucial element of distress was the loss of his assured and admiring reader.

In Memoriam is in large part a quest to repair that particular loss, and it is in this light that one should note the great incidence and variety of address throughout the poem. Of the 133 sections, no less than 80 contain some act of address. And these extend to almost 30 different objects, ranging from a yew tree to a ship, from the poet's heart to Time itself. We shall see more fully how this quest for a restored audience is part of the poet's quest to repair a wounded narcissism. The desperate succession of addresses represents the poet's need to bring himself back into the presence of some entity that will reflect his own image. Already in the prologue we note that Tennyson has chosen to regard the "Son of God" as being curiously conflated with Tennyson's ideal reader.

It is before this reader that the poet criticizes himself and his poem:

> Forgive these wild and wandering cries,
>   Confusions of a wasted youth;
>   Forgive them where they fail in truth,
> And in thy wisdom make me wise.

We are familiar with the mourner's impulse to self-abasement. As addressed to God, but also to the dead, this is partly the mourner's penitence for having survived, for choosing to live on, for having been unable to protect the dead, or simply for being unable to mourn him more effectively. As part of a quest for readership, the plea works especially well, for it entreats the kind of active scrutiny that must enter into relation with the poet and poem and respond with an actual judgment. The plea thus posits a superior reader who will somehow complete the poem.

As an introduction, this request is strangely proleptic, in the original sense of the term—it seeks to ward off, or at least preempt, criticism. [11] What is more important, it is a defense that works against time itself by seeking to cancel or outleap time's process. The prologue, which was, in fact, written after the entire poem, in 1849, speaks in retrospect about the poem that it nevertheless precedes. One of the most curious examples of an elegy's conventional self-commentary, this coda-prologue calls for an act of improvement that requires time, even while the call outleaps temporality with respect to the poem itself. The problem is central to the entire poem, and lies behind the first section.

> I held it truth, with him who sings
>   To one clear harp in divers tones,
>   That men may rise on stepping-stones
> Of their dead selves to higher things.

> But who shall so forecast the years
>   And find in loss a gain to match?
>   Or reach a hand thro' time to catch
> The far-off interest of tears?
>
> Let Love clasp Grief lest both be drown'd,
>   Let darkness keep her raven gloss:
>   Ah, sweeter to be drunk with loss,
> To dance with death, to beat the ground,
>
> Than that the victor Hours should scorn
>   The long result of love, and boast,
>   'Behold the man that loved and lost,
> But all he was is overworn.'

If the prologue implied a complicated attitude toward time, the first section of the poem proper immediately confronts the relation between that attitude and the work of mourning. Rather than accept the Goethean notion of constant self-surpassal, related as it is to the mourner's task, the poet clings to a self-definition that will not admit of change. Complaining precisely of his inability to overcome time by forecasting its yield, he chooses instead to defeat it by sheer resistance. At the very outset of the poem, these lines spell out the poet's greatest concern: not merely the loss of his friend but the threatened survival, in time, of his own selfhood. The question for the poet is how to mourn while retaining a sense of self.

In view of the Victorian passion for collectibles, for tangible guarantees of the unchanging and the idiosyncratic, it is interesting to note how Tennyson presents his struggle by images of physical touch or possession. He can not "hold" Goethe's truth because he cannot reach a hand through time to catch the interest of tears. So he chooses to "clasp" Grief instead. This fierce insistence on something to hold is similar to the demand for empirical knowledge, for proof positive, and relates, as we have seen, to the desire that must be broken and redirected during the process of mourning. Only thus can the poet relinquish his fixation on a certain attachment or knowledge and look instead to the more speculative rewards of time.

At this point, however, the poet's obsession with an unchanging identity is too strong. The second section therefore follows with an envious address to the yew tree, emblem not only of melancholy fixation and millenial constancy but also of physically apprehended connections ("Old Yew, which graspest at the stones . . . Thy fibres net the dreamless head, / Thy roots are wrapt about the bones"). Like the stifling, encrusted world of Mariana in her moated grange, this is a form of anti-pastoral, cutting against the grain of a conventional elegy. So, too, the recognizably elegiac images of texture here serve neither to conceal nor redress mortality nor to fabricate a substitute for the lost; rather, they serve as a literal bond, an integument that weaves the living to the dead. Instead of a consoling text we have a fibrous knot; in the place of a symbol of natural growth we find a stubborn stump with which the poet yearns to identify.

As though troubled by elements of projection in his address to the yew, the poet goes on to criticize an explicit case of projection, exposing it as a self-imprisoning danger besetting any griever. As in the previous section, images of texture do not suggest consoling fabrics. Rather, the poet continues, albeit via the distanced figure of Sorrow, to multiply negative versions of the elegiac craft. According to Sorrow, a web obscures the sky; Nature itself is a "hollow echo," a "hollow form" projected by Sorrow herself. The recognition that these expressions are themselves lies only carries us further into the melancholic's distrust of any expressions of grief. And the poet now thinks of repressing this figure of sorrow: "shall I . . . crush her, like a vice of blood, / Upon the threshold of the mind?" (3). The language is psychologically precise, stressing both the prohibition from consciousness and the stifling, rather than displacement, of natural vitality.[12]

In sleep, however, the censorship is lifted to the point where the poet can at least admit that the heart's melancholia involves not only a repression of grief but also another prominent feature of melancholy—what Freud termed unconscious loss:

> O heart, how fares it with thee now,
>   That thou should'st fail from thy desire,
>   Who scarcely darest to inquire,
> 'What is it makes me beat so low?'
>
> Something it is which thou hast lost,
>   Some pleasure from thine early years.
>
> (4)

To pass from melancholia to mourning, this "nameless loss," as Tennyson goes on to call it, must be defined and confronted. The congealment of affection must be broken and set in movement. So, too, the melancholic must overcome his icy resistance to the conventional expressions of grief: "Break, thou deep vase of chilling tears, / That grief hath shaken into frost!"

But the griever still distrusts his language, and although admitting its use as a narcotic, he once again stresses its opacity: "In words, like weeds, I'll wrap me o'er . . . / But that large grief which these en-fold / Is given in outline and no more" (5). We catch the similarity to Hamlet's rejection of the "suits of woe" in favor of an inexpressible inwardness, and the resemblance deepens in section 6 as the poet echoes Hamlet's mockery ("Ay, madam, it is common") of any consol-ing thoughts of grief's commonality. He does, however, allow several self-comparisons to other grievers—a father, a mother, and a young woman expecting her lover. But despite this apparent broadening of reference, the burden of the last comparison is one of extreme self-absorption, and it confirms our suspicion regarding the narcissistic element of the poet's grief. [13]

The woman admires herself in the mirror, and "glad to find herself so fair," prepares specifically for her visitor's admiration. She expects him to reinforce the mirror's complimentary imaging of her. As if to stress the somewhat compulsive attraction to the mirror, there is the detail not only of her turning to it a second time but of this turn being carefully associated with the instant of her visitor's death. By inver-sion, the scenario mirrors that of "The Lady of Shalott," confirming the incompatibility between the constraints of the mirror and the call of the outside world. In the earlier poem, a turn from the mirror destroyed the self, while here a return to the mirror destroys the other. In both poems, the incompatibility had hung in the air, as a "curse," waiting to fall. And in both, the woman had been immersed in creating artful textures—a magic web or an arrangement of golden ringlets. Tennyson's choice of this elaborate comparison suggests more than a continued assault on mediating texture. Now he seems also to express the guilt of one who was himself immersed in the self-reflection of his craft and who waited, like the woman, for the be-loved's approval.

Both narcissism and guilt dominate the following section, in which the poet creeps "like a guilty thing" to Hallam's house in Wimpole Street and asks the house and doors to "behold" him as if they could substitute for the mirroring friend. The present thwarting of past anticipations, the frustrated desire for a physical welcome, the sleep-less haunting of a limbo hour before dawn, the desperate placement of the poet not only on a barred threshold but on a middle ground between contemptuous attachment to the self and an equally con-temptuous and melancholy detachment from the outside world—these all contribute to the impact of this section. Its close is especially powerful:

> He is not here; but far away
>> The noise of life begins again,
>> And ghastly thro' the drizzling rain
> On the bald street breaks the blank day.

(7)

The poet gazes through a despised veil of rain onto a scene that his extreme detachment has rendered unreal but haunting, ghastly, as though a mocking substitute for the true ghost. The "noise" of life suggests nuisance as well as sound, and the unpleasant insistence of sound is itself caught by the near-mindless alliteration of the last line. Associated with time, the daybreak is hatefully "bald" and "blank," words whose connotations of barrenness, exposure, and ashen nullity apply as much to the poet as to the scene. [14]

Section 8 pursues these themes and brings them to the kind of temporary resolution necessary for the poem's continuance. Once again, like one who loses an admiring lover ("her that loves him well"), the poet is instantly disenchanted. "He saddens, all the magic light / Dies off at once. . . ." But now, instead of unadorned blankness, he seems to "find" his verse, or rather its value as an object like the flower once admired and fostered by his dead friend. The need for that fostering is as great as ever, but the poet is able to displace its focus slightly from himself ("my forsaken heart") to his poetry. And with the stress still on having "pleased a vanish'd eye," he offers his verse to the dead. Tentatively, the gesture hints at the ancient rites of tribute, and more specifically of sowing and hence of possible resurrection ("I go to plant it on his tomb, / That if it can it there may bloom, / Or dying, there at least may die").

As if to belie the notion of organic development, however, the poem shifts to a goup of sections addressing the ship that bears home the remains of Hallam. (The first of these sections was in fact written

175

earlier than the sections discussed above.) It is interesting that the stress now falls concertedly on calm sureness of motion. In describing what he desires, the poet gives his very lines the kind of ceremonious fluency that both he and his poem require. Instead of the melancholic's resistance to mobility and time, the ship moves so evenly in time that its "favorable speed" seems to tame or becalm time itself within its motion. Like the flower, and like the evolutionary myth that is to follow, the image of the ship's voyage thus indicates the kind of resolution that Tennyson will achieve. He soon describes how the sails appear to "linger weeping on the marge"; the waves will seem to "sway themselves in rest." Here—and later—Tennyson converts the melancholy fascination with the fixed instant to an assertion of a temporal flow that is somehow consonant with the fulness of any moment.

As yet, the poet falls far short of this achievement. He is still skeptical regarding the power or truth of his "idle dreams"; and he frames his "home bred fancies" of a quiet resting place for the dead with harsher references to the "vanish'd life" and to the often-clasped hands now tossing with tangle and with shells. So, too, his evocations of calm are imperiled by their own potential for a mere return to the fixity of despair and to the calmness of the dead (11). The fair ship yields easily to the poet's explicitly self-reflective image of an "unhappy bark" that "strikes by night a craggy shelf." In this description of traumatic shock, the conquest over time is only the nightmarish product of a delirium that fuses old and new. The poem is still marked by negative versions of its eventual success and by a repeated alternation, even within individual sections (e. g., 18 and 19) of hope and despair, resignation and protest.

Section 19 initiates a further series of doubts about craft. By way of a beautiful description of the tidal Severn, Tennyson repeats the melancholy preference for an unexpressed and supposedly inexpressible fulness rather than for the shallow mourner's empty vocalizing. With similar effect, he contrasts the volubility of servants to the silence of their master, and to the immobilized children with their "other griefs within / And tears that at their fountain freeze" (20). Again, the poem seems to seize up, as the melancholy poet discredits his own utterance; and in section 21 the skepticism turns specifically against the very genre of elegy, attacking this poet, who "take[s] the grasses of the grave, / And make[s] them pipes whereon to blow." Against charges of enervation, paraded constancy, and selfish opposition to an age of progress, the poet defends himself with a rather weak plea for the poetry of natural impulse: "I do but sing because I must, / And pipe but as the linnets sing." The simplistic terms of the defense surely strengthen the charges, while further depleting the reserves of traditional pastoral consolation.

And yet the generic conventions do allow moments of retrospect, in which the poet evokes the traditional idyll of shared joy (22–23). Here, with Pan and the flutes of Arcady, the survivor can at least surmise images of well-being while also submitting himself and his friend to the impersonal figures of Theocritean pastoral. The sections are, however, overshadowed by Death and by the poet's relentless skepticism, which characteristically turns to attack the idyll as mere idealization: "is it that the haze of grief / Makes former gladness loom so great?" (24). Once again, an intervening texture is distrusted rather than recognized as the potential medium of consolation. Similarly, in this section the traditional elegiac images of sun and star are robbed of their solacing effect by mention of sunspots and the distortive effects of distance. The poet appears to have adopted the disenchanted perspective of Sorrow's bitter claims, thus returning to the tone of section 3, while making ever deeper inroads into the resources of the genre.

Although section 26 confirms the element of guilt in the poet's melancholy, his paralyzing sensitivity to accusations of inconstancy or betrayal, the following section brings a crucial alteration:

> I envy not the beast that takes
>   His license in the field of time,
>   Unfetter'd by the sense of crime,
> To whom a conscience never wakes;
>
> Nor, what may count itself as blest,
>   The heart that never plighted troth
>   But stagnates in the weeds of sloth;
> Nor any want-begotten rest.
>
> I hold it true, whate'er befall;
>   I feel it, when I sorrow most;
>   'Tis better to have loved and lost
> Than never to have loved at all.

(27)

This momentary casting out of remorse, like that of Yeats's Self in "A Dialogue of Self and Soul," enables more than an act of *amor fati*. As Walter Benjamin suggested, a conviction of guilt, or of being unredeemably fallen, partly determined the melancholy fear that language could be no more than a fabric of opaque and unfulfillable signs.[15] The poet's affirmative revision of his "sense of crime" may, therefore, allow a more positive attitude toward the formal expression of grief. This is indeed what we discover in the immediately subsequent sections. As we know, they form one of the major dividing points of the elegy, marking the first of three Christmases. But the true nature of the crux should, I think, be seen in this altering attitude toward the forms of grief, and hence toward the medium of the poem itself.

At first, the poet's resistance blocks out the Christmas bells, "as if a door / Were shut between me and the sound" (28). He admits to having wished that his own death might have forestalled his hearing them again. But as the nature of mourning requires, the suicidal desire yields to an everlasting "canon gainst self-slaughter," and the poet does in fact submit to the bells, hearing them now as figures of an almost parental sway.

> But they my troubled spirit rule,
>   For they controll'd me when a boy;
>   They bring me sorrow touch'd with joy,
> The merry, merry bells of Yule.
>
> (28)

We have already begun to note how heavily Tennyson's consolation will depend on this achievement of an attitude whose childlike nature establishes a comforting relation to a superior authority. Here, the submission also works positively against, yet with, Time, bridging the gulf between boyhood and adulthood, allaying the poet's fear that time defeats identity. What might otherwise have been regarded as mere hollow sound thus yields a certain fullness. And this submissive revaluation of ritual forms and figures continues even more thoroughly in what follows.

Resembling a miniature elegy in itself, section 30 narrates how a nervous and faltering observance of traditional forms wins through to an affirmative crescendo. The elegiac images of weaving and of echoing song—it is as though the antiphonal bells ring on within the voices—are certainly those of Sorrow in section 3. But the attitude

toward them is now utterly different. What at first rang hollow now
takes on an impetuously released charge; and with a ceremonious
recommencement so typical of the genre, the song rises, like Virgil's
"Eclogue IV" or "Lycidas," to a "higher range":

> Our voices took a higher range;
>> Once more we sang: 'They do not die
>> Nor lose their mortal sympathy,
> Nor change to us, although they change;
>
> 'Rapt from the fickle and the frail
>> With gather'd power, yet the same,
>> Pierces the keen seraphic flame
> From orb to orb, from veil to veil.'
>
> Rise, happy morn, rise, holy morn,
>> Draw forth the cheerful day from night:
>> O Father, touch the east, and light
> The light that shone when Hope was born.

(30)

This denial of death addresses the precise terms of the mourner's
fear by asserting that a given identity may sustain rather than suffer
change. There will be many relapses before this position is consolidated, but for the moment, much is gained; and the poet can turn to
the Father, which his boyhood has implied, and encourage Him to
advance the passage of once-hated Time. The images of light and
sphere are now repaired. And whereas it had earlier been spurned, the
motif of dawn is heralded in a typically elegiac note of triumphant
elevation. Even the "touch" so often mourned, and again so tentatively hinted at by the "trembling fingers" of the poet, is here recuperated and augmented in a figure of regenerative power.

We should not, however, overlook the fact that the poet's celebration of the "happy morn" contains a powerful defense against the mere
unfolding of time. The welcomed light is, after all, the same light that
shone in the past. And the temporal rebirth of Christ counters the
very passage of time by revealing a persistent identity, making the
very motion of time a circular rather than an irrevocably linear process. This will be an essential element of the poet's consolation and
will determine the very category of rhetoric that he will employ. For as
we may already suspect, the ground is being prepared for a consoling

use of typology, or *figura*, which will allow the poet to reconcile his antipathy to temporal change with his myth of evolution. Unlike metaphor, which depends on the very substitution that Tennyson resists, and unlike metonymy, whose comforting contiguities Tennyson would accept were not all links felt to have been broken, a *type* appears to allow the retention of an identity that is as changeless in form and as fixed in time as Tennyson desires and yet that also participates in a higher existence fulfilled and revealed in time.

Hence the positive reappraisal of ritual and poetic forms continues, with specific attention to the principal figure of Christ as "type" (34). And dominated by this figure, the surrounding sections' (29–36) defense of religious fable and of the incarnation of the Word should be read as crucial elements of the poet's partial reconciliation with the devices of his mourning and his poem.

Tennyson will not use typology fully until later in the poem, and he characteristically interrupts the incipient mood of acceptance. His guilt (37) disrupts the positive attitude toward language that has been so painstakingly gathering force. Regarding the muse of Shelley and Milton as an aloof and hostile judge, the poet's saturnine Melpomene deprecates herself for having "darken'd sanctities with song." Nevertheless, not all the ground is surrendered, and with spring (38), the poet's songs offer a "doubtful gleam of solace." Similarly, in section 39, his revised description of the yew ("To thee too comes the golden hour / When flower is feeling after flower") is meant at least to suggest an alternative to Sorrow's continuing stress on gloomy fixation. With more success than in the harshly repressive section 3, the poet is still seeking to accommodate the univocal distress of melancholy within the antiphonal or eclogic form of elegy. But the following sections reveal how strongly melancholia continues to dictate the terms of the poet's grief.

Spring offers the image of a young bride, but the poet rejects the analogy between her departure from home and Hallam's death. He has introduced the figure only to lament "the difference" between its rhetorical nature and the reality that he discerns. The rejection of the image is thus itself a melancholy act, but the terms involved are even more significant. In fact, they are vital to an understanding of the poem.

The bride would become "A link among the days, to knit / The generations each with each" (40). In other words, the bride represents the kind of mediation ("knit" reminds us of the textual fabric) and evolution that might allow a happier relation to linear time. By contrast, the poet and his dead friend are held incommunicado, with no language, no "tidings," to connect them. The poet has "lost the links that bound Thy changes" (41). Contradicting section 30, he complains that Hallam has not remained "the same" but rather has "turn'd to something strange." And having denied the possibility of linkage, he desires to "leap the grades of life and light, / And flash at once, my friend, to thee." Again, the bias is against both the "stepping-stones" of intervening grades and a linked progression into the "secular to-be." The urge is for an *instantaneous* and unmediated leap or flash, an obliteration of grades, barriers, intervals, or links. The language is that of rebellious desire itself, which, as noted earlier, is associated with the passionate attachment to the dead and also with the urge for immediate, apprehensible knowledge—in particular, knowledge of what lies beyond the boundaries of the living and beyond the fabric of time or language.

It is precisely this melancholy desire that forms the subject of "Ulysses," which, as Tennyson admitted, "was more written with the feeling of [Hallam's] loss upon me than many poems in *In Memoriam*."[16] There, too, a griever rejects all "slow degrees" and rules, as well as all generational linkage, choosing instead a suicidal quest in which forbidden knowledge is again associated with the (lost) object of desire:

And this grey spirit yearning in desire
To follow knowledge like a sinking star,
Beyond the utmost bound of human thought.
                    (*Poems*, 563–64, lines 30–33)[17]

Within "Ulysses," the proleptic reverie itself seems to narcotize and hence safely retard forever the destructive quest that it envisions. But *In Memoriam* faces the issue more directly. The poet analyses more fully the relation between knowledge and unchecked desire, and he also spells out the mourner's need to subdue that wild urge:

Who loves not Knowledge? Who shall rail
   Against her beauty? May she mix
   With men and prosper! Who shall fix
Her pillars? Let her work prevail.

But on her forehead sits a fire:
   She sets her forward countenance

And leaps into the future chance,
  Submitting all things to desire.

Half-grown as yet, a child, and vain—
  She cannot fight the fear of death.
  What is she, cut from love and faith,
But some wild Pallas from the brain

Of Demons? fiery-hot to burst
  All barriers in her onward race
  For power. Let her know her place;
She is the second, not the first.

A higher hand must make her mild,
  If all be not in vain; and guide
  Her footsteps, moving side by side
With wisdom, like the younger child:

For she is earthly of the mind,
  But Wisdom heavenly of the soul.

(114)

As we have learned to expect in an elegy, these terms are close to those of oedipal submission. We have already suspected that much of Tennyson's consolation will depend on his assuming the position of a chastened child. These lines only confirm how closely that self-humbling is related to the mourner's necessary shift from the "earthly" to the "heavenly," from Knowledge to Wisdom, from an insistence on the timeless moment to a reconciliation with the gradual passage of time, and finally from a wilful rage for the immediate and graspable, to an acceptance of what the mediate can at best suggest.

Of course, this shift occurs neither smoothly nor by any single turning point. But we do see it gathering as an intermittent tendency that after several reversals and successes yields its rewards and allows a programmatic statement such as that in section 114. Returning to the earlier passage, in which the poet still yearns for the sudden leap, we do find, for example, that it is followed, in section 42, by a self-rebuke ("I vex my heart with fancies dim: / He still outstript me in the race") and a disavowal of knowledge ("one that loves but knows not"). In section 43, he would willingly concede not only to a period of delay, of "intervital gloom," but also to the highly literary device of a "figured leaf" on which the persisting identity of the dead would be inscribed and thus preserved until their final rebirth.

The poet also works now to replace the wilful desire for full knowledge by the chastened, more passive receptions of fragmentary "hints." Instead of the single and ultimate flash or leap into certainty, he now images "a little flash, a mystic hint," such as the remembering Hallam may receive "he knows not whence" (44). Apart from being diminished, the once-and-for-all singularity of the flash is dispersed over time—it is given out "at times." Both the diminution and the fracturing submission to time are crucial elements of the mourner's acquiescence. The word *hint* itself suggests the attendant shift from physical *bent* to mental apprehension, and this chastening of touch is emphasized in the succeeding lines ("some dim touch . . . such a dreamy touch"). So, too, the self-castrative nature of this entire acquiescence is emphasized by further images of fragmentation and of mediating textures that are both childlike and fragile:

> From art, from nature, from the schools,
>   Let random influences glance,
>   Like light in many a shiver'd lance
> That breaks about the dappled pools:
>
> The lightest wave of thought shall lisp,
>   The fancy's tenderest eddy wreathe,
>   The slightest air of song shall breathe
> To make the sullen surface crisp.
>
> And look thy look, and go thy way,
>   But blame not thou the winds that make
>   The seeming-wanton ripple break,
> The tender-pencil'd shadow play.
>
> (49)

These terms of the mourner's admission do more than describe his accommodation to language. They describe the very form of his particular poem—its fragmentary, intermittent "hoarding" of self-encircling but incomplete eddies or wreathes of song. This accurate self-commentary should not, however, lead us to suppose that the poet is happily at one with himself or with his poem. For even as he is setting forth the ideological vindication of its form and content, he is pointing, in melancholy fashion, to the essentially superficial nature of his own language: the eddy, the ripple, and the play of light on the crispening surface of the pool. And it is from just these characterizations of his own song that the last stanza of this section withholds assent:

> Beneath all fancied hopes and fears
> Ay me, the sorrow deepens down,
> Whose muffled motions blindly drown
> The bases of my life in tears.

(49)

With this reversal, we are back to the complaints of section 5, the Hamlet-like dismissal of language and the "forms of grief" as an inky cloak that muffles the inner life. While it is fair to speak of some "progress" in the poem thus far, we are forced to regard it as one of continuing debate, the antiphonal division that marks a grieving mind as surely as it structures any elegy's eclogic form. That division is of unusal depth, and as I have already suggested, it is rendered especially problematic because the resolution will depend more on an inter-penetration of melancholia and mourning than on a sheer replacement of one by the other.

Pursuing its argument, therefore, the melancholy voice of section 50 requests the closeness of the dead ("Be near me") and rages against both the tyranny of "Time, a maniac scattering dust," and the texture of human life ("men . . . weave their petty cells and die"). Instead, this voice hankers for the "twilight of eternal day," which marks "the low dark verge of life." In addition, the melancholic again raises the question of his guilt, "some hidden shame" (51), which is once more associated with his narcissistic attachment to the dead ("he for whose applause I strove"). And although he does establish the "clear eye" of the dead, the "larger other eyes than ours," this totemic power which Hallam now shares with God as ideal audience is primarily menacing: "the dead shall look me thro' and thro.'" There is the tentative hope for a milder attitude, an "allowance," but this is still far from the more complete prayer for a forgiving criticism such as he will make in the prologue. The poet has yet to argue more effectively against his own guilt and particularly against his conviction that recourse to language is itself a sin.

We have noted how the melancholy contempt for representation is associated with a distrust of Time and it is not surprising to find how much the continuing defense against the poet's self-prosecution entails an explicit defense of Time. Thus, although section 52 begins with the familiar attack on the superficiality and opacity of words ("My words are only words, and moved / Upon the topmost froth of thought"), the counterargument ("blame not thou thy plaintive song") opposes the image of maniacal Time by one of Time as the agent who will have "sunder'd shell from pearl."[18]

But even as the poet seeks to consolidate this optimistic defense, this hope "that somehow good / Will be the final goal of ill," his argument breaks down in a combination of ruptured syntax, cliché, self-doubt, and explicit attack on the inadequacy of his own language:

Behold, we know not anything;
  I can but trust that good shall fall
  At last—far off—at last, to all,
And every winter change to spring.

So runs my dream: but what am I?
  An infant crying in the night:
  An infant crying for the light:
And with no language but a cry.

(54)

As mentioned before, this self-chastening return to childhood is essential to the poem's consolation. Indeed, we have speculated earlier on the relation between elegy and the infant's cry of abandonment. But here this cry is one of sheer desolation: only later (124) will it evoke the comforting presence of a parental figure. The cry now introduces one of the poem's most bitter and most famous passages.

Sections 55 and 56 are familiar to all readers of the poem, but it is essential to recognize how the great denunciation of Nature, "red in tooth and claw," derives its force and function from the psyche of a mourner. From Theocritus's "First Idyl" to "Lycidas" and "Adonais," we have noted not only the place of anger in elegies but the relation of that anger to the mourner's loss of a mother figure. In each case, that loss is associated with images of castration, as though the mourner were being forced to recapitulate a moment of original separation, as well as the later moment in which he voluntarily renounced or curbed his own desire to abolish that separation. Section 55, therefore, follows the image of the abandoned infant with images of sharply attenu-

185

ated physical strength ("I falter where I firmly trod, / And falling with my weight of cares / Upon the great world's altar stairs . . . I stretch lame hands . . . And faintly trust. . . ." It is this drastically subdued questor who is crushed by the juxtaposed images of futile, frail mankind and of an at best indifferently ravenous Mother Nature (56). Here, then, is *In Memoriam*'s version of such passages as those in which a stricken Daphnis cursed his implacable tormentor Aphrodite; or Milton despaired, "What could the Muse herself" for her decapitated Orpheus? or Shelley set the figure of dead Adonais against that of the oblivious mother, Urania, sitting in paradise "with veiled eyes." As we have asked before, how but in relation to an immortal matrix should man most suffer his mortality? And how can the mourner avoid repeating his own necessary separation from that matrix?

Unable to merge or identify in an immediate way with such a source or setting, the poet must artificially weave what once had seemed a natural bond. And this woven fabric must interpose between him and the object of knowledge or desire. Hence the imagery in a soothing yet also frustrating answer to the poet's anguish in section 55: "What hope of answer, or redress? / Behind the veil, behind the veil" (56). As the word *redress* suggests, the veil will be a necessary part of any answer. It is there, not to be torn aside, but to be used precisely as a medium. And as we shall see, succeeding sections of the poem, particularly the moments of solacing vision, confirm how thoroughly any consolation must depend upon the texture of language. The very next words of the poem suggest as much: "Peace; come away: the song of woe / Is after all an earthly song" (57).

Here, in the calm with which so many elegies have followed anger, song's earthliness is meant to refer not only to its sphere of reference but to its materiality. And after several intervening passages that imagine Hallam looking back at the "dimly character'd" script and fading legend of his past, the poet arrives at the first of those consoling trances that so explicitly depend on the physical properties of language. Section 64 depicts the poet as one who "ploughs," "reaps," and "muses" in the earthly "furrow" of his song. The following section speaks of "painful phases wrought" to yield happiness. And section 66 defends an apparent gaiety as follows:

The shade by which my life was crost,
  Which makes a desert in the mind,

Has made me kindly with my kind,
And like to him whose sight is lost;

Whose feet are guided thro' the land,
Whose jest among his friends is free,
Who takes the children on his knee,
And winds their curls about his hand:

He plays with threads, he beats his chair
For pastime, dreaming of the sky;
His inner day can never die,
His night of loss is always there.

Pursuing his observance of the veiled ("shade") and earthly ("desert") quality of his mind, the poet shows an unusual acceptance of positive self-comparison. Blindness, as we know, suggests the chastened condition of a mourner, and the image "plays with threads" describes so many elegists, from Virgil to Stevens. "Winds their curls" takes the physical image of spinning or weaving further (we may recall by contrast the self-admiring virgin arranging her ringlets in section 6) and adds to it the important suggestion of an old man braiding his affectionate linkage to the younger generation. Similarly, "beats his chair / For pastime" drives home the physicality of the poet's rhythmic art while again stressing its potential reconciliation, or rather alliance with time.

In section 67, darkness is again an essential element. Indeed, it is as though the poet were now obeying such ancient elegiac rites as those at Eleusis, where revelations were received only by those who had descended into the dark. At night, he imagines (he is not there to see) how the moonlight illuminates the memorial tablet of his friend.

Thy marble bright in dark appears,
As slowly steals a silver flame
Along the letters of thy name,
And o'er the number of thy years.

The mystic glory swims away;
From off my bed the moonlight dies;
And closing eaves of wearied eyes
I sleep till dusk is dipt in gray:

> And then I know the mist is drawn
>   A lucid veil from coast to coast,
>   And in the dark church like a ghost
> Thy tablet glimmers to the dawn.

Apart from the "marble bright in dark" or the tablet glimmering under a "lucid veil" of mist, the emphasis on a physical script is striking. In fact, the slow passage of moonlight over the individual letters suggests the deliberate movement of the mind over the material nature of words. The script's emergence out of darkness thus figures not only the resurrection of the dead into a world of light but also the resurrection of language itself as the medium of that event. From our knowledge of the poem thus far, we could say that language itself is emerging from the darkness of the poet's melancholy disapproval. Furthermore, the "silver flame," which shines without burning, surely indicates that language is being not only resurrected but also trans-figured. [19] The meaning is clear: not transcendence nor ascension but rather transfiguration in which the mediating form is preserved but glorified.

This cluster of images and concerns helps to explain what is, nevertheless, the rather banal dream in section 69, and the more interesting dream in section 70. In the first, the poet weaves himself a crown of thorns which a glorious hand transforms to leaf. Similarly, in the following dream, after the poet seeks to "paint" Hallam's face on the fabric of "the gloom," the imperfect representation is transfigured to a perfect semblance. With consistent acuity, the poet stresses that this consoling image is still mediated by a woven screen ("thro' a lattice on the soul / Looks thy fair face"). It is significant that this apparition is said to occur "beyond the will," as if to emphasize how these acceptances of mediation depend on a chastening of the will. Later visions will return to this with programmatic clarity.

Before considering those later passages, we should note how the debate continues to allow melancholy its voice. There are the angry denunciation of the first anniversary of Hallam's death (72), the complaint that poetry can neither describe the dead (75) nor in itself survive (75–77), and the bitter lament that Death prevents all speech between the living and the dead (82). But interspersed with these are counterarguments in favor of continuing song (77, 83), the familiar rituals (78), and the passage of time (80, 83). [20] Only with section 85 does the balance shift conclusively away from melancholia. The section is the longest in the entire poem, and in its struggling oscillation of mood it seems to recapitulate much of the poem at large.

Indeed, this elegy within the elegy begins by quoting from an early section (27) and goes on to narrate the poet's shock at hearing of Hallam's death, the pain of survival, and the difficult necessity of breaking the fixation of this first attachment and "transfer[ring]" his affection to a new object. Despite the impossibility of conversation, the poet feigns responses from the dead, conceding that in this manner "shall grief with symbols play." Not only does he seem unusually at ease with his own devices but the answer he projects is a positive restatement of those ultimate rewards that he had rejected in section 1 ("I triumph in conclusive bliss, / And that serene result of all"). Finally, in response both to this reassurance and to Hallam's advice that he should form a new attachment, the poet offers his affections to his sister Cecilia's fiancé, Edmund Lushington. The description of this offer is as beautiful as it is canny:

> Ah, take the imperfect gift I bring,
>   Knowing the primrose yet is dear,
>   The primrose of the later year,
> As not unlike to that of Spring.[21]

Although he offers a lesser version of an original gift, this offering is of the same *type* of flower. Once again, the poet approximates the mode of rhetoric that we have expected to become the chief consoling device of the poem—that of typology (here, however, reversing its eventual movement from diminished to fulfilled identity). A single name or type identifies two individual flowers from different times. Once again, the *figura* thus works in time but against time's dissolution of identity, while the specific type, primrose, stresses the firstness whose conservation the poet has so highly prized.

This use of type introduces a series of sections marked by recollection, by an establishment of what is still "The same, but not the same" (87). And from recollection the mourner moves to invocation, courting a return of the dead. Of interest here is the self-chastening quality of this courtship—the stress that any manifestation will depend on the mourner's purity at heart, his ascetic receptivity to the unseen spirit, rather than his wilful grasping after any visible form. In fact, the mourner must strive for a level of spirituality matching that of the dead:

> No visual shade of some one lost,
>> But he, the Spirit himself, may come
>> Where all the nerve of sense is numb;
> Spirit to Spirit, Ghost to Ghost.
>
> . . . .
>
>> That in this blindness of the frame
>> My Ghost may feel that thine is near.

(93)

And at the beginning of section 94:

> How pure at heart and sound in head,
>> With what divine affections bold
>> Should be the man whose thought would hold
> An hour's communion with the dead.

By this preparation, reminiscent of the self-refining rituals of the elegiac cults, the poet approaches the celebrated trance of section 95:

> By night we linger'd on the lawn,
>> For underfoot the herb was dry;
>> And genial warmth; and o'er the sky
> The silvery haze of summer drawn;
>
> And calm that let the tapers burn
>> Unwavering: not a cricket chirr'd:
>> The brook alone far-off was heard,
> And on the board the fluttering urn:
>
> And bats went round in fragrant skies,
>> And wheel'd or lit the filmy shapes
>> That haunt the dusk, with ermine capes
> And woolly breasts and beaded eyes;
>
> While now we sang old songs that peal'd
>> From knoll to knoll, where, couch'd at ease,
>> The white kine glimmer'd, and the trees
> Laid their dark arms about the field.

If we allow the conjunction of line 9 ("And bats . . .") to erase the preceding period, these stanzas are all part of a single sentence, which in fact extends beyond them ("But when . . . "). There is, therefore, an unusual syntactic inclusiveness within these lines, a sense of their participating in one "linger'd" moment that becomes more scene than time. The unifying effect is reinforced by a subtle mesh of imagery: the "silvery haze," which shares its light with the tapers, fluttering urn, filmy moths, and glimmering kine—almost all of which represent the poet's mind, that delicate yet uncertain source of light that depends on the surrounding gloom for its definition and that, as we now recognize, is a light invariably associated with some veil or texture.

The atmosphere and elements are those of near-religious rites: tapers, urn, old songs that peal like bells. The word *knoll* is itself an inspired choice, offering its associated root meaning of "knot" (hence adding to the images of texture) while also blending *knell* and *toll*. But the heart of the ritual begins with the ceremonious departure "one by one" of the poet's companions and the extinction, "light after light," of all sources of illumination other than those already associated with the poet's mind. As in Gray's elegy, the poet is left in solitary custody of the night, a custody close to identification (compare Tennyson's "Withdrew from me and night" with "And leaves the world to darkness and to me"). This repetition of the mourner's earlier experience of abandonment brings a predictable pang ("A hunger seized my heart") and forces him to search once more for consolation.

Although we have been following the poet's struggle to accept his dependence on language, it is still perhaps a shock to see how directly he now turns to the very medium that his earlier imagery of lucid veils and illuminated scripts implied: "A hunger seized my heart; I read. . . ." Like Gray in the churchyard, he, too, reads, in this case the letters of his friend, the "fallen leaves which kept their green." (The metaphor only drives home the substitution of the literary for the natural.) His friend survives as a script whose silence is enforced despite the oxymoronic straining for voice:

And strangely on the silence broke
  The silent-speaking words, and strange
  Was love's dumb cry defying change
To test his worth;

This dependence on the written letter is even more firmly emphasized in what follows:

> So word by word, and line by line,
> The dead man touch'd me from the past,

The physical touch so long desired, and so reluctantly spiritualized, has finally become a literary impression, and the recovered presence of the dead in letters suggests the poet's own recovery of Hallam in the lines of his elegy.

For a moment, the communion rises to a height that apparently transcends mere letters:

> And all at once it seem'd at last
> The living soul was flash'd on mine,
>
> And mine in this was wound, and whirl'd
> About empyreal heights of thought,
> And came on that which is, and caught
> The deep pulsations of the world,
>
> Aeonian music measuring out
> The steps of Time—the shocks of Chance—
> The blows of Death.

Here "at last" is the instantaneous flash that fulfills the poet's desire not so much for reunion with Hallam as for the revelation of an eternal pattern ("that which is") in which the adversary, Time, is accommodated to measures of music. What he sees, or rather hears, is an ideal version of his own poem, a reconciliation of the timebound with the timeless in a music that smoothly encompasses the occasions of grief.

But with the mention of Death, the reverie breaks up with a specific reminder of its textual nature: "At length my trance / Was cancell'd, stricken thro' with doubt." It is as though the trance were no more than a canceled page of script. But now the poet's admission of his "matter-moulded forms of speech" coexists with an apparently residual faith in the vision to which these forms seem to have led. *Returning* to the "vague words" and to the materiality of language may finally be the poet's way of conceding the "word by word" ground from which the vision sprang. Hence, too, the return to the surrounding scene, the knolls, the trees, the kine now glimmering in the uncertain light before dawn. This time, a gentle breeze animates the scene and issues into the language of proclamation:

> 'The dawn, the dawn,' and died away;
> And East and West, without a breath,

Mixt their dim lights, like life and death,
To broaden into boundless day.

Apart from the assurance with which language now seems to usher
in the time of day, something of the all-encompassing trance persists
in the medley of lights. Like the Aeonian music, the twilight seems to
overcome what may otherwise appear to be the discontinuities of day
and night, life and death. [22] The poet celebrates the passage of time,
but within a chordlike compounding of its divisions. As always, the
lights are dim. And in the following section, the poet makes his most
explicit defense of this essential obscurity. The darkness, or veil, is
now meant to refer also to doubt, an easy extension, since we have all
along been associating darkness with accepted limitation, blindness,
or the material, "earthly" nature of language. The poet praises one
who, like Hallam or himself, has found a "stronger faith":

And Power was with him in the night,
Which makes the darkness and the light,
And dwells not in the light alone,

But in the darkness and the cloud,
As over Sinaï's peaks of old,
While Israel made their gods of gold,
Altho' the trummmpet blew so loud.

(96)

Intriguingly, the passage combines a defense of a mediating veil or
cloud like that of language with an allusion to the figure of Moses,
who in himself represents mediation and is, moreover, a prime example of the very kind of mediation, the precise mode of rhetoric, that
most enables the consoling resolution of this poem—*figura* or type.
For Moses, *the* type of the mediator, is himself a type prefiguring
Christ. Milton had captured this in his account of the Sinaitic instruc-
tion "by types / And shadows":

   . . . he grants what they besought,
Instructed that to God is no access
Without Mediator, whose high Office now
Moses in figure bears, to introduce
One greater, of whose day he shall foretell. [23]

Earlier, we began to suggest that the device of *figura* was particularly helpful to a poet who was struggling to reconcile the in-

stantaneous with the passage of time and who needed to preserve an assurance of identity despite temporal change. We had remarked how fully Tennyson subscribed to the Victorian insistence on a self defined as idiosyncratic personality and how completely he therefore shunned the traditional displacements by which a mourned self gave way to some new substitute. The appeal of *figura* is that it requires neither an alteration of identity nor a submission to time conceived as merely horizontal metamorphic linkage. Rather, it offers a preservation and fulfillment of any discrete moment or identity by a revelation of its higher, timeless character. As Erich Auerbach put it:

> In this way the individual earthly event is not regarded as . . . a link in a chain of development in which single events or combinations of events perpetually give rise to new events, but viewed primarily in immediate vertical connection with a divine order which encompasses it [Tennyson's "that which is"], which on some future day will itself be concrete reality. . . .
>
> For Dante the literal meaning or historical reality of a figure stands in no contradiction to its profounder meaning, but precisely "figures" it; the historical reality is not annulled, but confirmed and fulfilled by the deeper meaning. [24]

It is precisely this avoidance of the much doubted and much dreaded transformation or substitution that must have so appealed to the poet of *In Memoriam*. And in the remaining sections of the poem, he exploits the resources of *figura* with varied amplitude. For example, the consoling dream that attends the departure from his childhood home at Somersby centers upon successive encounters with the figure of Hallam. At first the figure is

A statue veil'd, to which they sang;

And which, tho' veil'd, was known to me,
  The shape of him I loved, and love
  For ever.

(103)

Like the first term of the *figura*, this is the shape that conceals within itself its true and essentially unchanging identity. In Auerbach's similar terms, "Thus, history, with all its concrete force, remains forever a figure, cloaked and needful of interpretation."[25] As statue, the shape is emphatically immobile. It has the frozen aspect that we earlier associated with the statuesque attitudes of melancholy.[26] As we know, however, Tennyson retains yet revises the elements of his melancholy. The veiled statue is, after all, interpretable, and it is succeeded by a revelation and enlargement of its identity. And the poet himself increases to gigantic size as he is ferried with his poems to meet his friend.

Elsewhere, the figures of typology are more straightforwardly employed:

> Till at the last arose the man;
>
> Who throve and branch'd from clime to clime,
>   The herald of a higher race,
>   And of himself in higher place,
> If so he type this work of time
>
> Within himself, from more to more;
>
> (118)

According to Tennyson's idiosyncratic blend of typology and evolution, a historical individual may have within himself an identity that resembles a veiled statue while on earth but would be fully apparent now and forever in heaven, or, in the fullness of time, by way of evolution, here on earth. By regarding evolution as a movement toward a manifestation of what certain types on earth have already prefigured, and of what exists already outside of time, Tennyson tempers what would otherwise be a merely linear series of substitutions. He maintains his stress on a lasting identity as surely as he continues his "check" against the "propulsion towards change." The final expression of this particular use of typology, in which Hallam himself is seen as the type of human perfection, will bring the poem to its conclusion.

Before turning to the epilogue, however, we should note some features of the preceding sections, particularly those that pursue and resolve such previously mentioned issues as the poet's melancholy narcissism, his adoption of a childlike posture, his need to repair a sense of audience, and his related need to conserve a stable image of his *own* identity.

The departure from Somersby is interestingly described, for the poet clearly displaces onto Somersby the wounded narcissism that he himself suffered at Hallam's death. By a series of repeated negations, he suggests that Somersby had no existence apart from its relation to Hallam or himself. His departure now seems, therefore, to repeat the devastating effect of Hallam's then: "And, leaving these, to pass away, / I think once more he seems to die." By leaving Somersby, he enacts his own abandonment by Hallam, not unlike the child who brings about a symbolic version of its mother's departure in order to master the experience. Somersby precisely represents the poet's forsaken self, a self deprived of love and audience: "Unwatch'd . . . Unloved . . . Uncared for" (101).

For Somersby, the only redress will be a new tenant, a substitute for the departing lover. And similarly, for the poet, redress will depend on the regained presence of his approving friend. An essential part, therefore, of the "departure dream" in section 103 is Hallam's welcome, extended both to the poet and to his works. Significantly, the poet cannot bid his own poems to enter. It is the ideal reader, Hallam, who must save them from neglect ("'And wilt thou leave us now behind?'")

In the light of this dream, the departure from Somersby thus takes on added complexity. The poet not only leaves behind his youth but detaches himself from that youth defined as a scenario of abandonment. In other words, the mourner is making that crucial movement beyond a prior state of desolation, beyond a melancholy fixation on the dead and on his own forsaken self.[27] Tennyson frees himself from the ego on to which his affections had refastened after Hallam's death—the ego that nevertheless had unconsciously, and melancholically, been associated with Hallam as a lost object. The poet's own sense of enlargement in the dream reflects his surpassal of that younger, arrested self. But it also represents his arrival at a repaired and enlarged narcissistic relation to the dead. As he had previously identified with the lost, so he now reidentifies with the found Hallam. And as the found Hallam is enlarged and unveiled, so the poet himself mirrors this new state.

Finally, by the images of the summons, the shallop-ferry, and the waters broadening to a grand "flood," the poet confirms that this dream passage prefigures his own death. And as in "Adonais," but without Shelley's blazing extinction of personality, it is the resource of transformed narcissism that enables the poet to use his new image of the dead as a mirror image of his own surviving self. Once again, the elegy yields its archaic reward—the elegist's invention and rehearsal of his immortality.

This augmentative mirroring, in which the poet projects and then tries to match a higher self-image or ideal ego, continues with the poet's attempts to imitate the wisdom of the dead. The reflective device is captured by approximate echoes: "'Tis held that sorrow makes us wise, / Whatever wisdom sleep with thee" (108); "High wisdom holds my wisdom less" (112); "And in thy wisdom make me wise" (prologue). And the culmination of this entire strategy is reached in the epilogue, where the poet describes himself in terms similar to those of the dream in section 103:

> No longer caring to embalm
>   In dying songs a dead regret,
>   But like a statue solid-set,
> And moulded in colossal calm.
>
> Regret is dead, but love is more
>   Than in the summers that are flown,
>   For I myself with these have grown
> To something greater than before;

While he retains the motif of enlargement, he has also carried over the image of the statue. That is, he imitates not only the fulfilled, colossal figure of the refound Hallam but also the statuesque figure of the dead Hallam in his life-size, shrouded state before fulfillment. So intent is the poet not to lose his or Hallam's familiar form that he clings, even in the midst of imaging his higher self, to the conservative condition of the statue. He thus carefully preserves the prior, historical figure within its later fulfillment. There could be no better example of his overall retention yet revision of his melancholia.

Throughout these last sections the poet is thus devising images that represent both Hallam and himself as being "the same, yet not the same," enlarged but not transformed. The masterful Hesper-Phosphor image in section 121 is one such image, relying yet again on a version of *figura* ("double name / For what is one, the first, the last"). And it is the inherent conservatism of such a passage, like that regarding the statue in the epilogue, that may make the reader a little skeptical of the apparent upsurge of belief, for the first time in the poem, in an impersonal version of immortality:

What art thou then? I cannot guess;
    But tho' I seem in star and flower
    To feel thee some diffusive power,
I do not therefore love thee less.

My love involves the love before;
    My love is vaster passion now;
    Tho' mix'd with God and Nature thou,
I seem to love thee more and more.

                                             (130)

Even if one were not a little skeptical, one should at least note how these assertions are situated in clauses that are not only subordinate but concessional. The emphasis throughout this and the surrounding sections bears firmly on the stable, obsessively stressed identity of the poet and of his still extremely possessive love: "Dear heavenly friend that canst not die, / Mine, mine, for ever, ever mine" (129).

The last section of the poem proper—before the epilogue—returns to several essential themes:

O living will that shalt endure
    When all that seems shall suffer shock,
    Rise in the spiritual rock,
Flow thro' our deeds and make them pure,

That we may lift from out of dust
    A voice as unto him that hears,
    A cry above the conquer'd years
To one that with us works, and trust,

With faith that comes of self-control,
    The truths that never can be proved
    Until we close with all we loved,
And all we flow from, soul in soul.

                                             (131)

The "living will," by which is meant "Free will, the higher and enduring part of man,"[28] is here assimilated, by way of the elegiac image of liquidity, to the will of Christ. The allusion is to 1 Corinthians 10.4: "For they drank of the spiritual Rock that followed them: and the Rock was Christ." This is itself a perfect example of *figura*, fulfilling the type in Exodus 17.6: "and thou shalt smite the rock, and there shall come water out of it, that the people may drink."[29] And this in turn takes us back to section 96, the defense of darkness, mediation, and *figura* in the reference to Moses. Like the Scriptures, the poem itself appears to be fulfilling its own prefigurations, exemplifying the very process on which its consolation depends.

The second stanza continues the image of miraculous liquidity, now mingling it with a representation of voice or cry. Since the beginnings of elegy, in which a shepherd's voice accompanied a murmuring stream, we have grown accustomed to this mingling. And since discussing how the earliest images for the spirit and the enduring will, or the powers of song, were drawn from images of an originally sexual force, we have come to recognize the complex nature of this figure. As his specific use of the above *figura* suggests, however, Tennyson has done far more than merely rely on a given convention. His cry has a highly individual character. It refers us back to the cry of the infant abandoned by its mother Nature in section 54 and to the entire issue of the poet's need for a regained sense of almost parental audience. In section 124, the achievement of just such a cry is carefully linked to the mourner's work of self-chastisement. And once again, that work seems to involve an oedipal resolution:

> And like a man in wrath the heart
> Stood up and answer'd, 'I have felt.'

> No, like a child in doubt and fear:
>   But that blind clamor made me wise;
>   Then was I as a child that cries,
> But, crying, knows his father near;

The abandoning and abandoned mother is thus replaced by a father, under whose aegis the mourning poet has apparently unmanned himself, but with consoling effects. Hence the final submission in section 131 of the "free will" to that of Christ, himself a martyr, and the replacement of the rebellious desire for knowledge with a milder attitude of "trust" and "faith that comes of self-control." Only in this way can the poet raise a voice "as unto him that hears." The use of simile hints at poignant uncertainty, a symptom of the continuing deferral of knowledge.

The epilogue, as Tennyson admitted, carries the poem from funeral to marriage, thereby concluding with the ancient rituals of sexual reunion and rebirth. But the marriage itself is described as though it were somehow a funeral in which the poet is compelled to give away or surrender his sister to her new life. Section 40 suggested some of the similarity between a bride and the newly deceased, and while the epilogue does repair the dissatisfaction of the earlier section, it nonetheless retains something of a mourner's resignation. There is the recollected idyll framed by its own fate:

> For I that danced her on my knee,
>   That watch'd her on her nurse's arm,
>   That shielded all her life from harm,
> At last must part with her to thee;

The presence of the dead surrounds her: "Their pensive tablets round her head." The marriage inscription, by contrast with the "living words of life," takes on an epitaphic cast ("Now sign your names, which shall be read, / Mute symbols of a joyful morn"). And the unavoidable moment of departure, however delayed, is abrupt and final:

> But they must go, the time draws on,
>   And those white-favour'd horses wait;
>   They rise, but linger; it is late;
> Farewell, we kiss, and they are gone.

In the wake of this farewell, the poet is repeatedly shadowed ("A shade falls on us . . . the shade of passing thought") until he is left alone, as in section 95, with the night. But the dark sets off the "shining vapour" of moonlight which moves like the poet's mind to bless his sister's marriage: "And breaking let the splendour fall / To spangle all the happy shores." True to its original sense, the blessing would grant a procreative strength, which yields the consoling figure of the reborn child. Whereas earlier in the poem the poet lamented the absence of linkage, the child now serves to connect "Betwixt us and the crowning race." But as always, the sheer linearity of linkage is modified by the insistence that Hallam had been "a noble type," prefiguring such a race, and that he continues to exist, to "live" as such, "in God." The "one far-off divine event, / To which the whole creation moves," is therefore not exclusively the product of evolution.

It is also the revelation of what has been and of that which is. Along with the elegiac image of vegetative ripening, merged now with the final use of *figura*, the poet draws his friend into the Aeonian music, which, like the poem's extraordinarily long final sentence, seems to envelop in itself the far-off reaches of time to which it points and moves.

Or rather *seems* to move. Like so many of Tennyson's resolutions, the end is a postponement. The final lines not only stave off consummation but seem to fall into a self-involved trance in which motion of any kind is laid to sleep or drugged. The syntactic advance is so exhausting that one tends to collapse upon the final word rather than advance according to its meaning. More precisely, the almost agglutinative caution with which the clauses are attached one to another ensures that the entire mass will move together if it moves at all. The motion is therefore as hard to perceive as that of the globe itself. And for all its splendidly climactic cadence, the poem ends with a suspended approach to, rather than a decisive apprehension of, the "far-off divine event." Certainly, elegies often end with an indication of further movement—the shepherd's rise and departure from the place of song, the uncouth swain's prospect of pastures new, Shelley's self-consuming drive beyond mortality. But these endings usually clinch or go beyond the culmination of the elegiac achievement, whereas *In Memoriam* remains at a long remove from the culmination to which it points. [30] And although the poem ends by creating the illusion that the act of pointing itself may sound or feel like an arrival, the prologue is there, as if it were the poem's true coda, to remind us of the poet's residual and no doubt comforting sense of incompletion in regard to both himself and his elegy:

> Forgive these wild and wandering cries,
>   Confusions of a wasted youth;
>   Forgive them where they fail in truth,
> And in thy wisdom make me wise.

Any appreciation of *In Memoriam* must recognize that its length is essential to its success. With such a burden of skepticism and such a passionate clinging to the empirical and personal, there was little chance of Tennyson's finding genuine consolation in an elegy of conventional length. Only the prolonged accretion, the ebb and flow of inner dialogue, the patient piecing together of visionary fragments, and the necessarily gradual deployment of typology could resist the tremendous counterpressure of melancholy. And yet we may wonder whether too much ground has been ceded to that counterpressure and whether the poem's length robs it of the energetic, processional drive that is so important to elegy. *In Memoriam* does not perform the kind of single, unified ceremony that pretends to accomplish the work of mourning in one action. Reading this poem in fact shows up the importance of the condensation and intense thrust of other elegies—how those poems leave the reader invigorated as well as comforted.

In "Thyrsis," Matthew Arnold, a dogged proponent, if not consistent practioner, of invigorating poetry, tried to deal with problems similar to those faced in *In Memoriam*, but in an elegy of conventional length. "Thyrsis" is, however, equally burdened by the Victorian elegist's almost novelistic fidelity to the empirical details of his own experience and by his need to win some pledge of untransformed personal continuity. Not surprisingly, despite moments of great beauty, the poem falls short of success.

"Thyrsis" neither has ecstatic moments of visionary communion with the dead nor prefigures a world of revealed permanence. Even more markedly than the conclusion of *In Memoriam*, Arnold's poem fails to close the distance between the mourner and a remote state or even sign of consolation. Having momentarily imitated the sequestering flight of the scholar-gypsy, Arnold sees the elm tree, emblem of that patient visionary's survival and hence of Arnold's own survival as a questing poet. But although the tree stands as the figure of survival, Arnold cannot reach it. His power is diminished by a personified nightfall, which, like age, "In ever-nearing circle weaves her shade," "let[ting] down her veil" between the poet and the object of his quest. This veil is no image of the elegist's powers of fabrication. Rather, as in Collins's elegy for Thomson or as in the negative versions of texture in "Adonais," it is the sign of frustrated separation from a more powerful poetic stance: "I cannot reach the signal-tree tonight."

The poem is marked, therefore, by several kinds of debilitating distance. The tree as an explicit emblem is at a remove from its natural identity and its surrounding landscape. As Alan Roper puts it concisely, the tree "ends as arbitrary sign, an allegorical object in a literal landscape."[31] As "allegorical object," the tree is also removed from the supposed gypsy to whom it points. The gypsy, himself waiting and hence separated from the vision he seeks, is derived, moreover, from a book written two centuries before the poem. These starkly allegorical aspects would not in themselves be inappropriate were it not that Arnold has elsewhere so carefully insisted on the more literal setting of the poem, with its attention to missing chimney stacks and its observation of "each, field, each flower, each stick."

It is therefore from a severally removed signal of a figure that Arnold keeps his own distance. There is a faint closing cheer ("happy omen, hail"), and the poet's solace is not insubstantial. But that untraveled ground is a sore symptom of what keeps the poem from a more comforting achievement. It is as though Arnold were reluctant to yield up his recalcitrant personality in favor of an immortal but allegorical identity. And as if to underline this refusal of a truly elegiac displacement, the poet twice invokes the traditions of pastoral elegy only to relegate them (along with the unfortunate Clough) to the realms of the remote and the irrelevant. To this graying elegist of a minutely inventoried rather than invented world the chants of Sicily are as distant, and as mocking, as the world of Death itself, beyond the "unpermitted ferry's flow."

Only by a change of requirements, only by disavowing the melancholy insistence on personality and the skeptical obsession with undisplaced particulars, could the Victorian elegist succeed in anything briefer than the exhaustive length of *In Memoriam*. It is to Hopkins and Swinburne that one may look for an example of such changes, as well as for a renewed success with the genre in its more conventional length. [32]

VIII

Swinburne: "Ave Atque Vale"

As for there being a "movement" or my
being of it, the conception of poetry as
a "pure art" in the sense in which I use
the term, revived with Swinburne.
Pound, "A Retrospect"

In 1866, the year in which Arnold published "Thyrsis," a false report
of the death of Baudelaire reached the young Swinburne. His elegy for
Baudelaire, begun that very year but not published until 1868, the
year following Baudelaire's actual death, occupies precisely the regions of elegiac mythology that Arnold had marginalized in his poem
for Clough. Although he could imagine Clough at ease in "a boon
Southern country . . . / Wandering with the great Mother's train divine," Arnold himself explicity refused to apply that kind of mythology to the concrete world of his own experience. Swinburne,
however, takes his stance, along with such supposed mourners as the
gods Apollo and Venus, in a highly imaginary place. I would like to
understand why Swinburne could do this and to appreciate the terms
on which he accepted and revised the traditions of the genre. By
doing so, I hope not only to explore one of the finest and least
understood elegies in the language but also to trace one of the routes
by which the elegy escaped the Victorian obsession with personality
such as we have seen exemplified by Tennyson and Arnold. [1]

When Swinburne finally withdrew, in 1861, from an erratic career
as a student at Oxford, he must have felt pressed to justify his departure. He had left to pursue a purely literary career, and since the kind
of poetry that he wished to write clashed with the prevailing literary
norms of the time, his desire to vindicate that poetry took on a
programmatic edge. In this year, a revised edition of Baudelaire's Fleurs
du Mal appeared, drawing from the twenty-four-year-old Swinburne a
review, published the next year in The Spectator, that included in its

appreciation a personal manifesto *and* a remarkable act of self-promotion.

The manifesto is straightforward: "A poet's business is presumably to write good verses, and by no means to redeem the age and remould society."[2] For Swinburne, Baudelaire exemplified an intense dedication to art itself rather than to "extraneous matters." Swinburne would also go on to discuss Baudelaire's morality, and in his own poetic career he would embrace political concerns. But for the moment, it is important to look beyond the review's contrast between aesthetic and didactic issues to Swinburne's plea for a restored confidence in the artistic imagination itself. He recognized that the Victorian poet's "meddling" with the "extraneous" was not so much an act of misplaced confidence as a symptom of self-doubt. And it was this legacy of crippling self-doubt that he wished to overcome, choosing instead the fiercer confidence of a Blake or a Shelley or, in his own time, a Baudelaire.

As for the self-promotion, it occurs in the curious reiteration that Baudelaire's excellence as a critic and reviewer heralded his subsequent success as a poet:

> From a critic who has put forward the just and sane view of this matter with a consistent eloquence, one may well expect to get as perfect and careful poetry as he can give. . . . In these early writings [Baudelaire's art criticism of 1845 and 1846] there is already such admirable judgment, vigour of thought and style, and appreciative devotion to the subject, that the worth of his future work in art might have been foretold even then.[3]

Why repeat this if not to suggest a potential identification between Baudelaire and his young admirer and to invite readers to expect a similar course of poetic achievement from the present young critic?

Swinburne's self-association with Baudelaire went beyond either the temporary espousal of aestheticism or the coincidence of a career that began with criticism rather than poetry. Swinburne appreciated the peculiarly spiritual quality of Baudelaire's art. He admired Baudelaire's quest for those situations in which personal passion surpasses human intimacy and in which the apparently idiosyncratic fascination with the macabre or the forbidden reveals itself to be a ritualization of the more than merely personal forces or structures that lie at the heart of the most personal experiences. Above all, Swinburne recognized the relationship between Baudelaire's essentially ascetic, if eroticized, quest and the extremely rigorous formal beauty of the poems. A self-effacing devotion to craft was inseparable from a larger, self-martyring dedication to a highly stylized image of life. After all, human life itself had worth and beauty only as it imitated the attributes of a god, however fallen, however demonic. Art was to be the mirror or theater in which imperfect individuals might perfect a godlike gesture.

In far-reaching ways, therefore, Swinburne regarded Baudelaire as a pioneer and model, and it is with this in mind that we should recognize how fully "Ave Atque Vale" exploits the elegy's generic association with issues of lineage and inheritance. This archaic aspect, together with both Baudelaire's and Swinburne's love for the impersonal forms of ritual and for a poetry *about* such rituals, in part explains the hieratic quality of this elegy. Indeed, Swinburne begins by asking, with reference to the ancient ceremony of floral tributes, what kind of a poem he should appropriately write.

> Shall I strew on thee rose or rue or laurel,
>   Brother, on this that was the veil of thee?
>   Or quiet sea-flower moulded by the sea,
> Or simplest growth of meadow-sweet or sorrel,
>   Such as the summer-sleepy Dryads weave,
>   Waked up by snow-soft sudden rains at eve?
> Or wilt thou rather, as on earth before,
>   Half-faded fiery blossoms, pale with heat
>   And full of bitter summer, but more sweet
> To thee than gleanings of a northern shore
>   Trod by no tropic feet?[4]

A brief note, first, on the form of this and other stanzas of the poem. As the indentation and rhyme scheme emphasize, each stanza has two matching quatrains rhymed *abba* and *deed*. These are separated by an intervening couplet, and the entire stanza is rounded off by an abbreviated line rhyming with the *ee* couplet. Profuse alliteration and assonance, together with an unusual degree of rhythmic variation, add to the effect of ingenious craftsmanship. Such a highly wrought form does more, however, than demonstrate the virtuosity of a poet who is admittedly aspiring to follow a great master. As already suggested, the technical constraints are important elements not only of this mourner's necessary self-discipline but of his and his subject's devotion to the stylized impersonality of ceremonial art. Beyond these general features, the form has specifically elegiac properties.

The indentations provide the antiphonal effect of ancient elegiac chants—an effect enhanced by the quatrains' counterpoise on either side of the near-choral couplet. More minutely, the indentations, together with the shifts between feminine and masculine endings in the first quatrains of each stanza, resemble the metrical structure of the Greek elegiacs, in which a dactylic hexameter was followed by a pentameter line with a masculine close. As with the metrical shifts within lines, these shifts contribute greatly to the poem's overall play with questions of resolution. So, too, the final line hovers between a stoical reining in on the one hand and a poignant echo and appeal to further lengthenings on the other. Its abbreviation emphasizes both the abrupt falling silent that the poem laments and the elegiac act of persistently renewed mourning with which every following stanza continues.

Swinburne begins his poem with far more than a straightforward question about the propriety of northern versus southern or Mediterranean verse. By asking his specific question, and by doing so with such elaboration, the poet carries himself eleven lines beyond the more general and more difficult problem of how to begin at all. Similarly, the proliferation of alternatives (six within the first four lines) distracts the mourner from the troubling question of whom or what he addresses and from the puzzling nature of the object onto which he would "strew" his offering. For even as the question creates the illusion of a present "thee," there is the disconcerting slip from "thee" to "this," from Baudelaire to a veil. By dwelling on the diversity of flowers, Swinburne postpones the poem's crucial confrontation with this precise issue, the substitution of a veil for a now absent person. The rich flourishing of alternatives is itself already an instance of the kind of fabricated masking whose necessity the poem will go on to define.

Of course the strewing of flowers, or, figuratively, of elegiac poetry, is an extremely conventional act, redolent of vegetation rituals and the origins of the genre. What is most interesting here is the ease with which Swinburne acts out the convention. Unlike Tennyson and Arnold, who insistently foregrounded their own empirical environment and experience, Swinburne has little difficulty in allegorizing his project. Performing the gesture, he becomes any mourner—indeed, the figure of a mourner. The facility with which he does this relies, as we shall see, on an idea of the poet as a participant in a community of poets who sing and have sung with the same voice. Hence, too, the assurance with which he addresses Baudelaire as "brother," although the exact nature of their shared parentage is still to be established.

Already Swinburne thus demonstrates a reduction or displacement of the self to a figured mouthpiece of song, a reduction that looks away from the Victorian morass of personality toward the aesthetics of impersonality later pursued by Pound, Eliot, Joyce, and in certain respects Yeats. As he would express it more explicitly in his highly mythologized spiritual autobiography, "Thalassius,"

> And with his heart again
> The tidal throb of all the tides keep rhyme
> And charm him from his own soul's separate sense
> . . . .
> . . . . .
> Being now no more a singer, but a song.
>
> (*Works*, 3: 302)

As Oscar Wilde confirmed, "He is the first lyric poet who has tried to make an absolute surrender of his own personality, and he has succeeded. We hear the song, but never know the singer."[5]

Looking more closely at the actual kinds of flowers / poetry from which Swinburne chooses in his first stanza, we note a deliberate preference for the Baudelairean varieties. The quatrain describing these has none of the multiplied alternatives that weakened the claims of all the earlier candidates, marked as those were by an air of open possibilities, a gentle, near-Edenic summer drowsiness in which even the rain is snowlike only in its softness, not in its cold. By contrast, the "half-faded fiery blossoms, pale with heat" indicate Baudelaire's and Swinburne's revision of the pastoral clichés. Here, the world of pastoral is made harsh; luxuriousness and sweetness are crossed with fervor and astringency. Furthermore, these southern flowers are more truly elegiac than the easily woven garlands of the north, for they are all reliquary, bearing the marks of a withering passion. They are the products of an artificer who has exhausted and turned away from the simple yield of the natural world. Both senses of the phrase "tropic feet" are thus relevant. Interestingly enough, Swinburne's description of these blossoms suggests that he may somehow span both north and south, that he may be among the first ever to tread on his cold shores with tropic feet.

Swinburne pursues the momentum of the first stanza by an explanatory conjunction that carries him far beyond mere explanation:

For always thee the fervid languid glories
    Allured of heavier suns in mightier skies;
    Thine ears krew all the wandering watery sighs
Where the sea sobs round Lesbian promontories,
    The barren kiss of piteous wave to wave
    That knows not where is that Leucadian grave
Which hides too deep the supreme head of song.
    Ah, salt and sterile as her kisses were,
    The wild sea winds her and the green gulfs bear
Hither and thither, and vex and work her wrong,
    Blind gods that cannot spare.

As though elaborating on Baudelaire's preference, Swinburne moves here into the kind of recollective celebration that is so typical of the early passages of an elegy. But the account is strikingly impersonal and figurative; and it rapidly refocuses on yet another, anterior object of mourning, Sappho. The displacement is certainly legitimized by Baudelaire's own fascination and empathy with Sappho, but the speed with which it is made is provocative. Partly, the fluent association hints at a deeper identity between such poets as Baudelaire and Sappho, an identity that Swinburne will explore later in the poem. For the moment, he does, however, insinuate one important element of such an identity. Baudelaire has a mourner's intimate knowledge of a mournful sea that grieves for Sappho, herself a passionate griever. The further connection with the presently mourning Swinburne implies not just the bond between all three but a certain relation between poetry itself and grief, between song and separation. Paradoxically, these poets are connected most by their passionate responses to disconnection.

The stanza also moves quickly from a celebration of totemic powers ("heavier suns in mightier skies" and "Thine ears knew . . . ") to a bitter outcry against a harshly castrative fate. Our study of the elegy at large helps us to appreciate the significance and aptness of this development. As we have often recognized, the experience of loss has at its core a castrative separation from an original matrix, a separation that any mourner is called upon to repeat. Despite her "salt and sterile. . . .kisses," Sappho represents an image of one such matrix, particularly in her close association with the sea. Apart from designating a relation between Baudelaire and Sappho, Swinburne is now repeating a form of the anterior loss. By a complex play of images, he represents that loss even while he displaces it onto Sappho herself, an instance of the previously mentioned strategy by which a child attempts to reverse and in fact avenge its abandonment. Here, then, a castrative separation from the mother is represented as the mother's own fate. Describing Sappho in these terms, Swinburne therefore mourns his own loss of "knowledge," his own sterility or vulnerability to blind gods, his own separation from the hidden head and source of song. The scenario is close to that in "Lycidas," with its blind Fury, and helpless mother-Muse, its "gory visage" of a dismembered Orpheus, and its sunken head of Lycidas. Swinburne's "which hides too deep the supreme head of song" is astonishingly close in content, meter, and syntax to Milton's "That sunk so low that sacred head of thine." In both instances, the elegist submits to a harshly chastening loss, without which no figure for what survives can be invented.

Returning to his celebration of Baudelaire, Swinburne focuses again on the poet's totemic faculties, this time of sight:

> Thou sawest, in thine old singing season, brother,
>> Secrets and sorrows unbeheld of us:
>> Fierce loves, and lovely leaf-buds poisonous,
> Bare to thy subtler eye, but for none other
>> Blowing by night in some unbreathed-in clime;
>> The hidden harvest of luxurious time,
> Sin without shape, and pleasure without speech;
>> And where strange dreams in a tumultuous sleep
>> Make the shut eyes of stricken spirits weep;
> And with each face thou sawest the shadow on each,
>> Seeing as men sow men reap.

Baudelaire's subtler eye perceived subjects "bare" for him alone, existing in a forbidden region where breathlessness and a tumultuous sleep marked a world like that of death itself. Coming after the second stanza, with its dark stress on what death hides, this emphasis on a faculty that sees beyond the limits of the apparent, natural world suggests that Baudelaire had the kind of vision that might have seen the supreme head of song. Similarly, Baudelaire had prophetically envisioned what lay in store for each person after life. Within this praise, however, one senses the troubled celebration of the martyr, one whose privileged intimacy with the head of song and with the realm of death required his own ruin. The celebration of totemic power is thus harshly qualified in this stanza, ending as it does with a grimly ambiguous harvest. The poem has yet to establish the terms, if any, on which a poet has access to such sights beyond the tomb.

The fourth stanza conjures an almost mesmerizing image of death as consummation and release:

> O sleepless heart and sombre soul unsleeping,
>> That were athirst for sleep and no more life
>> And no more love, for peace and no more strife!
> Now the dim gods of death have in their keeping
>> Spirit and body and all the springs of song,
>> Is it well now where love can do no wrong,
> Where stingless pleasure has no foam or fang
>> Behind the unopening closure of her lips?
>> Is it not well where soul from body slips
> And flesh from bone divides without a pang
>> As dew from flower-bell drips?

Death brings the desired extinction of desire, in a region where both spirit and body are gathered together with the springs of song. But despite their ease, these lines seem burdened by contradiction. When the definition of pleasure or beauty has already been so inextricably entwined with bitter passion, the undoing of that bond now seems to unravel the existence of pleasure and beauty themselves. Although "pleasure has no foam or fang," that consolation is surely offset by the image of her lips' "unopening closure." The complex enjoyments of the living seem here to have been drastically replaced by the anaesthesia of the dead.

A further ambiguity marks the final three lines. Again, the general impression is that of exquisite release, a blissful dissolution of opposites that had been bound together. But the identities of these separating elements are themselves hard to distinguish. The conjunction "soul from body slips / And flesh from bone divides" invites a puzzling association of soul and flesh. The association is then advanced and complicated by the simile "As dew from flower-bell drips." "As dew" compares the flesh to a traditional symbol of distilled purity, thus strengthening its curious association with the soul. Yet, as we know, dew came to represent spiritual purity only by an "upward" revision of its originally physical association with seminal power. By elaborating his simile "from flower-bell drips," Swinburne forcibly reminds us of this physical origin. This reminder, together with the above conjunction of soul and body, suggests that Swinburne is in fact revising the image of the soul downward to its originally sexual referent. Unlike many Victorian poets, Swinburne could point with confidence to some transpersonal element of identity, but only by returning to a distinctly pagan ideology. The poem itself will spell out the particulars of this revision.

In addition to its curious ambiguities, its images of depleted pleasure and deliquescent flesh, the fourth stanza is cast in the form of a repeated, almost taunting question. The condition of the dead may, after all, exist only as it is posited by the questions of the living. And although Swinburne moves by way of a partial self-rebuke ("It is enough") toward the less interrogative mode of the fifth stanza, his answer tends almost entirely to diminish the implied powers or satisfied repose of the dead. Here, for the first time, the dead poet is shown, by a series of negations, to lack the powers of his survivor—sight, hearing, touch, speech, and thought:

> It is enough; the end and the beginning
>   Are one thing to thee, who art past the end.
>   O hand unclasped of unbeholden friend,
> For thee no fruits to pluck, no palms for winning,
>   No triumph and no labour and no lust,
>   Only dead yew-leaves and a little dust.
> O quiet eyes wherein the light saith nought,
>   Whereto the day is dumb, nor any night
>   With obscure finger silences your sight,
> Nor in your speech the sudden soul speaks thought,
>   Sleep, and have sleep for light.

While the repeated negations pursue the mourner's early task of testing reality, they also eliminate the possibility that the elegist may have been guessing what the dead now see. With the dead so thoroughly stripped of senses, we recoil on the living poet as the sole envisioner of a world beyond the grave. Cataloguing the deprivations of the dead, the mourner thus accrues a power of his own, a power to pluck, win, triumph, labor, and lust, even while he is forced to recognize, with sharpened skepticism, the fabricated, hypothetical nature of his questions and replies. Of course he is also continuing his work

of self-limitation. The unclasped hand of Baudelaire implies the un-
clasping hand of Swinburne—a debility to be repaired later in the
poem. The unseen implies the unseeing friend, and Swinburne's attention to his own or any living person's repeated loss of sight allows
another elegiac submission, to the "obscure finger" of night. Even as
he confers sleep on Baudelaire, the poet's own disquietude prompts
him to question the dead man further.

> Now all strange hours and all strange loves are over,
>   Dreams and desires and sombre songs and sweet,
>   Hast thou found place at the great knees and feet
> Of some pale Titan-woman like a lover,
>   Such as thy vision here solicited,
>   Under the shadow of her fair vast head,
> The deep division of prodigious breasts,
>   The solemn slope of mighty limbs asleep,
>   The weight of awful tresses that still keep
> The savour and shade of old-world pine-forests
>   Where the wet hill-winds weep?
>
> Hast thou found any likeness for thy vision?
>   O gardener of strange flowers, what bud, what bloom
>   Hast thou found sown, what gathered in the gloom?
> What of despair, of rapture, of derision,
>   What of life is there, what of ill or good?
>   Are the fruits grey like dust or bright like blood?
> Does the dim ground grow any seed of ours,
>   The faint fields quicken any terrene root,
>   In low lands where the sun and moon are mute
> And all the stars keep silence? Are there flowers
>   At all, or any fruit?

If the origin of consoling visions is the imagination of the living
poet alone, can such a poet's imaginative solicitations be rewarded
after death? In Baudelaire's case, will he be united with the giantess for
whom he had so eloquently yearned in his poem "La Géante"? The
allusion to Baudelaire's poem, like the earlier reference to Sappho, is
the kind of tribute and memorial that an elegist may aptly make to an
admired poet. But it inevitably invites the reader to compare Swinburne's treatment of the giantess with Baudelaire's. An undertone of
contest, or at least of notified succession, therefore marks the passage,
making it especially appropriate to Swinburne's elegy.

It is not easy to adjudicate between "La Géante" and Swinburne's stanza. Each has a splendid combination of hypnotic languor and disciplined craft, of highly artificial language that is nonetheless uncannily allied to the natural cadence of the poet's desire. Swinburne has conjured up the giantess as graphically and with perhaps a more indulgent sensuality than did Baudelaire. But Swinburne's evocation is, after all, framed as a question, thus submitting Baudelaire's original to the scrutiny of the later poet's skepticism. To query the fulfillment is to undermine, however slightly, the expression of the desire, drawing attention to the rhetoric of its fantasy rather than to the repose whose *image* that fantasy engenders. Even as he imitates Baudelaire, Swinburne, therefore, persists in privileging himself. In particular, he stresses his peculiar wakefulness as opposed to the sleep that Baudelaire enjoys, as we noted earlier, only at the cost of a diminished power. For the first time in the poem, Swinburne has now insinuated a certain edge over the living as well as over the dead Baudelaire. Does Swinburne know more than Baudelaire knew regarding the impossibility of fulfilling one's desire, even in death? In general, I would say no. But this specific instance seems designed to have us answer in Swinburne's favor. He has both given and taken away—a typically elegiac gesture that he will continue to perform.

The description of the giantess is itself perfectly appropriate to an elegy. The female figure returns us to that of Sappho earlier in the poem, addressing once again that instance of original loss but now offering some vision of redress. So immense as to invite comparison with landscape, the giantess is clearly both the mother and the earth, the matrix to which the martyred vegetation deity returns—the Muse, the womb, a version of what we have elsewhere called the primary object for which all mourners are compelled to mourn again. She is the idealized maternal figure for whom so many elegists have sought and to whose protective presence so many have desired to return.

Thus Swinburne allows a representation of primary desire to emerge—as it must do—in his elegy. Yet as we know, the elegist must somehow also query or control such a desire. And Swinburne does this not just by his already implied skepticism but by the details of his description. Unlike Baudelaire, he calls the giantess a "Titan-woman," hence pointing to her fallen stature. She is herself a figure of loss. She evokes a landscape marked by weeping winds. Even her breasts, the source of nurturing power and the conventional site of calm union, are threateningly "prodigious" and marked by a "deep division." By such details, combined with a general atmosphere of gloom and awe, Swinburne continues to perform a crucial stage of the work of mourning, chastening his desire for a straightforward union such as that between child and mother. Choosing, however sadly, the detours of survival, he seeks to undermine or exorcise the erotic attractions of regression and death.

In the seventh stanza, Swinburne asks with explicit skepticism the question implied in the preceding lines. What can the words of the living evoke in the world of the dead? Can any language exist there? Will a poet find some testimony of his achievement there? If not—if poetic language cannot generate a likeness of itself "over there"— does this also mean that poetry cannot offer here, among the living, persuasive images of the dead? Is there to be no transfer of language between worlds, even at the level of imaginary representations? The extreme urgency with which Swinburne poses his question suggests a sad wisdom regarding the answers. And the following two stanzas pursue this wisdom yet more harshly:

> Alas, but though my flying song flies after,
>   O sweet strange elder singer, thy more fleet
>   Singing, and footprints of thy fleeter feet,
> Some dim derision of mysterious laughter
>   From the blind tongueless warders of the dead,
>   Some gainless glimpse of Proserpine's veiled head,
> Some little sound of unregarded tears
>   Wept by effaced unprofitable eyes,
>   And from pale mouths some cadence of dead sighs—
> These only, these the hearkening spirit hears,
>   Sees only such things rise.

> Thou art far too far for wings of words to follow,
>   Far too far off for thought or any prayer.
>   What ails us with thee, who art wind and air?
> What ails us gazing where all seen is hollow?
>   Yet with some fancy, yet with some desire,
>   Dreams pursue death as winds a flying fire,
> Our dreams pursue our dead and do not find.
>   Still, and more swift than they, the thin flame flies,
>   The low light fails us in elusive skies,
> Still the foiled earnest ear is deaf, and blind
>   Are still the eluded eyes.

For the first time since the second stanza, the tone of bitter anger returns. Significantly, this attends the poet's more contemptuous application to himself of the limitations he was presenting above. Just as Baudelaire's poetry cannot penetrate or take root in the next world, so Swinburne's cannot gather anything but mockery from that too distant region.

The manner in which Swinburne expresses this reveals that here, in these two stanzas, the elegist is performing the most drastic action of his work. Both stanzas accumulate imagery of blindness, deafness, and muteness, coupled with derided futility. In addition, there is the "veiled head" of Proserpine, enforcing yet another separation between the poet and a mourned or solicited female figure. Even more explicitly than in the cases of Sappho or the giantess, it is the veil of mediation itself that envelops the head and keeps the questor at bay. This, coupled with the images of general impotence, confirms that the moment is one not merely of self-mockery but rather of crucial self-curbing. Swinburne is repeating the essentially mournful decision to live, renouncing, as he must, the dream of unmediated union, whether with the dead or with a prior object of desire. Hence the images of voluntary symbolic impotence, accompanied by the presence of the veil. And having brought to a decisive and more personal close the long process of renunciation, among whose objects we have already counted Sappho and the Titaness, Swinburne can now move from withdrawal to reattachment. Here, at the very midpoint of his poem and of his work of mourning, he is finally prepared to accept a substitute for what he can neither grasp nor unveil. The chosen substitute appears to be the very material that intervenes, the veil itself:

> Not thee, O never thee, in all time's changes,
>   Not thee, but this the sound of thy sad soul,
>   The shadow of thy swift spirit, this shut scroll
> I lay my hand on, and not death estranges
>   My spirit from communion of thy song—
>   These memories and these melodies that throng
> Veiled porches of a Muse funereal—
>   These I salute, these touch, these clasp and fold
>   As though a hand were in my hand to hold,
> Or through mine ears a mourning musical
>   Of many mourners rolled.

With unusual emphasis and condensation, the first two lines enact the turn at the heart of any elegy: "Not thee . . . but this." . . . Despite the plangency of that repeated negative apostrophe, the very clearness and economy of the turn from personal to impersonal pronoun suggests much of Swinburne's freedom from the retarding Victorian obsession with personal survival. Admittedly, the act of substitution is notably similar to that of *In Memoriam*, section 95. But whereas Tennyson went beyond the actual letters to a moment of mystical reunion with Hallam, Swinburne remains resolutely with the scroll itself. The swell of compensatory verbs—*Salute, touch, clasp, fold*—may seem to redress the privations listed in stanzas 7–9. But the object of these verbs is only the sound, the shadow, the shut scroll, never the hand. The "As though" reminds us not just of the difference but of the fact that such a difference is precisely that of figuration itself. "As though" indicates the distance through which the mourner has turned. The act and fabric of that figuration lie between him and the dead. Swinburne holding the shut scroll could be Pan with the hollow reeds of Syrinx, or Apollo with his token of cut laurel.

The scroll is, of course, also the melodies that "throng / Veiled porches of a Muse funereal." The previously frustrating images of veiling are now redefined. Here, the veil is almost indistinguishable from the throng of memorial melodies, a throng from which death cannot estrange the living poet. It is a cunning formulation. Narrowly speaking, Baudelaire's death cannot keep Swinburne from the former's poems. But by choosing to write "not death" without specifying a particular death, Swinburne implies some larger victory over death itself—a victory that the poet himself seems to enjoy, achieving an immunity, even a version of immortality, as his *spirit* communes with the undying songs.

As in the ancient mysteries, the bewildered, even humiliated, initiate recognizes the tokens of his own immortality. As we shall see more explicitly in what follows, Swinburne's notion of immortality depends on his attitude toward poetry. For Swinburne, the spirit of poetry *is* the spirit of man. Thus the elegist's "spirit" emerges in stanza 10 as he recognizes the immortality of verse. The previously "foiled earnest ear" is repaired as it becomes a chamber for preceding music. Clearly, Swinburne is now commenting on his own elegy—the hand that holds the scroll in true communion is the hand that writes; the ear hears a medleyed music scarcely distinguishable from its own inventions.

In a manner already seen most fully in the Neoclassical elegies, Swinburne is here creating a sense of himself as a medium or persona for a voice or voices that transcend him. The simultaneous humbling and enlargement of the self is, of course, characteristic of the genre; but the purity of Swinburne's blend of submission and confidence, his assumption of a more than narrowly personal stance, is a crucial element that other Victorian elegies either lacked entirely or achieved with too much reluctance:

> I among these, I also, in such station
> > As when the pyre was charred, and piled the sods,
> > And offering to the dead made, and their gods,
> The old mourners had, standing to make libation,
> > I stand, and to the gods and to the dead
> > Do reverence without prayer or praise, and shed
> Offering to these unknown, the gods of gloom,
> > And what of honey and spice my seedlands bear,
> > And what I may of fruits in this chilled air,
> And lay, Orestes-like, across the tomb
> > A curl of severed hair.

The opening, with its repeated "I," contrasts boldly with the repeatedly denied "thee" of the previous stanza. Indeed, we suspect that the actual substitute for the lost Baudelaire may be the elegist himself. This would be fair, provided that we see the elegist correctly, not merely as the man, Swinburne, but as the representative poet-mourner possessed by an undying language not exclusively his own. Hence this moment of extreme hieraticism, together with the poet's emphatic placement of himself among other ritual mourners from ancient times. He takes on a timeless, deliberately Classical stance, as though he were a survivor from those times—the surviving voice of elegy itself.

And yet, just as the elegy or poetry at large has not continued unchanged, Swinburne diverges from those earlier mourners. He does reverence "without prayer or praise"; the gods of gloom are unknown to him; his seedlands may not necessarily yield the honey and spice of earlier times. The precise difference is not spelled out beyond a hinted diminution and lost certainty, mingled as these are, however, with a certain freedom and independence. It is difficult to distinguish modesty from pride, so successfully compounded are the tones. So too, the self-comparison with Orestes is glorifying, but we recognize the gesture of elegiac, filial submission in the offered lock. Swinburne's choice of Orestes is provocative, and in the light of the next stanza's denial, we must explore what lies behind the comparison.

But by no hand nor any treason stricken,
　　Not like the low-lying head of Him, the King,
　　The flame that made of Troy a ruinous thing,
Thou liest and on this dust no tears could quicken
　　There fall no tears like theirs that all men hear
　　Fall tear by sweet imperishable tear
Down the opening leaves of holy poets' pages.
　　Thee not Orestes, not Electra mourns;
　　But bending us-ward with memorial urns
The most high Muses that fulfil all ages
　　Weep, and our God's heart yearns.

Why Orestes and Electra? No doubt partly because they are among the most heroic grievers in Classical literature. But beyond this, they were revengers. For them, mourning itself was not sufficient. Now we have noted repeatedly that elegists must find ways of venting and surpassing vengeful anger. Swinburne does this by imitating Orestes and by immediately rejecting that model as inappropriate. He thus expresses and outdistances his own anger. But the precise terms of this comparison and of its treatment need to be uncovered. Orestes was a thwarted, disinherited son. For a moment, we may see Swinburne, imitating a would-be heir, vowing angrily to take revenge against his rightful predecessor's enemies—enemies such as those established critics and poets who had condemned and usurped the position of Baudelaire. (Swinburne's review had mentioned "the foolish and shameless prosecution" of Fleurs du Mal.) And yet this reading has to be corrected almost as quickly as it was formed.

Unlike Agamemnon, Baudelaire was not betrayed. This admission removes a charge of guilt, thereby freeing the mourner both from his own potential association with that guilt and from the burden of revenge. The picture of the dead Agamemnon is, however, highly suggestive, not least for its disqualifying frame. As though released by its allegedly negative relation to Baudelaire, the picture of the "low-lying head of Him, the King," raises the question of Swinburne's motive for describing this fall, particularly in such language. For a young poet, the death of a master, especially one from whom he seeks to inherit power, must provide an element of gratification, however ambivalent. And since that young poet's elegy for the master has already mourned the unavailability of the mother matrix, it is not impossible to imagine some resentful desire to lay the head of "Him, the King," as low as that of the lost Sappho or the veiled Persephone.

Unable to express this desire directly in relation to Baudelaire, Swinburne displaces it to Agamemnon, and he further distances that very
displacement by denying the force of the comparison. And despite
the suggested goodwill toward Baudelaire, this disclaimer goes on to
admit that no tears of the present mourner can quicken the dead man's
dust. If this is an aspect of necessary modesty and submission, it also
keeps the dead king down. Indeed, Swinburne's focus soon reveals
itself to be very much on the mourner and the company he keeps
rather than on the mourned.

It is not easy to say exactly by whom Orestes and Electra are
replaced. Are they replaced by "us," as the Muses bend our way
instead of toward Orestes? Or are the Muses themselves the replacement? Despite its awkwardness ("us-ward"), the confusion is significant, pushing toward a suggested closeness between the elegist and
the Muses. And the ambiguity of the final line (is it the heart of our
God, or do we yearn with a God's heart?) presses home the association
between human and divine mourners. It is entirely appropriate for an
elegy to center this connection on the heart, for as we have seen,
ancient elegiac rituals often focused on such an organ as a figure for
the surviving and resurrective element of the martyred god—a god,
moreover, with whom disciples might at moments of intense devotion
become identified. The following two stanzas explore the possibility
of just such an identification:

> For, sparing of his sacred strength, not often
>   Among us darkling here the lord of light
>   Makes manifest his music and his might
> In hearts that open and in lips that soften
>   With the soft flame and heat of songs that shine.
>   Thy lips indeed he touched with bitter wine,
> And nourished them indeed with bitter bread;
>   Yet surely from his hand thy soul's food came,
>   The fire that scarred thy spirit at his flame
> Was lighted, and thine hungering heart he fed
>   Who feeds our hearts with fame.
>
> Therefore he too now at thy soul's sunsetting,
>   God of all suns and songs, he too bends down
>   To mix his laurel with thy cypress crown,
> And save thy dust from blame and from forgetting.

Therefore he too, seeing all thou wert and art,
Compassionate, with sad and sacred heart,
Mourns thee of many his children the last dead,
And hallows with strange tears and alien sighs
Thine unmelodious mouth and sunless eyes,
And over thine irrevocable head
Sheds light from the under skies.

These stanzas clearly consolidate an identification between Apollo and the dead poet, as well as between the god and the elegist through whose "strange tears and alien sighs" he mourns. The terms of the identification are spelled out in the celebration of Baudelaire. For Swinburne, certain poets incarnate Apollo's heat and light in the passionate radiance of their work. The imagery of the sun and of sacred strength returns us to the physical origins of all spiritual images. And in a sense Swinburne is trying to return the Christian imagery to its pagan sources. The Eucharist and the refining fires are reinterpreted as Apollo's nourishment of a poet's soul—a soul that somehow comes into being by a combination of fame-hungering heart and divinely ignited spirit.

In a manner reminiscent of primitive mourners' ingestion of the dead god, incarnation occurs by way of the poet's feeding on divine attributes, imaged as bread and wine, or in less vegetal versions, fame and fire. Swinburne is proposing an ancient definition of the soul as a physical entity, a burning strength that derives from the god of heat and light. And although Swinburne is clearly describing a poetic strength, that strength is not far removed from its originally sexual definition. Indeed, it could be regarded as the genetically immortal strength of the father-god, passed on to such of his "children" as Baudelaire or, by implication, Swinburne.

Espousing neither Christianity nor Neo-Platonism, Swinburne finds his way back to transpersonal notions of genius and of the soul. Once again, he moves past the Victorian obsession with personality, providing a crucial link between Shelley's self-purifying idealism and such post-Victorian cultivators of impersonality as Eliot and Pound. The curious physicality of Swinburne's notion shows clearly in his following statement, as well as in the subsequent conjecture from Pound: "But the life that lives forever in the work of all great poets has in it the sap, the blood, the seed derived from the living and everlasting word of their fathers who were before them."[6] "It is more than

221

likely that the brain itself is, in origin and development, only a sort of great clot of genital fluid held in suspense or reserve . . . as a maker or presenter of images."[7]

We have seen how often an elegist's consolation depends on his celebration of and subsequent association with the power of the father. By his elaborate mention of divine nourishment and of the elegiac motifs of ingestion and inheritance, Swinburne has done more than merely succeed Baudelaire. Associated with Apollo, the father of Baudelaire, Swinburne figuratively takes on the powers of paternity, pronouncing a benediction on the dead the way a father might bless a child. "From the underskies," he sheds his admittedly lower portion of Apollo's own light. And pursuing this traditionally elegiac evocation of parental figures, Swinburne introduces Venus, Apollo's and now his consort in mourning.

> And one weeps with him in the ways Lethean,
>   And stains with tears her changing bosom chill:
>   That obscure Venus of the hollow hill,
> That thing transformed which was the Cytherean,
>   With lips that lost their Grecian laugh divine
>   Long since, and face no more called Erycine;
> A ghost, a bitter and luxurious god.
>   Thee also with fair flesh and singing spell
>   Did she, a sad and second prey, compel
> Into the footless places once more trod,
>   And shadows hot from hell.

Swinburne may thus have reassociated himself with both parental figures. But by a movement that again underlines the relation between the work of mourning and the oedipal resolution, Swinburne had identified with the father while forcefully rejecting or redefining his attachment to the mother. He can associate with Venus, but only in her present form, that is, only as she represents and bears the disfiguring marks of a *rejected* sexual appeal. This is not Venus Aphrodite or Venus of Erice but rather "that thing transformed," the Venus Horselberg, to which she has been reduced by a harshly repressive puritanism. The image of a perpetually stained and changing bosom puts the breast beneath the intervening print of grief while subjecting it to a process like the substitution or transformation by which the mourner turns from its original presence.

Exiled from her once natural pursuits, Venus has come to be perceived as an imprisoned and imprisoning seductress whose victims
labor in a passion of sterile fantasy. This portrait is in part designed to
expose and attack the barren, anti-pagan and anti-carnal prejudice of
the Judaeo-Christian tradition, particularly in its narrow, Victorian
phase. But the bitter anger and form of the attack surely flows from the
elegist's unavoidable submission to the very quelling of sexual energy
and of physical attachment that he mourns. Venus Horselberg may be
the product of a system that Swinburne detests, but she is the only
form in which he can refabricate the association that he desires. She is
his muse. Like Tannhauser and Baudelaire, Swinburne devotes himself
to the "barren" pursuit of images in the chilly precincts of Venus's
"hollow hill," the insatiable vacancy that represents the region of
poetic work itself.

The following stanza confirms this revision—one more in the
history of the genre—by which not only the images of consolation
but also the figure of the lost mother-lover-Muse is reinterpreted.
From her appearance as Aphrodite in the elegies of Theocritus, Bion,
and Moschus to Spenser's Neo-Platonic revision of her in "Astrophel"
or Jonson's Christian version of her as Mary in "On My First
Daughter", and from the helpless mother of Orpheus in "Lycidas" to
the veiled and ineffectual Urania in "Adonais" or the absorbed, self-
mirroring virgin and the finally surrendered bride of *In Memoriam*, the
Venus figure has been a crucial and continually evolving presence
throughout the genre's development. Swinburne's is one of the most
passionate, yet purely literary, of these reinterpretations:

> And now no sacred staff shall break in blossom,
>> No choral salutation lure to light
>> A spirit sick with perfume and sweet night
> And love's tired eyes and hands and barren bosom.
>> There is no help for these things; none to mend
>> And none to mar; not all our songs, O friend,
> Will make death clear or make life durable.
>> Howbeit with rose and ivy and wild vine
>> And with wild notes about this dust of thine
> At least I fill the place where white dreams dwell
>> And wreathe an unseen shrine.

This Venus represents no fertile matrix of recurrent natural life.
Nor can Swinburne offer, as in the Tannhauser legend, a spiritualized

version of that fertility. Baudelaire can function neither as a straight-forward vegetation deity nor as a Christian martyr. In contrast to the demands of nature or of faith, the hollow of Venus demands an even more heroic gift—an expense of passion and creativity that is made with no expectation of reward. To resurrect or redeem the giver would diminish the self-consuming generosity of his life's work. Swinburne insists that instead of a compensatory flowering of nature or belief, there can be only the barren wreath of a surviving poet's art.

And yet, in rendering powerless the conventional means of conso-lation, Swinburne's lines take on a definite authority of their own. The three lines at the center of the stanza ("There is no help . . . or make life durable"), with their steady balance of phrasing, their inserted apostrophe, and their limpid diction, underlie the poet's dignified search for an accurate as well as emotionally satisfying response. And the gesture in the last four lines is beautifully elegiac in its manner of assertion. After all the negations, the "Howbeit . . . " has the force of indomitable resistance, a dim echo of the satanic "What though the field be lost?" Of course, it follows closely the elegiac setting aside of untenable attachments in favor of a substitute—the precise movement of the tenth stanza's "Not thee . . . but this." Once again, it is the fabric of poetry that provides the new attachment, a fabric that is skeptically yet heroically held up against a clearly recognized absence or obscurity. Swinburne is now imitating Baudelaire's passionate devo-tion to the vacancy of Venus's tomblike region. And having reinforced the closeness between his own pursuit and Baudelaire's work, in the following stanza Swinburne moves yet further, to a consoling identifi-cation with the former powers of the dead poet.

> Sleep; and if life was bitter to thee, pardon,
>> If sweet, give thanks; thou hast no more to live;
>> And to give thanks is good, and to forgive.
> Out of the mystic and the mournful garden
>> Where all day through thine hands in barren braid
>> Wove the sick flowers of secrecy and shade,
> Green buds of sorrow and sin, and remnants grey,
>> Sweet-smelling, pale with poison, sanguine-hearted,
>> Passions that sprang from sleep and thoughts that
>> started,
> Shall death not bring us all as thee one day
>> Among the days departed?

Swinburne returns to the fifth stanza's mode of benedictory address, this time with the assurance of a mourner who has clearly established the limits and value of his offering. The benediction is, however, the minor burden of this stanza, whose true object is to make at least three claims on behalf of Swinburne himself: that he has, after all, inhabited the unearthly garden previously reserved for Baudelaire alone; that the wreathing of his tribute resembles and succeeds the barren braid of his master; and that he too will return to "the days departed." For a poet like Baudelaire, who defined lyric poetry as "un retour vers l'Eden perdu," this last promise is genuinely rewarding. [8] And the idea of sharing not only the poetic life but the restitutive fate of Baudelaire was no small claim for Swinburne to make. The tone of resignation and the philosophical musing on a universal human destiny serve well to introduce the final stanza of the poem. Here the benediction comes into its own.

> For thee, O now a silent soul, my brother,
>> Take at my hands this garland, and farewell.
>> Thin is the leaf, and chill the wintry smell,
> And chill the solemn earth, a fatal mother,
>> With sadder than the Niobean womb,
>> And in the hollow of her breasts a tomb.
> Content thee, howso'er, whose days are done;
>> There lies not any troublous thing before,
>> Nor sight nor sound to war against thee more,
> For whom all winds are quiet as the sun,
>> All waters as the shore.

The *ave atque vale* from Catullus reaffirms Swinburne's consistent attempt to adopt a "mourning musical of many mourners." With this most dignified expression, at once fraternal and formal, he continues to elevate both Baudelaire and himself to the timeless region of such gestures. And yet the revisionary impulse is at work here as elsewhere in the poem. Catullus had addressed his actual brother. For Swinburne to call Baudelaire his brother is, however, a right earned only by Swinburne's particular establishment of a metaphorical parentage and of a figurative relationship between the poets. This project is still very much at work in the final stanza's inclusion of the Niobean earth, mother of Baudelaire and hence also of Swinburne.

With relentless consistency, however, Swinburne again refuses to accept on easy terms the consolatory aspect of another maternal figure. Just as he qualified the garland as thin and chilly, so the earth mother is little more than a barren and wintry setting for a tomb. She is Ovid's petrified figure of inconsolable grief. Associated with Venus Horselberg and with the Titaness, Proserpine, and Sappho (I know no elegy that equals this prolonged play of substitutions for the lost mother), she testifies yet again to Swinburne's chastening of the tradition, his hollowing out of all otherwise comforting matrices so as to stress the heroism of the martyr and to bring himself as close as possible to the martyr's heroic act of wreathing an acknowledged void. Unwaveringly, it is not on the fate of the deceased but on this action, expressive of Apollo's immortal force of displaced creativity, that consolation rests.

And yet, in a finely tempered spirit of homage, the elegist still seeks to comfort Baudelaire. As in stanza 16, he turns from sober negations to a brave "Howso'er. . . . ," ending the poem with a stoical vision of the enviable calm of the dead. The last two lines of this gentle and sedately cadenced ending are of particular interest. Apart from their all-encompassing finality, pacifying the perilous floods of "Lycidas" and "Adonais" and settling the four elements themselves to a harmonious rest, there is a final reminder of the way in which the living and the dead are separated not only by the threshold of death but also by the veil of language. Baudelaire now lies on the far side of the braid of similarities and differences that constitutes language. For him, the essential differences that make all equations purely figurative have collapsed. The final lines' actual *elision* of "quiet" comes as close as language can to achieving a deathly release. As the specific tenor slips into silence, the comparison broadens out into an equation as wide and as embracing as the ocean and the shore themselves. Only the living, perpetually discontent but temporarily lulled, know that such a reconciliation depends on the fabric in which the dead now rest, forever shrouded and "content."

IX

Hardy: "A Singer Asleep" and *Poems of 1912–13*

> Whatever its character, the provincial
> England of 1907, when I was born,
> was Tennysonian in outlook; whatever
> its outlook the England of 1925 when I
> went up to Oxford was The Waste
> Land in character. I cannot imagine
> that any other single writer [apart from
> Hardy] could have carried me through
> from the one to the other.
> Auden, "A Literary Transference"

> She had learnt the lesson of
> renunciation. . . . Yet her experience
> had consisted less in a series of pure
> disappointments than in a series of
> substitutions.
> Hardy, *The Mayor of Casterbridge*

"The question was, where do we go from Swinburne?"[1] Thus T. S. Eliot, reviewing the predicament of those poets who sought to begin the twentieth century with a thrust beyond even Swinburne's surpassal of Victorian poetry. As already noted, Swinburne, together with Hopkins, had found his way out of the Victorian obsession with personality.[2] But Hopkins's poetry was not to be fully published or recognized until 1918; and Swinburne's achievement was marred for Eliot's generation by what they perceived as its old-fashioned ornamentation, its use of an inflated poetics of mere sound, too poor in thought and too remote from any given reality, let alone that of the modern world.

From what we know of the relation between the elegy and the project of inheritance, we might look for an answer to Eliot's question in an elegy for Swinburne. Several such poems were written, but one in particular stands out as being precisely the kind of absorption yet modernization of Swinburne that Eliot invoked. As such, the elegy accurately reflects its author's position as one of the most significant links, beyond Swinburne, between Victorian and modern poetry. The poet is Hardy, who within two years of his poem for Swinburne, "A Singer Asleep" (1910), wrote a series of haunting and unprecedented elegies for his first wife, Emma Gifford Hardy. In this chapter, I hope to observe, first, how the elegy for Swinburne offers an intriguing continuation of the earlier poet's style and ideology; and second, how Hardy's elegies for his wife shed the Swinburnean legacy and carry the elegy as a genre still further into the twentieth century.

"A Singer Asleep"

A Singer Asleep
(Algernon Charles Swinburne, 1837–1909)

I

In this fair niche above the unslumbering sea,
That sentrys up and down all night, all day,
From cove to promontory, from ness to bay,
The Fates have fitly bidden that he should be
    Pillowed eternally.

II

—It was as though a garland of red roses
Had fallen about the hood of some smug nun
When irresponsibly dropped as from the sun,
In fulth of numbers freaked with musical closes,
Upon Victoria's formal middle time
    His leaves of rhythm and rhyme.

III

O that far morning of a summer day
When, down a terraced street whose pavements lay
Glassing the sunshine into my bent eyes,
I walked and read with a quick glad surprise
    New words, in classic guise, —

228

IV

The passionate pages of his earlier years,
Fraught with hot sighs, sad laughters, kisses, tears,
Fresh-fluted notes, yet from a minstrel who
Blew them not naively, but as one who knew
      Full well why thus he blew.

V

I still can hear the brabble and the roar
At those thy tunes, O still one, now passed through
That fitful fire of tongues then entered new!
Their power is spent like spindrift on this shore;
      Thine swells yet more and more.

VI

—His singing-mistress verily was no other
Than she the Lesbian, she the music-mother
Of all the tribe that feel in melodies;
Who leapt, love-anguished, from the Leucadian steep
Into the rambling world-encircling deep
      Which hides her where none sees.

VII

And one can hold in thought that nightly here
His phantom may draw down to the water's brim,
And hers come up to meet it, as a dim
Lone shine upon the heaving hydrosphere,
And mariners wonder as they traverse near,
      Unknowing of her and him.

VIII

One dreams him sighing to her spectral form:
"O teacher, where lies hid thy burning line;
Where are those songs, O poetess divine
Whose very orts are love incarnadine?"
And her smile back: "Disciple true and warm,
      Sufficient now are thine." . . .

IX

So here, beneath the waking constellations,
Where the waves peal their everlasting strains,

And their dull subterrene reverberations
Shake him when storms make mountains of their plains—
Him once their peer in sad improvisations,
And deft as wind to cleave their frothy manes—
I leave him, while the daylight gleam declines
          Upon the capes and chines. [3]

By the title alone, Hardy has offered Swinburne the kind of death as repose that the latter had accorded Baudelaire. And the form of the stanzas, with their intricate rhyme schemes and nicely abbreviated "musical closes," provides another initial effect of homage and imitation. (While the abbreviations allude specifically both to Baudelaire and to his "singing mistress," Sappho, Hardy will pursue the elegiac effects of their antiphony in several of the poems for his wife.) The poem is indeed marked by Swinburne's style of writing, by his almost impersonal, hieratic gestures, and by his ideological view of the immortal continuity between such poets as Sappho and himself. We may question Hardy's ultimate sympathy with Swinburne's Hellenism or with his contrived scenarios; and Hardy *has* departed from Swinburne in several respects. But even those of the poem's moments that Hardy has made most his own yield a level of meaning that might escape notice if not read in the light of Swinburne and the tradition.

The first stanza is very much within Swinburne's world: the carefully and variously described coastline, including its promontory (as in "Ave Atque Vale" and, before that, "Lycidas"); the reference to the pagan Fates' ennobling decree; and the evocation of eternal repose, imaged with the beautiful sensuousness of "pillowed," possibly drawn from Swinburne's own "A Swimmer's Dream" ("I lean my cheek to the cold grey pillow")—all enfolded, as if by Swinburne himself, in the ceremonious cadence of a periodic sentence.

With the following four stanzas, however, we enter a world that is far more Hardy's own. The very abruptness of the break signals a peculiarly modern ellipsis—a jagged switch, as though mid-thought, breaking from the fairly objective, declamatory mode of the first stanza, with its timeless scene, to a specific, more private recollection presented not just with bewildering suddenness but with a curious, un-Victorian directness. The opening is colloquial, with an unexpected juxtaposition of conventional or even archaic poetic language ("garland of red roses," "fulth," "freaked") on the one hand and a rather daringly modern diction ("irresponsibly dropped," "some smug nun")

on the other. And with stanza 3, an elegiac fixing of a highly particularized and intense moment in the past, the poem has become almost
familiar to any reader of Hardy.

But traditional elegiac motifs and formulae, especially those transmitted by Swinburne, are at work throughout these stanzas: the Neoclassical focus on the poetic achievement of the dead; the use of
figures from pastoral elegy ("floral gardens," "flute-notes"); the association of the work, and only *thence* the poet, with the elegy's arch-
figure for the continuing source of physical or spiritual energy, the
sun.

Even the deliberate modernity of the urban terraces and pavements, together with Hardy's characteristic sensitivity to fugitive images of reflected light, carries forward the elegiac conventions. The
poet walked with his head down in order to read. But "bent eyes" also
suggests a gesture of humility or reverence. And the sunlight reflected
off the wet pavement is, of course, associated with the light "dropped
as from the sun," reflected in the pages of poetry. On a city street at
the beginning of the twentieth century, the elegist could be assisting
at a ritual two millennia ago: a mourner with lowered eyes bearing
witness to the dead, who, like some vegetation deity, has been identified, through his creative powers, with the sun. And by his response,
"I walked and read with a quick glad surprise," the elegist has performed that absorption of the dead man's power ("quick" meaning
vital, "glad" suggesting shining) so crucial to the work of mourning
and inheritance. Sealing the identification, "new words in classic
guise" could apply to this poem as well as to Swinburne's work.

The fifth stanza continues to celebrate Swinburne's achievement.
The praise is again in terms of a physical "power," one that swells in an
undying increase. But Hardy now adds a traditionally vengeful elegiac
contrast, attacking the hostile "brabble and the roar," much as Shelley
had cursed the enemies of Keats or Milton had assaulted the clerics'
grating on scrannel pipes. [4] The opposition of swelling power to spent
spindrift implies what we know to be the originally sexual basis for all
elegiac images of an undying force, while the passage through fire
provides an equally traditional image of refinement. As for the
shoreline setting, it is a handsome tribute, associating Swinburne not
only with the sun but with the sea, as Swinburne himself had so frequently done.

With the return to the shore, and with the image of a refined sexuality, the poet has prepared for the following stanzas' conjecture of a nightly meeting between the spectral forms of Swinburne and Sappho. Hardy's introduction of Sappho closely follows Swinburne, using the ancient image of physical genealogy ("mother of the tribe") and of Sappho's submersion beneath a veil that none can penetrate. Once again, an elegist is apparently unable to mourn without some-how recapitulating such a version of prior loss and such an attendant admission of limited knowledge or power. Only after this acceptance can he present a consolatory but spiritualized, phantasmic reunion of the pair.

Hardy is very much at home with the apparitional encounter of stanzas 7 and 8. In the very first line, he brings his own emphasis to bear on the scene: "And one can hold in thought." From our reading of Tennyson and Swinburne, we are familiar with the elegiac refinement not only of the dead, but of the survivor's physical attachment to the dead. The only touchable element of the dead is in their letters or poems. Hardy's "hold in thought" goes beyond these by suggesting more frankly that the dead exist, if at all, only in the tenuous conjec-tures of the mind. For Hardy, their apparitional nature derives, there-fore, not from some accepted fiction about ghosts, nor from their displacement into traceable letters, but from the fact that their existence is now purely mental or psychological. Hardy's elegies for his wife will fully explore this relation between the apparitional and the psycho-logical. For the moment, we see the poet at an interesting point, adding his measure of skepticism to the mythological fiction inherited from Swinburne.

Hardy's pressure on the tradition continues noticeably in his de-scription of Sappho as "a dim / Lone shine upon the heaving hydro-sphere." Little could be more conventional than to transform the dead into a source of natural light. But the aggressive modernity of *hydro-sphere* (the first date given in the *Oxford English Dictionary* is 1887) is a mark of Hardy's characteristically tough insistence on welding even the most delicate elements of his Romantic and Victorian legacy to the intractable reality of his own times. *Hydrosphere* is more appropriate than it may first appear. Its entirely Greek derivation suits Sappho, while its meaning—the waters and the aqueous vapor enveloping the earth—takes the element loved by Sappho and Swinburne, yet de-scribes it in such a way as to stress its filmy, veil-like quality. We have seen how often elegies refer to the mediating fabric with which their images for the dead are woven. Even within the scientific term, Hardy is thus paying attention to the arguments of his genre. Sappho appears as the dim light cast on an enveloping medium. And it is on this same watery screen, already shown to be held in thought, that she and Swinburne meet.

Hardy qualifies the encounter by the potentially ironic presence of unknowing seamen—a strategy repeated by the "ignorant" birds and seals in "After a Journey." And he restates the purely conjectural nature of the thought ("one dreams") before performing the fine impersonation of the succeeding dialogue. In an earlier chapter on the Neoclassical elegy, I discussed the relation between mourning and impersonation.[5] Much of that discussion is relevant here, for Hardy, too, is trying to invoke the undying voices of the past while himself sharing in their immortality. Not by chance, the actual dialogue, almost resembling a miniature eclogue, with its graceful antiphony of elegiac question and consoling answer, takes as its subject the very issue of discipleship and inheritance.

Apart from the attributed apotheosis of Sappho, Hardy also seems to adopt Swinburne's imagery for a physically transmitted, or even ingested, "line" of genius. *Orts* suggests fragments, particularly of food; and *incarnadine* carries forward the red of Swinburne's garland, while adding a sense of incarnation, as though to stress once again the embodied continuity. But the lineage, like Sappho's "burning line" itself, is also broken or hidden. The continuity may be expressed in terms suggesting a nutritive or genetic connection; but clearly Swinburne's songs must substitute for Sappho's, must recreate, in and of themselves, whatever power Sappho's poems embodied. A real loss is registered, even as it allows the gain of a true succession.

As in the codas of so many elegies, the poet is himself the focus of the last stanza. A line is added, perhaps to resemble the epical *ottava rima* close of "Lycidas," and here, too, the departing elegist moves in such synchrony with the daylight as to imply his association with the sun ("I leave him, while the daylight gleam declines"). In view of the relation between this gleam and the brighter lights of earlier elegies, or even the sun-dropped power of Swinburne or the shine of Sappho, we may note that Hardy's consoling identification with his predecessors is not without attenuation. Indeed, this unwillingness to disengage comfort from a surrounding gloom is one of the strengths of Hardy's elegies, particularly those for his wife. In those poems, even

233

the attenuated natural light or the enduring properties of a landscape will prove inadequate to the mourner's need.

For in addition to his association with the light, the poet depends heavily, at the close of "A Singer Asleep," on the heroic characteristics of the given scene. Through them, he establishes a sense of immensity and permanence. And it is this scene whose description, with all its carefully gathering clauses, moves beyond the associated figure of Swinburne to bear finally on the departing figure of the elegist, the only subject of the entire one-sentence stanza.

We may wonder how Hardy will mourn once he forgoes such consolations as those offered by Swinburne's myth of lineage or by the archaic and indeed totemic features of the external world. (*Capes* suggests heads, and *chines* spinal ridges—prominences that are durable and yet somehow severed.) How, also, will he mourn when the subject of his grief is not a poet translatable to the region of achieved works but rather his own first wife, with whom so much of his individual past was necessarily entwined?

Poems of 1912–13

When Hardy sheds the Swinburnean legacy, however modified, of "A Singer Asleep," he appears to move beyond *any* of the inherited ideologies or poetic forms that previously had supported an elegist's pursuit. Spenser, Milton, Gray, Shelley, and Swinburne, for all their originality, remained largely within a certain framework, a way of proceeding that we associate with the ceremonies of the genre. And even poets who appear to discard most of the traditional *manner* of the genre nevertheless draw on some external matrix of consoling beliefs or ideas, be it Jonson's odd mixture of stoicism and faith, Dryden's Augustan reliance on the immortalizing value of the classics, or Tennyson's laborious melange of evolutionary theory and scriptural typology. By contrast, Hardy's departure from convention is at first sight so radical as to place him and his poems in a strange, unhoused isolation with respect to the genre.

Isolation is, of course, a notable element of Hardy's work in general. The poems have a self-sustaining, home-crafted quality which marks them off as being not only discretely Hardy's but the product of an uncompromisingly independent, almost exiled mind. For the most part, this singularity is an attractive and moving feature of Hardy's poetry. When the subject is the sudden, wrenching loss of his first wife, and of the associated early years of courtship and marriage, Hardy's singularity takes on a more specific nakedness and vulnerability. Apart from their formal brilliance and their superb control of personal voice, it is the unsheltered nature of these poems, their openness to loss, and their apparent insistence on remaining outside the borrowed comforts of the genre that contribute to their position among the most affecting lyrics in the language.

If the poems in *Poems of 1912–13* are so singular, why read them with a generic approach? Indeed, will they reveal the limits of such an approach, perhaps forcing a redefinition of the genre? As I hope to show, their originality and modernity are considerable; but this sequence of poems nevertheless includes the elements most essential to the work of mourning and to the composition of an elegy. Despite their stark, individual beauty, their apparently erratic and fragmented ordonnance, their differing verse forms, and the perplexed wandering of their protagonist, these poems enact familiar tasks: proving the reality of loss, confronting guilt and anger, recollecting and then severing attachments to the dead, establishing substitutive figures for the lost object of love, curbing the mourner's desires by an act of self-purification that both redefines and reinforces his continuing identity. So, too, while our reading of the poems must do justice to their unique occasion and character, a generic approach will recognize their use of such elegiac features as repetition, antiphony, apostrophe, interrogation, procession, and eclogic division. By bringing our understanding of the genre to bear, albeit unevenly, on *all* the poems, I hope finally to show what they yield when read together.[6] As in the case of *In Memoriam*, most readings have too exclusively isolated certain moments of the work, thereby perpetuating a highly restricted understanding of Hardy's achievement.[7]

The epigraph to *Poems of 1912–13* reads "*Veteris vestigia flammae*," a quotation from the *Aeneid* 4.23, where Dido confesses that her new love for Aeneas has rekindled the "traces of an ancient flame." (The common translation of "ashes" for *vestigia* loses the sense of a signifying remnant.) As has been pointed out, the allusion is complex, summoning up not only Dido's relationship to her dead husband, Sychaeus, but also her impending betrayal by Aeneas, as well as Aeneas's future encounter with her mute form in the underworld.[8] In condensed form, all three elements are present in Hardy's relation to his wife Emma. Her death somehow rekindled Hardy's early love for her; that love had long since been betrayed or doomed by estrangement; and in his elegies he will repeatedly confront her "voiceless ghost." The consoling potential of allusion as an elegiac device is thus partially undercut by the ironic aspect of its usage here.

The precise wording of the quotation is itself of great interest. *Vestigia* means "tracks," or "signs," even "footprints"; also "stations" or "posts"; and finally, "moments." *Vestigo,* meaning "to investigate," "to track," or "to search out," is from the same root. To a great extent, Hardy's elegies will track down special stations or instants in his relationship with Emma, investigating traces of his wife and of himself and studying the nature of their persistence as a print or sign. Hardy will in fact investigate the degree to which human identity, at its most durable, is no more than such a trace. The word *flammae* is also intriguing, for it refers not only to fire—the blaze of passion, and the energy or light at the core of nearly all figures of consolation—but also to the ruin caused by fire. The mingling of these oppositions certainly accords with Hardy's offering of only the bleakest of comforts. And when we read the final poem in the series, we note how Hardy in fact ends with a quite unprecedented version of the generic figure, a version that exploits both senses of the Latin word.

The Going

Why did you give no hint that night
That quickly after the morrow's dawn,
And calmly, as if indifferent quite,
You would close your term here, up and be gone
    Where I could not follow
    With wing of swallow
To gain one glimpse of you ever anon!

    Never to bid good-bye,
    Or lip me the softest call,
Or utter a wish for a word, while I
Saw morning harden upon the wall,
    Unmoved, unknowing
    That your great going
Had place that moment, and altered all.

Why do you make me leave the house
And think for a breath it is you I see
At the end of the alley of bending boughs
Where so often at dusk you used to be;
    Till in darkening dankness
    The yawning blankness
Of the perspective sickens me!

    You were she who abode
    By those red-veined rocks far West.
You were the swan-necked one who rode
Along the beetling Beeny Crest,
    And, reining nigh me,
    Would muse and eye me,
While Life unrolled us its very best.

Why, then, latterly did we not speak,
Did we not think of those days long dead,
And ere your vanishing strive to seek
That time's renewal? We might have said,
    "In this bright spring weather
    We'll visit together
Those places that once we visited."

    Well, well! All's past amend,
    Unchangeable. It must go.
I seem but a dead man held on end
To sink down soon. . . . O you could not know
    That such swift fleeing
    No soul foreseeing—
Not even I—would undo me so!

The formal structure of each stanza and of the entire poem is uniquely Hardy's. The way in which its "home-crafted" quality— original, intricate, and beautiful—draws attention to the poet's technical skill is itself a familiar elegiac strategy. But as mentioned before, the consoling effect of this display of mastery is disturbingly tempered by the isolation implied by the very idiosyncracy of the craft.

Apart from controlling the emotional release, the actual intricacy of form has more precisely elegiac properties. As in most of the accompanying poems, the use of antiphony is one such property,

evident here in the alternation of line lengths both within and between stanzas. Such alternations have greatly nuanced and varied
effects, in addition to referring to the alternations of ancient Greek
elegiacs, to the shifts between restraint and release or curtailment and
compensation, and to the rhythms of eclogic question and reply.
Here, too, the second, fourth, and sixth stanzas begin with inset,
short couplets, suggesting a broader antiphony in the relation between these stanzas and those immediately preceding them. In fact,
each of the odd-numbered stanzas begins with a question, which the
other stanzas either expand, address, or reject.

While a questioning mode is certainly appropriate for the beginning of an elegy, Hardy's opening question is alarmingly abrupt.
There is no preparatory staging or frame, no sense of a ceremony that
will contain either what has happened or what is to follow. And the
question is, after all, precisely *about* the absence of warning or preparation. It is a particularly painful question, since it addresses more than
just the unexpected and hence incredible nature of the loss ("So
unforeseen that I can scarcely realise it at times even now"). [9] Beyond
this, as the fifth stanza and succeeding poems prove, the opening
question probes the very nature of Hardy's progressively incommunicative relationship with his wife, a relationship that for many of
its final years was marked by the very minimum of conversation. The
"no hint" refers in part to this breakdown, which thus obtrudes, at the
very outset, as a central object of grief.

Most elegies take up subjects besides those of mortality and loss.
What is so moving about Hardy's other subjects—his ruined marriage, for example, and his courtship days—is that they are seen in
their terribly close resemblances to death and to mourning. The
marital estrangement was a kind of death-in-life. And Hardy's
courtship was, as we shall see, marked by the same kind of fictionalizing of its object as occurs in the poet's work of mourning. [10] The suitor,
like the mourner, is engaged with "a phantom of his own figuring."
The heart-rending closeness, or rather overlap, of these main subjects—death and estrangement, mourning and courtship—is therefore far greater than one of sheer ironic juxtaposition or shadowing.
And it is partly this doubling of significance that makes Hardy's elegies so emotionally powerful.

Hardy's opening question is remarkable for more than its
abruptness. Beginning with a line of one-syllable words, it seems to

have the frank, unadorned bearing that marks much of what follows. But the unimpeded freshness of address is deceptive. The question passes into an almost incantatory rhythm and length, taking on a musing, involuted drift away from its addressee toward the baffled desires of the questioner himself. And this movement away from a speechlike beginning toward a distinctly uncolloquial close confirms and reenacts the realization that the supposedly addressed presence of his wife has in fact been fictional or inapprehensible. This dialectic between the wife's presence and absence, or rather the way in which the poet's evocations of her repeat her "going," is subtly replayed throughout several of the poems.

We have already studied how and why an elegy conventionally repeats, by statement and often by narrative, the death that it mourns. While Hardy's use of such repetition has less overt ritualism than those of Bion, Milton, and Shelley, it, too, arises partly from the mourner's need to break down his own denial of the actual death. Such reality testing is by nature repetitive, for it must not only drive home the resisted fact of the death but also constantly undo the repeated illusions that the dead are still present. With Hardy, this need was especially intense, partly because he was by temperament an unremitting and fascinated undoer of illusions at large but more importantly because Emma's death came as such an extreme shock. To the task of reality testing there was therefore added the condition of compulsive repetition, often associated with shock. Having had "no hint" when Emma retired for the night that she would die early the next morning, Hardy had prepared none of the defenses that might have cushioned the blow. Afterwards, but too late, he was compelled to repeat the loss, trying retrospectively to create the defenses that he had so utterly lacked.

It is this traumatic aspect of the loss, rather than the loss itself, that underlies the first question: not Why did you go? but Why did you go without warning? As already mentioned, the question moves beyond the primary occasion of grief, Emma's death, to the immense regret that Hardy felt regarding their relationship. "Why did you give no hint?" is inseparable from "Why, then, latterly did we not speak?" or from the numerous other moments in which Hardy mourns both a death and a vanished love. To the other reasons for the repetitive recollection, evocation and loss, we should therefore add Hardy's thwarted impulse not only to review but to *revise* his marriage. [11]

The second stanza expresses the complex object of Hardy's grief—
the loss of his wife, but more specifically the loss of a particular blend
of eroticism and communication ("lip me the softest call") even when
she was alive. Hardy laments in his marriage precisely the deprivation
that any mourner must accept: the loss of an attachment that is
originally sexual in nature and the closely related turn from a certain
ease of physical or vocal contact to more heavily mediated forms of
communication or reference. As we shall see, Hardy will continually
perform this complex elegiac task, deflecting his own desires away
from the physical presence of his wife to a phantasmal figure for her
while at the same time moving from motifs of voice to those of
vestigial sign or trace.

Apart from its resemblance to the demise of his marriage, this
movement is unusually bleak for Hardy because he posited no valued
force or authority under whose aegis such a submission could be
made, and because the movement traverses such a vast and well-
evoked interval of blankness, the "dark space wherein I have lacked
you." Hardy's refusal to imagine an ultimately benign, ongoing power
whose design enforces and guarantees the transaction of renunciation
and reward is, of course, a measure of his departure from the conventional elegiac myths. In itself, this departure considerably darkens the
poems. But the situation is still more troubling. For the only ongoing
enforcer of his losses is Time, whose chief characteristic, according to
Hardy, is sheer indifference. And it is indifference that Hardy regards
as his own greatest shortcoming in the marriage. Whatever its cause
(inevitable disenchantment after a too idealized romance, or a legitimate response to Emma's querulous snobbishness and jealousy, or just
the harsh singularity of Hardy's nature), Hardy's indifference so un-
comfortably resembles that of Time, or that of the uncaring backdrop,
that it must have been difficult for him to avoid confronting his own
guilt in what would otherwise have been a more straightforward description of context and event.

The first stanza of "The Going" refers to Emma's going "calmly, as if
indifferent quite." Projected or not, the issue of indifference is thus
broached at the very outset. And the second stanza pursues this issue
yet more clearly. Opposing the erotic intimacy of "lip me the softest
call," Hardy sees "morning harden upon the wall / Unmoved, unknowing." The check against speech and desire and the self-limitation
of "unknowing" are familiar elegiac gestures. But the image of morning

on the wall, hard against the soft-lipped call, with which it cruelly rhymes, also represents the indifference of the unknowing Hardy himself. Bleakly revising the genre's convention of pathetic fallacy, the poet associates the setting, not with his grief, but with his imperviousness. Similarly, in the image of hard sunlight, Hardy certainly recognizes and submits to the overruling power of the sun, but with none of the compensation that such a conventional elegiac gesture would normally earn.

Developing from the first two stanzas, Hardy's second question describes a devastating instance of the kind of repetition whose several determinants—shock, remorse, disbelief—we have already noted. "Why do you make me . . ." suggests the compulsion; and the account itself may remind us of how closely the mourner's repetition of loss resembles the child's *fort-da* game, mentioned earlier. Indeed, Hardy's scenario, however dismal, has something of a gamelike quality. A trick is being played, if only by the mourner upon himself. Despite the guise of passivity, the mourner is trying to master the experience of unexpected abandonment. While needing to dispel his illusions of her actual presence, he is repeatedly conjuring and banishing his wife, much as the child repeatedly retrieves and discards the image of its mother. Once again, however, Hardy reverses the strategy of compensation. Whereas the child plays at losing a substitutive symbol for the mother (the wooden reel), Hardy does not yet mediate his loss in that way. It is the illusion of actual presence ("it is you") that he loses. Nor does he yet seem to manage the reassuring task of retrieval. In this phase of sheer deprivation, Hardy has not yet begun the mourner's task of inventing a figure for what he has lost.

And yet the stanza itself is such a masterpiece, so perfectly modulated in rhythm and rhetoric, that we look there for signs of the mastery and invention that are to come. Once more, within a single sentence, the diction and phrasing turn away from an opening freshness toward highly contrived and enclosed effects, which undermine the initial ease and nearness of address. Several details are striking. The poet is drawn outside, into that remarkably unhoused condition that governs both himself and his poems. "For a breath," reminding us of the difference between the living and the dead, is inescapably poignant when measured in its brevity and urgency against the near-timeless routine of the "so often" or against the colossal indifference of the "yawning blankness."

241

This contrast between the "yawning blankness" and the single breath is similar to that between the broad hardening of sunlight and the fugitive glimpse or glimmer. *Yawn* is an ironic rejoinder to the urgent poet, a harsh repetition of the charge of indifference brought against the world and himself. Continuing to explore the interruption of spoken language, the yawn perfectly negates the desired word or call of preceding lines. It also captures the abysmal, absorptive nature of the disappearance—not just vacancy but vacuum—which seems to suck the poet (much as death may be said to suck away the living breath) down the long alley toward a perspectival vanishing point. The abbreviated lines, with their relentless rhythm and rhyme, serve to seal the vacuum. What "sickens" the poet, therefore, is a sensation like that of vertigo, of falling into a gaping hole from which there is as little escape as from the narrowing lines of perspectival recession. It is this sickness that recurs so powerfully in the poem's final image of the "dead man held on end / To sink down soon."

The fourth stanza answers the third in two ways. It explains why the dead woman has such a hold on the poet, and it responds to the negative moment of loss by an attempted retrieval. Significantly, the retrieved image does not represent the woman in the alley at dusk but rather an image of her as the young woman that she had long since ceased to be. Hardy's twofold mourning is thus clearly at work as he returns to the scenes of his courtship in Cornwall forty years before.

In keeping with this remoteness, the language is now archaic ("abode," "beetling," "nigh") and highly figurative ("You were the swan-necked one"). The setting and actions are those of chivalric romance ("reining nigh me"), enchantment ("Would muse and eye me"), and elevation ("the beetling Beeny Crest"). We cannot help suspecting that Hardy's image of the young Emma is not just the construction of an old mourner but rather the equally fictive product of the young lover. "Swan-necked" in itself suggests how much he had transfigured her, how remote from himself he had held her. And so we may register a slight unease in this recollected idyll. Like those in "Astrophel" or "Lycidas," the idyll is not only highly fictionalized but also highly vulnerable—almost a setup for the disaster to come. As a retrieved image, therefore, this legendary "she" will not suffice, for she exists, if at all, only before the double loss of romance and of life.

Spenser and Milton went on to substitute figures for Astrophel and Lycidas after death, figures on the far side of catastrophe. No such image of Emma Hardy, no figure that has her death somehow inscribed upon it, is yet in sight. That will come later, in other poems of the sequence. For the moment, we have only the idyll, of which further details confirm our unease. The "red-veined rocks," for all their colorful relief of the second and third stanzas' monochromes, are perhaps a little too mortal for comfort—they are not yet the primeval recorders found in a later poem. The "beetling . . . Crest," for all its Shakespearean aura and totemic strength, is disquietingly close to the "yawning blankness" of a sudden drop. And finally, there is the eerie and subtly incongruous juxtaposition of the reined-in lovers and unrolling Life, as though the lovers were somehow, even at this moment of great promise, being stranded and outdistanced by an unstoppable, even mechanical, force.

As if to stress the fragility and insufficiency of the retrieval, the fifth stanza dispels the idyll with yet another painful question, one that cuts yet more closely to the core of the Hardys' estrangement. Again, the focus is on a failure of speech, the absence of what they " might have said." As in the first stanzas, spoken words themselves thus seem to be part of the complex object of mourning, together with "those days long dead" and "Those places that once we visited." There is little assurance that Hardy *could* have renewed those times and places, even during Emma's lifetime. The very difference in diction between the almost nursery-rhyme simplicity of " 'In this bright spring weather / We'll visit together' " on the one hand and the artificial, hieratic splendor of the idyll on the other suggests the impossibility. Surely, Emma's death has robbed Hardy of that illusion of actual renewability. Her death has forced him to recognize that his renewals or recollections can only take place across, or rather against, the "blankness" of a deathlike space. And as the final stanza drives home, just such a space now yawns within Hardy's own life.

The very form of the final stanza matches Hardy's intensified recognition of both loss and discontinuity. The lines are broken up by abrupt declaration, ellipses, interruptions. And the crucial burden is Hardy's apparent completion of the mourner's first tasks—those of confronting, defining, and actively renouncing what has been lost. But now Hardy seems to have added himself to the object of his loss. The sickening in the third stanza was mortal, and Hardy's disillusioning knowledge that time cannot be renewed leaves him with a sense that his own life has suffered irrevocable divisions. What is most alarming here is Hardy's suggestion that life or identity is dependent on illusions of continuity, illusions that mask the fact that a life is perhaps pieced together, "held," or "done up" out of discrete moments. Should a piece be removed or an unbridgeable gap be exposed, the construction is "undone", the already dead man sinks down.

Reversing the usual coda of an elegy, which focuses on the elegist's established power, often imaged as a rise or advance, the poem ends with the poet's own fall and disintegration. In a sense, this is the unmanning or self-chastening moment whose importance we have often noted. That moment is usually followed by a recompense or reward. But since the individual lyrics within Hardy's series are poems in their own right, they give us a frighteningly intense, unappeased view of how an *isolated* early stage of mourning might feel. "The Going" performs the first tasks of mourning but stops on a note of extreme deprivation and self-denial, without suggesting a comforting context to come. Here, the painful reenactment of his loss has undermined the very foundations of the poet's life. If the following poems are to invent a consoling figure for his dead wife, they will have to construct some trace that can withstand and outlast the poet's *own* undoing. In few other elegies has the poet gone so far to undermine his own identity or had to fight so desperately for his own survival.

Most of the eleven poems between "The Going" and "After a Journey" pursue elements of the opening poem. With the exception of "Rain on a Grave" and "I Found Her Out There"—and even here the comforts are restrictive and dubious—the poems conjure Emma's presence only to repeat and emphasize her unexpected death. Yet again, Hardy's present distance from his wife sadly resembles both the estrangement between them in the recent years and the alarming division within Hardy himself. With a "sickening" and falling, Hardy brings his own selfhood and voice more deeply into question.

"Your Last Drive" returns to a moment in which Emma is utterly unaware of her coming death. Hardy exaggerates and ironizes her unawareness by describing her drive past her actual burial ground. As in "The Going," the unawareness is expressed by harsh words such as *heedless* and *alien*, which not only stress Emma's pitiful unpreparedness but harp again on the uneasy relation between such unpreparedness and the perhaps more culpable state of indifference. The irony of the poem actually swings around to bear on her husband, who would not have perceived her fate had he been with her at that moment. Hardy writes *now* the words that he claims not to have been able to read on her face *then*. This language is thus in a strange and ironically remote relation to the poet himself. It is as though Hardy were obsessed with situations in which he and his language were somehow not quite present to themselves, situations in which each was split by specifically temporal divisions. He looks back now at a moment in which he would not have been able to look forward. The self is severally fractured by time, and the poem recreates, rather than heals, the division.

The words that Hardy claims to read now might have been addressed to him by Emma, so that the voice of the poem divides between his and his wife's, between that of the living and that of the dead. But even to call these words Emma's is doubly inaccurate. Apart from being ascribed to her by the poet, they were written on her face without her having any knowledge of their presence. The speakers' words thus are and are not their own.

The third poem, "The Walk," is another attempt to capture the actual sensation of loss. Returning to the theme of his division from Emma while she was alive, Hardy asks how a solitary walk now differs from one then. Once again, he divides himself in time, to measure the discontinuity. The actual difference, "that underlying sense / Of the look of a room on returning thence," is difficult to describe. And Hardy's almost incommunicative terseness, his refusal to explain or elaborate, increases his separation from both Emma and the reader. Obviously, the room has a vacant look, a "yawning blankness." But the way that the room looks *to* Hardy is less alarming than the way that it looks *at* him. For it looks at him in the same way as it looks at his absence. He is both there and not there. With another queasy sensation, Hardy is thus again somehow "undone," his own self-presence undermined by a hollowness like that of death, disclosing itself within his own house.

While "Rain on a Grave" and "I Found Her Out There" have their intensely ironic and bleak moments, their endings are so conventionally consoling that we may wonder whether Hardy includes such poems only to emphasize the more arduous, skeptical work that surrounds them. For that purpose, an elegy often allows a moment of "false surmise," also using such moments for a needed respite. Since these two poems are separate lyrics, however, it is difficult to decide how to integrate them with the other poems. Again, this is an important feature of *Poems of 1912–13*. Even more than *In Memoriam*, these poems unsettle our notions of a coherent and sequential work of mourning. Hardy's sequence does have a general movement toward resolution, but that movement does justice to the erratic and awkward alternations of mood that mark the groping course of a mourner who lacks normative rituals. It is not surprising that Hardy follows "Rain on a Grave" and "I Found Her Out There" by a brief lyric entitled "Without Ceremony." The two poems' traditionally consoling figures of the child's heart, flowers, stars, and "life's round" are now starkly superseded by a return to the opening poems' obsession with Hardy's inability to "notice" Emma's silent departure. With a courteous, yet ironic, restatement of apparently reciprocal neglect, the poem again brings the entire elegiac project into question: "'Good-bye is not worth while!'"

"Lament" continues to undo the fictions of the fourth and fifth poems. The child's love of flowers is mentioned only to drive home the dead woman's separation both "From sights she loved best" and from her own "eager glance" of childhood. The poem is made up of a series of conjurings and banishings in which Emma's bright, imagined presence at a garden party, or at a dinner, or among February flowers is repeatedly negated by reminders of her death. Throughout the first three stanzas, the irony focuses exclusively on Emma, imprisoned and excluded from the scenes she loved. In a movement similar to that of "Your Last Drive," the last stanza widens the ironic focus to include Hardy himself. The effect is one of continued self-limitation, expressed here in the language of melancholia:

> And we are here staying
> Amid these stale things,
> Who care not for gaying,
> And those junketings
> That used so to joy her,
> And never to cloy her
> As us they cloy! . . . But
> She is shut, she is shut
> > From the cheer of them, dead
> > To all done and said
> > In her yew-arched bed.

"How weary, stale, flat and unprofitable. . . ." The sentiment is familiar, and there is little promise that Hardy will move beyond this mood. He has not yet (or so he claims) attached his affections else-where, and remains almost as shut off as Emma from all the uses of this world. Hardy's use of the word *cloy* is of special interest, repeated as it is in an exclamatory way. Interested as Hardy was in archaic words and etymologies (he even wrote an elegiac tribute to Liddell and Scott), he may well have known the relation of *cloy* to the Middle English *acloien*, "to lame," as well as to the Middle French *enclouer*, "to drive in a nail," from the Latin *en+clavus*.[12] Such associations of lameness and of a nailed, perhaps coffined or crucified restraint carry forward Hardy's unusually overdetermined course of self-chastisement.

Well situated between "Lament" and "The Voice," "The Haunter" takes up Emma's counter song. And while the attribution itself under-mines our sense of Hardy's unitary voice or power, the poem is in fact *about* this kind of undermining. Hardy does not know, nor can he see—two familiar aspects of the mourner's self-curbing—nor can "the words he lifts her" elicit a direct response from the unseen ghost. Her voice in turn lacks "the power to call to him." Emma's ghost can only appeal to the reader: "What a good haunter I am, O tell him!" The limitations of voice, of knowledge, of sight, are thus accompanied here by the reliance on mediation, on the mediation precisely of the reader, and hence of the poet's written word. And with this crucial elegiac acceptance (displaced onto Emma, however, as though Hardy himself were not yet quite endorsing it) comes a tenuous promise of faith, of love, of peace, and of a continuation of the mourner's path:

Tell him a faithful one is doing
    All that love can do
Still that his path may be worth pursuing,
    And to bring peace thereto.

Emma's confession that she is "Always lacking the power to call to him" renders both clear and poignant the imaginary nature of Hardy's hearing in "The Voice." And we may think of the first three stanzas of this poem as being made up of what Emma has just referred to as the ineffectual "words he lifts me":

Woman much missed, how you call to me, call to me,
Saying that now you are not as you were
When you had changed from the one who was all to me,
But as at first, when our day was fair.

Can it be you that I hear? Let me view you, then,
Standing as when I drew near to the town
Where you would wait for me: yes, as I knew you then,
Even to the original air-blue gown!

Or is it only the breeze, in its listlessness
Travelling across the wet mead to me here,
You being ever dissolved to wan wistlessness,
Heard no more again far or near?

Thus I; faltering forward,
Leaves around me falling,
Wind oozing thin through the thorn from norward,
And the woman calling.

The poem is hauntingly musical, with its antiphonal line lengths, its alternation of masculine and feminine rhymes (the latter echoing each other with a dying fall), its persistencies of assonance and alliteration, and its undulant yet altering rhythms. But much of the poem's emotional effect rises from the gradual damaging of the more melodic and lilting aspects of its music. Ironically enough, this music, with its triple dance rhythm, allegedly derives from one of the favorite songs of the young couple, "Haste to the Wedding."[13] And while the poem again mentions the Hardys' estrangement, the mourner is now even more concertedly troubled by the loss of voice. It is therefore appropriate that the form itself should move further and further away from the songlike quality of its opening, toward a halting expression of utter loss.

By a superb stroke, Hardy addresses Emma as "Woman much missed." While the inversion and participial phrase have an understated, almost analytical tone, "woman" has both the totalizing force (as in "all to me") and the intimate familiarity that this generic use can allow. "Call to me, call to me" is a beautiful reverse invocation in which the self-echoing element reinforces the ghost's call even as it subversively suggests that this calling is only an echo, or rather projection, of the mourner's voice. Addressing the prior object of Hardy's loss, that of his close relationship with her, she says that she is now as she had been before their estrangement. But there is something troubling and ironic in the fact that this restoration has been achieved only by virtue of a greater, more final loss. Also, the identification of the early beloved and the ghost questions once again the quality of the young Hardy's first images of her. So, too, while "all to me" amplifies Emma's renewal and maintains the echoing presence of "call to me," the attenuation in the loss of the consonant moves the call's sound closer to the airiness into which it will soon dissolve ("Or is it only the breeze?").

At this point, the mourner seeks that forbidden physical closeness with the dead, the unmediated apprehension of actual sight. Since Orpheus this has been a topos in many scenarios of mourning. And we have studied how elegists have had to accept the chastening loss of sight in favor of the mediated fabrics of their own invention. Similarly, the immediacy of voice must be displaced by the woven figures of consolation. "The Voice" is about these losses of sight and voice, although the compensation is still painfully withheld.

Hardy's image of the young Emma is affectingly described, the phrasing itself passing from a deliberate, stressed appeal to the more fluent yield of recollection, which moves on to the sudden catch and surge of "yes, as I knew you then, / Even to the original air-blue gown!" But as before, the restoration is subtly undone. The consoling originality and specificity of Emma's blue gown evaporates ("air-blue"), as though even the original had been a phantom.

Thus robbed of their substance, both the call and the "viewed" figment are easy prey to the poet's more explicit skepticism and to the passage of the air that they have each come to resemble. The third stanza describes their dissolution, so much more troubling than a mere disappearance and especially haunting for being described in lines still somehow addressed to Emma. As Shelley had lamented of his own image, " . . . even whilst we speak / Is it not broken?" The sensation of loss is thus again represented with terrible accuracy, as though the loved object were literally slipping from Hardy's grasp here and now. "You being ever dissolved" suggests both continuously and forever—not only the loss but also the losing is permanent.

More than voice and sight are being renounced here. As we have noted in all elegies, the mourner must also renounce or curb desire itself, as well as his will to knowledge. Although not applied directly to himself, the strange nouns *listlessness* and *wistlessness* express both of these further losses. [14] And the stanza closes with a last farewell to Emma's voice, which no intervals of time or space can restore.

With a distinctly elegiac coda, similar to Milton's "Thus sang,"

Hardy abandons the now impossible address to his wife and turns to describe himself. "Faltering" continues the self-crippling gesture of these poems, a gesture pointed to by the reduced length of the indented lines. And the poet falters among falling leaves, part of a large and unavoidable scheme of desiccation and decay. The description of the wind is almost unbearably bleak. It oozes as though from a wound and as though with the viscous but now thinned substance robbed from the poet, from his wife, and from the leaves. The alliterating *th* stresses the uncomfortable constriction, while the wind's sharpness must seem more piercing than the thorn bushes it penetrates.

And yet despite this desolation, the ghost's voice returns in the final line. The effect is complex, since on the one hand this is only the presence of a voice being ever dissolved, while on the other hand the voice seems to survive its dissolution and to mock the poet's attempted renunciation. Instead of truly renouncing, Hardy imperfectly represses the voice, allowing it to hover in the uncertain limbo between his skepticism and his need. Although he has travelled the immense distance from "Woman" to "the woman," forsaking both address and familiarity, and although he has so thoroughly qualified sight, voice, desire, knowledge, and physical strength, he seems unable to relinquish entirely or to transform the lingering voice. He falters forward with a stubbornness that amounts, despite all counter-assertions, to a kind of intrepid strength. Positioned ninth in a series originally comprising eighteen poems, "The Voice" is resolutely unresolved, a memorably drawn stalemate between the conflicting forces within Hardy's work of mourning.

Three poems now intervene before "After a Journey," the next major poem in the sequence. These poems carry forward several important elements. In "The Visitor," Hardy follows the eclogic alternation of voice yet again to impersonate Emma. The poem is far darker than "The Haunter," however, for it widens the gulf between ghost and mourner. Instead of her earlier promise of faithful accompaniment, Emma now speaks of feeling rebuffed by the new and alien life of her husband. And her voice, which once was characterized by a "softling song," returns to the explicitly "mute" grave. As in "The Going," "Lament," "The Voice," and several poems to come, the war between past ease and present devastation dominates the poem and draws the speaker himself nearer death. Finally, Emma's supposition of Hardy's "re-decked" comfort is ironically out of touch with his unhoused desolation just portrayed in "The Voice."

Deceptively slight, "A Circular," in which Hardy receives a fashionable clothing advertisement addressed to his wife, offers more than the obvious ironies. Beyond juxtaposing the "up to date" garments with the shroud, the poem continues several larger motifs of the series. Although the circular is addressed to his wife, it comes to Hardy as her "legal representative" in her absence. Now this alteration of address is not unlike those in several of the preceding poems in which Hardy's speech appears to address his wife only to recoil on himself in her absence. He is the only possible recipient of his words, which are marked by their failure to have kept "up to date." Like the circular, many of these poems are in the form of correspondence that has not quite come to terms with the death of its addressee. Furthermore, Hardy's uneasy position as "representative" resembles his impersonation of Emma in the poems set in her voice. In all, Hardy, as the reader of this circular, is the unhappy mediator between the living and the dead.

In discussing "The Haunter," we noted Hardy's obvious dependence on forms of mediation, in that case those of the reader and of his own text. "A Circular" attends to this dependence, not just by examining Hardy's position as mediator (a position itself created by the mediation of the law), and not just by showing that a "spring-time shout" is in fact a written missive, but also by its interest in the actual content of the circular: "New designs . . . tints as shown. . . . Here figure blouses . . . gay-pictured." These are all representations of clothes, figures for articles that are themselves made up of fabrics. This is a written circular addressed by professional fabricators to a woman who is dead—a wry item to include in these elegies. We can almost call it a gloss, its effect not so dissimilar from that of E. K.'s comment on certain "lively icons and representations" in *The Shepheardes Calender.*

"A Dream or No" repeats central elements of "The Going" and "The Voice," conjuring a highly contrived and in this case extremely archaized image of the young Emma only to repeat its disappearance. This time, however, the poet's melancholy has reached a narcissistic extreme in which the entire landscape associated with Emma loses reality—surely one of the most extreme versions of pathetic fallacy in the history of the genre. [15] Since "The Going," several poems have demonstrated a narcissistic melancholy in the poet's identification between his lost wife and a lost self ("I seem but a dead man. . ."). Now, even familiar parts of the external world are being drawn into identification with this loss. According to Freud, such a condition can arise from the mourner's utter withdrawal of affection from the world around him, followed by his reattachment of that affection to a self that is nevertheless identified with the lost object. While I would not characterize Hardy as a narcissist, I do think that he is working through this cluster of problems in his course of mourning. And I find it both interesting and comprehensible that the following poem marks a turning point in the series precisely by virtue of Hardy's recovery, first and foremost, of a hitherto lost self. The poem is "After a Journey":

> Hereto I come to view a voiceless ghost;
>   Whither, O whither will its whim now draw me?
> Up the cliff, down, till I'm lonely, lost,
>   And the unseen waters' ejaculations awe me.
> Where you will next be there's no knowing,
>   Facing round about me everywhere,
>   With your nut-coloured hair,
> And gray eyes, and rose-flush coming and going.
>
> Yes: I have re-entered your olden haunts at last;
>   Through the years, through the dead scenes I have
>   tracked you;
> What have you now found to say of our past—
>   Scanned across the dark space wherein I have lacked
>   you?
> Summer gave us sweets, but autumn wrought division?
>   Things were not lastly as firstly well
>   With us twain, you tell?
> But all's closed now, despite Time's derision.
>
> I see what you are doing: you are leading me on
>   To the spots we knew when we haunted here together,
> The waterfall, above which the mist-bow shone
>   At the then fair hour in the then fair weather,
> And the cave just under, with a voice still so hollow
>   That it seems to call out to me from forty years ago,
>   When you were all aglow,
> And not the thin ghost that I now frailly follow?

Ignorant of what there is flitting here to see,
   The waked birds preen and the seals flop lazily;
Soon you will have, Dear, to vanish from me,
   For the stars close their shutters and the dawn whitens
      hazily.
Trust me, I mind not, though Life lours,
   The bringing me here; nay, bring me here again!
      I am just the same as when
Our days were a joy, and our paths through flowers.

The very title of the poem suggests an arrival, although initially the traveler seems more lost than found. He begins by apparently accepting the truth that had so troubled him in "The Voice": that Emma is now a "voiceless ghost." With this concession comes a further relinquishment of will and knowledge, as Hardy submits to her whim, not knowing where she will next appear. But "the unseen waters" cry out as though with the denied voice of the dead, a sound whose "ejaculations awe" the poet no doubt with the force of the unconsciousness to which he had repressed them. This is not the comforting displacement achieved by the work of mourning but rather the overwhelming return of what the poet had too ambivalently sought to negate without substitution. While he has not announced a similar denial of the ghost's form, its omnipresence exerts a similar, if milder, effect, overwhelming any attempt to reduce it to a fixed or even denied place. Both negation and fixation thus give rise to an uncontrollable surplus of near-hallucinatory sounds and sights.

The second stanza assumes greater control, as Hardy remarks on the vast temporal and spatial distance between him and his wife. The verbs *tracked* and *scanned* stress a more mediated contact, based on vestigial marks. And from this distance, Hardy can imagine the most frank comments thus far to pass between him and Emma on the subject of their marriage. Despite its ironic simplicity and its faintly taunting note, Hardy's language implies that the two have somehow come to terms with their failure. Presumably, Emma is now saying what neither of them had actually said while she was alive. By silence, they had repressed and hence made unnegotiable the path, so to speak, of their estrangement. Thus, too, they had made absolute the gulf between their later and earlier selves. The present confrontation goes over the forbidden ground in such a way as to make it available, thereby somewhat reconnecting the very selves that they had "firstly" and

253

"lastly" been. It is this crucial step, I think, that prepares for Hardy's recovery of his identity ("I am just the same") at the poem's end.

"But all's closed now" may seem to echo "The Going" ("All's past amend"). But whereas the latter phrase brought a deathly end to its poem, the former gesture of resignation marks only the halfway point of "After a Journey" and seems to clear the way for a continuing and shared entry into the happier days of courtship.

While Hardy follows the ghost to the scenes of their past, he nevertheless inserts several ironic wedges between the present and the "then fair hour in the then fair weather." The covenantal "mist-bow" is made brief and remote; the young lovers themselves were haunters, even then; the comforting survival of the waterfall's call is qualified by "so hollow"; and the once glowing woman is finally contrasted with the thin ghost whom Hardy now frailly follows. Although Hardy suggests the consoling survival of certain "haunts," he has not yet fully marked those haunts with lasting signs of his and Emma's presence. The hollow voice belongs too much to the waterfall alone, and the significance of the scene is too dependent on the frail revenant. Not until "At Castle Boterel" and "Where the Picnic Was" will these memorials be given an autonomous durability.

Ironically framing his subjective experience by the ignorant and indifferent presence of seals and birds, Hardy accedes to the ghost's departure. But this departure is entirely different from Emma's earlier "goings." Hardy now has time to prepare for her vanishing ("Soon you will have, Dear, to vanish from me"), and he integrates it with a highly ceremonious account of dawn. Unlike the bald, unceremonious hardening of light in "The Going," the dawn "whitens hazily," an image of softness *and* mediation. And the gentle transition is softened yet further by the promise of future appointments. With this comes the poem's final yield—the most positive thus far—an assertion of continuous identity and of Hardy's recommitment to his early love. It is a persuasive moment, weighing courageously against the knowledge of disruption and disenchantment. From here, Hardy has only to invent a figure—outside his frail self and beyond Time's derision—to *represent* this reestablished identity.

As we shall see in "At Castle Boterel" and "Where the Picnic Was," the final figures of persistence seem to be inscribed on certain places in nature. To stress this, Hardy precedes the first of those poems by two poems whose discomforting effects arise from the fact that no human impressions had been made on the natural scene. Asking why Nature had betrayed the heart that loved her, "A Death-Day Recalled" shows Emma's favored places totally indifferent to her death. And "Beeny Cliff," for all the beauty and momentum of its scenic recollections, repeats this indifference between the human and the natural orders. Admittedly, it is now Emma who "nor knows nor cares for Beeny." But as the very swift movement of the poem suggests, there is nothing in the scenes to retard or compensate for the poet's rapid arrival at the final negation, "and will laugh there nevermore." As so often in these poems, Hardy specifically mourns the loss of a human voice—the laughter, the "sweet things said." Nothing in the scene retains that voice, and the poet is still unwilling or unable to substitute for it some nonvocal and hence more lasting trace. Instead, there is the mockery of the waves, "engrossed in saying their ceaseless babbling say."

Although enduring attributes of the scene are described ("Still in all its chasmal beauty bulks old Beeny to the sky"), they have no lasting connection with Emma or Hardy, and the poem even turns to mock its own words: "What if still in chasmal beauty looms that wild weird western shore." The substantial "bulk" and elevation is here replaced by a weird looming, while only the chasmal beauty is reemphasized, with "chasmal" not only suggesting an abysmal absence but also reminding us of that "yawning blankness" of "The Going." The scene itself hollows out, falling away, as does the woman, described with an abrupt loss of specificity and within a gaping parenthesis as merely "elsewhere."

Apart from bringing several themes and motifs of the earlier poems to a conclusion, "At Castle Boterel" finally invents a durable figure for Emma and for Hardy himself. In many ways, therefore, the poem completes the work of mourning, although Hardy will yet qualify and refine upon his resolution. Through the fine mist of a drizzle, Hardy looks back to a spot where he and Emma had walked in dry weather more than forty years before. He sees the two forms "distinctly yet," which leads us to suspect that his vision has been assisted rather than hindered by the veiling rain—an instance of the poem's reliance on particular intervening textures. We know that an acceptance of this reliance requires the renunciation of an immediate relationship to the dead. That renunciation usually occurs under the aegis of a law or power, one that forces a chastening redefinition or deflection of the mourner's attachments and desire. In this poem, it is Time, whose "unflinching rigour, / In mindless rote, has ruled from sight the substance now." "Ruled from sight" suggests both having forbidden—and in a sense blinded—by rule and having actually canceled, as by a written stroke. (We may recall Tennyson's "At length my trance / Was cancell'd, stricken thro' with doubt.") And it is in place of that lost substance and sight that Hardy conjures not only a "phantom figure" but also, and what is more important, the figure of a memorial sign:

> Primaeval rocks form the road's steep border,
>   And much have they faced there, first and last,
> Of the transitory in Earth's long order;
>   But what they record in colour and cast
>   Is—that we two passed.

Forgoing the substances of both Emma and his early self, forgoing his so frequent insistences on voice ("what we talked of / Matters not much"), Hardy thus turns finally to a silent trace, like that of written language, a record "in colour and cast." Having submitted to Time's rule, he can claim a mediated reference to his lost love and past self, a reference that itself stands beyond Time on the primaeval rocks. Whereas in "Beeny Cliff" he had written with Shelleyan scorn of how "the Atlantic dyed its levels with a dull misfeatured stain," Hardy now accepts the uses of the mediated stains, finding through them at last the very means for establishing a persistent record and for repairing the hitherto ironic division between the human and natural worlds. Despite the careful limitation of his claim ("to one mind . . . to me"), there is great confidence in Hardy's assertion. This is the confidence of the resurgent elegist declaring the singular importance of his recollected moment while also referring to his own powers of recording, of making his rocklike counterstatement to Time and death.

"At Castle Boterel" also makes crucial use of the self-division so often associated with the elegy. We have seen largely ironic forms of this in Hardy's preceding moments of self-mockery or self-accusation and in passages where his own voice is undercut or even supplanted. Now, however, Hardy discriminates an old and sinking self from the young man whose presence is forever recorded by the scene. Indeed, the poem is largely about Hardy's taking leave of that persistent figure of himself. The single phantom figure is Emma's; but Hardy, too, is there, indelibly inscribed within "old love's domain." The actual image of his departure—"my sand is sinking"—is nicely offset by the ageless rocks. And although the phrase reminds us of "The Going" ("sink down soon"), we recall that the earlier poem supplied no token of anything that might survive. The perspective had yawned blankly at that time. Now, the record of them both is there, together with the figure of Emma, which seems to shrink only because the poet leaves.

With the exception of "St. Launce's Revisited," the remaining five poems continue to emphasize the aging poet's faith in his admittedly invented fictions of enduring identity, the "phantom of his own figuring." The generally bleak tone of the series is, however, unremittingly present in Hardy's harsh awareness of his own decline ("He withers daily") and of the "beneaped and stale" quality of his remaining days.

Increasingly, with "Places" and "The Phantom Horsewoman," Hardy writes about his present self as though from a great distance. The self-reference is appropriate to the closing stanzas of an elegy. But in addition, Hardy seems to be using an almost eclogic self-division in order to objectify and detach himself from this aging, ghostly self. As in most elegiac self-surpassals, a final, achieved speaker moves beyond the representation of a less adequate version of himself. The speaker of "Places" and "The Phantom Horsewoman" suggests that he has taken on a voice that is already somehow surviving the old man whom it describes. This voice, produced entirely by the mediation of his text, is in a sense the voice of narration itself. And as a surviving recorder, it would seem to join the signatory associated with the "primaeval rocks." Of course, this voice is projected by the old mourner; but it nevertheless represents the side of him that can take a stand within language alone, together with the reestablished figure of his youth, and his immortally recorded wife. The old man "withers daily, / Time touches her not."

"The Spell of the Rose" ironically examines Hardy's thwarted desire to recapture in life the love he and Emma had lost. The motifs of "too late," of a barrier between husband and wife, both in recent years and now, mock the conventional figure of the rose, with its associations of love and (here) of rebirth. Following this poem, "St. Launce's Revisited" cuts against the yield of early revisitings, with Hardy now violently dispelling the gathered belief in some token of the days long dead. Of course, there had never been a suggestion that either Emma or those earlier days had been recaptured in anything but the traces of their earlier presence. While "St. Launce's Revisited" would seem to remind us of the deprivation that any trace implies, merely by the nature of its existence as trace, the poem also allows the poet a last outbreak of anger over that very deprivation. With this, he clears the ground for the final poem of the series.

"Where the Picnic Was" follows the motif of the poet's revisitation of earlier scenes. But now the scene is not from the distant past of courtship days but rather from the last year of marriage. This implies a slight gesture of reconciliation, as though Hardy were willing to set this scene alongside those of celebrated joy. Hardy's movement in the poem is an ascent, a deliberate version of the ascent that so often marks the close of an elegy. This is, however, no public ritual but rather the characteristically lonely search for a personal track. The preserved motif of such tracking ("I slowly climb . . . And scan and trace") emphasizes Hardy's continuing dependence on intervening marks of his earlier passage. And the seasonal change further stresses his distance from the former visit.

The object of the quest is remarkably similar in function to the primaeval rocks of "At Castle Boterel."

> But the spot still shows
> As a burnt circle—aye,
> And stick-ends, charred,
> Still strew the sward
> Whereon I stand,
> Last relic of the band
> Who came that day!

The spot is a burnt circle, one of the most primitive marks for a particular place. Indeed, Hardy relies on this primitive aspect, as in "At Castle Boterel," to suggest timeless permanence and perhaps at last to give his elegies, here at their end, the ritual quality that he had so thoroughly withheld. After all the images of himself as a forlorn pilgrim, this last scene makes him appear to be the last in a procession of selves, a solitary version of what would otherwise be the procession of a funeral or of an early elegy.

The charred stick-ends which "strew the sward" as though it were a grave (again the diction is archaic and ritualistic) are almost totemic symbols, representing the burned-out, shortened stumps of what had fed the fire. As such, they accord well with the nature of almost any elegy's figure for survival. But apart from marking the violence, the loss, and the refinement inherent to the construction of such a figure, the branded circle points to the *flammae*, the passion and its ruin, of which these elegies have been the vestige. Like the rocks, the circle is a figure for the past and perhaps for the elegies themselves—a harsh version of wreath or garland. Here all the poems' elegiac images of light, from the hardening sunlight to the glowing woman to the glimmerings of memory, terminate in an extraordinarily apt but revisionary figure for the light, for its extinction and its trace. With this ending, so far from the conventionally resurrective suns or stars of the tradition and yet so true to Hardy's own admixture of comfort and desolation, the elegist foregrounds himself as the survivor on his grassy rise, making his last assertion of persistent identity ("Yes, I am here / Just as last year") and finally closing forever the eyes of the dead. [16]

X

Yeats: "In Memory of Major Robert Gregory"

One year after Hardy had completed his *Poems of 1912–13*, the First World War broke out, obliterating much of the Edwardian afterlife of Victorian England and greatly intensifying what Ezra Pound called the "accelerated grimace" of the age. Hardy himself wrote several poems about the war, and his tough accuracy and irony influenced some of the best war poets, such as Owen and Sassoon. So, too, Pound, Eliot, and Yeats were each deeply affected by the war. Pound's "Hugh Selwyn Mauberley" elegizes at once a self, a culture, and a massacred generation:

> Died some, pro patria
>   non 'dulce' non 'et decor' . . .
> walked eye-deep in hell
>
> . . . .
>
> disillusions as never told in the old days,
> hysterias, trench confessions,
> laughter out of dead bellies.
>
> . . . .
>
> There died a myriad,
> And of the best, among them,
> For an old bitch gone in the teeth,
> For a botched civilization. [1]

The old consoling formulae now seem not only obsolete but hypocritical. In these few lines alone we see the outright negation of "'dulce' . . . 'et decor'"; [2] the macabre revision of that generic myth by which the dead still yield an ongoing music ("laughter out of dead bellies"); even the degradation of the elegiac Venus-mother-lover figure to "an old bitch gone in the teeth." With such intense "disillusions," there seemed to be few options apart from Pound's ironic withdrawal behind a highly wrought persona. [3] This was certainly the

260

option taken by Eliot, whose *Prufrock and Other Observations* was dedicated to the young French doctor and poet Jean Verdenal, "mort aux
Dardanelles," whom Eliot much later, but with unabated bitterness,
described as having been "mixed with the mud of Gallipoli." As critics
increasingly demonstrate, Verdenal's death was certainly part of the
private and public devastation mourned in *The Waste Land*.[4]

Yeats, on the other hand, decided to ignore the war as a subject for
poetry. "On Being Asked For a War Poem" briefly explains, "I think it
better that in times like these / A poet's mouth be silent, for in
truth / We have no gift to set a statesman right."[5] Yeats sent the poem
to its solicitor, Edith Wharton, as well as to Henry James. At the end
of the letter to James (20 August 1915), Yeats declared, "It is the only
thing I have written of the war or will write, so I hope it may not seem
unfitting."[6] And yet within three years, the isolation at Coole Park
estate, from where he had written to James, was shattered by the news
that Yeats's young and admired friend Robert Gregory, son of Yeats's
patron Lady Gregory and heir to her estate, had died in action on the
North Italian front.

Yeats's first poem on Gregory's death, the pastoral elegy "Shepherd
and Goatherd," is in one respect similar to the poems by Pound and
Eliot mentioned above: it makes use of overtly artificial personae.
While this was an important aspect of the modernists' strategy of
impersonality, their attempt to avoid the excesses of Victorian senti-
mentality, such contrived uses of persona would *not* in fact prove
influential on elegies of the twentieth century. The same may be said
for the strictly pastoral version of the genre. Few poets of this century
have even tried to write such a poem. The preference has been for a
less disguised voice, located in a more immediate and contemporary
setting. In the wake of a "botched civilization" and amidst "disillusions
as never told in the old days," our century has found scant solace in
imagined dialogues of mourning herdsmen or in ceremonies based too
explicitly or too derivatively on such fictions as that of the martyred
god.

As if to acknowledge this inappropriateness of the pastoral elegy,
Yeats himself turned from "Shepherd and Goatherd" to the nonpastoral "In Memory of Major Robert Gregory"—a poem that both
Yeats and his readers have singled out as one of his best works.[7] In an
undisguised, conversational voice and with an apparent lack of traditionally consoling beliefs, Yeats nevertheless established here a per-

sonal sense of ceremony and a domestic or everyday ground for
residually mythic figures and gestures.

This chapter briefly notes "Shepherd and Goatherd" before examining "In Memory of Major Robert Gregory" in detail. In addition to
commenting on one of the last strictly pastoral elegies in the language, I hope to show once again that even the nonpastoral elegy
depends heavily on elements more obviously present in the pastoral
mode. More generally, our preceding study of the genre as a whole,
both pastoral and nonpastoral, should greatly deepen our understanding of the poem. Examples of important but as yet incompletely
analyzed aspects of the poem include the following: What determines
Yeats's choice of Johnson, Synge, and Pollexfen as figures to accom-
pany Gregory? What do they have in common? How do they help to
define the qualities of Gregory? And even more significantly, how do
they help to carry forward the work of mourning? How should we
understand the poem's ending? How can it be seen to revise one of the
genre's conventional figures, and how does it represent a consoling
imitation of the qualities of the mourned hero?

Among Yeats's first written responses to Gregory's death were a
letter to John Quinn, on 8 February 1918, and an obituary appearing
nine days later in *The Observer*. Although I will refer to them later, I
quote these remarks now for the light that they shed on Gregory and
on the poems that they precede:

> News will have reached you before this of Robert Gregory's death in
> action. I feel it very much for his own sake, still more for his mother's. I
> think he had genius. Certainly no contemporary landscape moved me as
> much as two or three of his, except perhaps a certain landscape by Innes,
> from whom he had learnt a good deal. His paintings had majesty and
> austerity, and at the same time sweetness. He was the most accomplished
> man I have ever known . . . he could do more things well than any other.
> He had proved himself a most daring airman, having been particularly
> successful in single combat with German planes. . . . (*Letters*, 645–46)

> I have known no man accomplished in so many ways as Major Robert
> Gregory, who was killed in action a couple of weeks ago and buried by his
> fellow-airmen in the beautiful cemetery at Padua. His very accomplish-
> ment hid from many his genius. He had so many sides: painter, classical
> scholar, scholar in painting and in modern literature, boxer, horseman,
> airman—he had the M. C. and the Légion d'Honneur—that some among

his friends were not sure what his work would be. To me he will always remain a great painter in the immaturity of his youth, he himself the personification of handsome youth. I first came to understand his genius when, still almost a boy, he designed for Lady Gregory's *Kinkora* and her *Image* and for my *Shadowy Waters* and for Synge's *Deirdre of the Sorrows* decorations which, obtaining their effect from the fewest possible lines and colours, had always the grave distinction of his own imagination. When he began to paint, accustomed to an older school of painting I was long perplexed by what seemed to me neglect of detail. But in a few years I came to care for his paintings of the Clare coast, with its cloudy shadows upon blue-grey stony hills, and for one painting of a not very different scenery by his friend, Innes, more than for any contemporary landscape painting. A man of letters may perhaps find in work such as this, or in old Chinese painting, in the woodcuts and etchings of Calvert and Palmer, in Blake's woodcuts to Thornton's *Virgil*, in the landscape background of Mr. Ricketts' *Wise and Foolish Virgins*, something that he does not find in the great modern masters, and that he cares for deeply. Is it merely that these men share certain moods with great lyric poetry, with, let us say, *The Leech Gatherer* of Wordsworth; or that their moods, unlike those of men with more objective curiosity, are a part of the traditional expression of the soul? One always understands by something in his selection of line and colour that he had read his Homer and his Virgil and his Dante; that they, while giving something of themselves, had freed him from easy tragedy and trivial comedy.

Though he often seemed led away from his work by some other gift, his attitude to life and art never lost intensity—he was never the amateur. I have noticed that men whose lives are to be an ever-growing absorption in subjective beauty—and I am not merely remembering Calvert's philosophy of myth and his musical theory, or Verlaine's sensuality, or Shelley's politics—seek through some lesser gift, or through mere excitement, to strengthen that self which unites them with ordinary men. It is as though they hesitated before they plunged into the abyss. Major Gregory told Mr. Bernard Shaw, who visited him in France, that the months since he joined the army had been the happiest of his life. I think they brought him peace of mind, an escape from that shrinking, which I sometimes saw upon his face, before the growing absorption of his dream, as from his constant struggle to resist those other gifts that brought him ease and friendship. Leading his squadron in France or in Italy, mind and hand were at one, will and desire. [8]

Eight days after writing to Quinn, Yeats wrote a brief poem entitled "Tom O'Roughley." The poem has not been counted amongst those

for Gregory, but it immediately precedes "Shepherd and Goatherd,"
and its date lends a particular focus to its second stanza:

'If little planned is little sinned
But little need the grave distress.
What's dying but a second wind?
How but in zig-zag wantonness
Could trumpeter Michael be so brave?'
Or something of that sort he said,
'And if my dearest friend were dead
I'd dance a measure on his grave.'

(*Poems*, 141)

Despite the heroic bluster, this is a chilling moment—Yeats using a
highly theatrical persona to establish a near-impervious, eccentric
gaiety. We find this elsewhere in Yeats's work, but in this context the
artifice takes on a disturbingly hard sheen. By a wilful avoidance of
emotional complexity, this particular use of persona seems to bypass
the entire process of mourning and to arrive almost a priori at a
deliberately "wanton" resolution. The poem is worth noting not only
because it seems to introduce "Shepherd and Goatherd" but also
because the second poem also suffers from a chilly impersonation, as
well as from a curiously unemotional and dogmatic rigidity which
locks the poem to its solution. Clearly, if Yeats is to write a persuasive
elegy, he will have to reduce the distance between the voice of his
poem and the more personal feelings expressed in the letter and
obituary. He is closer to the shepherd, and particularly the goatherd,
than he was to Tom. But not until "In Memory of Major Robert
Gregory" will he finally write his poem.

On 22 February 1918, Yeats wrote to Lady Gregory, "I am trying a
poem in manner like one that Spenser wrote for Sir Philip Sidney"
(*Letters*, 646). And on 19 March he added, "I have to-day finished my
poem about Robert, a pastoral, modelled on what Virgil wrote for
some friend of his and on what Spenser wrote of Sidney. My wife
thinks it good. A goatherd and a shepherd are talking in some vague
place, perhaps the Burren Hills, in some remote period of the world. It
is a new form for me and I think for modern poetry" (*Letters*, 647).

Several factors made the pastoral form of "Shepherd and Goatherd"
a reasonable first choice. Beyond his ambition to excel in a conventional genre and to achieve a "new form for . . . modern poetry," Yeats
looked upon traditional ceremony itself as a bastion against the in-

coherence and degradation of the contemporary world. Often, he associated such ceremony with the old world of rural Ireland, and with the few aristocratic families, such as the Gregorys, whose estate offered some continuation of that world. Certain historical periods had also enjoyed what Yeats regarded as "cultural unity," one such period being that of Elizabethan England. By setting a Renaissance pastoral elegy in a rural region of ancient Ireland, Yeats sought to combine these instances of cultural integrity, thus furthering the concept of an Irish Renaissance while also celebrating this ideal compound as an appropriate context for Robert Gregory's life.

Gregory himself suited the genre. Apart from his association with a defined rural setting, he was not much older than Sidney had been and at thirty-seven was therefore still perhaps close enough in age to the martyred vegetation deities who had been the original subjects of the elegy. Like Sidney and the early martyr-heroes, Gregory was an exemplary figure in Yeats's eyes—a man of physical and aesthetic achievements whose versatility further associated him with the Renaissance ideal. And Gregory, too, had abandoned his rural and aesthetic pursuits for "an outrageous war," thus again resembling Sidney and, obliquely, their common archetype, Adonis.

The opportunity to use a myth, such as that of Adonis, must itself have drawn Yeats to the pastoral elegy. Just as the generic use of pastoral personae might carry the elegist beyond the idiosyncracies of his own private voice, so an inherited elegiac myth might not only offer a consoling theme but also assimilate the individual dead to a more than personal figure. Several of Yeats's poems do in fact feature Adonis, Dionysus, and Atthis, and it is therefore surprising to find that "Shepherd and Goatherd" makes no real use of these figures. [9] This is one of the problems of the poem. While its traditional form invokes such familiar mythic figures, and while several allusions link the unnamed Gregory to Astrophel and hence to Adonis, Yeats substitutes a myth of his own making, one that has little connection to the generic context of the poem. Yeats's myth, that of the soul's "dreaming back" and "return," derived from the visionary material that he and his wife had recently begun to receive. "Shepherd and Goatherd" is, in fact, one of the first of Yeats's poems to make explicit use of his new "metaphors for poetry." Presumably, the remote, impersonal, and mythic aspects of the old convention appealed to Yeats as a good vehicle for his new material.

Before looking further at Yeats's myth and at other problematic elements of his elegy, I should mention one other probable reason for his choice of the pastoral form: his increasing obsession with old age. *At the Hawk's Well* was written in this year, and many poems, apart from the elegies, in *The Wild Swans at Coole* address this specific anxiety. [10] "Shepherd and Goatherd" offered Yeats the chance to confront and yet to distance the concern by means of a Virgilian eclogue between an old and a young herdsman.

Many elements, therefore, conspired to make the pastoral elegy an appropriate form for Yeats. And yet the poem is a disappointment. That such a set of favorable conditions for such a masterful poet should nevertheless fail to yield a successful poem surely signals what we in retrospect can confirm as the virtual disappearance of the pastoral elegy in the twentieth century.

"Shepherd and Goatherd" disappoints on numerous counts. Much of the problem is already indicated in Yeats's letter to Lady Gregory: "in some vague place . . . in some remote period of the world." This multiplied lack of specificity prevents the poem from ever taking root. It floats at a vague remove, never persuading us to suspend our disbelief, never inviting us to locate its action or its speakers in a given situation that is persuasively bound (as, for example, those in "Astrophel" or "Lycidas" had been) by a world of contingency or strongly felt mortality. Their grief itself is therefore somehow artificial, and their language does little to allay this sense of unreality or contrivance. Both speakers seem to step awkwardly into position, carefully adjusting their costumes and masks to fit their preconceived roles. And the stilted conversation is self-conscious to an almost absurd degree:

> I thought of rhyme alone,
> For rhyme can beat a measure out of trouble
> And make the daylight sweet once more; but when
> I had driven every rhyme into its place
> The sheep had gone from theirs.

> (*Poems*, 142)

Apart from the admitted incompatibility, these lines have a clumsy literalness, a near arithmetical insistence on trying to insert poetry into the shepherd's world. This typifies the poem at large. The speakers' remoteness from their allegedly natural context and roles adds to their distance from the dead shepherd, and this is surely the most severe problem of the poem. We receive such a vague, conventional, and generalized sketch of the dead youth that nothing invites us to mourn the absence of an actual man. Admittedly, one of the tasks of an elegy is to arrive eventually at some reconciliation between the individual dead on the one hand and a more consoling universal figure on the other. But the painful toil of that arrival is crucial, as is a residual tension between the claims of the historical person and the ideal figure to which he has been assimilated. Neither such toil nor such tension lends weight to "Shepherd and Goatherd." It is as though Robert Gregory himself had never lived or died among these hills.

The consoling myth that Yeats appends in the form of the old goatherd's song only reduces Gregory yet further toward an abstract cypher. For the song describes the soul's return, through the reversed sequence of its recent incarnation, to the "cradle-side" where it had entered life. But none of this applies with much specificity to Gregory. It is the prospect facing *any* soul, an almost dogmatic resolution. And although familiar elements of consolation are at hand—the self-conscious reference to achieved songs, the restored relation to a parental figure, the image of repaired narcissism ("he dreams himself his mother's pride"), the suggestion of rebirth and ongoing procreation (confirmed by the final description of Gregory's children "spring-[ing] up shoulder-high")—nothing saves the poem from its detachment. It remains a formulaic exercise, expressing little of the man whom it mourns and still less of the man who mourns him. In his next elegy, Yeats will find ways to combine these latter, expressive demands with the numerous concerns and motifs carried forward from the earlier poem.

One of these continued concerns is Yeats's determination to write a Renaissance poem for his Renaissance man. As is well known, Yeats took the stanzaic form of "In Memory of Major Robert Gregory" from Cowley's elegy "On the Death of Mr. William Hervey." I shall examine the stanzaic structure of that poem in a moment; but we should also note that Yeats was doing far more than borrowing an appropriate form. If he was searching for a *nonpastoral* elegy that was nonetheless of the Renaissance, Cowley's poem was a good choice. Cowley, after all, was elegizing a "Renaissance man" of versatile excellence. The versatility appealed to Cowley not so much for its variety as for the concentration of that variety in one person: "all the Virtues there did come / As to their chiefest seat." The word *all* in fact appears in Cowley's poem no less than eleven times; and although its application varies, the word drives strongly toward a consoling image of totality. Yeats's poem depends even more heavily on this drive toward regarding its dead hero as a unifying image of totality. And Yeats, too, as we shall see, makes a remarkably repetitive use of the word *all*, which appears thirteen times in his poem.

More broadly, Cowley's poem offered an example of an elegy whose rejection of the pastoral form did *not* mean a rejection of ceremony or dignity. Cowley's decorum is at once formal and personal, a good model for a poet trying to adjust the claims of impersonal remoteness and more private emotion. "On the Death of Mr. William Hervey" moves with great dignity, with the kind of self-assurance that even permits a simply expressed but authoritative personal refrain ("Dark as the grave wherein my friend is laid"). Yeats will also use an occasional refrain, and *his* words, too, will often come to rest in the simple gravity of near-monosyllabic lines.

Yeats's decision to go beyond his pastoral elegy reflected his impatience with its heavy frame and outworn fictions, as well as his search for a more direct kind of expression. Here again, Cowley was important, for he had been highly deliberate in his dismissal of "senseless Fables" and of the assorted "cold-meats of the Antients, new-heated, and new set-forth."[11] He had been a friend, and subsequent biographer, of that most stringent reformer of language, Thomas Sprat, passages of whose *History of the Royal Society* are remarkably close to Yeats's declarations more than two centuries later:

> . . . to return back to the primitive purity, and shortness, when men deliver'd so many things, almost in an equal number of words. They have exacted from all their members, a close, naked, natural way of speaking; positive expressions, clear senses; a native easiness; bringing all things as near the Mathematical plainness, as they can: and preferring the language of Artizans, Countrymen, and Merchants, before that, of Wits, or Scholars.[12]

In his notes for a 1900 lecture on Lionel Johnson, Yeats referred to poetry as "the speech of a man," and towards the end of his life, he wrote, "I tried to make the language of poetry coincide with that of passionate, normal speech."[13] "In Memory of Major Robert Gregory" is a triumph of such speech, although of course it gathers up the "passionate, normal" currents and accents of that speech and drives them into the highly wrought stanzas borrowed from Cowley. For as Yeats added to his remarks about personal speech, "All that is personal rots; it must be packed in ice or salt. . . . I must choose a traditional stanza, even what I alter must seem traditional. . . . Talk to me of originality and I will turn on you with rage. . . . Ancient salt is best packing" (EI, 522).

The ice or salt pack of Cowley's eight-line stanza has two quatrains, rhyming *aabb* and *cddc*, respectively. The lines are iambic pentameters, except for the fourth, sixth, and seventh, which are tetrameters. We are familiar with the elegiac alternation of line lengths, with its traditional antiphony and its interplay of contraction and expansion, loss and gain. Here, the fourth line has the more particular effect of aborting a pair of heroic couplets. And as though in response to this abrupt deprivation, the second quatrain reorganizes its structure so as to rhyme in the more contained or even defensive way, *cddc*, protecting its inner couplet and keeping its curtailed lines within the pentameter rather than remaining open to a final abbreviation. Less specifically, the irregularities temper and personalize what might otherwise have sounded too unshakably formal.

But "even *what I alter* must seem traditional" (my emphasis). Despite their formal similarity, Yeats's stanza works differently from Cowley's. [14] An appreciation of this difference takes us quite deep into the poem. Whereas Cowley pauses frequently in his stanza, invariably coming to a full stop after each quatrain, Yeats drives *through* his stanzas with extraordinary momentum. Cowley's syntax quite passively meets the demands of most lines and of every quatrain, whereas Yeats's entire stanza gives the illusion of being charged or even domineered by an irresistible syntactic will. In most cases this will is single and unbroken. Eight of the twelve stanzas have only one period each. Yeats seems to have crossed the form of Cowley's stanza with the syntactic momentum of another elegist he admired, Shelley. We have seen how forcefully the later stanzas of "Adonais" press and mount to their end, and we shall discuss the thematic relation between that poem and Yeats's elegy. For the moment, the stylistic similarity is already suggestive.

Yet another influence on the momentum of Yeats's stanza must surely have been Walter Pater. Pater's presence is definitely implied by that of Lionel Johnson, one of the heroes of this elegy; and Yeats often acknowledged the power of Pater's cadenced prose, even to the point of versifying *one* of its periods into a single sixteen-line stanza. [15] As we shall see, Pater joins Shelley in affecting far more than the syntax of Yeats's poem.

Why this great urge to unify period and stanza? An obvious answer is the inherently consoling display of some kind of mastery—a display whose importance we have noted in almost every elegy. In Yeats's case, riding a powerful syntax through the course of each stanza might also be his version of what he later represents by the horsemanship of George Pollexfen and Robert Gregory—a combination of skill and daring, a glamorous *sprezzatura*. We shall see how closely the elegist will try to imitate the admired qualities of the dead. Here, at the level of syntax and stanzaic form, Yeats is already performing his elegiac emulation.

What is more important, the thrust of a period is, for Yeats, an embodiment and shaping of passion itself. As he would write twenty years later, "It was a long time before I had made a language to my liking; I began to make it when I discovered twenty years ago that I must seek, not as Wordsworth thought, words in common use, but a powerful and passionate syntax, and a complete coincidence between period and stanza" (*EI*, 521–22).

Yeats celebrated passion, like mastery and daring, throughout his poetry. But passion was at the very center of his praise for Johnson, Pollexfen, Synge, and Gregory. These men exemplified not only passion but discipline, a combination captured by the syntax of the poem. So, too, for the celebration of totality and unity, with the stanza-period grasping and molding its elements into a single gesture. This in turn is very close to Johnson's yearning for "consummation" and to Gregory's having "consume[d] / The entire combustible world in one small room." A stanza is, after all, a room, and Yeats tries hard, particularly in the closing reaches of this poem, to simulate the achievement of his hero.

To call Gregory's death an achievement is already to have fallen under Yeats's spell, and later I will look at the thematic nature of that spell. For the moment, however, the sheerly formal working of the spell should be noted. Each long period's drive creates a hunger for the end; it makes us regard the end as a quarry, a place of triumph and repose. In a poem about restless dreamers, racers, hunters, and travelers, even stanza ends become alluring. It is as though each stanza, and the poem at large, has a kind of lust for its own close. And the satisfaction of this lust transvalues the abrupt ending of the poem and of the life that it mourns.

It would be wrong to suppose that this formal drive toward consummation is entropic or deadly. Admittedly, the poem is at one level a displacement, as any elegy must be, of the mourner's "longing for the tomb." And a great source of the almost irresistible power of much of Yeats's poetry is certainly its satisfaction of this hunger for finality. But one cannot disregard the other aspect of this period-stanza coincidence: its celebration of passionate energy expressed in the rhythmic momentum itself. For here we approach that other familiar elegiac motif, the assertion of a force that seems to outlast individual death, a more than personal life-force associated with happiness and joy. If this sounds far-fetched, we may read Yeats on the subject of "natural momentum in the syntax": "Because I need a passionate syntax for passionate subject-matter I compel myself to accept those traditional metres that have developed with the language. Ezra Pound, Turner, Lawrence wrote admirable free verse, I could not. I would lose myself, become *joyless*" (*EI*, 522, my emphasis). And elsewhere, discussing the rhythm of Elizabethan lyricists and quoting, of all poems, a verse commendation of Sir Philip Sidney: "Yet if one were to put even these lyrics beside a fine modern song one would notice that they had a stronger and rougher energy, a featherweight more, if eye and ear were fine enough to notice it, of the active will, of the happiness that comes out of life itself" (*EI*, 381).

After stopping at Glendalough, among the Burren Hills, where he wrote "Shepherd and Goatherd," Yeats and his wife returned to Ballylee. They stayed at Lady Gregory's Ballinamantane House while making final preparations to occupy the nearby tower. Here Yeats wrote his elegy. The theme of settling into the tower opens the poem.

> Now that we're almost settled in our house
> I'll name the friends that cannot sup with us
> Beside a fire of turf in th' ancient tower,
> And having talked to some late hour
> Climb up the narrow winding stair to bed:
> Discoverers of forgotten truth
> Or mere companions of my youth,
> All, all are in my thoughts to-night being dead.

(Poems, 132)

As opposed to the impersonation of herdsmen "in some vague place . . . in some remote period of the world," here is the direct, conversational voice of the elegist, situating himself and his poem within his very house. This domestic intimacy determines much of the emotional pressure of the poem: it is quite literally close to home. But as suggested earlier, Yeats's achievement was to wed this personal domestic world with that of a more than personal, mythological character. The ancient tower, as we know, is one such compound. Apart from its connection with Robert Gregory himself, who had encouraged Yeats to buy it, the tower's elegiac properties are particularly impressive. On the simplest level, it is an image of defensive fortitude (we recall Wordsworth's elegiac castle "cased in the unfeeling armour of old time"). Not only has the tower withstood time but it has remained as though at the center of time, a kind of temporal as well as spatial omphalos measuring the movements of the sun and moon. As Yeats would later claim:

> Alexandria's was a beacon tower, and Babylon's
> An image of the moving heavens, a log-book of the sun's
>   journey and the moon's;
> And Shelley had his towers, thought's crowned powers he
>   called them once.
>
> I declare this tower is my symbol; I declare
> This winding, gyring, spiring treadmill of a stair is my
>   ancestral stair;
> That Goldsmith and the Dean, Berkeley and Burke have
>   travelled there. [16]

Associated with the ancient centers of philosophy and astronomy, Yeats's tower is thus also closely bound up with a specifically Irish history. The concern for national heritage, thus embedded in the very stones of his house, will be important to the elegy, partly determining the selection of its mourned heroes. [17] But in addition, the tower suggests the isolated but lofty retreats of Shelley and of that other elegiac idealist, "Il Penseroso"'s Platonist, who "toiled on / In some like chamber, shadowing forth / How the daemonic rage / Imagined everything."[18] We shall see how thoroughly Yeats's elegy confronts not only Shelley and Milton but also the questions of isolation and of "daemonic rage," the daemon itself being in many ways an elegiac construction. In all respects, then, Yeats's opening focus on the tower is deep and complex. Even his attention to the winding stair reminds us not only of the purgatorial ascent of that visionary mourner, Dante, but also of the soul's spiraling "return" described in "Shepherd and Goatherd" and of the turning gyres of history itself, as Yeats had begun to envision it.

All these symbolic connections to otherworldly philosophers and questors and to longstanding structures of defense or research are, however, nicely balanced by the touching admission of a personal, highly mundane condition of incomplete settlement. Yeats is just about to settle, and it is in the very interval of that uncompleted settlement that the poem arises. Indeed, we suspect that this elegy is a rite essential to that settlement. Like a member of an ancient or so-called primitive society, Yeats cannot take possession of a home until he has summoned his dead and settled them, too, in the new place.

It is striking that Yeats's opening line alone thus seems to reverse or redefine the alleged occasion of the poem. Rather than seeming to write under the pressure of Gregory's recent death, Yeats creates the impression that this death, like those of Johnson, Pollexfen, and Synge, has somehow been waiting upon *him*, waiting until *he* is ready to give it its due. Yeats often does this, maneuvering himself into a central position from which the world and the events of history seem curiously dependent upon *him*. They await his ceremonies of integration and his conferrals of meaning as though he and his poetry were no less than their destiny. For a mourner, this reversal is itself an important achievement.

Without being ultimately ambiguous, the first stanza allows for a momentary but significant confusion of reference. While certainly performing the mourner's necessary submission to reality ("friends that cannot sup with us . . . being dead"), the stanza twice lets us blur the demarcation between the living and the dead. For just a moment we wonder whether the fourth and fifth lines continue, as do the line and a half above them, to refer to the dead friends. But no, it is Yeats who will "talk" (the verb points precisely to the conversational quality of this elegy's passionate speech), and it is *he* who will climb the stair to bed (although, added to the syntactic blur, that image suggests the winding ascent of the dead to *their* repose). Similarly, the final line, "All, all are in my thoughts to-night being dead," allows another moment in which we wonder whether it is somehow the poet who is dead. These are, admittedly, passing ambiguities, but they register early in a poem whose project will in large part be an emulation of the chosen dead and whose poet begins by giving these dead a present life within his thoughts.

Other elements of the first stanza will be mentioned when we discuss later moments in the poem. But one deserves early notice: the repetition "All, all" in the final line. This initiates the poem's almost compulsive use of the word, the elegist grasping time and again for a consoling image of totality. In fact, the stanza moves away from a fractional use of the word in a prefix to denote a partial state ("almost"), and within eight lines it reaches instead this bold assertion of a unifying and complete embrace.

> II
> Always we'd have the new friend meet the old
> And we are hurt if either friend seem cold,
> And there is salt to lengthen out the smart
> In the affections of our heart,
> And quarrels are blown up upon that head;
> But not a friend that I would bring
> This night can set us quarrelling,
> For all that come into my mind are dead.

The second stanza opens with a positive use of the *al*-prefix and closes with another final *all*. The motif of domesticity is continued, with an advance now from the transitional hesitancy of "almost settled" to the discussion of routine ("always"). Hospitality is the subject, reminding us of the protocol between host and guests and reinforcing the ceremonious nature of the poem's invitation. As in Yeats's pastoral elegy, courtesy is highly valued throughout the poem, in this case being assimilated to the elaborate courtesy of a private seance.

The curious lines about the salt and smart gain weight if we recall that salt both burns and preserves, two actions crucial to the poem, particularly as these are applied to the affections of the heart. And while the *heart* will emerge as an essential protagonist of this elegy, its ideally unifying interplay with the *head* is nicely insinuated by these two words, positioned as they are at the end of two consecutive lines at the core of the stanza.

With the last three lines, as often in the poem, Yeats cuts back across his stanza following a *but* or an *and yet*. The effect partly preserves the dialogic antiphony of early elegies, while the gesture of moving "withershins," to use Yeats's word, acts as a bracing cross-weave or cross-stitch, tautening the fabric of the stanza. In this case, the actual statement is a poignant repetition of the fact that the dead are, after all, dead. By echoing the last line of the previous stanza, this end sounds like a refrain, perfectly suited to the form of an elegy and performing what we have noted elsewhere as the repetitive task of reality testing. There is, however, a calmness to the admission, for it moves beyond the realm of possible quarrel into a conciliatory reassurance of peace.

Finally, Yeats has raised the energy of his invocation to "I would bring." Now, too, the dead not merely "are" but rather "come" into the mind. The refrain is, after all, as much a chanted summons as it is a truthful reminder. And emerging directly out of this repeated spell, the first guest enters the poem. The traditional elegiac procession, revised to include the dead rather than the mourners, begins to move through the poem as Yeats starts to represent the qualities that, partially embodied in the following three figures, will finally converge in the unifying figure of Robert Gregory.

> III
> Lionel Johnson comes the first to mind,
> That loved his learning better than mankind,
> Though courteous to the worst; much falling he
> Brooded upon sanctity
> Till all his Greek and Latin learning seemed
> A long blast upon the horn that brought
> A little nearer to his thought
> A measureless consummation that he dreamed.

Here, as in the two succeeding stanzas for Synge and Pollexfen, the single-period stanza is at full stretch, working with great effect. The one thrust embodies Johnson's ongoing quest for consummation, while the unitary quality captures an image of the dead man as if in the once-and-for-all frame of a portrait.

"Johnson comes the first to mind," having been one of Yeats's earliest friends, a mentor whose poetry, beliefs, and life profoundly affected the younger poet. A dominant member of the Rhymers' Club, his poetry exemplified the blend of passion and austerity that Yeats saw as a path beyond his own juvenile, "soft" Victorianisms toward a harder, more mature clarity of style. Ezra Pound described Johnson's poems in these terms: "Their appeal is not so much to the fluffy, unsorted imagination of adolescence as to more hardened passion and intellect of middle-age."[19] And Yeats's comments on the Rhymers, and on Johnson's poetry in particular, refer very closely to formal characteristics that we noted earlier with regard to this elegy. The Rhymers sought "to rediscover in verse the syntax of impulsive common life." "Johnson's poetry, like Johnson himself before his last decay, conveys an emotion of joy, of intellectual clearness, of hard energy; he gave us of his triumph" (A, 202, 207).

Impulse yet syntax, passion yet discipline and law—these terms will characterize Robert Gregory's art as well. Johnson's appearance and character were no less important to Yeats. Indeed, as Yeats wrote, these were similar in nature to the poetry:

> He became for a few years my closest friend, and what drew me to him was a certain elegance of mind that seemed to correspond to his little, beautifully formed body, the distinction, as of a Greek carving, in his regular features. He was the first disciple of Walter Pater whom I had met, and he had taken from Walter Pater certain favourite words which came to mean much for me: "Life should be a ritual," and we should value it for "magnificence," for all that is "hieratic."[20]

The connection to Pater is crucial, but for the moment this mention of Johnson's physical appearance is itself worth regarding. Yeats had elaborated elsewhere: "He has the delicate strong features of a certain filleted head of a Greek athlete in the British Museum, an archaistic Graeco-Roman copy of a masterpiece of the fourth century, and that resemblance seemed symbolic of the austere nobility of his verse" (A, 149). The figure of Johnson thus contributes greatly to a poem that is trying to celebrate the timeless image of an ideal man. The obituary had spoken of Gregory as "the personification of handsome youth." The athletic figure recurs in the portrayals of Pollexfen and Gregory, while the description of an actual person in terms of a work of art touches the heart of what we shall recognize as this elegist's general ambition to imitate an artistically constructed "mirror-resembling dream."[21] That the work of art in question above should be a copy of a masterpiece is itself extremely apt. The resemblance between Johnson's face and the artwork is appropriate in other ways, for it links Johnson not only to the heroes and art of the Classical world he studied but also to the style of art ("stern color and delicate line") that Gregory had begun to practice. Johnson looked the way Gregory painted, and his appearance at the outset of the poem therefore begins to characterize both the figure and the work of the young man, connecting both to the ideal image of a Classical work of art.

Johnson's hieratic ritualism and his discipleship to Pater were even more important. We have already noted the influence on Yeats of Pater's prose style. In addition, Pater's intense but priestlike appreciation of art had an immense appeal for Yeats, who was himself searching to make "a new religion, almost an infallible church of poetic tradition, of a fardel of stories, and of personages, and of emotions, inseparable from their first expression, passed on from generation to generation by poets and painters with some help from philosophers and theologians" (A, 77). In Pater, as in Johnson, Yeats admired the blend of fervor and asceticism, of passion and style, both in their work and in their near-monastic life.

More specifically, in these cases Yeats admired life's attempted imitation of a work of art—an imitation arising partly from acts of appreciation so devoted as to mirror, in their intensity and concentration, the very qualities of the objects that they appreciate. The conclusion of The Renaissance is only the best known of Pater's many formulations of this ideal project; but its exhortation to "ecstasy," to burning with a "hard, gem-like flame," is an intriguing forerunner of the concluding images of fire, however revisionary, of Yeats's poem.

And yet, the pathos of Johnson's life exposed the contradictory nature of Pater's celebration. One has only to contextualize the quotation from The Renaissance to confirm its elegiac quality—its brave attempt to salvage moments that are in essence reliquary and to recognize the brief lusters in unmistakably divided lives.[22] Furthermore, submission to ritual, or to the imitation of perfect images discovered in art or scholarship, demands renunciation, an ascetic chastity that we have seen to be closely related to the work of mourning, with its unavoidable deflections of desire. A fascinating but hitherto unnoticed feature of this elegy is its thorough presentation, through Johnson, Pollexfen, and Synge, of just this elegiac theme.

As Yeats's portrayal shows, Johnson had displaced many of his natural affections onto the objects of his learning, objects that could only indicate a consummation yet to come. And this power of indication could itself arise only by Johnson's disastrous falling to brood upon sanctity. The "falling" of course alludes to Johnson's "Mystic and Cavalier" ("Go from me: I am one of those who fall"). It no doubt applies to Johnson's alcoholism, the cause of several collapses. But it applies as much to Yeats's picture of a tragic generation of poets whom he saw falling between unattainable dreams and the lives that those very dreams had shattered. Set off against "a measureless consumma- tion," the phrase "a little nearer" is at once sympathetic and bitter. A passage in Yeats's *Memoirs* provides a remarkable summary of these issues. It sheds light on the stanza as well as on the larger concerns of the poem:

> Under some censored need to people that solitude, he invented innumera- ble conversations with people he had never met, and would tell them for truth, and at the end, I do not doubt, to believe their truth. . . .
> So far as theory went, he was an extreme ascetic . . . as he emptied each glass of wine his doctrine became more exalted, winding up with a eulogy upon St. Jerome who, that he might live undisturbed the life of the soul, had unmanned himself. And once too he had read me a story, never to be published, of some scholar led at last to suicide by his longing for what may be beyond death. I remember nothing of it now but that the scholar's dying words were in Latin, and ecstatic praise of those splendours. . . .
> Johnson had refused rather than failed to live, and when an autopsy fol- lowed his accidental death during intoxication it was found that in him the man's brain was united to a body where the other organs were un- developed, the body of a child. (*M*, 95–96)

The invention of imaginary conversations or audiences is not too remote from Yeats's present pursuit. And a self-castrative unmanning or "refusal," one that yields an ecstatic gain in spirituality—this is a familiar topos for an elegy. Clearly the *life* of Johnson thus exhibits aspects of the elegist's task. By confronting the tragedy of such a life, Yeats performs a substantial portion of his work of mourning. Simi- larly, in the portraits of Synge and Pollexfen, Yeats will continue not only to assemble valued qualities later concentrated by Gregory but also to summon, and mourn, lives whose own sacrificial transactions exemplify the nature of his own poem.

IV
And that enquiring man John Synge comes next,
That dying chose the living world for text
And never could have rested in the tomb
But that, long travelling, he had come

Towards nightfall upon certain set apart
In a most desolate stony place,
Towards nightfall upon a race
Passionate and simple like his heart.

The stanza's movement is similar to but even more fluid than that of the stanza on Johnson. Long, unsatisfied brooding and dreaming now give way to traveling, discovery, and repose. But the elegiac dynamic is the same. Yeats even repeats the grammatic style, in which a present participle expressing loss in terms of physical suffering or submission ("falling," "dying") is followed by the verb that refers to the act of consequent displacement ("brooded," "chose"). Just as Johnson, physically disabled by alcohol and dreamy seclusion, turned to brood on sanctity, so Synge, weakened by a mortal illness (he died of Hodgkins disease at thirty-eight), turned to the compensatory activities of literature. His choice of "the living world for text" may seem to refer to a choice different from Johnson's. Synge turned, not to scholarship, but to an immersion in the daily life of Ireland and the Aran Islands. And yet the similarity reemerges as we recognize that Synge's immersion was a means to an end and that this end was, after all, a displacement from life to literature, from "living world" to his dramatic "text" about that world. Yeats's essay on Synge underlines the elegiac quality of this displacement, its similarity to the castrative or sacrificial substitutions associated with mourning:

> It is possible that low vitality helped him to be observant and contemplative, and made him dislike, even in solitude, those thoughts which unite us to others. . . . What blindness did for Homer, lameness for Hephaestus, asceticism for any saint you will, bad health did for him by making him ask no more of life than that it should keep him living, and above all perhaps by concentrating his imagination upon one thought, health itself. I think that all noble things are the result of warfare; great nations and classes, of warfare in the visible world, great poetry and philosophy, of invisible warfare, the division of a mind within itself, a victory, the sacrifice of a man to himself. I am certain that my friend's noble art, so full of passion and heroic beauty, is the victory of a man who in poverty and sickness created from the delight of expression, and in the contemplation that is born of the minute and delicate arrangement of images, happiness and health of mind. (*EI*, 321)[23]

Like Johnson, who "loved his learning better than mankind," Synge "dislike[d], even in solitude, those thoughts which unite us to others."

Yeats is exploring here the costs of what he had referred to in the Gregory obituary as a plunge into the abyss of solitary contemplation, an abyss associated with the subjective pursuit of art and literature. Gregory, we remember, hesitated before making that plunge. By enlisting in active service, he chose, unlike Synge and Johnson, to "strengthen that self which [united him] with ordinary men." While sharing qualities and tendencies of the other two men, Gregory thus managed to experience a kind of instantaneous completion, an active unity of being which the others had forgone. Over against their solitude, and counter-acting "the growing absorption of his dream," Gregory had won a few months' "ease and friendship." As was true of the deities originally celebrated by the elegy, Gregory seems to satisfy desires ("will and desire") that no mortal (in this case, no artist) can fulfill. That he could do so only at the cost of his own life is of course part of the ancient bargain. We shall return to this fulfillment and its cost later, but the comparison of Yeats's comments on Synge's and Johnson's solitude, on the one hand, and Gregory's fellowship, on the other, shows again how carefully Yeats has selected his *dramatis personae*.

Apart from the choice of solitude, Synge has suffered a fate similar to those of Homer and Hephaestus, or for that matter of the ascetic, "undeveloped" Johnson. From our view, the point of the allusions is fairly obvious. But the conclusion of the quoted passage is more specific. Yeats defines Synge's compensatory substitutions precisely as the figurings forth of qualities *opposite* to those of his nature or condition: in "poverty and sickness" he created "happiness and health of mind." This formulation is crucial to our understanding of Yeats's elegy. It is again stressed later, in his *Autobiography*, where we find an explicit connection made between oppositional or antithetical self-imaging and the motif of death and rebirth: "A writer must die every day he lives, be reborn, as it is said in the Burial Service, an incorruptible self, that self opposite of all that he has named 'himself.' . . . Synge was a sick man picturing energy, a doomed man picturing gaiety . . ." (A, 307). [24]

By repeating the word *picturing*, Yeats emphasizes a dependence on artistic mediation, just as he had in the preceding references to the "delight in expression" and "the contemplation that is born of the minute and delicate arrangement of images." By means of an artistic figure, the self finds or creates an image of its opposite, which it may then strive to imitate in an act of contemplative self-transformation or self-completion. This represents a mediated, aesthetic version of what Gregory did in an actual, unmediated way. We have seen forms of this antithetical mirroring in Shelley and Tennyson, and the poem will pursue the theme on several levels. But already we recognize that Yeats is working here with his emerging concept of daemon, or mask.

"Ego Dominus Tuus," Yeats's first poetic expression of the doctrine, was published along with the two Gregory elegies in *The Wild Swans at Coole*. In this poem, *Ille* supposes that Dante and Keats, very much like Synge, conjured images of their own opposites. *Ille* himself is such a conjurer, seeking the figure that is at once his "double" and his "anti-self." In *Per Amica Silentia Lunae*, to which "Ego Dominus Tuus" is the introduction, Yeats speaks of this double or anti-self as the daemon or mask; and intriguingly enough, the discussion of this concept early in the essay is followed by the example of Synge.

Even more intriguing is the expressly elegiac element of the daemon. Not only is it a compensatory strategem devised to complete a partial self but it is constructed out of the chosen dead. As Robert Langbaum described it: "The term for the external self which Yeats took over from the Neoplatonists, and which he introduces for the first time in *Per Amica*, is *Daimon*. According to Plutarch, Yeats's main source, the souls of certain illustrious dead men become purified to the point where they 'are exalted into Daimons' and champion those living men who 'strive for the same attainments'—communicating with them in sleep or waking trance."[25]

"In Memory of Major Robert Gregory" is itself a form of waking trance in which the elegist strives for the attainments of the illustrious dead, reducing them (particularly Gregory) into a daemonic image that he can imitate. Yeats thus performs not only a work of mourning but also the ritual of symbolic death and self-resurrection that that work may resemble. As in the primitive rites, the devotee or griever is reborn. Expanding on the earlier comment on Synge ("A writer must die every day he lives, be reborn, as it is said in the Burial Service, an incorruptible self, that self opposite"), Yeats added in "The Death of Synge": "I think that all happiness depends on the energy to assume the mask of some other self; that all joyous or creative life is a re-birth as something not oneself . . ." (*A*, 340).

Returning to the stanza, we can regard Synge's "long travelling" as an antithetical quest—a quest largely prompted by Yeats, who on meeting Synge in Paris had felt that the latter "needed something to take him out of his morbidity and melancholy" (A, 230). It was as though Synge had needed to move to a more vigorous phase of some work of mourning. Yeats pressed Synge to "go to the Aran Islands and find a life that had never been expressed in literature, instead of a life where all had been expressed" (A, 230). And in "that desolate stony place" Synge found so complementary an image of his heart that he could finally be at rest.

The "desolate stony place" recalls the description in "Shepherd and Goatherd" of Gregory's location and art: "it was their loneliness / The exultation of their stone, that cried / Under his fingers." The crying of the stone is, literally, an echo. And in the ninth stanza of the poem, the motifs of both stern landscape *and* a discovered likeness, echo, or mirroring will figure prominently. Finally, the stanza's powerful culmination with the passionate and simple heart looks forward to the elegist's own ultimate focus on *his* heart. He, too, will have arrived "towards nightfall upon certain set apart." He, too, will have discovered or created his resemblance to an ideal image of passion, simplicity, and unity.

Meanwhile, continuing to "gather the limbs" of his ideal image, Yeats summons another guest:

> V
> And then I think of old George Pollexfen,
> In muscular youth well known to Mayo men
> For horsemanship at meets or at racecourses,
> That could have shown how pure-bred horses
> And solid men, for all their passion, live
> But as the outrageous stars incline
> By opposition, square and trine;
> Having grown sluggish and contemplative.

Yeats describes the athletic prowess of his uncle, stressing the horsemanship at which Gregory, too, excelled. The figure of the athletic youth looks back within the poem toward Johnson's appearance and forward toward Gregory. But Pollexfen also suffered his version of Johnson's and Synge's particular ills. And his life, too, strongly resembled aspects of the work of mourning. Very much like them, Pollexfen suffered a form of physical decline that yielded a compensatory gift. While their "falling" and "dying" is matched by his "having grown sluggish," Johnson's spiritual dream and Synge's choice of complementary text match his "contemplative" astrology.

The movement from muscular youth to contemplation and to brooding age is a submission to time. And the elegiac submission itself is heavily underscored by the exact subject of Pollexfen's thought: man's will is subject to a power beyond his own control; his passion is qualified by the outrageous rule of a larger force. (Yeats's transfer of the word *outrageous* from the war in "Shepherd and Goatherd" to the stars here is noteworthy, suggesting a lingering bitterness in this image of submission.)

With startling consistency, Pollexfen's submission, too, has its association with a mourner's displacement of physical, specifically sexual, energy. Like the much falling and "undeveloped" Johnson, or the Synge who had been compared to blind Homer, lame Hephaestus, or a man "condemned to the life of a monk,"[26] the declining Pollexfen had his chastened aspect: "Some love affair had gone wrong when he was a very young man; he had now no interest in women; certainly never sought favour of a woman, and yet he took great care of his appearance. He did not let his beard grow, though he had, or believed that he had, for he was hypochondriacal, a sensitiveness of the skin that forced him to spend an hour in shaving . . ." (A, 172).

The second sentence does more than merely intensify implications of the first. Certainly, the compulsive, exaggerated act of shaving is, in context, almost absurdly appropriate. But beyond the gesture of castrative or even funereal sacrifice, there is the important suggestion that Pollexfen, no less than Johnson or Synge, cultivated a certain image of the self by means of an elaborate and distinctly ascetic ritual. The sentence quoted above continues, "and he would take to club and dumb-bell if his waist thickened by a hair's breadth." (The adjacency, together with the image of the hair's breadth, confirms the relation between Pollexfen's shaving and his weight lifting.)

Like Johnson and Synge, Pollexfen cultivated an image that was antithetical to his actual condition. In a preceding passage, Yeats wrote: "His furniture had not been changed since he set up house for himself as a very young man, and in a room opposite his dining-room were the saddles of his youth, and though he would soon give up riding, they would be oiled and the stirrups kept clean and bright till the day of his death" (A, 172). In his rituals of shaving and weight lifting and in the saddles and bright stirrups of his youth, Pollexfen cultivated a masklike image of what he had ceased to be. Not only do the self-division and the mask resemble those of Johnson and Synge but they look ahead to the figure of Gregory, who died before suffering this kind of decline, and before having to cultivate this kind of image. Once again, therefore, the early guests of the elegy present positive attributes of the hero—here youthful athleticism and riding skills—but in a mode of divisiveness that only the ideal figure of Gregory will unify. "What made us dream that he could comb grey hair?"

VI
They were my close companions many a year,
A portion of my mind and life, as it were,
And now their breathless faces seem to look
Out of some old picture-book;
I am accustomed to their lack of breath,
But not that my dear friend's dear son,
Our Sidney and our perfect man,
Could share in that discourtesy of death.

In a poem so attentive to questions of division and totality, Yeats's description of his friends as "a portion of my mind and life, as it were" takes on particular force. Their deaths presumably robbed him of a portion that he is even now trying to reintegrate. Indeed, the mention of a "picture-book," with its stress on artifice and image, invites us to see Yeats, too, constructing his own version of a mirror or rather complementary mask, a set of portraits that enables him to complete his "life and mind."

But now, at the very midpoint of the poem, Yeats introduces a death that threatens the very habit of compensatory picturing and mirroring. Gregory cannot so easily be transformed to a breathless image. Nor can he reflect Yeats as straightforwardly as had Johnson, Synge, and Pollexfen. Their cases of self-division, of yearning for spiritual consummation, of struggling for images of gaiety and strength, of obsessively trying to combat the pathos of old age—all these reflected aspects of Yeats himself. But Gregory represented something quite different. He had attained an apparent unity of being, a completion within life, that Yeats and the others lacked. And while Yeats will continue to mirror the dead in his poem, the method of this mirroring will have to change if it is to provide a resemblance of Gregory.

Gregory is not named anywhere in the poem. As in the most traditional elegies, this allows him to be more easily assimilated to a mythic or legendary figure. Unlike Spenser, Milton, or Shelley, Yeats does not, however, rename Gregory; rather, he uses the Augustan device of allusion. Like Dryden's Oldham, "Marcellus of our tongue," Gregory is called "our Sidney and our perfect man," the allusion serving to elevate him to the status of an already immortalized Renaissance man. Spenser's complex praise of Sidney is thus neatly brought to bear on Yeats's own object of various celebration. And the beautiful understatement "that discourtesy of death" preserves the association with the exemplary courtier, even while it suggests that Yeats is reaching for an astonishingly elevated protocol or courtly system of his own—one whose grandeur would relegate even Death to the low rank of a discourteous bungler. While denigrating Death, Yeats thus acquires for himself a measure of the superior courtesy for which he praises Gregory.

> VII
> For all things the delighted eye now sees
> Were loved by him; the old storm-broken trees
> That cast their shadows upon road and bridge;
> The tower set on the stream's edge;
> The ford where drinking cattle make a stir
> Nightly, and startled by that sound
> The water-hen must change her ground;
> He might have been your heartiest welcomer.

Returning more fully to his immediate location, Yeats develops his own closeness to Gregory. The *For* construction echoes Milton's similar movement of identification, "For we were nursed upon the self-same hill," and the poem here moves quite close to the pastoral mode, associating elegist and elegized with a particular shared locale. That locale even includes the traditional presence of livestock and of a soothing current of liquidity. Other details however, are less comforting. A familiar elegiac image of almost totemic power and continuity, the old tree is present only in storm-broken forms. And these ruins subtly menace ("cast their shadows upon") the otherwise moderating

285

images of passage and transition ("road and bridge"). Similarly, the reassuring routine of cattle drinking at the ford is offset by the startled water-hen, and her sudden displacement, so near to the ancient settlement of the tower, thematizes the elegist's own need to change and fortify his ground.

The last line, "He might have been your heartiest welcomer," raises several possibilities. "Your" may refer to the poet, the new arrival who might have been most heartily welcomed by Gregory. But "your" may also refer to the landscape, now having lost its potentially greatest appreciator. This last would be a conventionally elegiac use of the pathetic fallacy to link the griefs of poet and place. But it would also confirm that Yeats himself has already begun to substitute for Gregory as the appreciative audience of this scene. Yeats's delighted eye has replaced that of Gregory. And if we accept Yeats's association with his new home, we see that he is repairing, by his own delighted appreciation and welcome, the loss of his friend's love. Exactly one year later he would pray not only that his daughter find "a house / Where all's accustomed" but, more important, that her soul would learn at last that it was "self-delighting."[27] We have already studied the relation between narcissism and mourning, and the subject will arise again later in the poem.

VIII
When with the Galway foxhounds he would ride
From Castle Taylor to the Roxborough side
Or Esserkelly plain, few kept his pace,
At Mooneen he had leaped a place
So perilous that half the astonished meet
Had shut their eyes, and where was it
He rode a race without a bit?
And yet his mind outran the horses' feet.

The celebratory flashback is conventional, but critics are wrong to see this stanza only as a regrettable capitulation to Mrs. Gregory's request for some praise of her late husband's horsemanship. The stanza is well integrated with that on George Pollexfen, and it begins the work of recuperating and amalgamating, in the figure of Gregory, the different virtues of the other three dead men. The pacing of the lines is superb and further stresses Yeats's aesthetic imitation of Gregory's headlong drive, his recklessness and mastery. Letting his lines seem to run loose and leap, Yeats nevertheless keeps his rhythms, his rhymes, and his strong hold on a stanza that must be pulled in suddenly with a question at the end of the seventh line so as to release the final sprint of the eighth. Clearly, Yeats's mind outruns the feet of his own stanza. After the painful "falling," "dying," "much travelling," and "having grown sluggish," these lines soar with an apparent release of pent-up energy. They refer, after all, to uncurbing, leaping, racing without a bit—all images of unchecked desire.

Early in our study of the genre, we saw how the martyred deity can appear to have given free rein to a desire that the survivors themselves must always inhibit. This desire could be for union with the mother earth, for a state preceding individuation, or more simply "for the tomb": an "impulse of delight" driving toward death. By transgressing the necessary limits of this desire, the martyred deities display their embodiment of a more than personal life-force. And by representing and mourning that martyrdom, the survivors celebrate the existence of that life-force even as they exorcise their own yearning for its unchecked expression. We have already noted how the momentum of Yeats's single-period stanza suggests an aesthetic version of such a force. And we observed how carefully the frustrations or renunciations of Johnson, Synge, and Pollexfen are matched by the apparent fulness of Gregory's undeferred satisfactions. Here, in the eighth stanza, these strands coalesce as Yeats eulogizes, with awe and even a residue of archaic reverence ("half the astonished meet / Had shut their eyes"), this youth who, like his model, Sidney-Astrophel, and like all that model's mythological forebears, had so thoroughly exhibited a force that seemed to drive beyond the bounds of individual life. For all its local place-names, and for all its reference to the sporting scene of Irish rural aristocracy, the stanza is thus extremely close to the primitive origins and functions of the genre.

IX

We dreamed that a great painter had been born
To cold Clare rock and Galway rock and thorn,
To that stern colour and that delicate line
That are our secret discipline
Wherein the gazing heart doubles her might.
Soldier, scholar, horseman, he,
And yet he had the intensity
To have published all to be a world's delight.

The first five lines condense a theory of symbolic landscape painting, a theory closely related both to Gregory's work and to the crucial
elegiac motif of the disciplined heart doubling its might. This requires
some investigation. The stanza's opening, "We dreamed . . . ," seems
odd in an austere poem apparently so set against the dreamlike fictions
of Yeats's earlier verse. And "what made us dream" in the eleventh
stanza certainly has a mocking tone. Is this an elegist's admission of his
"false surmise," in this case a recognition that Gregory never in fact
lived to fulfill his potential? One cannot say that after reading the
obituary: "To me he will always remain *a great painter* in the immaturity
of his youth" (my emphasis). For Yeats, Gregory's greatness declared
itself early and would merely have matured. The greatness itself is not
in question. "We dreamed . . ." may therefore not impugn but rather
render fragile or poignant the dreamers' expectations of Gregory. But
perhaps there is another reason for this opening, one connected to the
stanza's support of that visionary school of landscape painting that
seeks to represent more than mere imitations of nature. So, too, the
stanza does move Gregory himself far closer to the symbolic status
that he will have gained by the end of the poem.

Being "born / To cold Clare rock and Galway rock and thorn" is
itself to have an almost mythological status, that of a god born directly
out of the natural elements. The region, however, is described in
terms that apply as much to a kind of painting, as though what Yeats
sees is already an abstraction from the landscape: "that stern colour
and that delicate line." Yeats describes Gregory's works, the works his
obituary had described as "obtaining their effects from the fewest
possible lines and colours" and as being in the tradition of Blake,
Calvert, and Palmer.

As Marion Witt has shown, Yeats was immersed in a study of these
painters at the very time that he heard of Gregory's death. [28] He prized
not only their austere clarity of style but also their insistence on
representing what the imagination, rather than the merely physical
senses, could perceive. In fact, a reduction of the merely sensuous
("the fewest possible lines and colours") was seen to yield an increase
of spiritual vision or depiction. This relation is, of course, extremely
close to the elegiac transactions associated with Johnson, Synge, and
even Pollexfen. The words *austerity, discipline, asceticism,* and *ecstacy* recur
like a litany throughout Yeats's descriptions of these men and of Gregory. By submission to the "stern" rigor and clarity (described as if

these were indeed parental figures), the artist and viewer gain a purified apprehension of the world. Blake, Calvert, and Palmer all had striven to see "through not with the eye," the movement from physical to spiritual organ that we have so consistently recognized in the elegy as a genre. Yeats's mention of "the gazing heart" stresses this substitution as though the eye were now merely a lens through which a more significant organ could gaze.

This purifying transaction at the center of symbolic landscape painting was, for Yeats, a "secret discipline," the kind of arcane ritual whose ceremonies of ascetic submission and revelatory compensation recall aspects of the work of mourning and of the mystery cults associated with the origins of the elegy. And it is by just such a ritual that "the gazing heart doubles her might." The phrase is fascinating, and its diverse meanings are immensely important to the poem. Once again, the heart is the protagonist, continuing a role that will culminate at the end of the poem. We have already understood why it is the heart and not the eye that gazes. "Doubles her might" means on the one hand that the heart multiplies her power, which is exactly the compensatory gain we expect. But "doubles" also suggests a kind of mirroring, and the elegy has already introduced such a notion. In fact, the play between reflection and amplification is at the center of this poem, as the cases of Johnson, Synge, and Pollexfen suggested. Each gazed into a mirror that was at the same time a mask depicting an augmented or more desirable image of the self. In a passage adjacent to that on Synge in *Per Amica Silentia Lunae*, Yeats tells how the daemon may encounter one not only in the form of Dante's visitant declaring "ego dominus tuus" but also in the form of "some fine landscape . . . where we eternally solace ourselves."29

Just as the landscape picture is more than merely mimetic, so it mirrors something more in the given self of the painter or viewer. It reflects the creative power that can envision and represent a scene stripped down to its essential form. As mention of "the heart" suggests, this creative power is seen as a function of desire, but of desire only under the aegis of discipline, the heart's passion deflected into aesthetic work. In fact, the idea of this chastening is itself present in yet another implication of "doubles," whereby the word also means "halves." And with this recollection of a chastening gesture, associated with a blinding yet purifying displacement from physical to spiritual vision and with compensatory rather than mimetic self-imaging, we could scarcely be closer to the elegy's performance of the work of mourning.

"Soldier, scholar, horseman, he. . . ." With the initiation of the refrain, Yeats reinforces the poem's ceremonious movement of idealization. Gregory becomes an even more symbolic figure, caught up again in association with Sidney (even Hamlet is perhaps alluded to— "The courtier's, soldier's, scholar's, eye, tongue, sword"), [30] and finally established as the point of convergence for the virtues of Johnson, Synge, and Pollexfen. This convergence is still seen as difficult and rare, attainable and communicable only by an intensity that, as Yeats had elsewhere said, allowed for the kind of concentration and simplification (similar to that of Gregory's painting) that could have "published all to be a world's delight."

The phrase "a world's delight" is a direct quotation of Fulke Greville's elegy for Sidney. [31] But now the delight is not so much in the man as in all that he could "publish." Beneath the vagueness of this term, it is worth noting that Yeats cannot escape stressing a familiar displacement, from the life to the created or published work. *Published*, of course, applies more sensibly to Yeats's rather than Gregory's work, and perhaps the elegist is obliquely drawing attention to his own performance—a traditional gesture—here reminding us that he, too, can give delight as well as receive it, as earlier in "all things the delighted eye now sees."

      X
What other could so well have counselled us
In all lovely intricacies of a house
As he that practised or that understood
All work in metal or in wood,
In moulded plaster or in carven stone?
Soldier, scholar, horseman, he,
And all he did done perfectly
As though he had but that one trade alone.

The tenth stanza carries forward the celebration of this "most accomplished man" who "could do more things well than any other." Again, Yeats admires Gregory's power to overcome the kind of fragmentation that had so deeply marked the lives of the other friends. But the celebration has its mournful aspects. Yeats is about to occupy the very house whose purchase Gregory had encouraged (even to the point of having suggested particular renovations). The irony of this dominates the stanza and the poem at large, while also broadening the nature of the poet's loss to include the familiar motif of the departed guide. As the use of *counselled* confirms, Yeats can here overtly defer to the younger man, thus performing, however mildly, an elegiac gesture which otherwise might have been unconvincing coming from an older, famous poet to a man "in the immaturity of his youth."

The lines emphasize the slow labor of craft and texture, the turning aside from passion to artifice, a turning accented within or *between* the words "lovely intricacies."32 And the elegiac stress on artifice and its materials (metal, wood, plaster, stone) becomes almost funereal in the phrase "In moulded plaster or in carven stone." In this context, the repeated refrain "Soldier, scholar, horseman, he . . ." becomes un-avoidably epitaphic, especially when followed by the terse finality of "did done." While the attendant adverb *perfectly* describes the work, it surely points back to the harsher perfection of those two verbs' tense itself. Finally, *trade*, recalling *published*, has a nagging connotation not just of energy channeled into craft but also of exchange, with its interplay of cost and gain, of work and reward. The elegy as a work of mourning and as a product offered for publication is itself a form of trade.

Thus far, the poem has gathered abundant testimony of Gregory's worth, and there is much that is already consoling in his embodiment of unity and completeness. What justification, however, can be offered for his early death? This question forces the great response of the eleventh stanza:

> XI
> Some burn damp faggots, others may consume
> The entire combustible world in one small room
> As though dried straw, and if we turn about
> The bare chimney is gone black out
> Because the work had finished in that flare.
> Soldier, scholar, horseman, he,
> As 'twere all life's epitome.
> What made us dream that he could comb grey hair?

Here, for the first time, the fact of Gregory's death and the brevity of his life are transformed to a source of consolation. The emphasis on totality, unity, and completion are already familiar. But only now do these seem to emerge from and depend on what might otherwise have seemed a disastrous brevity. The brevity and concentrated unity gain much of their additional value by contrast to the drawn-out falling, dying, traveling, and aging of the earlier, divided heroes of the poem. But this stanza does more than counterpose images of entirety and completion to those of disunity and fractured desire. Johnson had dreamed of a measureless consummation, and Yeats had thought of Synge's soul as the stage of a final but continuous scene of judgment ("He was one of those unmoving souls in whom there is a perpetual 'Last Day,' a perpetual trumpeting and coming to judgment") [M, 205]). Gregory brings these motifs to an utter conclusion by consuming "the entire combustible world" in one apocalyptic flare.

The fire imagery is traditional for an elegy, but Yeats's revision is disturbingly original. Associated with light and heat, and with the sun and stars, fire has served most elegists as a figure for the physical or spiritual powers that exist within and beyond individual men. Usually, the destructive aspect of fire is suppressed to create a pure image of regenerative or unconsumed force. Examples would include Spenser's "And kindling love in him above all measure / Sweet love still joyous, never feeling paine" ("Astrophel"); or Milton's "And tricks his beams, and with new-spangled Ore, / Flames in the forehead of the morning sky"; or, from Yeats's stanzaic model, Cowley's elegy for Hervey: "He like the Stars, to which he now is gone, / That shine with beams like Flame, / Yet burn not with the same, / Had all the light of Youth, of the Fire none." Shelley, as we recall, brought into decisive play the figure's immortal *and* destructive attributes. Adonais's soul is forever "burning through the inmost veil of Heaven." To reach it, and to join the "unquenchably" burning fountains of "the Eternal," Shelley allows this "fire for which all thirst" to "beam on [him], / Consuming the last clouds of cold mortality." Hardy abandoned the Neo-Platonic assurances, emphasizing instead the burnt circle and charred stick-ends of a former fire. But these still served as vestiges of a valued flame. Yeats, however, stresses only the conflagration, implying neither transcendence nor trace: "And if we turn about / The bare chimney is gone black out." It is a startling and bleak revision of an entire legacy.

With such a grasp of the tradition, and with such an admiration for Shelley, who, he later admitted, "had shaped my life," clearly this harsh revision was deliberate (*EI*, 424). In fact, Yeats's first elegiac tribute to Synge in his journal drew directly upon "Adonais" for comfort: "We pity the living and not such dead as he. He has gone upward out of his ailing body into the heroical fountains. We are parched by time" (M, 205). Yet now, in the elegy for Gregory, Yeats turns against such idealizations. Instead of what he himself named "Nature's pure unchanging light" (in "Tom the Lunatic"), he proposes the brief but entire combustion of the individual life.

This apparent rejection of transcendence or even persistence may seem peculiarly modern. But Yeats is describing a state close to the traditional condition of ecstacy, which in turn implies transfiguration, if only for the instant. Indeed, even the lines' bleakest image, that of the chimney "gone black out," relates closely to Yeats's understanding of this state: "How often had I heard men of my time talk of the meeting of spirit and sense, yet there is no meeting but only change upon the instant, and it is by the perception of a change, like the sudden 'blacking out' of the lights of the stage, that passion creates its most violent sensation" (A, 218). Or even more memorably:

Gaiety transfiguring all that dread.
All men have aimed at, found and lost;
Black out; Heaven blazing into the head. [33]

The achievement of ecstacy, like that of unity and consummation and like the practice of asceticism and austerity, has been one of the salient values and aspirations of the heroes of this elegy. As Yeats quoted Synge, "There are three things any two of which have often come together but never all three; ecstasy, ascetism, austerity; I wish to bring all three together" (A, 232). Once again, the figure of Gregory gratifies desires that have been at work throughout the poem. And yet, as we continue to see, the elegiac transaction demands that such satisfaction be attainable only at disastrous cost.

Even Yeats's final praise of Gregory as "all life's epitome" expresses this contradiction. As so often before, the elegist's consoling image of the dead, like the closely related construction of a totem, cannot avoid testifying to the peculiarly castrative fate that enabled that very construction. In this case, the honorific *epitome*, even while it seems to encompass and signify "all life," cannot disguise its original relation to a "cutting short" (*epitemnion*). Once again, an elegist has represented the dead in terms of a particular figure or trope, in this case that of synecdoche. (Yeats even draws attention to the figurative turn by his

293

introductory, conditional simile "as 'twere.") But once again, the trope cannot conceal that from which it turns. For all its claim to totality, the epitome, like the vehicle of any synecdoche, is inevitably partial and abbreviated.

Against this sorrowful recognition of the sheared or cut-short character of his epitome, Yeats poses the wistful, self-chastening question, "What made us dream that he could comb grey hair?" Apart from the familiar elegiac dispelling of surmise, the question takes on added meaning if we recall the general opposition of youth and age in this poem, together with the elegist's current obsession with his own increasing age. The question forces him to renounce not only his own youth but also the possibility of any easy mirroring between the living and the dead. And yet we know how often an elegist strives for just such a relation between himself and the idealized figure whom he celebrates. The success with which Yeats concludes his elegy is in large part a result of his determined achievement of that relation, not in any direct way, but by a displacement onto the medium of his very art. Before examining that feat in the twelfth stanza, we should look further at Yeats's sober recognition of how little he and Gregory could have in common.

The unsustainable dream of grey hair was only a small, though familiar and poignant, part of what necessarily separated the poet from his hero. The line is effective because it is so understated. It admits more than it says, while it also performs those inescapable elements of the work of mourning—the overruling of the griever's prior desires and dreams *and* the enforcing of a detachment and distance between him and the dead. This is Yeats's "Aye me I fondly dream," his "false surmise." It is not just that he, living, cannot resemble the distant dead. Rather, he can never simply resemble the man Gregory was when alive. For even while he admired the all-consuming flare of Gregory's life, Yeats saw its incompatibility with his own life and practice as a poet. The terms of this recognition are crucial to the elegy:

> [Dowson, Johnson, Horne, Symons] taught me that violent energy, which is like a fire of straw, consumes in a few minutes the nervous vitality, and is useless in the arts. Our fire must burn slowly, and we must constantly turn away to think, constantly analyse what we have done, be content even to have little life outside our work, to show, perhaps, to other men, as little as the watch-mender shows, his magnifying glass caught in his screwed-up eye. Only then do we learn to conserve our vitality, to keep

our mind enough under control and to make our technique sufficiently flexible for expression of the emotions of life as they arise. (A, 212)

This statement, so similar in language to the elegy, points accurately and comprehensively to elements of the work of mourning: the renunciation of unlimited energy, the preference for a bounded and therefore conserved vitality, the detours by which one must "constantly turn away," the reduction or displacement of life in the interests of the work, even the artificial and perhaps painful mediation of physical sight ("his magnifying glass caught in his screwed-up eye"). Once again, the very medium of an elegist's poem stands between him and his own otherwise unchecked desires. The text intervenes between the living and the dead, but also between the living and their own unlimited immersion in life. Over against Gregory's flare of dried straw, Yeats has all along, since the opening stanza of his elegy, been quietly burning "a fire of turf." His poem, by its very nature as well as by its content, has all along been coming to terms with his inability, as a poet, to make the kind of "plunge" into action and into unity of being for which he had celebrated Gregory. This, as much as Gregory's death, has been the poem's true object of mourning: Yeats's acceptance that he can never write of himself what he had written of Gregory, namely, that "mind and hand were at one, will and desire."

And yet, Yeats does drive toward some resemblance between himself, or rather his poem, and the heroic figure that he has created. He tries to close the gap between the very texture of his verse and the unified life of action. As already mentioned, the single-period stanza and the momentum of passionate syntax themselves approximate an act of all-unifying consummation. Beyond this, in the final stanza, Yeats makes his very act of writing the poem resemble as closely as possible a kind of lived action—in particular, the passionately abbreviated action that characterizes the life and death of Gregory.

XII
I had thought, seeing how bitter is that wind
That shakes the shutter, to have brought to mind
All those that manhood tried, or childhood loved
Or boyish intellect approved,
With some appropriate commentary on each;
Until imagination brought
A fitter welcome; but a thought
Of that late death took all my heart for speech.

Following the conventions of the genre, Yeats turns, in a form of coda, to focus on himself and on his performance. As conventionally, the description of his performance suggests an act of self-surpassal or at least of shifting from an initial to a subsequent stance ("I had thought . . . but . . ."). The shift is presented as a curtailment, the kind of self-limiting that marks part of the mourner's work. But this is no simple act of limitation, for it is the very means by which the poet most establishes both the final value of his performance and its resemblance to the figure of Gregory.

The stanza begins slowly, with just the kind of delay or turning away that Yeats associated with the slow burning of composition ("I had thought, seeing how bitter is that wind / That shakes the shutter . . ."). The delay returns the poet to his own surroundings, menaced as they are by a bitter wind that agitates a shutter, oblique emblem both of protective mediation and of a perhaps abrupt closure. His categorization of his intended guests is itself oddly deranged, moving from manhood back to childhood, then forward again to boyhood, as though the very notion of sequence were now disturbed. "Some appropriate commentary on each" sounds curiously dull and remote, hinting at a poetry that is precisely *not* like action but rather like commentary itself, something secondary and mediate. Against this, he opposes a response that gives the illusion of being more immediate and active, certainly "fitter" and more imaginative. The shift from the ponderous Latinism of "appropriate commentary" to "fitter welcome" is itself a movement toward what sounds like a more vital act.

Finally, and closer yet to action, the thought of Gregory's death abruptly ends the poem by taking all the poet's heart for speech. It is as though the poem, like Gregory, "plunges" abruptly to its end. Like the epitome, it is allegedly cut short. And yet again like Gregory, this abbreviation is the result of a sudden intensity that finishes the work in a flare. Knowing that more than age and more even than death, marked him as different from Gregory, Yeats chose to regard his image of the younger man as a daemon, a mask that he could mirror only by transforming himself. Without Shelley's Neo-Platonic ardor, he could not "consume his own mortality" in a final self-immolation. Rather, he deflected such a radical or literal imitation away from himself onto his poem. He himself would burn slowly in order to craft a poem whose end would simulate the sudden conflagration of Gregory's life and death. It is a brilliant and distinctly elegiac solution.

The final phrase, "took all my heart for speech," is even more deeply elegiac than it at first appears. It is ambiguous, meaning on the one hand that the thought robbed Yeats's desire for further speech (yet another instance of the mourner relinquishing a portion of desire) and on the other hand, that the thought entirely consumed Yeats's heart, "taking" it, almost as if it were fuel for the preceding, now exhausted speech.[34] As Yeats wrote elsewhere, "Whatever flames upon the night / Man's own resinous heart has fed."[35] In this sense, Yeats has fed his heart to his poem. The sacrificial movement from desire to language could not be more elegiac. Nor could the archaic image of offering up the heart.[36] Just as he has imitated Gregory's abrupt end, and just as he has now imitated Gregory's totalizing unity ("all my heart"), so, too, Yeats is imitating the gesture by which the archtypical elegiac martyr, the vegetation deity, offers up his heart as figure for the fertilizing power that outlives him. If we doubt Yeats's familiarity with this detail of the conventional myth, we need only read "Parnell's Funeral" or recall "Two Songs from a Play," as quoted earlier, in chapter I.

> I saw a staring virgin stand
> Where holy Dionysus died,
> And tear the heart out of his side,
> And lay the heart upon her hand
> And bear that beating heart away;
> And then did all the Muses sing
> Of Magnus Annus at the spring,
> As though God's death were but a play.

While Yeats seems to have ended his elegy with a sudden check against the ceremonious unfolding of his original intentions, he has in fact reined in hard at the very core of the genre.

Gregory's prototype, Sidney, had ended the first sonnet of *Astrophil and Stella* by charging himself to "look in [his] heart, and write!" Yeats ends more radically, suggesting that the heart can enter language only at the cost of its own extinction or drastic transfiguration. Indeed, narrating this "taking away" of his heart, as though explaining his death, Yeats assumes an almost posthumous voice, an assumption pointing to the elegist's ultimate form of self-surpassal, his rehearsal or achievement of some token of his own immortality. If the original vegetation deities were given to the earth, and if the heart of Dionysus was torn out and borne away in the hands of a "staring virgin," or in the *Liknites* basket, to prepare for his rebirth, Yeats has given his heart to

297

that other surviving ground, poetic "speech." And it is there that he, or rather his heart, or rather his words—this again being *the* elegiac displacement—will continue to exist, however modified, "in the guts of the living."[37]

Epilogue: The English Elegy after Yeats; a Note on the American Elegy

I shall follow briefly the two lines of enquiry suggested by the chapter title: What happens to the English elegy after Yeats? and What bearing does our study have on the American elegy? My responses to these questions are not designed to be comprehensive. Rather, they seek to indicate how the preceding study of the genre may be extended beyond its chronological and national limits. At the same time, they serve to reemphasize certain elements of our theoretical approach.

Returning to Yeats, we recall that "In Memory of Major Robert Gregory" was written at a moment when the traditional elegiac myths and ceremonies were regarded with a new level of incredulity or contempt. The tendencies noted then continue throughout the century, eroding the generic resources of consolation. Apart from developments within the history of this century's poetry—much of it marked by a continuing subversion of traditional poetic goals and means—recent attitudes toward death have made it increasingly difficult to write a conventional elegy. Sociologists and psychologists, as well as literary and cultural historians, consistently demonstrate the ways in which death has tended to become obscene, meaningless, impersonal—an event either stupefyingly colossal in cases of large-scale war or genocide, or clinically concealed somewhere behind the technology of the hospital and the techniques of the funeral home. [1]

In this situation most elegists either have withdrawn yet further behind masks of irony or have maintained personal accents at the cost of admitting their reduced circumstances—forswearing traditional procedures of mourning, adopting deliberately unidealized settings, making smaller and more credible claims, if any, for the deceased and for themselves. Occasionally the mourned subjects of recent elegies include not only the deceased but also the vanished rituals of grief and consolation themselves. As Seamus Heaney has written in "Funeral Rites," "we pine for ceremony, / customary rhythms."[2]

Admittedly, "In Memory of Major Robert Gregory" dispensed with many of the comforting fictions of the genre, disallowing even the supposition of an afterlife. But we also noted the poem's personal ceremony and its refiguration of the most archaic elements of the genre. Even by 1918, however, the glamorous, idealizing achievement of Yeats's elegy was beyond the reach of other poets.

Ironically enough, Yeats himself followed "In Memory of Major Robert Gregory" by one more poem for Gregory, a poem that bitterly undoes the consolation of the earlier work. So harsh is "Reprisals" in its revelation of how the brutal facts of history may mock the claims of verse, and so terrifying is its reversion from elegiac grief to merely vengeful anger, that Lady Gregory requested Yeats not to publish the poem. It remains uncollected, even in Richard Finneran's enlarged edition of Yeats's verse.

> Some nineteen German planes, they say,
> You had brought down before you died.
> We called it a good death. Today
> Can ghost or man be satisfied?
> Although your last exciting year
> Outweighed all other years, you said,
> Though battle joy may be so dear
> A memory, even to the dead,
> It chases other thought away,
> Yet rise from your Italian tomb,
> Flit to Kiltartan cross and stay
> Till certain second thoughts have come
> Upon the cause you served, that we
> Imagined such a fine affair:
> Half-drunk or whole-mad soldiery
> Are murdering your tenants there.
> Men that revere your father yet
> Are shot at on the open plain.
> Where may new-married women sit
> And suckle children now? Armed men
> May murder them in passing by
> Nor law nor parliament take heed.
> Then close your ears with dust and lie
> Among the other cheated dead.[3]

Raging against the uncontrolled violence of the Black and Tans, Yeats inveighs contemptuously against the idealizing attitude that "called" Gregory's death good and "imagined" his cause as fine. The elegist's necessary blend of humility and assertion is here replaced by the exaggerated self-chastisement of sheer impotence; and this uncompensated impotence is all the more devastating in a poem that exposes the threat against those traditional elegiac elements—on the one hand reverence for the father and for the law, on the other such figures for continuity and regenerative power as that of new-married women suckling their children.

Yet more desolating are the cruel subversion of the power of the dead and the failure on the part of the elegist to invent any figure or substitute for such power. Yeats's impotence is projected onto Gregory, whose ghost is invited to watch the degradation of his country and his people before being smothered in the dust. In place of the previous high courtesy of host and guest, Yeats now supplies a sordid ritual of humiliation. The elegiac contract between the living and the dead is cynically revised to a transaction between deceiver and deceived. Gregory has been disinterred only to be more devastatingly buried.

Of course, Yeats did not lapse irrevocably into this distrust of an elegist's ennoblement of the dead. Nor did he always remain as acidly aware of how dead heroes may be cheated by the subsequent squalor of history. While "Under Ben Bulben" forbids grief and commands "a cold eye," the magisterial, administrative quality of the poem installs its subject in the secure position of an influence on succeeding generations. Yeats's testament not only dictates the ideal practices of future poets and artists but testifies to the perfectly elegiac purpose that "Bring[s] the soul of man to God" and "Make[s] him fill the cradles right."[4]

And yet it was just this Yeatsian hieratic confidence, even arrogance, that other elegists found difficult to match. Before looking briefly at Auden's elegy for Yeats, we might pause over Ezra Pound's travesty of "Under Ben Bulben":

Neath Ben Bulben's Buttoks Lies

Neath Ben Bulben's buttoks lies
Bill Yeats, a poet twoice the soize

> Of William Shakespear, as they say
> Down Ballykillywuchlin way.
>
> Let Saxon roiders break their bones
> Huntin' the fox
> thru dese gravestones.[5]

By an anti-elegiac displacement downward from mountain top to buttocks, Pound begins by mocking the totemic eminence of Yeats's ancestral mount. The humorous denigration continues with the subversion of another elegiac convention, the naming or renaming of the dead. Instead of a repetition of Yeats's full name, or instead of the attribution of a universalizing name (Daphnis, Lycidas, Adonais, Thyrsis), Pound clips William Butler down to Bill. Pursuing the play on size, Pound mock-aggrandizes Yeats in relation to Shakespeare— another anti-elegiac allusion (subverting, for example, "Marcellus of our tongue" or "Our Sidney and our perfect man"). The effect is intensified by the suggestion, (particularly following "buttoks"), of a crudely physical rather than literary comparison, one that reverses the genre's traditional allegorization of merely physical powers.

The Brooklyn accent and the almost leering attribution, "as they say," are both cunningly apt (attribution itself having been used cynically in "Reprisals" and used here to dissipate the authority of a strong individual voice such as Yeats's own). So, too, Pound mocks Yeatsian place-names, robbing them of mythic associations and dissipating the proud self-rooting of the poet by relocating him, if at all, in the vague reaches of gibberish. If one task of an elegy is to repeat or represent the child's entry into language, Pound's parody includes an apparent regression, however controlled by mockery, to the nonsense syllables of the nursery.

The poem ends with an elegiac curse, but one that belies its seeming protectiveness towards Yeats. For the curse degrades Drumcliff churchyard to a scene for fox hunters' mishaps (no doubt playing against Yeats's epitaphic address to the horseman and against his admiration for aristocratic riders and hunters like Gregory). Finally, Pound blunts the carefully quarried, incised gravestones of Yeats's directive by mockingly eroding them from *these* to *dese*. Language itself, the true ground of Yeats's survival, is subjected to inglorious accents and decays.

Although far from Pound's aggressive travesty, Auden's "In Memory of W. B. Yeats" also attacks Yeats's grandiose posture, as well as his claims for the powers of poetic language. So, too, Auden questions the conventions and idealizing ceremonies of the elegy as a genre. Lawrence Lipking has shown how precisely Auden controverts so many of Yeats's assertions, particularly those of "Under Ben Bulben."[6] For example, Auden "robs Yeats of property rights in his own death," dislocating him from a distinct rural setting to a generalized urban or suburban scene. He "internationalizes" the nationalistic poet, and by "scatter[ing him] among a hundred cities," "Auden makes his resurrection impossible," while also "demonstrating the essential unimportance of tombs." Similarly, Auden rejects Yeats's claim to the perfectibility of poetic work, and while replacing Yeats's mythic terrains with the very world of banality and formlessness that Yeats detested, Auden emphasizes that "poetry makes nothing happen."

Auden thus cuts deeply against the grain of the traditional elegy. Certainly, he turns in the final section of the poem to a style and position that is far more traditional. Eclogically trying to surpass the looser, skeptical voice of the preceding two sections, he turns to the insistent, ceremonious slow march of Yeats's rhymed tetrameter quatrains. Echoing Tennyson's phrase for the dead duke of Wellington, and drawing on Yeats's own high notions of hospitality, he now commits Yeats as "an honored guest" to the earth.[7] In retrospect, earlier images of dislocation and scattering now signify an elegiac *sparagmos*. And in these closing stanzas Yeats indeed comes to resemble the allegorized vegetation or agricultural deity, whose death may "With the farming of a verse / Make a vineyard of the curse" and whose fertile, liberating influence may thaw the earlier frozen brooks and disfiguring snow in order to renew the elegiac image of liquidity, thus starting the "healing fountain" in "the desert of the heart."

This recuperation confirms and augments the recovery that ended the second section of the poem, where once again an elegist has followed a harshly disconnective and chastening gesture—here against Yeats and the supposed potency of verse, including Auden's own—by positing a disconnected but immortal figurative organ of such potency, "a mouth." Concentrating increasingly on that which survives, as we have come to expect, precisely by its being "punished under a foreign code," Auden celebrates "the words of a dead man," exhorting the dead poet to continue his persuasions. Having "disappeared in the dead of winter," having been "scattered among a hundred cities" and "modified in the guts of the living," the poet has returned to "teach the free man how to praise."

And yet this most traditional section of the elegy is the least satisfying. After the fluent and urbane skepticism of the opening sections, after the so deftly portrayed world of banality, and after that voice of supple qualifications and almost mocking understatement ("fairly accustomed," "almost convinced," "slightly unusual"), it is difficult not to resist much of the final section's highly formal pomp and ceremony, together with its rather hollow impersonation of the Yeatsian mode. The poem falls apart into the opening voice of Auden, on the one hand, skeptically setting a standard of credibility that the almost caricatured version of Yeats's voice, on the other, cannot quite survive. (In elegiac fashion, but at the cost of marring his poem, Auden has thus suggested the terms on which he may succeed the figure he has mourned.)

It is not surprising, therefore, to find that Auden's more successful elegies, such as those for Ernst Toller, Freud, and Henry James, work by moving further away from the hieratic ceremonies and rhetoric of the genre. Here, too, Auden is unafraid to cut against the traditional idealizing of the dead. As he called Yeats "silly," so he describes Toller as "egotistical"; and Freud "wasn't clever at all," indeed was often "wrong and, at times, absurd." Similarly, the exclamations and the intricate syntactic labyrinths of James's late style are affectionately but effectively mocked in Auden's imitation (for example, in stanzas 3–5 of "At the Grave of Henry James"). [8]

In these poems, particularly those for Freud and James, it is not some immediately recognizable elegiac ceremony or renewed myth but rather the astonishingly poised and urbane conversation that masters us. Moving fluently across the nonetheless carefully measured syllabic lines, Auden's voice consoles as much by its manner as by what it says. Calm, civilized, flexible, and seemingly inexhaustible, its current "flows on," pausing only for the occasional crystallization of an aphorism or the solution of a carefully posed series of problems. It is the voice one may imagine continuing unperturbed during an air raid. Like the voice Auden ascribed to Eliot, Auden's elegiac manner suggests a poet "who, not speechless from shock but finding the right / language for thirst and fear, [does] much to / prevent a panic." [9]

Concentration on the unconventional and apparently demystifying style of Auden's elegies, as well as on his de-idealizing and modernizing of the traditional claims and contexts of the genre, should not, however, lead us to overlook how deeply generic these works remain. We have already seen this with regard to the elegy for Yeats. But we might note as well how the poems for Freud and James present images of a child's submission to a certain authority or law (in one, the present, as a child, must learn to recite the past until it "falters"—a word we found in similarly chastening moments in Tennyson's and Hardy's elegies; in the other, James's "hand submitted / To those formal rules that help a child to play"). Such submission is, of course, related to that by which Auden erects his "disciplinary image" of the dead James to hold himself back from "agreeable wrong." With the concluding stanzas of these poems Auden arrives at such traditional figures as the weeping Aphrodite and the interceding Master. And without suggesting an afterlife, Auden nonethless abstracts a virtue or standard of achievement from the dead, suggesting that while the particular flawed life has forever "lost its uniqueness," it evinced qualities that our lives should preserve or approximate. [10]

The above are drastically abridged readings of Auden, but I hope that they chart his skeptical inroads against the traditional elegy and show how those inroads were somewhat checked by the consoling aspects of his discursive manner and by the residue of generic strategies at work in each poem. But as one moves away from Auden's elegies toward the "climate of opinion" that other mourners of this century have expressed against the genre, one is likely to carry away such lines as those that open the poem for Freud:

> When there are so many we shall have to mourn,
> When grief has been made so public, and exposed
>   to the critique of a whole epoch
>   the frailty of our conscience and anguish,
> of whom shall we speak?
>
> (CSP, 166)

or those near the beginning of the elegy for James: "What living occasion can / Be just to the absent?" (ibid., 198).

With these questions, we return to the discomforting strain of queries and forays that have been gathering force against the genre, especially since the First World War. We have already noted the

section of "Hugh Selwyn Mauberley" beginning "Died some pro pa-
tria / non 'dulce' non 'et decor.'" And we have seen how much of that
section systematically subverted the old fictions of elegy, as if they
were not only useless but somehow culpable. To Pound's attack we
could add Wilfred Owen's poem ironically titled "Dulce et Decorum
Est" or his "Greater Love" or "Anthem for Doomed Youth": "No
mockeries now for them; no prayers nor bells, / Nor any voice of
mourning save the choirs, — / The shrill, demented choirs of wailing
shells. . . ."11

Such poems, like Isaac Rosenberg's "Dead Man's Dump" or Edward
Thomas's "Tears" (which begins "It seems I have no tears left"), appear
to signal a drying up or a deliberate termination of the familiar expressions of grief. 12 They reach forward to Edith Sitwell's "Dirge for
the New Sunrise," which flatly declares, "But no eyes grieved— / For
none were left for tears," and goes on to annihilate those two arch-
elegiac figures, the sun and the "heart of Man."13 In this vein, we may
also point to Dylan Thomas's "A Refusal to Mourn the Death, by Fire,
of a Child in London":

I shall not murder
The mankind of her going with a grave truth
Nor blaspheme down the stations of the breath
With any further
Elegy of innocence and youth. 14

It would be absurd, however, to suggest that these refusals and
those of the preceding poets cancel out the survival of the genre. Even
the stanza just quoted; with its own version of elegiac formal antiphony, implies that if the elegist refuses to "murder the mankind of her
going," this "mankind" or virtue must somehow still survive. And the
following stanza mythologizes the child, evoking both a legendary
parental figure and an imagined community of the dead that "robes"
the daughter in friendship:

Deep with the first dead lies London's daughter,
Robed in the long friends,
The grains beyond age, the dark veins of her mother,
Secret by the unmourning water
Of the riding Thames.
After the first death, there is no other.

Even if it is said to be "unmourning," the riding Thames recalls the
river deities whose daughters were transformed to reeds or laurel. And

in a poem mourning a death by fire, such a figure carries even more assuagement than its suggestions of continuity and ongoing fertility. Finally, the poem closes, in traditional fashion, with a claim that both admits and hyperbolically contrives to deny the power of death: "After the first death, there is no other."

But how do elegies more recent than those of Auden or Thomas continue the genre? How do they reach beyond the specificity of a particular death and of a particular poet's loss? How do they offer a surviving ritual with renewed figures of consolation that readers at large can share? I shall bring these questions to bear very briefly on several elegies of Geoffrey Hill, looking at the early poem "In Memory of Jane Fraser," then noting related elements of "Requiem for the Plantagenet Kings," "Two Formal Elegies," and "Of Commerce and Society" before closing with "Veni Coronaberis."

In Memory of Jane Fraser

When snow like sheep lay in the fold
And winds went begging at each door,
And the far hills were blue with cold,
And a cold shroud lay on the moor,

She kept the siege. And every day
We watched her brooding over death
Like a strong bird above its prey.
The room filled with the kettle's breath.

Damp curtains glued against the pane
Sealed time away. Her body froze
As if to freeze us all, and chain
Creation to a stunned repose.

She died before the world could stir.
In March the ice unloosed the brook
And water ruffled the sun's hair.
Dead cones upon the alder shook. [15]

Even a cursory glance notes how thoroughly traditional an elegy this is. In an abbreviated version of Gray's elegiac quatrains, Hill sets out a pastoral context that associates the winter landscape with the human situation. Prolonging the period of the first quatrain, he creates a syntactic and stanzaic suspension that emphasizes the setting's apparent dependence on the subject, Jane Fraser. This surprising dominance attributed to the dying woman is stressed further by her resemblance to a bird of prey. Apart from beginning the mourner's task of transforming or substituting for the dead, Hill already performs a displaced version of the reversal of mastery that we have noted in the vegetation rites, the *fort-da* game, and several elegies: the victim becomes the powerful agent or aggressor, although here that aggression is perhaps tempered by the allusive echo of Milton's Spirit "brooding on the vast abyss."[16]

But in case we thought this merely an archaic poem, Hill now introduces the apparently unpoetic kettle, proof of the unexalted world in which contemporary elegists have to work. The kettle nevertheless serves as more than a detail of significant realism, for its power to fill the room suggests, however humbly, the possible association between the displaced breath of the dying women and an infusing power. And yet, while "refining" the element of water upwards to air, the kettle's breath also spreads the kind of veil-like medium that we have seen as crucial to many elegies. Indeed, the image is pursued in that of curtains glued against the window—an elegiac admission of an opaque fabric that may be the stuff of consolation but also seals off transparency or immediate connection.

The damp curtains, sealing time away, recall the shroud covering the moor, and they serve to disconnect the dying woman from the world of time. As such, they seem to have no role as figures of consoling fabrication and instead resemble Shelley's rejected curtains either of death or of mediation in a fallen world. Such negativity is pursued in the following menace of universal death, as if Jane Fraser were some vegetation deity whose demise threatened to congeal Creation itself. The mourner's danger of identification with the dead is thus also confronted, even as it is held at bay by its very articulation and by the distancing admission that its threat is only figuratively "as if" present. Finally, in this stanza, the description of death as an extinction of warm life into "stunned repose" may recall Shelley's "intense atom . . . quenched in a most cold repose." Even if we were not already primed by the pastoral setting, the recollection of "Adonais" may encourage us to expect some counterassertion of surviving vitality.

The last stanza fulfills this expectation. Jane Fraser dies, but the

world breaks from congealment. The images of renewal are themselves essentially elegiac—renewed liquidity and a particularly
totemic figure of the sun, necessarily new-washed or purged, its hair
suggesting the "new-spangled" repaired head of the sun in "Lycidas" or
the laved locks of Lycidas himself. With the concluding image of dead
cones shaking on the alder, we return to the center of elegiac myth,
the dead cones, totemically rigid and inert, shaking abroad the fertilizing pollen they have preserved.

The poem is not, however, entirely successful. Ironically, this is
owing to its being so deeply generic as to appear almost formulaic, a
piece of writing whose engagement with the generic conventions too
far exceeds its engagement with a particular loss. One might have said
as much of "Lycidas," but that poem was tense with grief and anger,
and a strong current of emotion drove Milton to the powerful revision
of an entire legacy. While it speaks of a final unloosing and ruffling,
"In Memory of Jane Fraser" remains congealed within the tradition it
has so skilfully employed. Perhaps it is for such reasons that Hill
himself has come to dislike the poem; and it is to other of his works
that we should look for a yet more vigorous survival of the genre.

"Requiem for the Plantagenet Kings" reactivates the inert effigies of
the dead precisely by bringing them to a powerful scenario of judgment that is rife with images of purgatorial refinement and with the
kind of castrative submission that we have noted at the core of the
genre:

Before the scouring fires of trial-day
Alight on men; before sleeked groin, gored head,
Budge through the clay and gravel, and the sea
Across daubed rock evacuates its dead.

(*Kingdom*, 18)

While mention of the apocalyptic trial day completes the poem's
earlier concern with justice, the last line augments the poem's opening
ambiguity regarding the sea's litter. That earlier ambiguity, suggesting
delivery or debris, informs the final image of evacuation, again suggesting on the one hand rescue or salvation, on the other a mere
voiding. Such ambiguity marks the extreme toughness of Hill's elegiac
stance in this and succeeding poems, a refusal to console without first
stressing decimation and the bleak harshness of judgment—a
harshness as intransigent as rock, however daubed.

The stress on submission to the law and to judgment also characterizes "Two Formal Elegies," particularly the first. Here Hill moves beyond a traditional image of the martyr's blood nourishing the rebirth of nature and song, and works instead toward the figure of the "fierce heart" brought to judgment (ibid., 19). That judgment takes on special force by its association with "Jehovah's hand," an elegiac image of the creative but also authoritative power of the god.

Jehovah is indeed the presiding deity of these elegies, the Old Testament god of judgment, closely related to Jove and seeming to require no less of a sacrifice as the price of comfort. In the fourth section of "Of Commerce and Society," we learn of the "need to demonstrate / Jehovah's touchy methods, that create / The connoisseur of blood, the smitten man" (ibid., 39). The following section speaks explicitly of the need to "appease the terse gods," while the entire sequence concludes with a deliberate focus on a barely Christianized martyrdom.

These poems themselves thus seem to be "engrossed in the cold blood of sacrifice" (ibid., 41). Their great success derives from their vigorous adoption of primitive mythic calculi or rituals, in which death has its justification in a bleak economy of atonement. The horrifying deaths of war and even of the extermination camps are thus supplied with the kind of generic context whose absence had seemed to place such subjects beyond the reach of elegy. Under the terrible and yet ultimately consoling aegis of Jehovah or Jove, Hill returns to a persuasive form of mourning.

Such observations raise the possibility that during a period when consolation is hardest to achieve, the successful mourner is one who performs most thoroughly the very *harshest* aspects of the work of mourning. We saw in our study of revenge tragedies and of "Lycidas" that the issues of justice and of judgment become prominent precisely when the inherited fictions and modes of consolation have grown weakest. And as "Lycidas" revealed, only the bleakest scenarios of dismemberment, drowning, and divine vengeance could reinstate a language of comfort. Hill's power draws on this situation. His elegies are sacrificial and expiatory in the extreme. By recognizing not only the connection between the horror of contemporary history and the violence of ancient theology but also the necessity of extreme chastisement for the gain of any solace, he has written some of the few consoling poems of our time.

To bring these brief notes on Hill to a milder close, let us look at the recent "Veni Coronaberis" (1978), subtitled "A Garland for Helen Waddell."

> The crocus armies from the dead
> rise up; the realm of love renews
> the battle it was born to lose
> though for a time the snows have fled
>
> and old stones blossom in the south
> with sculpted vine and psaltery
> and half-effaced adultery
> the bird-dung dribbling from its mouth;
>
> and abstinence crowns all our care
> with martyr-laurels for this day.
> Towers and steeples rise away
> into the towering gulfs of air. [17]

The title alone is a fine choice for this elegy, for it immediately presents the elegist's submission to a preceding language not his own. More specifically, it pays homage to Helen Waddell as a scholar and translator of Latin; and by requiring translation, it brings about a repetition and survival of her work. The meaning itself, "Come and you will be crowned," suits the elegy, with its solacing conferral of reward; and while evoking an ancient ceremony, it also draws attention, in traditional fashion, to this elegy itself as a form of crowning "garland."

Couched in the protectively self-enclosed quatrains of *In Memoriam*, the poem opens with conventional images of returning spring. But instead of formulaically repeating the pastoral tradition, Hill now integrates his reference with a careful presentation of love's submission to time and to mortality. In other words, the comment on the seasonal moment also performs the mourner's submissive recognition of the inevitable defeat, almost from birth, of "love." As we have seen so often, an admission of that defeat is crucial to the establishment of any consolation.

The precise description of spring mingles a tone of resignation with a nonetheless resilient clarity and toughness in its talk of adultery and bird dung. The echo of Horace's *diffugere nives* continues the tribute to Helen Waddell as translator even as it alludes to Horace's elegiac masterpiece. Once again, the elegist draws attention to the medium of his craft and to his elegiac entry into the "foreign code" of language. Related to this entry, the entanglement of natural growth and cultural artifice is itself explored in the image of the "sculpted vine;" and "half-effaced adultery" alludes to the sexual aspect of that entanglement, here chastening the adultery by drawing it under the eroding power of time and by moving the word *adultery* itself toward its additional meaning, so central to elegy—that of becoming something other. While the punitive aspect of this effacement is intensified by the image of "bird-dung dribbling from its mouth," that image may itself provide the point of entry into the cycle that includes decay or waste, as well as the seeding or fertilizing associated with rebirth.

This last suspicion is confirmed by the final stanza, where the abstinent martyr gains the laurel crown. With the last two lines, "Towers and steeples rise away / into the towering gulfs of air," the work is accomplished. Here, as the imagery of eroding stone is countered by the soaring towers, the traditional figure for an erected power of dominance and endurance reinforces the consolation even as it cannily plays between solidity and sheer emptiness. Like the fertility gods, or the totemic images of elevated fortifications, or the tropes of light, or all the genre's major figures of consolation, the final "towering gulfs of air" point to the mourning mind's construction of a virtual presence in the space of absence. In this case, absence—the gulfs of air—becomes the very material of those towering constructs. [18]

To undertake a study of the American elegy would be to open yet another book. A very brief discussion may, however, suggest some of the ways in which our approach to the genre might be brought to bear on American elegies. These poems do differ from their English counterparts, and we can sketch some of these differences; but American elegists, too, perform the work of mourning, and they, too, depend in various ways on the conventions of the genre. While helping us to see precisely what is characteristic of American elegies, our approach would, therefore, also take us to the center of these works.

One of the striking, but not surprising, differences between the English elegy and the American is the latter's loss, rejection, or radically transformative borrowing of the traditional myths and contexts of the genre. Partly because of obvious geographical and ideological

differences, but also because of a strong compulsion toward originality and privacy, American elegists could not easily situate their
poems in the familiar pastoral settings or even within the familiar ritual
procedures of the genre. American elegists have had not only to
reinvent the forms (if not the functions) of elegiac mythology but also
to establish their own literal and figurative settings.

Both the mourners and the dead have therefore been somehow
exiled from the old precincts of the elegy. From her condition of
"polar privacy," Dickinson positions herself directly "Before the door
of God."[19] Whitman leaves the domestic dooryard (itself a distinctly
Americanized setting) and departs from the communal scenes of Lincoln's funeral procession in order to wander alone near the cedars and
pines of a secluded swamp. The speaker in Allen Tate's "Ode to the
Confederate Dead" stands *outside* the shut gate of a cemetery wall,
while Robert Lowell stands outside "the new barbed and galvan-
ized / fence on the Boston Common."[20] And most recently, Amy
Clampitt mourns along the uniquely American reaches of Route 80. In
each case, the elegist is explicitly on the margins, dislocated, vagrant,
or expelled.

The unfamiliar placement, or rather *dis*placement, of the American
elegist reflects not merely an exclusion from the traditional settings of
grief but also a marked distance from the comforts of community
itself. If American poets have a greater tendency than other poets to
write about the unique and isolated self, this isolation is particularly
troubling in the case of the elegist. For since its origins in a Puritan
society marked by the severe repression and rationalization of grief,
and partly owing to its schooling in the almost exclusively forward-
looking orientation of a long pioneer experience, American culture
seems to have had particular difficulty in accommodating genuine
mourning.[21] As often as not, therefore, the American elegist is at
pains to justify the very expression, not simply the occasion, of his
grief. Hence William Vaughn Moody "striv[ing] to evade" a "furtive"
grief that sets him at odds with a "heedless" public; or Tate writing an
elegiac ode whose true subject is "solipsism"; or Roethke closing his
"Elegy for Jane" with the expressed anxiety that he has "no rights in
this matter."[22]

To the American elegy's more overt and uneasy focus on the isolated self of the griever, we should add its more nakedly expressive
style. This is in part a result of the general departure from constraining

conventions and decorums, a valuing not only of originality and freedom but also of greater directness, of trying (in Whitman's words) "to put a Person, a human being (myself . . . in America) freely, fully and truly on record."[23] From the outbreak in the second stanza of Whitman's elegy for Lincoln or Dickinson's terrifyingly direct rup- tures of her own formality ("Burglar! Banker—Father!") to the mur- derous immediacy of Plath's "daddy, you bastard, I'm through" or Berryman's "O and O I mourn / again this complex death," American elegies often have a frighteningly raw and immediate feeling, as if their speakers were fighting not just for an aesthetically acceptable form of consolation but for their own literal survival.[24]

Further factors make the intense, personally expressive nature of the American elegy yet more vivid and more troubling. These poems are often volatile, and rebellious, as if the poets were unusually re- sistant to the very submission that we now recognize as crucial to the work of mourning. With less of a tradition of authoritarian hier- archies, and with an opposite legacy of egalitarianism, the elegist may be hard-pressed to accept or invent the kind of overruling figure of authority to whom his desires must be subjected. In this predicament, not only will the mourner find it difficult to achieve consolation but he may tend to oscillate erratically between postures of defiance on the one hand and exaggerated victimization on the other.

Whether as a result of this lack of inherited, hieratic figures or as a consequence of a related cultural longing for origins (discussed be- low), American elegists have often sought either to ignore the elegy's traditionally totemic figure of rule or to redefine it as a member of the family. Even associated as it is with the image or powers of death, the figure of rule recurs in American elegies as a remarkably parental presence. While this creates a far more direct, personal, and unstable relation between the elegist and such a figure, it comes much closer to the probable genesis of such figures in the first place, thus consider- ably reinforcing what we have begun to see as the American radi- calization of the genre.

Furthermore, while returning to the foundations of the genre in this way, the Americans have also tended to return more directly than other elegists to the origins of loss itself. For almost as a corollary of the turn to more obviously parental or familial figures, the American elegists frequently adopt *for themselves* the position of the child.[25] This may be done by association, as we shall see in the case of Whitman's use of the lilac, or far more directly, as we shall also see in the case of Lowell's elegy for Devereux Winslow. But from Dickinson to Plath, Stevens, or James Merrill, American elegists return the mourning mind to an unusually radical closeness to that of a child. They repeat more directly the kinds of early desolations and searches for comfort that we have seen recapitulated, however indirectly, by almost every other elegist. We have already cited part of Dickinson's "Burglar! Banker—Father! / I am poor once more!" And we shall soon note Whitman's and Lowell's less theological association of elegist and child. But we could cite the close of Stevens's elegy for Church: "It is a child that sings itself to sleep, / The mind, among the creatures that is makes, / The people, those by which it lives and dies."[26] Or Allen Grossman's yet more direct "On the bed lies a shadowy boy who must / Be consoled, / and also a man who must / Believe the consolation. . . ."[27]

While the absence or distrust of generic figures of authority sets the elegist at odds with the dictates of his work, this unhappy relation is aggravated by the American poet's distinctive attitude to the question of origins. For the drive toward originality and the insistent cultural need to cling or return to a "new world" scene of origins (be it political, psychological, or literary) are deeply incompatible with the elegy's enforcement of an accepted distance between the mourner and any such scene or sense of origins. As we have noted repeatedly, the elegy establishes at most a highly mediated relation between the mourner and an original scene or attachment from which he has been irrevocably torn. So, too, we have seen how the elegist is forced to recapitulate his entry into a language and a network of codes that he may at best revise but never originate.

These dilemmas and incompatibilities have driven several American poets to powerful and new contributions to the elegy; but they have also placed the elegist in a particularly vulnerable relation to death itself. As we might have supposed, the distrust of figures of authority (and of the displacements and mediations they enforce), the intense recoil upon the isolated mourning self, and the resistant yearning for origins combine to render the mourner especially susceptible to the appeal, and not merely the threat, of death. From Dickinson and Whitman to Crane, Berryman, and Plath, the American elegist has drawn uncommonly close to what Whitman called "the sure-enwinding arms of cool-enfolding death."[28] The history of the American elegy is in large part the story of such poets' hard-won, highly revisionary, and independent defenses against this attractive threat.

Turning from these generalizations, we should ask what our approach to the genre might yield when applied to particular American elegies. In the remaining pages, I can choose only a few examples, and my remarks will be far from attempted readings of these poems. Rather, I will suggest, a few of the questions and observations that might arise from our understanding of the genre.

In approaching Whitman's "When Lilacs Last in the Dooryard Bloom'd," we might begin by asking how the specific historical occasion of the poem interacted with the generic concerns and tasks of almost any elegy. How could an egalitarian elegist dedicated to ideals of universal brotherhood come to terms not only with a war between brothers but with the alien supposition that perhaps only a highly differentiated, totemic figure of authority and justice—the kind of figure traditionally essential to elegiac consolation—could curb such conflict? How could Whitman mourn without reinstating some form of such a figure? How could he devise an elegy of brotherhood and comradeship as opposed to the more traditional poem of reestablished fatherhood? Why is it, after all, that his elegy is so marked by figures of brothers and imaginary companions, while it avoids apotheosizing or adequately substituting for the figure of Lincoln? Similarly, why was Whitman driven (as almost no elegist before him) to appear to commune with, rather than submissively obey, the figure of death? To what extent was this communion politically as well as psychologically motivated? Why is the figure of death divided into two companion forms (in addition to that of the "dark mother"—a triad recurring in Stevens's elegy for Henry Church) rather than conceived as the unitary power imagined by most elegists? To these topics and to the question of how Whitman came to write a fraternal rather than traditionally authoritarian elegy, we might add the equally generic question of how, if at all, he resisted the attraction not only of death but of the return to a "state of union" preceding the ruptures of individuation *and*, in this pressing moment, of recent civil war.

Within the poem itself, we would obviously note conventional elements of the genre, however fragmentary and revisionary Whitman's use of them might be—such elements as the use of pastoral, of cropped flowers, of stellar and solar imagery, of covering the coffin or grave, of procession, of reality testing, of repetition and antiphony, of eclogue and self-surpassal. But we would also be alert to the issue of the mourner's sexuality. Is the painful cry in the second stanza the cry of an elegist who does not yet realize or accept the elegiac necessity of some form of symbolic impotence? And is the "black murk" and "harsh surrounding cloud" a negatively perceived version of the kind of mediation of desire that the poet will finally have to embrace? As for the sprig of lilac, our discussion of the castrative work of mourning enables us to investigate the full significance of Whitman's offering and to recognize this signalled beginning of the kind of acceptance just mentioned.

Whitman's association of the lilac with his own childhood and with a part of his own body should strike us as necessary, given what we know of the elegist's recapitulation of his earliest experiences of loss and substitution. [29] But we would understand just how that offering or "tally" serves as the sexual renunciation that in turn provides the freeing and the measurement not only of the bird's song of the bleeding throat but also of the poet's soul. So, too, while recognizing just how that song should be construed as "Death's outlet song of life," we would know why Whitman's long-deferred translation of the song into language requires the prior disruption of his erotically dyadic fantasies and the acceptance instead of a triadic relationship such as that between himself and the two companion forms of death, or that between himself, the bird, and the dark mother. In this elegiac and eclogic (by way of the bird's song) acceptance of positionality, Whitman has moved beyond the moment of sexual sacrifice to a more socialized, less erotic vision of relationship—a vision that also encompasses the poet's mediation between the unique and the universal (Whitman "in the middle" between the particular thought and the general knowledge of death who comes "to all, to each").

The self-consciously dramatized performance in which the poet translates the bird's song represents the elegist's familiar recapitulation of his entry into language—in this case a scenario even more than usually fraught with questions of echo in tension with originality. And the form of the song, with its "limitless," inclusive, almost undifferentiated flow, is a carefully wrought aesthetic displacement and figuring of the actually undifferentiated flux of reunion, "the flood of . . . bliss" that the poet both desires and renounces. In fact, we might see the bird as an unusual reminder of the vegetation deity, one whose power and whose transgressive, even incestuous, yearning for a sur-

passal of differentiation the elegist comes to imitate only within the
mediating fabric of his language. Only after this consoling translation
and imitation, this establishment of "the voice of [his] spirit," can
Whitman finally confront the historical images of castration and carnage ("the staffs all splinter'd and broken . . . the debris and debris of
all the slain soldiers"). And only then can he complete the elegiac
movement of self-surpassal, traveling beyond the self that sang, beyond the companions, and beyond the carefully "twined" achievement of his song.

   Offered in this highly schematic and reductive way, such suggestions are in no way designed to present the complexity or individual richness of Whitman's poem, but they at least indicate some of
the ways in which our generic approach may be applied. Already
several topics have arisen that would recur in a study of such later
elegies as Moody's neglected "Ode in Time of Hesitation," Tate's "Ode
to the Confederate Dead," and Lowell's "For the Union Dead." As we
read these poems, yet other elements of our understanding of the
genre would come into play, such as that concerning the relation
between narcissism and melancholia, a subject crucial to both Tate
and Lowell. So, too, many of these generic topics and elements would
be essential to a reading of yet other elegies, such as Crane's "Voy-
ages," Stevens's "The Owl in the Sarcophagus," Plath's poems for her
father, Berryman's Dream Songs for Delmore Schwartz, or Lowell's
elegies for several of the Winslow members of his family.

   It may be worth pausing on one of these elegies by Lowell, "My
Last Afternoon with Uncle Devereux Winslow," from *Life Studies.* I
choose this poem partly because it is not as overtly generic as, for
example, "The Quaker Graveyard in Nantucket" or "In Memory of
Arthur Winslow" and partly because the comprehensive readings that
it has already received nevertheless leave room for certain generic
considerations, several of which I shall put forward as brief, supple-
mentary questions. [30]

   What is the importance, within an elegy, of Lowell's self-presentation as a child? Why should the poem open with an outbreak of
rebellion against the poet's parents—a rebellion curiously mingled
with allegiance to the figure of the grandfather? Why should the child
be looking through screens as he listens to the sound of a clock? Why
should that clock be "Alpine, Edwardian . . . / slung with strangled,
wooden game"? Why should the child be playing with black earth and

white lime? And why should he be surrounded by his grandfather's decor, described as "overbearing, disproportioned"? What holds these details together? By answering such questions from our generic perspective, we would recognize that Lowell's apparently casual opening stanzas address the child's (and the mourner's) need to distance himself from prior, parental attachments while also submitting to an overruling figure of authority. That detachment and submission involve the acceptance of intervening mediations or screens, the entry into a systematic game of differentiations, and the obedience to the rule of time—time itself associated here with a distinctly totemic figure (mountainous, royal, decorated with wooden carvings of dead birds) to which the grandfather and his "overbearing, disproportioned" decor are definitely assimilated. [31]

In the cryptic second section of the poem, we would note the child's self-estranging identification, as in the mirror stage, with an apparently perfect external image ("My perfection was the Olympian / poise of my models in the imperishable autumn / display windows . . ."). Regarding this identification as a potentially imprisoning rehearsal both for the acceptance of a socially coded and positioned self and for the construction of a self that can more realistically be associated with surviving figures or powers, we would understand why Lowell's earliest kind of self-imaging is therefore painfully disrupted ("Distorting drops of water / pinpricked my face in the basin's mirror") and why it gives way to an image that may be far less flattering, but that is governed in a compensatory way by its association with the previously described figure of totemic rule ("I was a stuffed toucan / with a bibulous, multicolored beak").

Continuing the work of mourning, the third section pursues the traditional strategy by which an elegist summons female figures only to repeat his required detachment from them. As so often, these figures are familial, as well as associated, however ironically here, with art or music, as if they might indeed recall the protective mother-Muse who necessarily fails her charge. Great Aunt Sarah is associated, again ironically ("risen like the phoenix / from her bed of troublesome snacks and Tauchnitz classics"), with the undying goddess who outlives a younger mortal. And while she practices *Samson and Delilah*, a work with obvious elegiac connotations, she is herself appropriately surrounded by images of veils, gauze curtains, and "naked Greek statues draped with purple." Finally, Great Aunt Sarah fulfills her association with the mothers, muses, and nymphs of whom so many elegists have asked Where wert thou?—at the critical moment on recital day "she failed to appear."

Even by way of these schematic remarks, we recognize how deeply generic Lowell's poem remains and how its apparently arbitrary array of anecdote and decor is organized not simply by a pattern of images but by a carefully structured adaptation of the devices and strategies of the traditional elegy. This is no less true of the fourth and final section of the poem, which begins with the elegist's exorcistic account of the child's yearning for release. As he sits picking at the anchor on his sailor blouse (an inversion of the traditional image of the elegist as weaver or embroiderer), the child wishes to undo not only what Stephen Yenser has correctly read as the stain or imperfection of mortal life but also the very system of differentiated signs and codes to whose anchoring rule both child and poet have submitted.[32] Of course, the poet's submission is not a unilateral surrender. He, too, may be seen as picking at a given fabric, in this case the codes and resources of the genre that he adapts to the details of his particular world.

Much in this final section of the poem would support our generic approach. But I shall pass over many exemplary details—motifs of halving and doubling, of intervening clouds and boarded windows, of camouflage and decoys, of a cowering child, of submission to daylight, as well as to societal emblems and regulatory codes—to note the elegist's traditional self-measurement in relation to the dead and to mortality, and his final assimilation of the dead man to the carefully manufactured "animated, hierarchical" figure of totemic power.[33] Finally, with one last reference to the child's and the poet's play with differences, Lowell places Devereux Winslow in a realm where such differences seem to fall away: "Come winter, / Uncle Devereux would blend to the one color." While the dead man has moved as if beyond the world of contrasting signs and determinants, the poet is left with the symbols of life and death, the dark soil and the white lime, the schematically opposed marks of the language he has once again entered and reshaped.

Before concluding, I would like to refer to Amy Clampitt's "A Procession at Candlemas," a poem that asks us not only to repeat some of our assumptions about the work of mourning but also to question some of the prejudices that have been inherent in the tradition of the elegy itself.[34]

To put it most simply, Clampitt reminds us that so many traditional elegies perform a multiple exclusion or occlusion of figures representing the mother. The first such exclusion derives, as we know, from the mourner's inescapable repetition of his or her detachment from and substitution for the mother. The second, however, derives from a male culture's establishment of an almost exclusive relation between masculinity and the figures of authority—figures whose intervention between the child and its mother and whose upholding of the symbolic codes (including the arch-symbols of consoling power) have been highly important to the elegy and the work of mourning. But such figures—particularly those of consolation and even more especially those associated with male figures of fertility—have monopolized a role once shared by female counterparts. Allegorized or not, the consoling figure of the female fertility goddess or procreative mother, once so prominent in the ancient world, has been pushed to the margins of the elegy, surviving, if at all, only in unconsoling versions of itself.

It is extremely difficult, however, to decide how far or how clearly one can disentangle this secondary, prejudicial occlusion from the prior, psychological necessity for detachment from or concealment of the mother. (Indeed, how *much* of this "necessity" is itself the product of cultural bias?) While Clampitt tries quite programmatically to rescue the mother figure from its secondary, cultural banishment, her work is complicated by her necessity as a mourner to detach herself from and, indeed, finally to cover over such a figure with no less of a disconnective mediating veil than traditional male elegists have used. (Admittedly, Clampitt will have preceded that final covering by a remarkable act of uncovering, as we shall see.) So, too, her reinstatement of the figure of the female goddess as a potentially consoling trope, whether of fertility or of wisdom, requires no less of the chastening gesture required for the creation of its masculine counterparts.

Learning that her mother has been placed in Intensive Care, the poet travels homeward to visit her. She travels under the pressure of threatened bereavement, a bereavement that will be actual by the time she has arrived. Under this pressure, the mourning mind reinterprets the night traffic along Route 80, altering it "to a processional, a feast of Candlemas." Although unorthodox in setting and private in nature—

typically American revisions—this subjective alteration situates the action and meaning of the poem in a more than personal context of traditional ritual. (The poem's tercets are especially appropriate for this—recollecting such elegiac processionals as those of Stevens, Shelley, and Dante.) The specific ritual, however, raises immediate problems. Candlemas commemorates the presentation of the Christ child in the temple (an allusion not only to the kind of elegiac myth that we have already studied but also to the dominance of such myths by male figures—a dominance Clampitt wishes to challenge). Furthermore, within Catholicism, Candlemas recalls the originally Judaic ceremony by which Mary was purified after delivery—the "Mosaic insult" whose chastening limitation of the mother Clampitt opposes as early as in the eighth stanza of her poem. While presenting her cultural polemic, Clampitt thus complicates her elegy by seeming to resist the elegiac procedures both of purification itself and of the submission of the mother—including the child's relation to her as origin—to the repressions of law. The poem returns to this quarrel several times.

The journey itself resembles the ritual elegiac descent, a painful entry into the dark, self-limiting state of disability that precedes any consoling revelation. Hence the accepted rewrapping of the self (earlier in the poem Clampitt had drawn potentially subversive attention to the fragility of the ego, the "integument, layer / within layer" whose texture we know that both child and mourner should accept). Hence, too, the specific ordeal as the traveler "clamber[s] down, numb-footed, half in a drowse / of freezing dark, through a Stonehenge / of fuel pumps. . . ." The reference to Stonehenge reinforces the sacrificial nature of the ritual, whose elegiac aspect is pursued by the following question: "What is real except / what's fabricated?" While the query suggests the mourner's necessary acceptance of artifice and mediation, it also indicates an American poet's radical desire to question the fictional nature of even her own constructions.

The strangely conjoined submission to and subversive questioning of elegiac procedures continues ("Who / can assign a trade-in value to that sorrow?") as the elegist broadens the scope of her grief to encompass the losses suffered by American Indians whose dislocation from their lands forced them on a similar, more tragic journey of loss. This very broadening of sympathy carries the mourner beyond the confines of the ego toward the object for which so many American elegists have so explicitly admitted their longing, the transpersonal "rest-in-peace of the placental coracle," the deathlike repose within a scene of origins. It is the very scene that the mourner must resist, the scene toward which she may return for consolation but away from which she must travel for survival. Appropriately enough, it marks the midpoint of the poem.

The second section begins by elegiacally admitting a limited knowledge of the dead and of the past, fittingly described as a "fabric" of antecedents. And it is in this context that the effigy of Athene is introduced. Here is the object of devotion, the figure of the female goddess. But as was true for male totemic objects, this figure is "wizened," inert, not only dead but somehow chastened or chastized. It is kept "out of sight like the incontinent whimperer / in the backstairs bedroom"—backstairs suggesting both relegation and elevation, and incontinent nicely capturing both disability and the uncontained transgressive quality for which the related figure of the god is revered yet punitively disabled. [35]

Clampitt has unquestionably rescued the effigy from cultural obscurity (certainly an obscurity within the genre), and it is a compelling figure, enjoying processional worship and sacrificial offerings. Since Clampitt is traveling toward her own mother, there is already a potentially consoling association between the mother and the divine figure. But the effigy has been recuperated as an originally and residually sequestered figure, resembling an incontinent whimperer—whimpering suggesting the very opposite of consolation. And even at its moment of greatest power, it is explicitly associated with intervening veils. The chief offering given it is a linen peplos—not merely a fabric, but a piece of drapery worn folded across the upper body and fastened with a brooch. Worse still, the mourner herself feels shut out, unable to "unpeel the layers" or repeated rituals that intervene between her and the sacred figure. With a typically American desire, she seeks impatiently to move beyond cultural memory to a more original, immediate, and personal revelation.

Clampitt thus continues to move within and yet apparently against the traditional current of the elegy. Resuming her account of the journey, she again embeds aspects of the work of mourning within the details of description. [36] These include not merely observations of urban decay and roadside squalor but, more precisely, reflections of the painful separation between parent and child. The most powerfully

323

described of such separations is that of birth itself. Here Clampitt's imagery of heaving birth canal and disgorged infant provides precisely the kind of uncovering of the female powers of procreation and the kind of honesty about the physical nature of birth that a male culture has tended to evade. For a genre so dependent on myths of birth and rebirth, it is remarkable that this prejudicial evasion has continued for so long. By attacking male notions of "purity" as she has done ironically earlier in the poem, Clampitt restores a wealth of specifically feminine imagery to the genre.[37] The reference to birth as separation, however, and the subsequent descriptions of gulfs between parent and child prevent any straightforwardly consoling sense of return to the mother here. So, too, the very landscape is described in terms of cadavers and of such textured overlays as frozen mush, quilting, and dragnets.

But the poem returns to its insistent search for some consoling testimony beyond or behind these separations and obscurements. With renewed elegiac anger, Clampitt tries again to penetrate "the shucked-off / bundle, the hampered obscurity that has been / for centuries the mumbling lot of women." At some crucial moment now hidden or lost, a moment Clampitt wishes to relocate, "the thread of fire . . . relinquish[ed] / the seed of possibility." The consoling elegiac images of fire and seed are thus reclaimed for women and reassociated with female creative powers even as women's loss of these is mourned. Once again we face the difficult task of discriminating two overlapping kinds of loss—on the one hand, women's loss of power, on the other the inescapable, castrative loss of actual power suffered by any subject who is raised to the level of a consoling *figure* for power. Even so, whereas the male figure's castrative loss of actual force is compensated by its subsequent wielding of symbolic power, the female figure has been robbed, by its cultural occlusion, of even this latter compensation. While Clampitt's polemic—one that brilliantly exploits the genre's traditional place for such critically directed sorrow—cannot seek to abridge the unavoidable quotient of loss that either gender must suffer, it urges us to redress the considerable social or political aggravation of this loss in the case of women.

How does Clampitt finally approach her revealed clue, and what is the nature of that clue? As we may expect, the approach requires a continued ordeal of self-limitation—a "blunder[ing], stumbling," with a familiar reduction of the claims of knowledge (the mourning memory "like a migrant bird that finds the flyway / it hardly knew it knew except by instinct"). The epiphanic encounter itself confronts the recollected image of "a small, / stilled bird, its cap of clear yellow / slit by a thread of scarlet." Since the remembering mind was itself compared to a bird, this encounter resembles a first recognition not only of mortality but of one's own mortal nature. While the clear yellow cap may recall the flame of promise, it is slit (we could almost say decapitated) by the scarlet thread of death, the thread that necessarily provides the fabric for all the poem's images not only of mediating textures (from the red-tassled llamas and the rug-piled mounts of other migrant animals to the ego's layers of integument, the peplos, and the curtain in Intensive Care) but also of the flame of original, vital possibility itself, the *"thread* of fire" (my emphasis).

Given this mortal submission of the epiphanic image to the thread of death and mediation, the "nucleus of fire" that it evokes (the vivid, Whitmanian apprehension of life's essence as revealed by the first perception of death) is explicitly "untouched." It represents both connection and severance—the "lost connection" that in turn "hallow[s] the wizened effigy, the mother / curtained in Intensive Care." Generative power, necessarily marked by the chastening, disconnective thread of death and mediation, is thus precisely what hallows both the dead mother and the figure of the goddess to whom she has been so closely joined. The poem may have sought reentry to an immediate, unhampered apprehension of the mother's power of origination, and it has in fact revealed more fully than preceding elegies the actual physical characteristics of that power. And yet it has closed by hallowing her in and by an inescapable veil like that of the peplos, or indeed like the curtain in Intensive Care—a peplos and curtain that could well represent the offered poem and the mourning mind themselves.

Any reader of contemporary American poetry will be struck by the large number of elegies published in books and periodicals each year. There is a still larger number of poems that, while not elegies, seek to express and come to terms with general feelings of loss and sorrow. Taken together, these poems would seem to represent a distinctly elegiac age. And yet while this may be the case, how many elegies console more readers than the poet, the particular bereaved, and their immediate circle? This question suggests both a problem besetting the contemporary elegy and a criterion by which to judge its individual examples. Often, these poems are too narrowly based, too private in their expression of grief and too idiosyncratic in their use of anecdote, description, or recollection. Well crafted, scrupulous, and intense in feeling as they may be, such poems fail to connect their highly particularized worlds with a generic and hence more general frame of reference. They connect neither to the recognizable motifs and elements of the work of mourning nor to the myths and ceremonies associated with that work.

By contrast, our successful elegies are those most able to connect the actual details of their occasion, however particularized, intractable, or unpoetic (Lowell's items of clothing and summerhouse furniture, Clampitt's Route 80 and Intensive Care curtain), to the ritual and psychological underpinnings of the genre. We have recognized how repetition itself and the submission to codes are crucial elements of the work of mourning; and the most successful elegists are in fact those least afraid to repeat the traditional procedures of the genre. In "The Owl in the Sarcophagus" Stevens returns to the core of elegiac ceremony by narrating a ritual descent, like that of Orpheus, or Dante, or the initiates in ancient elegiac mystery cults. And the obscure consolation that he offers derives from a deep understanding of the most ancient and hieratic elements of the genre. While his fraternal forms of Sleep and Peace are deliberately "modern," they nevertheless make up the *"mythology* of modern death" (my emphasis)—a mythology that goes back at least to Homer's account of the death of Sarpedon. So, too, Berryman's elegies for Delmore Schwartz describe the dead poet in terms that surely recall the figure of the vegetation deity: "Flagrant his young male beauty . . . the whole young man / alive with surplus love."[38] And Merrill's "The Changing Light at Sandover," a poem whose mastery and revision of elegiac conventions I have studied elsewhere, repeatedly mourns and celebrates its figures of the dead by assimilating them to "the latest / Recurrent figure out of mythology / To lend his young beauty to a living grave / In order that Earth bloom another season."[39]

Such instances of repetition bring to mind this study's epigraph in which the Angel of Zeal reminds Dante of the beatitude: "*Qui lugent* affermando esser beati.*" For just the words "those who mourn," Dante chooses to return from his own language to the preceding Latin. This does far more than suggest the mourning or penitent poet's submission to a preexisting code, or the very definition of mourners by the words of such a code—*qui lugent*. For the Latin words actually repeat the words of Aquinas, who in turn quoted them from a Latin translation of the words of Matthew, who in turn quoted the words of Christ: "Beati qui lugent, quoniam ipsi consolabantur."[40] The very words thus position the action and the agents of mourning within a series of repetitions that are themselves the grounds for sorrow and consolation—a sorrowful admission that no mourner enjoys an unmediated relation to an original state preceding repetitions either of grief or of a received language; and the consolation that such repetitions themselves may provide a sense not only of timeless community (including that between the living and the dead) but also of a relation, however mediated, to some notion of source or origin after all.

"Grief / is original, but it / repeats itself; there's nothing / more original that it can do."[41] Once again we recall our first discussion of the various kinds and determinants of elegiac repetition, and we remember how so many elegies have followed the way in which Theocritus's "First Idyl" presented its lament as being itself a repetition. Since the occasion for elegy will not disappear, and since the elegist's work of mourning itself requires repetitions and acceptances of codes and traditions, and, finally, since consolation itself comes usually in the form of an acquired legacy or sense of continuity, it seems as though the elegy, of all the genres, would have the strongest prospect of a continuing life. More than other poems, elegies are indeed condemned to repeat themselves and their predecessors. In an amusingly ironic instance, even an elegist's *claim* for originality (Swift's self-praise, "To steal a Hint was never known, / But what he writ was all his own") in fact repeats a former elegist's lines (Denham's praise for Cowley: "To him no Author was unknown, / Yet what he wrote was all his own").[42]

But having said that our best elegies repeat the conventions of the genre, we should recognize that the most satisfying of such repetitions have always been the most revisionary. The preceding study has pointed to a range of such revisions, one longstanding category of which appears to be of particular prominence in recent examples of the genre. This category relates to the elegist's skepticism regarding the inherited means of consolation. We saw how this skepticism itself became traditional after Spenser and Milton, and we may well ask how it can continue to be revisionary. By way of answer, one might note that contemporary elegists tend to voice their skepticism far more directly than do their predecessors, and they subvert more thoroughly the very underpinnings of their poetry at large rather than merely dispel local fictions or surmises within the poems. So, too, despite this skepticism, recent elegists tend to suggest their willingness to work within a fictional world rather than point confidently to a world of "truth" beyond the frame of fiction. Thus Merrill, carefully staging his elegiac rituals within the mirror of acknowledged speculation, writes of how "our own otherwise / Dumb grief is given words. DJ: Or lies?" And in the words attributed to the posthumous Auden, "FOR FACT IS IS IS FABLE."[43] Similarly, we heard Clampitt ask, "What's real except what's fabricated?" And Stevens takes us as if backstage in the theater of the genre to display, "in their mufflings, monsters of elegy" and to expose the very trappings by which such monsters are not only costumed but constituted, each figure now seen "In the manner of its stitchings, of its thread, / In the weaving round the wonder of its need." Reconstituting the "mythology of modern death," Stevens also demythologizes these mythic figures, exposing them as the fabricated products of need and as "the forms of dark desire."[44]

While such poems seek to balance our needs against our skepticism, our desires against our knowledge, they perform a constant renegotiation between the individual elegists and their inherited tradition. As we have seen, this is itself an essential aspect of the work of mourning. It is the aspect that lends force to the paradoxical compound of echo with origination or invention in Whitman's echo-translation of the bird's song in his elegy for Lincoln. It is expressed and enacted with extraordinary emphasis in Elizabeth Bishop's elegy for Robert Lowell: *"repeat, repeat, repeat; revise, revise, revise."*[45] And it lends particular significance to Stevens's account of how "the ear repeats, / Without a voice, inventions of farewell."[46]

Notes

Preface

Walter Benjamin, *The Origin of German Tragic Drama*, trans. John Osborne (London: New Left Books, 1977), 103.

1. William Wordsworth, *Poetical Works*, ed. Thomas Hutchinson, rev. Ernest de Selincourt (Oxford: Oxford University Press, 1904; reprint ed., 1973), 737.
2. Ibid., 701.
3. I am referring here to tendencies found most obviously, but by no means exclusively, in deconstructionist criticism, for which "literature is precisely that use of language which can *purge pathos*, which can show that it too is figurative, ironic or aesthetic" (my emphasis) (Geoffrey Hartman, *Deconstruction and Criticism*, with Harold Bloom, Paul de Man, Jacques Derrida, and J. Hillis Miller [New York: Seabury Press, 1979], ix).

   Other critics, operating from a more political perspective, such as that of Althusser, for example, have often conducted their attempt to dismantle the bourgeois ideology of the self by attacking traditional notions of the authorial subject. For an almost exact reversal of Benjamin's warning see, for example, the recent statement by Antony Easthope: "A major reason why the theory of discourse I shall put forward ought to be preferred is that it can explain the author as product or effect of the text, whereas conventional criticism accepts the notion of the author as unquestionable and pre-given in order to be able to define how the text should be read" (*Poetry as Discourse* [London: Methuen, 1983], 7). My own approach tries to bring out the ongoing tension and sense of reluctant *process* within what I see as a far more vexed and dialectical relationship than that of a unilateral production of the author by his text.

   Alongside, or in many respects preceding both deconstructionists and Althusserians, is the figure of Lacan. And another direct reversal of Benjamin's warning is formulated as follows, by one of the clearest explicators of Lacan's work: "One could, therefore, say that the human being is an effect of the signifier rather than its cause" (Anika Rifflet-Lemaire, *Jacques Lacan*, trans. David Macey [London: Routledge & Kegan Paul, 1977], 68). But Lacan's view of the production of that "effect" focuses on repeated conflicts and "splittings" and is constantly aware of what remains outside of, or as a vacancy within, the texture of signifying codes. If, for Lacan, the unconscious and desire are in part generated by the reductive submission of need to the (necessarily linguistic) "defile" of demand—a reduction that leaves desire as an unsatisfiable remainder, clamoring in self-misrepresentative language for total self-recognition—neither the unconscious nor desire is totally reducible to language, nor can we slight their constant counterpressure within and against language. For a fuller account of the need / demand / desire sequence see Jacques Lacan, *The Language of the Self: The Function of Language in Psychoanalysis*, trans. with notes and commentary by Anthony Wilden (New York: Dell, 1968), 185–96. See also Rosalind Coward and John Ellis, *Language and Materialism: Developments in Semiology and the Theory of the Subject* (London: Routledge & Kegan Paul, 1977), 117 ff.; Juliet Mitchell and Jacqueline Rose, *Feminine Sexuality* (New York: Norton, 1983), 6, 32.

4. For the major source of such prophecies see the conclusion of Michel Foucault's *The Order of Things* (New York: Random House, 1970), 386–87. Admittedly, Foucault is speaking of a certain view or manner of man, but his notion that "man had been a figure occurring between two modes of language" and his wager that altered arrangements of knowledge would leave man "erased, like a face drawn in sand at the edge of the sea," have led many to define man perhaps too exclusively as a construct of discourse. Of course man is inevitably conditioned by language; but that conditioning should be seen as a continuous conflict, not as an unequivocally decided conquest that has left man utterly dependent on subsequent changes in an autonomous order of signs.

5. "An Ordinary Evening in New Haven," in Wallace Stevens, *The Collected Poems of Wallace Stevens* (New York: Knopf, 1954; reprint ed., 1971), 473.

6. Robert Hass, "Meditation at Lagunitas," *Praise* (New York: Ecco Press, 1979), 4.

Chapter I. Interpreting the Genre: The Elegy and the Work of Mourning

Rainer Maria Rilke, *Duino Elegies*, trans. J. B. Leishman and Stephen Spender (New York: Norton, 1939), 27.

1. Sigmund Freud, "Mourning and Melancholia" (1917), trans. Joan Riviere, in *General Psychological Theory*, ed. Philip Rieff (New York: Macmillan, Collier Books, 1963), 164–79.

Studies of the genre are few in number, and while some (particularly Smith's and Lambert's, cited below) are more interpretive than others, none shares the approach of the following study. Two early articles focus on the pastoral elegy in particular: James H. Hanford, "The Pastoral Elegy and Milton's 'Lycidas,'" *PMLA* 25 (1910), 403–47; and G. Norlin, "The Conventions of the Pastoral Elegy," *American Journal of Philology* (hereafter cited as *AJP*) 32 (1911), 294–312. More extensive, and unusual for its attention to historical context, is John Draper, *The Funeral Elegy and the Rise of English Romanticism* (New York: New York University Press, 1929). Thomas Perrin Harrison, Jr., has a brief introduction but many useful notes and cross references in *The Pastoral Elegy: An Anthology* (Austin: University of Texas Press, 1939), translations by

Harry Joshua Leon. I shall use Harrison's edition repeatedly when citing early examples of the genre.

Focusing primarily on the seventeenth century, Ruth Wallerstein has made an excellent study of the changing norms within a sequence of elegies, *The Laureate Hearse*, pt. 1 of *Studies in Seventeenth Century Poetics* (Madison: University of Wisconsin Press, 1950). Scott Elledge includes much of interest to any student of the genre in *Milton's "Lycidas": Edited to Serve as an Introduction to Criticism* (New York: Harper & Row, 1966). A wide-ranging study of "elegiac" poetry (rather than of elegies per se) is Abbie Findlay Potts, *The Elegiac Mode: Poetic Form in Wordsworth and Other Elegists* (Ithaca: Cornell University Press, 1967). Donald Mell concentrates on the Augustan period in *A Poetics of Augustan Elegy* (Amsterdam: Mouton, 1974). Ellen Lambert's fine study of the genre does interpret several aspects of its conventions, but her examples and applications are mainly within the European pastoral tradition from the Classical period to the Renaissance (*Placing Sorrow: A Study of the Pastoral Elegy from Theocritus to Milton* [Chapel Hill: University of North Carolina Press, 1976]). Overlapping more closely with my chosen period, Eric Smith in *By Mourning Tongues: Studies in the English Elegy* (Ipswich: Boydell Press) offers good readings of several elegies from "Lycidas" to *In Memoriam*. He, too, stresses the "dramatic" aspects of the genre; but his project does not move toward a psychoanalytic understanding of the mythology of the genre, and several of the elegy's conventions remain uninterpreted. Finally, a more specialized but excellent study of certain elegies written *for poets*—a subgenre he calls "Tombeau"—is found in the chapter entitled "Tombeau" in Lawrence I. Lipking, *The Life of the Poet: Beginning and Ending Poetic Careers* (Chicago: University of Chicago Press, 1981).

2. Maurice Bowra believes the word *elegy* to be related etymologically to an ancient name for the flute, a name that survives in the Armenian word for flute, *elegn-*. He favors this proposed derivation, itself doubtful, over that which relates the word to the Greek phrase *e e legoi*, "to speak well of." Bowra, *Early Greek Elegists* (Cambridge, Mass.: Harvard University Press, 1938). Yet another etymological theory, close to that of the *e e legoi*, involves the phrase *ai ai legoi*, linking the genre to the cry of grief over Hyacinth or that of Hercules over Linus (see, for example, Scaliger, *The Poetics* 1.1, quoted in Elledge, 107).

3. Margaret Alexiou, *The Ritual Lament in Greek Tradition* (Cambridge: Cambridge University Press, 1974), 104.

4. For a recent survey of these changes in the generic definitions see Alastair Fowler, *Kinds of Literature: An Introduction to the Theory of Genres and Modes* (Cambridge, Mass.: Harvard University Press, 1982), 156 ff. For accounts of the prosodic adaptations of elegiacs see Findlay Potts, *The Elegiac Mode;* and John Hollander, *Vision and Resonance: Two Senses of Poetic Form* (New York: Oxford University Press, 1973), 172–73, 200–202, 268–69.

5. The funerary function of the flute, as well as its legendary origins, is widespread, appearing also, for example, in the beliefs and practices of Brazilian Indians. In China, the New Music, of the fifth century B.C., was characterized by wind instruments replacing the earlier percussive music. Critics of the New Music protested against its enervating, decadent, and erotic qualities, claiming that it was more appropriate for mourning.

6. James Merrill, *Braving the Elements* (New York: Atheneum, 1972), 72.

7. In the light of what follows, we should notice that Apollo's relation to Daphne is, from its very inception, punitive. Instigated by Cupid and executed by Daphne's father, it is as if the metamorphosis that follows were designed in part to reveal and to inflict on Apollo the nature of erotic desire as it is governed and deflected by the father.

8. Ovid, *Metamorphoses*, trans. Frank Justus Miller, Loeb Classical Library (London: Heinemann, 1916; reprint ed., 1960), 40–41. All further quotations from Ovid are from this edition.

9. By showing how Apollo's invention of the sign includes his projection of its future use, Ovid stresses the temporal disjunction at the core of the sign. Pan, too, will project the signifying function of his pipes into the future. For the relation between temporality and signification see Paul de Man, "The Rhetoric of Temporality," in *Interpretation: Theory and Practice*, ed. Charles S. Singleton (Baltimore: Johns Hopkins Press, 1969), 173–209.

10. Argos's fate is no less significant as a frame for the Syrinx episode. His failure to sustain an attentive regard for Mercury's order of signs leads to a literal decapitation; whereas by their submissive acceptance of a system of signs, Apollo and Pan suffer only mild, symbolic versions of this fate.

    After Argos is beheaded, his blinded eyes are converted to the decorative motif on a peacock's feathers. While this conversion is itself highly elegiac (cf. "Those are pearls that were his eyes"), it exemplifies the displacement from a physical organ to an aesthetic object or sign to be displayed. As we shall see, few elegies fail to perform variants of such transformations.

11. Sigmund Freud, *Letters*, trans. Tania Stern and James Stern, ed. Ernst Freud (New York: Basic Books, 1960), 386.

12. For an excellent discussion of Pan and the "functional interdependence between poetic power and erotic failure" see Harry Berger, Jr., "Orpheus, Pan, and the Poetics of Misogyny: Spenser's Critique of Pastoral Love and Art," *ELH* 50 no. 1 (Spring 1983), 27–60; see also Louis Adrian Montrose, "'The perfecte paterne of a Poete': The Poetics of Courtship in *The Shepheardes Calender*," *Texas Studies in Language and Literature* (hereafter cited as *TSLL*) 21 (1979), 34–67.

    One of the most persuasive *visual* testimonies to the phallic nature of the flute is Titian's *Allegory of the Three Ages of Life*. National Gallery of Scotland, Edinburgh. Cf. also Leo Frobenius's account of a Mande folktale, which begins:

    > A maiden refused to marry, refused to marry any one. This came to the ears of a man who liked her. Thereupon he changed himself into a flute, and laid himself, in the shape of a flute before the maiden's door. The maiden found the flute, picked it up, ran to her mother, and showed it to her. Her mother said: "What a lovely flute you have. No one in the village has so fine a flute." The maiden took the flute into the house and leaned it against the wall.

    (Frobenius, *African Genesis* [Berkeley: Turtle Island Foundation, 1983], 174–75).

13. For fuller accounts of these stages see Jacques Lacan, "The Mirror Stage as Formative of the Function of the I as Revealed in Psychoanalytic Experience," in *Écrits: A Selection*, trans. Alan Sheridan (New York: Norton, 1977). See also the works by Lacan, Rifflet-Lemaire, Coward and Ellis, and Mitchell and Rose, all cited in the Preface (n. 3). To these add John P. Muller and William Richardson, "Toward Reading Lacan: Pages for a Workbook," *Psychoanalysis and Contemporary Thought* 1, no. 3 (1978), 323–72.

14. For example, repetition, power reversal, and revenge.

15. For Freud's account of the *fort-da* game see his *Beyond the Pleasure Principle* (1920), trans. James Strachey (London: Hogarth Press, 1950). Lacan returns to this account often, but a principal reading is in "The Function and Field of Speech and Language in Psychoanalysis," in *Écrits*, 30–113.

16. Freud, *Beyond the Pleasure Principle*, 34.

17. Freud himself did not originally stress the element of castration in the oedipal drama. His gradual recognition of this component is described by Juliet Mitchell in Juliet Mitchell and Jacqueline Rose, *Feminine Sexuality* (New York: Norton, 1983), 12 ff.

18. Juliet Mitchell, *Psychoanalysis and Feminism* (New York: Random House, Vintage Books, 1975), 395.

19. Lacan calls the phallus "a ghost" in "Desire and the Interpretation of Desire in *Hamlet*," *Yale French Studies* 55/56 (1978), 50. The quotation from Jacqueline Rose is from Mitchell and Rose, 40.

20. Anika Rifflet-Lemaire, *Jacques Lacan*, trans. David Macey (London: Routledge & Kegan Paul, 1977), 82.

21. *The Complete Poems of Emily Brontë*, ed. C. W. Hatfield (New York: Columbia University Press, 1967), 223.

22. Sigmund Freud, *The Ego and the Id* (1923), trans. Joan Riviere, rev. and ed. James Strachey (New York: Norton, 1960; Norton Library, 1962), 48.

23. Jacques Lacan, *The Four Fundamental Concepts of Psycho-Analysis*, ed. Jacques-Alain Miller, trans. Alan Sheridan (New York: Norton, 1981), 198.

24. Freud, *The Ego and the Id*, 37.

25. See Freud, "Mourning and Melancholia," 168 ff.

26. Phaeton, seeking his identity in relation to his father, Phoebus, fails to accept the mediated nature of that relation and insists instead on becoming the father, to the extent of steering the sun. He wants exclusively the very thing that Phoebus would withhold, and he refuses an extensive list of offered substitutes. Phoebus's yielding brings on the death of his overreaching son, who thus joins the ranks of all those characters whose rejection of substitutes brings them to ruin. Phaeton is caught between the ungovernable nature of his own desire, represented by the unchecked horses, and the wrath of the absolute Father, Jove, whose thunderbolt finally annihilates Phaeton. We recall, too, the way in which the inconsolability of Phaeton's sisters and of his cousin turns them into poplars and a swan, respectively. Phoebus's own dark melancholy is itself only dispelled by the coaxing *and threats* of Jove. As we shall see, the fact that this scenario involves the sun, of all figures, is far from fortuitous.

27. Shakespeare, *Cymbeline* 4.2.235–38. This and subsequent quotations from

Shakespeare are from *The Riverside Shakespeare*, ed. G. Blakemore Evans (Boston: Houghton Mifflin, 1974).

28. Wallace Stevens, "The Owl in the Sarcophagus," in *The Collected Poems of Wallace Stevens* (New York: Knopf, 1954; reprint ed., 1971), 434.

29. James Wright, "Devotions," in *Collected Poems* (Middletown, Conn.: Wesleyan University Press, 1972), 72.

30. Theocritus, "First Idyl," in Harrison, 28.

31. Freud discusses the survivor's guilt not only in "Mourning and Melancholia" but also in his earlier *Totem and Taboo* (1913), trans. James Strachey (New York: Norton, 1950), 60 ff. In the latter, Freud recognizes the role of guilt in the genesis of the "pathological form of mourning," later to be analyzed as melancholia.

32. One further determinant of elegiac questioning will be studied with specific reference to *In Memoriam*. This involves the mourner's attempt to repair a damaged narcissism. By means of repeated questions and apostrophes, the mourner tries to reposit the approving audience that he has suddenly lost.

33. Quoted from Harrison, 34.

34. See Freud, *Beyond the Pleasure Principle*, 28–63.

35. Harrison, 36.

36. Freud, "Mourning and Melancholia," 166.

37. The quotation from Ronsard is from Harrison. Bryskett's elegy may be found in Edmund Spenser, *Poetical Works*, ed. E. de Selincourt (Oxford: Oxford University Press, 1912; reprint ed., 1969), 550 ff.

38. Specifically, I am anticipating the discussions about Jonson and Dryden in chapter V. For the best discussion of the rhetorical use of the echo figure see John Hollander, *The Figure of Echo: A Mode of Allusion in Milton and After* (Berkeley and Los Angeles: University of California Press, 1981).

39. Spenser, 461; Milton, *The Complete Poems and Major Prose*, ed. Merritt Y. Hughes (Indianapolis: Odyssey Press, 1957; reprint ed., 1975), 120.

40. Alexiou, 137.

41. Ibid., 109.

42. William Wordsworth, *Poetical Works*, ed. Thomas Hutchinson, rev. Ernest de Selincourt (Oxford: Oxford University Press, 1904; reprint ed., 1973), 701.

43. John Berryman, Dream Song 147, *His Toy, His Dream, His Rest* (London: Faber & Faber, 1969), 76.

44. The vegetation deity thus exercises an obviously cathartic power; and this element relates closely to the cathartic or apotropaic gestures in several elegies. See, for example, the discussion of "In Memory of Major Robert Gregory," in chapter X.

45. R. B. Onians, *Origins of European Thought* (Cambridge: Cambridge University Press, 1951); Jacques Choron, *Western Attitudes to Death* (New York: Macmillan, Collier Books, 1963).

46. E. R. Dodds, *The Greeks and the Irrational* (Los Angeles: University of California Press, 1951).

47. Erwin Rohde, *Psyche: The Cult of Souls and Belief in Immortality among the Greeks*, trans. W. G. Hillis (London: Routledge, 1925).

48. Homer's "Hymn to Demeter," quoted in ibid., 219.
49. By way of Pliny's description, a ritual like this may well have migrated to such imagined reconstructions of druidic practices as that found in Drayton's *Poly-Olbion*. There, too, the sacrifice of a bull is associated with the assumption of spiritual immortality:

> On th'unhew'd Altar layd, put to the hallowed fires:
> And whilst in the sharpe flame the trembling flesh
> expires,
> As their strong furie mov'd (when all the rest
> adore)
> Pronouncing their desires the sacrifice before,
> Up to th'eternall heaven their bloodied hands did
> reare:
> And, whilst the murmuring woods even shuddred as
> with feare,
> Preacht to the beardlesse youth, the soules
> immortall state; . . .

(9.421–27, in *The Works of Michael Drayton*, ed. I. W. Hebel, 5 vols. [Oxford: Blackwell and Mott, 1931–41; corrected ed. 1961], 4:180).
50. Ezra Pound, *Collected Shorter Poems* (London: Faber & Faber, 1952; reprint ed., 1973), 206; William Butler Yeats, "Two Songs from a Play," *The Poems*, ed. Richard J. Finneran (New York: Macmillan, 1983), 213.
51. While the martyrs by *sparagmos* have been predominantly male, this need not be exclusively so. Nor need it be an exclusively male victim whose sacrificed physical power yields the figurative immortal capacity allegorized, for example, as that of poetry or song. One version of Echo's fate has her, like Linus, suffer the punishment inflicted by a rival musician, in this case Pan, whose envy we are told is sharpened by erotic frustration. As quoted by John Hollander in *The Figure of Echo* (8):

> Pan sees that, and takes occasion to be angry at the maid, and to envy her music because he could not come at her beauty. Therefore he sends a madness among the shepherds . . . and they tore her all to pieces and flung about them all over the earth her yet singing limbs [*adonta ta melê*, punning on limbs and songs]. The Earth in observance of the Nymphs buried them all, preserving to them still their musical property, and they by an everlasting sentence and decree of the Muses breathe out a voice.

52. Harrison, 28.
53. Wordsworth, 454.
54. Compare the Spirit's lines in Wordsworth's "Invocation to the Earth," a poem included near the elegies for John, together with the other "Epitaphs and Elegiac Pieces":

> 'False parent of Mankind!
> Obdurate, proud, and blind,
> I sprinkle thee with soft celestial dews,

> Thy lost, maternal heart to re-infuse!
> Scattering this far-fetched moisture from my wings,
> Upon the act a blessing I implore. . . .

(ibid., 455).

55. Mircea Eliade, *A History of Religious Ideas*. Vol. 1, trans. Willard R. Trask (Chicago: University of Chicago Press, 1978).

56. *Iliad* 18.243–44, trans. Alexander Pope, in *The Poems of Alexander Pope*, ed. John Butt, 10 vols. Vol. 7, ed. Maynard Mack (New Haven: Yale University Press, 1967), 334.

57. For a study of the solar figure in elegies see Findlay Potts, *The Elegiac Mode*. And for a deconstructive reading of the metaphorical nature of our images for the sun and light see Jacques Derrida, "White Mythology," *NLH* 6, no. 1 (Autumn 1974).

58. *Iliad* 24.900–903.

59. Alexiou, 13. Alexiou's reference is to Aristotle's *Poetics* 12.1452b.

60. In the study of "Lycidas," I shall refer to this aspect of the poem, and to the dispute it has provoked among recent critics (See chap. IV, n. 8).

61. Sir Philip Sidney, *Miscellaneous Prose of Sir Philip Sidney*, ed. Katherine Duncan Jones and Jan Van Dorsten (Oxford: Oxford University Press, 1973), 95.

62. Alexiou, 21.

63. W. H. Auden, "In Memory of W. B. Yeats," *Collected Shorter Poems, 1927–1957* (London: Faber & Faber, 1966; reprint ed., 1969), 141.

Chapter II. Spenser: *The Shepheardes Calender* and "Astrophel"

1. Edmund Spenser, *Poetical Works*, ed. E. de Selincourt (Oxford: Oxford University Press, 1912; reprint ed., 1969), 471. Subsequent quotations from Spenser are from this edition, henceforth referred to in both text and notes as *Works*.

2. For an account of the self-imprisoning effects in "Ye Goatherd Gods" see William Empson, *Seven Types of Ambiguity*, rev. ed. (New York: New Directions, 1947), 34–38.

3. Sir Philip Sidney, *Miscellaneous Prose of Sir Philip Sidney*, ed. Katherine Duncan Jones and Jan Van Dorsten (Oxford: Oxford University Press, 1973), 81.

4. William A. Oram warns against too close an association of Alcyon with Gorges. He also argues persuasively that Alcyon is in part a fictional construct designed to portray and to exorcise the dangers of excessively self-absorbed grief. Oram admits, however, the poem's lack of a comforting resolution; and apart from the ignored words of Alcyon's dying Daphne, there is no articulated source of consolation in the poem (Oram, "*Daphnaida* and Spenser's Later Poetry," *Spenser Studies* 2 [1981], 141–58).

5. The illustrations to the eclogues present their own visual account of the pipe's career. It lies broken in "January" and "June," eclogues in which Colin himself is present; in "April" and "August" it is played, but by Hobbinol and Cuddie in Colin's behalf; in "October" Cuddie carries a worn panpipe in his hand, having

stopped playing it and having turned away from the palace toward the valleys; in "November" Colin is at last seen actually playing a pipe and is about to be crowned with laurel by Thenot; and finally in "December" Colin is again present, but his abandoned pipe is nowhere to be seen. For a study of the illustrations see Ruth Samson Luborsky, "The Illustrations to *The Shepheardes Calender*," ibid., 3–53.

6. For the large number of nearly contemporary mournful and frustrated heirs cf. Harry Levin, *The Question of Hamlet* (Oxford: Oxford University Press, 1959), 117: "It is significant that Malevola, like Hamlet, like most of Marston's heroes, and like so many protagonists of Jacobean drama, is a disinherited prince."

7. Closely related to the question of inheritance is the issue of Spenser's ambition, particularly as it was affected by the political ramifications and determinants of his profession. Louis Adrian Montrose has made the most penetrating exploration of *The Shepheardes Calender* from this perspective, illuminating the complex and often contradictory interplay between the poet's professional aspiration, pastoral poetry, and political power (see "'The perfecte paterne of a Poete': The Poetics of Courtship in *The Shepheardes Calender*," *TSLL* 21 [1979], 34–67; "'Eliza, Queene of Shepheardes,' and the Pastoral of Power," *English Literary Renaissance* 10, no. 2 [Spring 1980], 153–82; "Interpreting Spenser's February Eclogue," *Spenser Studies* 2 [1981], 67–74; and "Of Gentlemen and Shepherds: The Politics of Elizabethan Pastoral Form," *ELH* 50, no. 3 [Fall 1983], 415–59).

   The work of Harry Berger, Jr., is also indispensable for any thorough understanding of the strong currents of frustration (erotic as well as vocational and political) and compensatory displacement in *The Shepheardes Calender* (see "The Prospect of Imagination: Spenser and the Limits of Poetry," *Studies in English Literature, 1500–1900* (hereafter cited as *SEL*) 1 [1961], 93–120; "Mode and Diction in *The Shepheardes Calender*," *Modern Philology* 67 [1969], 140–49; and "Orpheus, Pan, and the Poetics of Misogyny: Spenser's Critique of Pastoral Love and Art," *ELH* 50, no. 1 [Spring 1983], 27–60).

8. Thomas Perrin Harrison, Jr., *The Pastoral Elegy: An Anthology* (Austin: University of Texas Press, 1939), 34.

9. Apart from the general attack against the corrupt clergy, "July" has several phrases or motifs that recur in Milton's poem: "And now the Sonne. . . . St. Michels mount [referred to in the gloss as a "promontorie"]. . . . What neede hem caren for their flocks. . . . weltre in welths waves. . . ." Most significant is Milton's resolution of the opposed attitudes toward the sun. He moves from a Thomalin-like shady idyll to the almost solar self-assertion of the concluding passage.

10. Cf. "November," where Thenot uses similar images for a more explicit reference to poetic influence: "Nay, better learne of hem, that learned bee, / And han be watered at the Muses well: / The kindlye dewe drops from the higher tree, / And wets the little plants that lowly dwell" (*Works*, 460, lines 29–31).

11. In its own terms, "November" is triumphant, and my following remarks do indicate a level of genuine success in the poem. In view of the focus on the

theme of inheritance in the *Calender* and of the relation between that theme and the elegy as a genre, it is worth recognizing that it is within this elegy that Colin most successfully combines the traditions of Chaucer, Virgil, and more recently Marot. I shall, however, suggest that "November" masks several problems confronted far more masterfully in "Astrophel." And the later elegy is far more radical and thorough in its revision and inheritance of an entire elegiac mythology.

12. Shakespeare, *A Midsummer Night's Dream* 5.1.276–87. *The Riverside Shakespeare*, ed. G. Blakemore Evans (Boston: Houghton Mifflin, 1974).

13. Marot, quoted from Harrison, 142.

14. It is worth recollecting the more sinister meaning of the word *glosse.* In 1548 Udall wrote: "Like as by a glosse ye subverte the commaundement." And Bishop Hall in 1608: "Neither doth his tongue . . . make good a lie with the secret glosses of double or reserved senses"; while in 1695 Kennett concisely writes that "the gloss indeed destroys the text" (quotations from *Oxford English Dictionary*).

15. Henceforth line numbers will be cited alongside text.

16. For example, Bryskett's "Mourning Muse of Thestylis" had been entered in the *Stationer's Register* in 1587. The elegies of Raleigh, Roydon, and Greville had appeared in *The Phoenix Nest* in 1593.

17. Arguments for Spenser's composition of the "Lay" have been convincingly presented in P. W. Long, "Spenseriana," *MLN* 31 (1916), 79–92; and C. G. Osgood, "Doleful Lay of Clorinda," ibid., 35 (1920), 90 ff.

18. Chap. I.

19. Lines 3–22. Henceforth lines from this section of the poem will be numbered as, e.g., "C 3–22."

20. *The Works of Thomas Nashe*, ed. Ronald B. McKerrow, 5 vols. (Oxford: Basil Blackwell, 1966), 3:283. The particular section of "Summers Last Will and Testament" from which these lines are taken is often referred to as "A Litany in Time of Plague."

Chapter III. Where Words Prevail Not

This quotation from *The Spanish Tragedy* and subsequent quotations from Kyd are from the edition by Andrew S. Cairncross, Regents Renaissance Drama Series (Lincoln: University of Nebraska Press, 1967).

This quotation from *All's Well That Ends Well* and subsequent quotations from Shakespeare are from *The Riverside Shakespeare*, ed. G. Blakemore Evans (Boston: Houghton Mifflin, 1974).

1. Quoted from Thomas Perrin Harrison, Jr., *The Pastoral Elegy: An Anthology* (Austin: University of Texas Press, 1939), 140.

2. Quoted in Ellen Lambert, *Placing Sorrow: A Study of the Pastoral Elegy from Theocritus to Milton* (Chapel Hill: University of North Carolina Press, 1976), 146.

3. Ruth Wallerstein, *The Laureate Hearse*, pt. 1 of *Studies in Seventeenth Century Poetics* (Madison: University of Wisconsin Press, 1950).

4. Cf. Frances Yates, *Astraea: The Imperial Theme in the Sixteenth Century* (Boston: Routledge, 1975).

5. John Eusden, *Puritans, Lawyers, and Politics in Early Seventeenth-Century England* (New Haven: Yale University Press, 1958).

6. Emile Durkheim, *The Elementary Forms of Religious Life*, trans. Joseph Swain (New York: Collier, 1961), 446.

7. See Lily Campbell, "Theories of Revenge in Renaissance England," *Modern Philology* 28 (1931), 281–96; and Fredson Bowers, "The Audience and the Revenger of Elizabethan Tragedy," *Studies in Philology* 31 (1931), 160–75. See also idem, *Elizabethan Revenge Tragedy* (Princeton: Princeton University Press, 1940).

8. See, e.g., John Scott Colley, "*The Spanish Tragedy* and the Theatre of God's Judgments," *Papers on Language and Literature*, 10 (1974), 241–53; Michael Henry Levin, "Vindicta Mihi! Meaning, Morality, and Motivation in *The Spanish Tragedy*," *SEL* 4 (1964), 307–24; and Ernst de Chickera, "Divine Justice and Private Revenge in *The Spanish Tragedy*," *MLN* 57 (1962), 228–32.

9. E. R. Dodds, *The Greeks and the Irrational* (Los Angeles: University of California Press, 1951).

10. Walter Benjamin, *The Origin of German Tragic Drama*, trans. John Osborne (London: New Left Books, 1977). Benjamin does not cite *Titus Andronicus*, and he makes the merest mention of *Richard III*, together with a few remarks on *Hamlet*. However, as I hope to suggest, his insights have important bearing on the plays discussed here.

11. *Gorboduc*, edition by Irby B. Cauthen, Jr., Regents Renaissance Drama Series (Lincoln: University of Nebraska Press, 1970).

12. Cf. Aaron's programmatic reversal of any work of mourning:

> Oft have I digg'd up dead men from their graves,
> And set them upright at their dear friends' door
> Even when their sorrows almost was forgot,
> And on their skins, as on the bark of trees,
> Have with my knife carved in Roman letters
> "Let not your sorrow die, though I am dead."
> (5.1.135–40).

13. Of interest here is the text of Lacan's seminars on *Hamlet* (1959), translated and published as "Desire and the Interpretation of Desire in *Hamlet*," *Yale French Studies* 55/56 (1978), 11–52. Lacan demonstrates how Hamlet's search for the lost (symbolic) object of desire necessarily "impeaches" the entire system of signifiers. Apart from shedding light on Hamlet's unhappy relation to language, Lacan confirms that a play about mourning must, as we noted in *Titus Andronicus*, revolve around the questionable location of a castrated yet potentially consoling figure of totemic power. For reflection on Lacan's study see John P. Muller, "Psychosis and Mourning in Lacan's *Hamlet*," *NLH* 12, no. 1 (Autumn 1980), 147–65.

14. Cf. especially the Christianized sexuality of the beautiful Middle English lyric "I Sing of A Maiden," in which Christ "cam also stille / Ther his moder was / As dewe in Aprille / That falleth on the gras"; or Wordsworth's lines quoted above, in Chap. I: "I sprinkle thee with soft celestial dews / Thy lost, maternal heart to re-infuse"; or Swinburne's "Is it not well where soul from body slips / And flesh from bone divides without a pang / As dew from flower-bell drips?" from "Ave Atque Vale," quoted below.

15. Sigmund Freud, "Mourning and Melancholia" (1917), trans. Joan Riviere, in *General Psychological Theory*, ed. Philip Rieff (New York: Macmillan, Collier Books, 1963), 165.

16. Benjamin, 158.

Chapter IV. Milton: "Lycidas"

1. Quoted in Scott Elledge, ed., *Milton's "Lycidas": Edited to Serve as an Introduction to Criticism* (New York: Harper & Row, 1966), 174.

2. Ibid., 208.

3. Ibid., 213.

4. *Shatter* is certainly the strongest verb in the opening of the poem, and Milton has placed it in such a way as to reinforce its effect. The fate of the men, and Bastwick's threat, should raise the question of the symbolic importance of the ear, so prominent in "Lycidas." Finally, we may recall Prynne's words in Milton's "sunk low, but mounted high."

5. Trans. from the Latin by David Masson, in *The Works of John Milton*, ed. Frank Patterson, Vol. 12 (New York: Columbia University Press, 1936), 19.

6. Ibid., 27.

7. "Let him live sparingly, like the Samian teacher: and let herbs furnish his innocent diet. . . . Beyond this, his youth must be innocent of crime and chaste, his conduct irreproachable and his hands stainless. . . . By this rule it is said that the wise Tiresias lived after the loss of his eyes, and Ogygian Linus, and Calchas when he was a fugitive from his doomed home, and Orpheus in his old age. . . . For truly, the bard is sacred to the Gods and is their priest. His hidden heart and his lips alike breathe out Jove" (Milton, "Elegy VI," in *The Complete Poems and Major Prose*, ed., Merritt Y. Hughes [Indianapolis: Odyssey Press, 1957; reprint ed., 1975], 52. Subsequent quotations from "Lycidas" are from this edition).

8. For the allusive echoing within Milton's "Yet once more" see John Hollander, *The Figure of Echo: A Mode of Allusion in Milton and After* (Berkeley and Los Angeles: University of California Press, 1981), 127–29; and Louis Martz, *Poet of Exile: A Study of Milton's Poetry* (New Haven: Yale University Press, 1980), chap. 3.

   More generally, for the relation of "Lycidas" to the traditional pastoral elegy see James H. Hanford, "The Pastoral Elegy and Milton's 'Lycidas,'" *PMLA* 25 (1910), 403–47; Thomas Perrin Harrison, Jr., *The Pastoral Elegy: An Anthology* (Austin: University of Texas Press, 1939); Ellen Lambert, *Placing*

Sorrow: A Study of the Pastoral Elegy from Theocritus to Milton (Chapel Hill: University of North Carolina Press, 1976); and Richard Mallette, *Spenser, Milton, and Renaissance Pastoral* (Lewisburg, Pa.: Bucknell University Press, 1981), chap. 4.

For the most recent, and in many respects the most subtle, study of Milton's use of generic conventions see Paul Alpers's *"Lycidas* and Modern Criticism," *ELH* 49, no. 2 (Summer 1982), 468–96. This essay also contains a thoughtful response to previous studies of the poem, such as those by Abrams, Friedman, and Fish (M. H. Abrams, "Five Types of *Lycidas," in Milton's Lycidas: The Tradition and the Poem,* ed. C. A. Patrides, rev. ed. [Columbia: University of Missouri Press, 1983], 216–35; Donald M. Friedman, *"Lycidas:* The Swain's Paideia," ibid., 281–302; Stanley Fish, *"Lycidas:* A Poem Finally Anonymous," ibid., 319–40. Patrides' collection contains other essays, which I will refer to later. It also offers an excellent bibliography of studies on the tradition and the poem).

In the course of *"Lycidas* and Modern Criticism," Alpers seeks to rebut Fish's contention that "the energy of the poem derives not from the presence of a controlling and self-contained individual, but from forces that undermine his individuality and challenge the fiction of his control" (Fish, 322). Where Fish suggests the obliteration of personal voice, Alpers points to that voice's careful convening of the antecedent voices of the genre. My own argument offers the view of an eclogic, self-surpassing voice composed, as Alpers demonstrates, of conventional strands but submitted to a process similar to that which Fish describes. Fish, however, does not integrate his perception with a psychological view of self-suppression as a crucial element of the work of mourning. I believe that there *is* considerable self-abasement and self-suppression in the poem; but I see this as a phenomenon that is suffered and worked through by an individual mourning mind. Elegies are in large part about this kind of self-chastening, just as they require the elegist's personal accommodation to the impersonal code of language and the symbolic order. In the following chapter, I shall be looking closely at the ways in which a mourner seeks precisely to merge his personal voice with the inherited voices of the dead. The difficulty in such moments is to distinguish self-definition or even self-aggrandizement from a more strictly submissive gesture. Indeed, the elegy as a genre shows how necessarily intertwined such seemingly antithetical elements must remain.

9. The most comprehensive reading of the imagery of "Lycidas" is still that of Rosemund Tuve, *Images and Themes in Five Poems by Milton* (Cambridge, Mass.: Harvard University Press, 1957). See, too, essays by Wayne Shumaker, Josephine Miles, and Richard P. Adams, in Patrides.
10. Hesiod, *Theogony,* trans. Dorothea Wender (London: Penguin, 1973), 23.
11. Rev. 22.1.
12. The sun itself is not sighted during the course of this ideal day: predawn appearances give way to midday sounds, and sight returns only with the view of the descending evening star.
13. Cf. the earlier discussion of narrative repetition in mourning. In Milton's case, this is played out with greatest scope in *Paradise Lost.* Milton even inserts his own warning cry, or rather his desire for such a cry ("O for that warning

voice"), a perfect instance of a combined preparation for, yet refreshing of, loss. We are told that it is about to happen, but it happens as if for the first time.

14. The passage is thus a brilliant accomplishment of what Freud calls the mourner's recalling yet undoing of remembered bonds. As Karl Abraham and others have stressed, this recalling is usually done once the memories have been introjected, and it is interesting to relate what we noticed as the oddly englobed quality of the idyll to the phenomenon of introjection. Also, the ability to catch or roll up time in this way is a crucial heralding of the poem's later perspectives on mere time, perspectives gained as though from the vantage of eternity.

15. Cf. the relation between the serpent and the ear in *Paradise Lost*, or the extensive imagery in *Hamlet*: " 'Tis given out that, sleeping in my orchard, / A serpent stung me" (1.5.35–36). Claudius is the serpent who, like Satan, pours his leprous distillment in the porches of the ear. Similarly, "the whole ear of Denmark / Is by a forged process of my death / Rankly abus'd" (1.5.36–38).

16. While the association of blinding with castration is familiar, Jonathan Swift reminds us of the similar association with injuries to the ear. His meditation, interestingly enough, begins with reference to such victims as Bastwick, Burton, and Prynne. After speaking of the "many loppings and mutilations, to which the ears of our fathers, and our own, have been of late so much exposed," Swift continues: "It is held by naturalists, that if there be a protuberancy of parts in the superior region of the body, as in the ears and nose, there must be a parity also in the inferior. . . . Hippocrates tells us, that when the vein behind the ear happens to be cut, a man becomes a eunuch" (*The Tale of a Tub*, in *Prose Works of Jonathan Swift*, ed. Herbert Davis, 9 vols. [Oxford: Basil Blackwell, 1939], 1:129).

17. Calliope is, of course, the muse of epic poetry, to whom Milton had been dedicating and, in a sense, sacrificing himself. The threat of her removal or helplessness is, therefore, particularly devastating.

18. He has had to face what Adam will express as perhaps the harshest aspect of his and therefore of all human loss:

> . . . how glad would I lay me down
> As in my Mother's lap! There I should rest
> And sleep secure; his dreadful voice no more
> Would thunder in my ears. . . .
>
> *Paradise Lost* 10.777–80.

The words "dreadful voice" of course echo the "dread voice" in the elegy.

19. Leslie Brisman has discussed this delay in his comments on the poem in *Milton's Poetry of Choice and Its Romantic Heirs* (Ithaca: Cornell University Press, 1973).

20. The shift from Camus to Saint Peter is appropriate. They are like two border figures, ushers from one realm to the next: Camus at the edge of his river and the idyllic world, Peter at the gates of heaven. Each is a quasi-deity of water—the Cam and the Galilean lake, respectively.

21. As we shall see, the two-handed engine invites reference to the sword of divine

vengeance in Hebrews, Revelation, and Psalm 149, but it is worth speculating on this curious trait of doubleness in the keys, the engine, and the miter's form. We know doubling to be a sign of castration, and it is not unlikely that these totemic objects somehow bear the sign of their status as products of castration.

22. "Socrates: 'And shall we not find them replete with immense pleasures? Or need we remind ourselves of that feature of passion and anger—of the lines: "Wrath that spurs on the wisest mind to rage, / Sweeter by far than stream of flowing honey," or of the pleasures mixed up with the pains in lamentation and longing'" (*Philebus* 47e in *Collected Dialogues of Plato*, ed. Edith Hamilton and Huntington Cairns, Bollingen Series, 71 [Princeton: Princeton University Press, 1961], 1128–29).

23. On the amaranth and other flower imagery see Tuve. Alpers, too, has excellent comments on this entire passage.

24. Cf. the similar status of Peele Castle, in Wordsworth's "Elegiac Stanzas Suggested by a Picture of Peele Castle." Notice even the emphasis of the "look":

> And this huge Castle, standing here sublime,
> I love to see the look with which it braves,
> Cased in the unfeeling armor of old time,
> The lightning, the fierce wind, and trampling waves.

> (*Poetical Works*, 453).

25. As mentioned in chapter II, n. 9, "Lycidas" bears a significant relation to Spenser's "July." Apart from the several verbal echoes and repeated motifs, "Lycidas" revises the earlier eclogue's unresolvedly opposed attitudes toward the sun.

26. The "Mantle blue" also recalls a line in a poem of George Herbert, published four years before "Lycidas." From *The Temple*, a lyric entitled "The Bag" describes Christ's descent to earth and itemizes his simultaneous disrobing. We are told that the "sky his azure mantle gain'd." In "Lycidas" it is the swain who seems to gain the mantle.

Further light on the significance of the mantle could be shed by a section of Yeats's *Autobiography*, quoted and commented on by Avrom Fleishman. Yeats writes of having opened at random a copy of Burkitt's *Early Eastern Christianity* and finding a "Gnostic Hymn that told of a certain King's son who being exiled, slept in Egypt—a symbol of the natural state—and how an Angel while he slept brought him a royal mantle. . . ." Fleishman remarks, "If the 'image of him who sleeps' is only tentatively to be identified as the king's son or Emmanuel, it is surely the soul awaiting resurrection, just as the angelic gift of a higher form of clothing is clearly redemptive" (*Figures of Autobiography: The Language of Self-Writing in Victorian and Modern England* [Berkeley and Los Angeles: University of California Press, 1983], 330–31).

27. This question haunts the entire history of religious beliefs, from the violent succession of deities in Greece to the contests of different nations' gods. In Milton's work, it is particularly and consistently problematic, extending from the "Nativity Ode" to *Paradise Lost* and *Samson Agonistes*.

28. *The Works of John Ruskin*, ed. E. T. Cook and Alexander Wedderburn, Library Edition, 39 vols. (London: George Allen, 1903–12), 7:262.

Chapter V. Jonson, Dryden, and Gray

1. For a survey extending from Congreve to Bewick and Cunningham see Raimund Borgmeier, *"The Dying Shepherd": Die Tradition der englischen Ekloge von Pope bis Wordsworth*, vol. 2 (Tübingen: Niemeyer, 1976), 2.
2. Ruth Wallerstein, *The Laureate Hearse*, pt. 1 of *Studies in Seventeenth Century Poetics* (Madison: University of Wisconsin Press, 1950).
3. John Dennis, *Critical Works*, ed. E. N. Hooker, 2 vols. (Baltimore: Johns Hopkins Press, 1939–43), 1:2.
4. Thomas Tickel, in *The Guardian* 30 (15 April 1713).
5. In choosing these poems, I have had to pass over other Neoclassical elegies such as Cowley's "On the Death of Mr. William Hervey" (which I shall mention when discussing Yeats) or Samuel Johnson's "On the Death of Dr. Robert Levet." These works share several properties of the poems under discussion here. Different in kind, and no less difficult to pass by, are several other elegies of the period. These would include at least Jonson's poems for Lady Jane Paulet, Venetia Digby, and Cary and Morison, as well as Dryden's "To the Pious Memory of the Accomplished Young Lady, Mrs. Anne Killigrew" and Pope's "Elegy to the Memory of an Unfortunate Lady." My reason for excluding these derives partly from limited space but also from my wish, in this chapter, to test my approach to elegy on the more restrained, epigrammatic poems, poems as different as possible from the more expansive, more traditionally expressive works discussed elsewhere.
6. Ben Jonson, *Poems*, ed. Ian Donaldson (Oxford: Oxford University Press, 1975), 26.
7. These questions have been posed, in some cases with close attention to the Scholastic and Church Father traditions, by such critics as W. David Kay ("The Christian Wisdom of Ben Jonson's 'On My First Sonne,'" *SEL* 11 [1971], 205–20), Arthur Marotti ("All About Ben Jonson's Poetry," *ELH* 39, no. 2 [June 1972], 207–37; and J. Z. Kronenfeld ("The Father Found: Consolation Achieved through Love in Ben Jonson's 'On My First Sonne,'" *Studies in Philology* 75 [1978], 64–83).
8. Sigmund Freud, *Jokes and Their Relation to the Unconscious*, trans. and ed. James Strachey (New York: Norton, 1963).
9. Paul Alpers reminds us that Milton's phrase "moist vows" recalls "the vows, *vota*, promised to Virgil's Daphnis and Sannazaro's Androgeo" (*"Lycidas* and Modern Criticism," *ELH* 49, no. 2 [Summer 1982], 488).
10. Martial, *Epigrams*, bk. 6, epigram 29, line 8.
11. John Dryden, *The Poems of John Dryden*, ed. James Kinsley, 4 vols. (Oxford: Clarendon Press, 1958; reprint ed., 1970), 1:324.
12. Any reader of Dryden's satire will recall his contempt for shapeless souls, such

as those of Absalom and Architophel, which have either rejected or never known a mould.

13. *Aeneid* 5.456–57, trans. in Vol. 3 of Dryden.

14. Ibid., 5.462–65.

15. Arthur Hoffman, *John Dryden's Imagery* (Gainesville: University of Florida Press, 1962). See also Christopher Ricks, "Allusion: The Poet as Heir," in *Studies in the Eighteenth Century*, vol. 3, ed. R. F. Brissenden and J. C. Eade (Toronto: University of Toronto Press, 1973).

16. The abundant critical literature on Gray's poem includes heated debates as to the reference of the epitaph: is it Gray, the narrator, or is it "the stonecutter"? I would agree with John Sutherland against Herbert Starr, Frank Ellis, Morse Peckham, and others that it must be the poet-narrator himself. These arguments are conveniently found in *Twentieth-Century Interpretations of Gray's Elegy*, ed. Herbert W. Starr (Englewood Cliffs: Prentice-Hall, 1968). Also included there are the important readings by Brooks, Jack, and Empson. An essay supporting the notion of Gray's self-epitaphic project is Bertrand Bronson's "On a Special Decorum in Gray's Elegy," in *Facets of the Enlightenment*, ed. Bronson (Berkeley and Los Angeles: University of California Press, 1968). See also Howard Weinbrot, "Gray's *Elegy*: A Poem of Moral Choice and Resolution," *SEL* 18 (1978), 537–51.

17. Anyone enjoying formal symmetries may recognize an almost perfectly achieved ratio of 4:2:1 between the three sections outlined above. This reflects perhaps the poem's regulated movement not only of continuing supersession but of self-condensation. The life and poem reduce to almost proportionate residues of themselves.

18. See such studies as Amy Reed, *The Background of Gray's Elegy* (New York: Columbia University Press, 1924); Eleanor Sickels, *The Gloomy Egoist* (New York: Columbia University Press, 1932); and more recently, John Sitter, *Literary Loneliness in Mid-Eighteenth-Century England* (Ithaca: Cornell University Press, 1982).

19. For Gray's specific sense of inferiority to Milton see his "Stanzas to Mr. Bentley." Also, Gray's concern with Milton is reflected in his having deliberately substituted this poet's name for that of Cicero (Tully). More generally, see Walter Jackson Bate, *The Burden of the Past and the English Poet* (Cambridge, Mass.: Harvard University Press, 1970).

Chapter VI. Shelley: "Adonais"

1. William Collins, *The Works of William Collins*, ed. Richard Wendorf and Charles Ryskamp (Oxford: Oxford University Press, 1979).

2. An interesting and deliberate use of the ode title for a distinctly un-odelike, elegiac poem is Allen Tate's confessedly ironic "Ode to the Confederate Dead." For a comparison between ode and elegy, particularly during the eigh-

teenth century, see Paul Fry's excellent *The Calling of the English Ode* (New Haven: Yale University Press, 1980).

3. In one of the best readings this poem has received, Lawrence Lipking argues that Collins's sense of remoteness from a Druid's powers is part of an actual critique of Thomson's more confident assumptions of poetic power (see *The Life of the Poet: Beginning and Ending Poetic Careers* [Chicago: University of Chicago Press, 1981], 146–51). For other studies of the poem see Richard Wendorf, *William Collins and Eighteenth-Century English Poetry* (Minneapolis: University of Minnesota Press, 1981), 167–75; J. M. S. Tompkins, "'In Yonder Grave a Druid Lies,'" *Review of English Studies* (hereafter cited as *RES*) 22 (1946), 1–16; E. M. W. Tillyard, "William Collins's 'Ode on the Death of Thomson,'" *Renaissance English Literature* (hereafter cited as *REL*) 1, no. 3 (1960), 30–38; and P. S. Sherwin, *Precious Bane: Collins and the Miltonic Legacy* (Austin: University of Texas Press, 1977), 105–9.

4. William Wordsworth, *Poetical Works*, ed. Thomas Hutchinson, rev. Ernest de Selincourt (Oxford: Oxford University Press, 1904; reprint ed., 1973), 7; henceforth referred to as *Works*.

5. The suspended or erected oar is, of course, a memorializing symbol in such works as the *Odyssey* (Elpenor's oar), "Hugh Selwyn Mauberley" ("Then on an oar / Read this: / 'I was / And I no more exist'"), and Pound's reworking of Homer in *Canto I*. Wordsworth brings to the convention a naturalistic yet symbolic richness in the almost archtypically elegiac image of measured but easily dispensed liquidity.

6. "I have been engaged these last days in composing a poem on the death of Keats, which will shortly be finished, and I anticipate the pleasure of reading it to you. . . . It is a highly wrought *piece of art*, perhaps better in point of composition than anything I have written" (Shelley to John and Maria Gisborne, 5 June 1821, in *Letters*, ed. Frederick L. Jones, 2 vols. [Oxford: Clarendon, 1964], 2:294).

7. Earl Wasserman, *The Subtler Language* (Baltimore: Johns Hopkins Press, 1959). Other studies that I have found helpful include the following: Lloyd Abbey, *Destroyer and Preserver: Shelley's Poetic Skepticism* (Lincoln: University of Nebraska Press, 1979); Carlos Baker, *Shelley's Major Poetry: The Fabric of a Vision* (Princeton: Princeton University Press, 1948); Ronald E. Becht, "Shelley's *Adonais*: Formal Design and the Lyric Speaker's Crisis of Imagination," *Studies in Philology* (hereafter cited as *SP*) 78, no. 2 (Spring 1981), 194–210; Harold Bloom, *The Visionary Company: A Reading of English Romantic Poetry*, rev. ed. (Ithaca: Cornell University Press, 1971); Jean Hall, *The Transforming Image: A Study of Shelley's Major Poetry* (Chicago: University of Illinois Press, 1980); Angela Leighton, "*Adonais*: The Voice and the Text," *Keats-Shelley Memorial Bulletin* (hereafter cited as *KSMB*) 31 (1980), 39–51; Milton Wilson, *Shelley's Later Poetry: A Study of His Prophetic Imagination* (New York: Columbia University Press, 1959); Ross Woodman, *The Apocalyptic Vision in the Poetry of Shelley* (Toronto: University of Toronto Press, 1964); John Williams Wright, *Shelley's Myth of Metaphor* (Athens: University of Georgia Press, 1970). Two additional studies, while not focusing on "Adonais," address Shelley's problematic attitude toward rhetoric:

Paul de Man, "Shelley Disfigured," in *Deconstruction and Criticism*, ed. Harold Bloom et al. (New York: Seabury Press, 1979), 39–74; and J. Hillis Miller, "The Critic as Host," in ibid., 217–53.

8. William Butler Yeats, "Lapis Lazuli," in *The Poems*, ed. Richard J. Finneran (New York: Macmillan, 1983), 294.

9. Percy Bysshe Shelley, *Poetical Works*, ed. Thomas Hutchinson, corrected by G. M. Matthews (Oxford: Oxford University Press, 1970), 720; henceforth referred to as *Works*.

10. See James A. Notopoulos, *The Platonism of Shelley* (Durham: University of North Carolina Press, 1949). Notopoulos discusses "Adonais," regarding it as the purest example of Shelley's Platonism. But he does not take up the question of the problematic relation between Shelley's ideology and his dependence on poetic figures.

11. Shelley had, in fact, translated parts of Moschus's elegy, in addition to Bion's "Lament for Adonis." He had also translated part of Virgil's elegiac "Eclogue X." Perhaps no-one since Milton and Spenser had so closely reengaged the origins of the genre.

12. John Milton, *The Complete Poems and Major Prose*, ed. Merritt Y. Hughes (Indianapolis: Odyssey Press, 1957; reprint ed., 1975), 58–59.

13. John Keats, "Hyperion," lines 51–69, in *The Poetical Works of John Keats*, ed. H. W. Garrod, 2d ed. (Oxford: Oxford University Press, 1958), 278.

14. The relation between "Adonais" and Spenser's poetry is, of course, far greater than one of a copied stanzaic form. Besides the Neo-Platonism, there is what one might call the romance of resignification, that of crossing thresholds by a process of redefining certain figures. While the form recalls *The Faerie Queene*, the practice of resignification (particularly within an elegy) closely resembles that of "Astrophel." That poem, too, worked from one inadequate delegate-mourner to a successor who rejected and redefined the meaning of the first mourner's tropes. "Adonais," however, will not share "Astrophel"'s apparently achieved acceptance both of the figuration itself and of the attendant distance between the survivor and the ideal image of the dead.

15. Impatient with mere comparisons, the curse disrupts not only the "pageantry of mist" but also the elaborate texture of similes itself, together with the conventionally elegiac comparisons to which those similes allude (cf. Moschus's "Lament for Bion").

16. Curiously, Shelley's outbreak of grief turns to the question of theatricality. So much of this elegy is seen through the eyes of a spectator at a scene of mourning, and Shelley's self-presentation in stanzas 21–34 only exaggerates this characteristic. The concluding sections of the poem attempt to move beyond theatricality, associating it with the undesirable material of rhetoric and with all fabrics that distance Shelley's relation to his object of aspiration. We recall the antitheatrical thrust of revengers, who seek a literal act of redress beyond the interventions of language or law (see above, chap. III).

17. However compassionate, the ironic manner in which Shelley describes Urania's enforced separation from Adonais not only separates Shelley and her from Adonais and divides Shelley from his own potentially inadequate response but

also widens the distance between Urania and Shelley, thereby furthering his work of mourning.

18. Sigmund Freud, "Mourning and Melancholia" (1917), trans. Joan Riviere, in *General Psychological Theory*, ed. Philip Rieff (New York: Macmillan, Collier Books, 1963), 164–79.

19. Shelley again uses explicitly sexual images to show what must be rejected. If Adonais survives, it will not be as a fertility god bequeathing his procreative legacy to the erotic Mother. While the figure of the martyred deity *is* used, the terms of his divinity are yet to be redefined.

20. Freud, 170.

21. This is Shelley's internalization of the conventional elegiac division of voices. The singing match is now against himself, in an even more radical way than had been the case in "Lycidas."

22. Heinz Kohut, "The Forms and Transformations of Narcissism," *Journal of the American Psychoanalytical Association*, 1966, 265.

23. *The Letters of John Keats 1814–1821*, ed. Hyder E. Rollins, 2 vols. (Cambridge, Mass.: Harvard University Press, 1958), 2:102.

24. This sonnet also prefigures the closing imagery of "Adonais": "Thou wert as a lone star, whose light did shine / On some frail bark in winter's midnight roar." In a sense, "Adonais" restores that vanished star, or rather replaces it with an idealized image of Shelley himself. Shelley's reasons for rejecting Wordsworth in "Adonais" exceed that of his disagreement with Wordsworth's attitude to loss. As Keats's elegist, he is surely drawn into the question of succession or inheritance, the competitive motif more obviously present within funeral games or early elegiac eclogues. Implicitly, he adds Wordsworth to the list of mourners (Byron, Thomas Moore, Leigh Hunt) against whose "veiled" or "mantled" mourning he will oppose his more vigorous poem.

25. See Richard Holmes, *Shelley: The Pursuit* (London: Weidenfeld and Nicolson, 1974), 729.

26. Ironically, the word *beacons*, derived as it is from the Old English term for a sign (*beacen*), reinforces our recognition that even while the "soul of Adonais" and its star appear to burn beyond or through the veils of nature or of signification, they nevertheless function precisely as signs. Similarly, the image of the spirit's bark not only depends on a metaphor but may be seen to present a traditional image for metaphor itself. Commenting on Aristotle's account of metaphor, Derrida has noted "the traditional recourse to the boat, its movement, its oars and its sails, to represent figuratively the figure of metaphor—itself a means of 'carrying over'" (Jacques Derrida, "White Mythology," *NLH* 6, no. 1 [Autumn 1974], 42).

Chapter VII. Tennyson: *In Memoriam*

1. Several critics have remarked on Tennyson's (and more generally, the Victorian poets') problematic concern with an exclusively defined personality, as

opposed to the Romantics' definition of a more universal self (see Patricia Ball, "Tennyson and the Romantics," *Victorian Poetry* 1, no. 1 [January 1963], 7–16: "The Wordsworthian independent and, in this sense, unselective, ego is [now] modified by a more specific and exclusive concept of the self" [12]; and, with greater scope, idem, *The Heart's Events: The Victorian Poetry of Relationships* [London: Athlone Press, 1976]. See also U. C. Knoepflmacher, "Dover Revisited: The Wordsworthian Matrix in the Poetry of Arnold," *Victorian Poetry* 1, no. 1 [January 1963], 17–26). With specific regard to the theme of compensation, Lawrence Kramer, too, notes how the Victorian poets lacked the Romantics' more replaceable (because less contingently defined) sense of identity (see "The 'Intimations' Ode and Victorian Romanticism," ibid. 18, no. 4 [Winter 1980], 313–35). Similarly, referring to *In Memoriam*, section 82, James R. Kincaid has written, "The inescapable insistence on personality keeps intruding, even here in the center of renewal" (*Tennyson's Major Poems: The Comic and Ironic Patterns* [New Haven: Yale University Press, 1975], 103).

Although Tennyson himself claimed that "it is a very impersonal poem as well as personal," I would therefore suggest that Tennyson's alleged "cry of the whole human race" expressed his age's as well as his own preoccupation with the self as a highly personalized identity (quotations from Hallam Tennyson, *Alfred Tennyson: A Memoir by His Son*, 2 vols. [New York: Macmillan, 1897], 1:396; henceforth cited as *Memoir*).

For a thorough survey of recent criticism on *In Memoriam* see Joseph Sendry, "*In Memoriam*: Twentieth-Century Criticism," *Victorian Poetry* 18, no. 2 (Summer 1980), 105–18. Sendry points to the then imminent, now published, critical edition of the poem by Shatto and Shaw, cited below in n. 2. Of the studies reviewed by Sendry, the following have had the most bearing on my work (this is to exclude some excellent books and articles that shed light on other aspects of the poem): A. C. Bradley, *A Commentary on Tennyson's "In Memoriam"* (London: Macmillan, 1901); T. S. Eliot, "In Memoriam," in *Essays, Ancient and Modern* (New York: Harcourt, Brace, 1936); Graham Hough, "The Natural Theology of *In Memoriam*," *RES* 23 (1947), 244–56; Eleanor B. Mattes, *In Memoriam: The Way of a Soul* (New York: Exposition Press, 1951); E. D. H. Johnson, "*In Memoriam*: The Way of the Poet," *Victorian Studies* 2 (1958), 139–48; John D. Rosenberg, "The Two Kingdoms of *In Memoriam*," *Journal of English and German Philology* (hereafter cited as *JEGP*) 58 (1959), 228–40; R. A. Foakes, *The Romantic Assertion: A Study in the Language of Nineteenth-Century Poetry* (New York: Barnes and Noble, 1971); Jerome H. Buckley, *Tennyson: The Growth of a Poet* (Cambridge, Mass.: Harvard University Press, 1960); Christopher Ricks, *Tennyson* (New York: Macmillan, 1972); A. Dwight Culler, *The Poetry of Tennyson* (New Haven: Yale University Press, 1977); Kincaid (cited above); Alan Sinfield, *The Language of Tennyson's "In Memoriam"* (Oxford: Basil Blackwell, 1971); W. David Shaw, *Tennyson's Style* (Ithaca: Cornell University Press, 1976); Harry Puckett, "Subjunctive Imagination in *In Memoriam*," *Victorian Poetry* 12, no. 2 (Summer 1974), 97–124; Eric Smith, *By Mourning Tongues: Studies in the English Elegy* (Ipswich: Boydell Press, 1977); Joseph Sendry, "*In Memoriam* and *Lycidas*," *PMLA* 82, no. 5 (October 1967), 437–43; Ian Kennedy, "*In*

Memoriam and the Tradition of Pastoral Elegy," *Victorian Poetry* 15 (1977), 351–66; and Robert Langbaum, *The Modern Spirit: Essays on the Continuity of Nineteenth- and Twentieth-Century Literature* (Oxford: Oxford University Press, 1970).

In addition to the studies surveyed by Sendry, Allan Danzig's "The Contraries: A Central Concept in Tennyson's Poetry," *PMLA* 77 (1962), 577–85, offers a view of the conflictual character of Tennyson's work, a view supported by my own sense of the divisive, eclogic debate within *In Memoriam*. Two other articles focus well on Tennyson's attitude toward his own language, thus overlapping with one of my areas of concern. These are Dolores Ryback Rosenblum's "The Act of Writing *In Memoriam*," *Victorian Poetry* 18, no. 2 (Summer 1980), 119–34; and Peter Allan Dale's "'Gracious Lies': The Meaning of Metaphor in *In Memoriam*," ibid., 147–67. Robert Dilligan carries further the stylistic approaches of Sinfield and Shaw, and his article ("Computers and Style: The Prosody of *In Memoriam*," ibid., 179–96) offers several suggestive ideas about this elegy's use of such rhetorical figures as repetition, apostrophe, and prosopopoeia. In his chapter on *In Memoriam*, Robert Pattison adds to the work by Sendry, Kennedy, and Smith regarding Tennyson's relation to the traditional pastoral elegy (see Pattison, *Tennyson and Tradition* [Cambridge, Mass.: Harvard University Press, 1979], chap. 5).

2. *In Memoriam* (47). Quoted from the most recent scholarly edition, *Tennyson: "In Memoriam,"* ed. with commentary by Susan Shatto and Marion Shaw (Oxford: Oxford University Press, 1982). Quotations of the poem, cited by section numbers in parentheses, will be from this edition, subsequently referred to as *T:IM.* Other poems by Tennyson will be quoted from *The Poems of Tennyson,* ed. Christopher Ricks, Annotated English Poets (London: Longmans, 1969), henceforth referred to as *Poems.*

For Tennyson's interest in an individualized survival after death see his comment: "The individuality lasts after death, and we are not utterly absorbed into the Godhead. . . . If the absorption into the divine in the after-life be the creed of some, let them at all events allow us many existences of individuality before this absorption. . . ." (*Memoir,* 1:319).

3. Matthew Arnold, "Stanzas from the Grand Chartreuse" ll. 107–8, in *The Poetical Works of Matthew Arnold,* ed. C. B. Tinker and H. F. Lowry (Oxford: Oxford University Press, 1950).

4. *Memoir,* 1:304–5. For a carefully postulated chronology of the poem's composition see most recently *T:IM,* 6–25.

5. "Tennyson is too noble, too Anglais; when he should have been brokenhearted, he had many reminiscences" (Paul Verlaine, quoted in *The Autobiography of William Butler Yeats* [New York: Macmillan, 1938; reprint ed., Collier Books, 1971], 229).

6. Not by chance, *In Memoriam* was written during the heyday of collectibles and souvenirs, when rooms, like selves, became little more than accumulations of highly discrete particulars and upholstery muffled the "ideal" forms of furniture beneath highly particularized fabrics. The Victorians clung to individualized things. Confronted by a new level of urban anonymity and by the accelerated tempo of "progress," one resisted by personalized accretions.

We may think, too, of the almost myopically detailed interiors and landscapes of many mid-century paintings. (Millais's painting of Tennyson's Mariana would be an appropriate example—Mariana having been a figure with whom the widowed Queen Victoria [*the* figure of the mourner in her century] identified.) Both in interior decor and in many paintings, the Victorians sought to obstruct the openness of space and to arrest the fluidity of time by a clotted, persistently detaining assemblage of details.

A confining use of impediment also marked the burial customs of the time, particularly those of the wealthy or the great. The corpse of Prince Albert was sealed within five coffins (one more than the duke of Wellington), and funeral carriages such as his were so heavy that teams of drayhorses could hardly move them. Like elegies of the period, the coffins and hearses seemed designed almost to detain the remains of the dead. Elaborate and years-long cultivation of mourning dress and the cult of souvenirs and relics were other symptoms of this general attitude.

For an account of Arthur Hallam's funeral see Alfred Gatty's description, quoted by Shatto and Shaw: "The corpse was landed at Dover, and was brought by sixteen black horses all the way to Clevedon. . . . Besides the coffin, there was a square iron box, deposited in the vault, which may have contained 'The darken'd heart that beat no more.' . . . the funeral procession consisted of a hearse and three mourning coaches, each of which was drawn by four horses" (*T:IM*, 180).

7. A. H. Hallam, "On Some of the Characteristics of Modern Poetry and on the Lyrical Poems of Alfred Tennyson," first published in *The Englishman's Magazine*, August 1831, reprinted in *Victorian Poetry and Poetics*, ed. Walter E. Houghton and G. Robert Stange (Boston: Houghton Mifflin, 1968), 852. Note that Hallam's comment is part of his explanation of "the melancholy which so evidently characterises the spirit of modern poetry."

8. Henry James, "Tennyson's Drama," *The Galaxy*, September 1875, reprinted in *Views and Reviews*, 1908, 171. The dilatory aspect of Tennyson's style is well described in Ricks, 228.

9. W. H. Auden, "Tennyson," in *Forewords and Afterwords* (New York: Random House, 1973), 222.

10. *Memoir*, 1:97.

11. Erich Auerbach, *Scenes from the Drama of European Realism: Six Essays*, trans. Ralph Manheim (Gloucester, Mass.: Peter Smith, 1973), 26.

12. Shatto and Shaw suggest that Tennyson's phrase "the threshold of the mind" may have been derived from "a famous German psychological term coined in the 1820s, *Schwelle des Bewusstseins* ('threshold of consciousness')" (*T:IM*, 165).

13. An unpublished section of the poem included the following lines:

So, friend, when first I look'd upon your face
Our thought gave answer each to each, so true—
Opposed mirrors each reflecting each—

(quoted in *The Works of Alfred, Lord Tennyson*, ed. Hallam, Lord Tennyson, Eversley Edition, 9 vols. [London: Macmillan, 1907–8], 1:103). These lines do not appear in Shatto and Shaw's edition of the poem and its variants.

For the mourner's potential regression to the mirror stage of an earlier narcissism, we may recall the general discussion in chapter I and remember the particular instance of "Adonais." Tennyson, too, moves from images of mirroring to those of fragmentation or shipwreck, indicating a necessary, but by no means final, disruption of this primitive narcissism.

14. Both *bald* and *blank* are etymologically related to *fire* and even *pyre*. Milton, Wordsworth, and Coleridge all used *blank* to refer to subjective as well as objective desolation. Cf. also Hardy's "The Death of Regret," which tells of the "same blank bald routine" of a mourner (*The Collected Poems of Thomas Hardy,* 4th ed. [London: Macmillan, 1930], 271).

    A telling note on the physical appearance of Wimpole Street is in *T:IM*, 170: "The unusual length of Wimpole Street is enhanced by the perspective of an almost unbroken line of flat Georgian housefronts, particularly along the west side, where is number 67. Georgian domestic architecture in London streets was often regarded with disdain by the Victorians. Cf. for example, Disraeli, *Tancred, or the New Crusade:*

    > It is Parliament to whom we are indebted for your Gloucester places, and Baker Streets, and Harley Streets, and Wimpole Streets, and all those flat, dull, spiritless streets, resembling each other like a large family of plain children."

15. Walter Benjamin, *The Origin of German Tragic Drama,* trans. John Osborne (London: New Left Books, 1977), 224.
16. Quoted in Ricks, 122.
17. Dante, Tennyson's admitted model for his own role as grieving questor, had of course regarded Ulysses as a negative example for any explorer. It was Ulysses' unbridled ardor for experience and knowledge (*conoscenza*) that drove him and his falsely counseled crew to transgress the appointed barriers.
18. Whereas before (41), Tennyson made a merely unconsoling allusion to Shakespeare's "sea-change / Into something rich and strange" (*The Tempest* 1.2.400), now he seems to restore the "rich" yield, as of "Those were pearls that were his eyes."
19. The gospel accounts of Christ's transfiguration refer both to his resplendent image and to his "shining raiment," as well as to God's voice within an overshadowing cloud (see, for example, Mark 9.1–8).
20. In passing from section 82 to section 83, one notes, as before in "Lycidas" and "Adonais," that an expression of vengeful anger (here "feud" and "I wreak / The wrath") leads to a "sweet" passage, often describing flowers and a release of natural energy: "That longs to burst a frozen bud / And flood a fresher throat with song."
21. In his insightful article mentioned above, Kramer regards this gesture toward Lushington as a turning point in the poem. One must contextualize that gesture within Tennyson's shifting attitude toward mediation, Time, and his own language.
22. And yet *twilight* itself is a curiously elegiac state, in which light, the consoling arch-image of the genre, most thoroughly bears the chastening mark of loss, a

castrative division or doubling (*twi-light*). Also, the figure of twilight often blends the image of light with the otherwise antithetical texture of mediating veils.

23. Milton, *Paradise Lost*, 12.238–42.

24. Auerbach, 73.

25. Ibid., 58.

26. See above, chap. III. Perhaps the melancholic can now be seen as one who regards himself and the objects of this world as the first terms of an aborted and forever unfulfilled typology.

27. Not only does the dream repair a wounded narcissism by an act of self-transformative mirroring but it performs the familiar elegiac movement away from female figures of previous, easy alliance (here the sisterly, muselike figures of his earlier poems) toward male figures, often of authority, with whom alliance must somehow be earned. As William E. Buckler has written, "It is not easy: aesthetic withdrawal . . . is as attractive as the womb ('And when they learnt that I must go, / They wept and wailed'); but, though painful, it is essential, and its compensation is development, growth, magnification of both art and the individual" ("*In Memoriam* in Aesthetic Context," in *The Victorian Imagination: Essays in Aesthetic Exploration*, ed. Buckler [New York: New York University Press, 1980], 169). It is in keeping with what we have seen as Tennyson's reluctant and particularly melancholy embrace of the work of mourning that he manages to transport his earlier attachments along with him as he moves toward the commanding figure of Hallam.

28. *Memoir*, 1:319.

29. George Landow notes this example of typology in *Victorian Types, Victorian Shadows: Biblical Typology in Victorian Literature, Art, and Thought* (London: Routledge & Kegan Paul, 1980).

30. At the outset, we discussed the nonlinear, dilatory quality of Tennyson's style in *In Memoriam*. To Henry James's remark, quoted earlier, we may now add his description of Tennyson reading "Locksley Hall": "With all the resonance of the chant, the whole thing was yet still, with all the long swing of its motion it yet remained where it was—heaving doubtless grandly enough up and down and beautiful to watch as the self-posed veils of its long self-consciousness" (quoted in Ricks, 325). A similar point, particularly in relation to Tennyson's evasion of closure, is made by W. David Shaw in "Tennyson's Late Elegies," *Victorian Poetry* 12, no. 1 (Spring 1974), 1–12.

31. Alan Roper, *Arnold's Poetic Landscapes* (Baltimore: Johns Hopkins Press, 1969), 228. For a thorough study of Arnold's elegies see A. Dwight Culler, *Imaginative Reason: The Poetry of Matthew Arnold* (New Haven: Yale University Press, 1966). Although Culler sees a mythological structure governing the elegies, he also notes the persistent and often narrowly self-interested intrusion of Arnold's personality into these poems. See also Richard Giannone, "The Quest Motif in 'Thyrsis,'" *Victorian Poetry* 3, no. 2 (Spring 1965), 71–80.

32. Apart from Swinburne, Hopkins is the other Victorian who most carries the elegy beyond the predicament studied above. Like Swinburne, Hopkins writes *about* the revelation of a more than personal element of identity—a

revelation even more consistently sacrificial and elegiac than in Swinburne. For the nuns of the *Deutschland,* as for the windhover, the burst sloe, or even the cut soil, it is a buckling or battering self-martyrdom that yields the individual creature's identity with Christ. Behind the practice of such self-christening, one sees the ancient rituals of identification with the martyred god. An understanding of the elegy as a genre, with its strong and complicated current of sexual energy, its submissive readjustment to the claims of language (here a violent "charactering," the act of naming as an elegiac stigmatizing, in which language itself, apart from what it names, seems to yield its essence), would deepen the appreciation of much of Hopkins's work.

One may suggest Browning as a poet who went beyond the insistence of mere personality. But his dramatic monologues, even while they may mask features of the poet, are themselves intense expressions of idiosyncratic personality. And Browning wrote almost no elegies. "La Saisiaz," his most serious venture in the genre, has moments of great beauty and interest, but it does not truly engage the tradition, and its tentative consolation depends above all on the personality of its proponent. The poem is even more doggedly and exhaustingly entrenched in the Victorian dilemma than were the elegies of Arnold and Tennyson.

Chapter VIII. Swinburne: "Ave Atque Vale"

Ezra Pound, "A Retrospect," in *Pavannes and Divisions* (New York: Alfred A. Knopf, 1918), 106–7.

1. Studies of "Ave Atque Vale," like studies of Swinburne's poetry at large, have been relatively few and disappointing. The best reading of the poem is Jerome J. McGann's in the appendix to his *Swinburne: An Experiment in Criticism* (Chicago: University of Chicago Press, 1972). Surprisingly few readings intervene between McGann's and that of Samuel C. Chew in *Swinburne* (Boston: Little, Brown & Co., 1929). Apart from McGann's study, the following works, however, offer serious attempts to break the still reigning prejudice against Swinburne's allegedly mindless artistry: Ross C. Murfin, *Swinburne, Hardy, Lawrence, and the Burden of Belief* (Chicago: University of Chicago Press, 1978); Leslie Brisman, "Swinburne's Semiotics," *Georgia Review* 31 (Fall 1977), 578–97; David Riede, *Swinburne: A Study in Romantic Mythmaking* (Charlottesville: University Press of Virginia, 1978); Thomas Connolly, *Swinburne's Theory of Poetry* (Syracuse: SUNY Press, 1964); Marvel Smiefsky, "Swinburne's Anti-Establishment Poetics," *Victorian Poetry* 9, no. 3 (Autumn, 1971), 261–76; Meredith B. Raymond, *Swinburne's Poetics: Theory and Practice* (The Hague: Mouton, 1971); Robert L. Peters, *The Crowns of Apollo: Swinburne's Principles of Literature and Art* (Detroit: Wayne State University Press, 1965); John D. Rosenberg, "Swinburne," *Victorian Studies* 11 (1967), 131–52; George M. Ridenour, "Time and Eternity in Swinburne: Minute Particulars in Five Poems," *ELH* 45, no. 1 (Spring 1978), 107–29; and Anthony H. Harrison, "Swinburne's Losses: The Poetics of Passion," ibid., 49, no. 3 (Fall 1982), 689–706.

2. Quoted in Walter E. Houghton and G. Robert Stange, eds., *Victorian Poetry and Poetics* (Boston: Houghton Mifflin Co., 1968), 686.
3. Ibid., 686.
4. *The Complete Works of Algernon Charles Swinburne*, ed. Sir Edmund Gosse and Thomas James Wise, Bonchurch Edition, 20 vols. (London: William Heinemann, 1925), 3:44; henceforth referred to as *Works*.
5. Oscar Wilde, "Mr. Swinburne's Last Volume," reprinted in Richard Ellmann, ed., *The Artist as Critic: Critical Writings of Oscar Wilde* (New York: Random House, 1968), 148.
6. *New Writings by Swinburne*, ed. Cecil Y. Lang (Syracuse: Syracuse University Press, 1964), 70–71.
7. Ezra Pound, *Pavannes and Divagations* (Norfolk, Conn.: New Directions, 1958), 203.
8. Charles Baudelaire, *Oeuvres complètes*, ed. Y.-G. Le Dantec (Paris: Gallimard, 1961), 737.

Chapter IX. Hardy: "A Singer Asleep" and *Poems of 1912–13*

W. H. Auden, "A Literary Transference," *Southern Review* 6 (1940–41), 80. Thomas Hardy, *The Mayor of Casterbridge* (New York: Harper & Row, 1905), 213–14.

1. Quoted in Hugh Kenner, *The Invisible Poet: T. S. Eliot* (New York: McDowell, Obolensky, 1959), 55.
2. For remarks on Hopkins, see chap. VII, n. 32.
3. Thomas Hardy, *The Collected Poems of Thomas Hardy*, 4th ed. (London: Macmillan, 1930), 304–5. Subsequent quotations are from this edition.
4. Hardy actually associated his own fate at the hands of reviewers with that of Swinburne. One critic had written, "Swinburne planteth, Hardy watereth, and Satan giveth the increase." As Hardy recalls, he and Swinburne once "laughed and condoled with each other on having been the two most abused of living writers" (quotations from Ross C. Murfin, *Swinburne, Hardy, Lawrence, and the Burden of Belief* [Chicago: University of Chicago Press, 1978], 82). Murfin writes well of the relation between the two writers, and he includes a brief account of Hardy's visit to Swinburne's grave at Bonchurch—a visit that partly occasioned this elegy. Whereas my turn from "A Singer Asleep" to *Poems of 1912–13* may give the impression that Hardy disengaged quite rapidly from Swinburne's influence, Murfin's study offers a valuable corrective, showing just how qualified and gradual that disengagement was.
5. See above, chap. V.
6. Hardy wrote numerous poems treating of Emma's death. Amongst those not included in *Poems of 1912–13* are the following: (page numbers are from *Collected Poems*) "Something Tapped" (436); "He Prefers Her Earthly" (466); "The Figure in the Scene" and "Why Did I Sketch?" (447); "Old Excursions" (489); "Paths of Former Time" and "The Clock of the Years" (496); "The Shadow on the Stone" (498); "In The Garden" and "The Tree and the Lady" (499); "An

Upbraiding" and "Looking at a Picture on an Anniversary" (501); "The Man Who Forgot" (504); "The Frozen Greenhouse" (698); "Two Lips" (699); "Her Haunting-Ground" (770); "Penance" (596); and "The Last Performance" (457).

7. Even critics who have perceived, or who claim to discuss, the structural pattern of *Poems of 1912–13* do not give an adequate reading of the entire sequence. One exception is William Morgan, who shows how the poems are arranged according to their placement in the distant past, the recent past, and the present and relates this arrangement to the poems' development from blame and expiation to forgiveness and reconciliation ("Form, Tradition, and Consolation in Hardy's *Poems of 1912–13*," *PMLA* 89, no. 3 [May 1974], 496–505). Another exception is William E. Beckler, who points to a "basic movement of Hardy's elegy" and suggests a "mythic subtext" to the series, namely, that of Orpheus and Eurydice (*The Victorian Imagination: Essays in Aesthetic Exploration* [New York: New York University Press, 1980], 297–309). Most recently, the sequence has been read sympathetically and insightfully by M. L. Rosenthal and Sally M. Gall in *The Modern Poetic Sequence: The Genius of Modern Poetry* (New York: Oxford University Press, 1983), 82–95. While these readings have many points of interest, they leave room for an interpretation of the series from a perspective of the genre and of the work of mourning. Irving Howe and J. Hillis Miller have both indicated that the sequence is in fact organized. But their readings, while excellent, are condensed and selective (Irving Howe, *Thomas Hardy* [New York: Macmillan, 1967], 181–86; J. Hillis Miller, *Thomas Hardy: Distance and Desire* [Cambridge, Mass.: Harvard University Press, 1970]). For his comments, particularly on "The Voice" and "After a Journey," F. R. Leavis is a valuable reader (see "Hardy the Poet," *Southern Review* 6 [1940–41], 87–98; and more important, "Reality and Sincerity," *Scrutiny* 19, no. 2 [Winter 1952–53]). For a similar but more extended and more critical appreciation see R. P. Blackmur, "The Shorter Poems of Thomas Hardy," *Southern Review* 6 (1940–41), reprinted in *Form and Value in Modern Poetry* (New York: Doubleday & Anchor, 1957).

   Other studies that I have found particularly helpful include: Paul Zietlow, *Moments of Vision* (Cambridge, Mass.: Harvard University Press, 1974); James E. Richardson, *Thomas Hardy: The Poetry of Necessity* (Chicago: University of Chicago Press, 1977); Dennis Taylor, *Hardy's Poetry, 1860–1928* (New York: Columbia University Press, 1981); Samuel Hynes, *The Pattern of Hardy's Poetry* (Chapel Hill: University of North Carolina Press, 1961); Jean Brooks, *Thomas Hardy: The Poetic Structure* (Ithaca: Cornell University Press, 1971); Murfin, cited in n. 1; Donald Davie, *Thomas Hardy and British Poetry* (London: Routledge & Kegan Paul, 1973); David Perkins, "Hardy and the Poetry of Isolation," *ELH* 26, no. 2 (June 1959), 253–70; and John Bayley, *An Essay on Hardy* (Cambridge: Cambridge University Press, 1978).

8. Miller, 248.

9. Quoted in Taylor, 22.

10. This last point is noticed by Zietlow: "What happened to Hardy after Emma's death is similar to what happens to the lovers in his poems after their first meeting" (191).

11. I differ here from Irving Howe, who claims that Hardy is free from the pride of

"relentless self-accusation" (185). Howe's position has been endorsed by Richardson: "Hardy's regret is not for what he has done or left undone but for the passing of what was good and beautiful" (131).

12. Etymologies given in Webster's *New Collegiate Dictionary*, 1980. For *lame* cf. Tennyson's chastening moment in *In Memoriam* (55): "I stretch lame hands of faith, and grope, / And gather dust and chaff. . . ."

13. Brooks, 83.

14. Precisely because of its suggestion of lost knowledge, or lost "knowingness," I would defend Hardy's revision (of "wistlessness" for "existlessness") against F. R. Leavis's complaint (see *Southern Review* 6, 93).

15. "Does there even a place like Saint-Juliet exist? / Or a Vallency Valley / With stream and leafed alley, / Or Beauty, or Bos with its flounce flinging mist?" (cf. above discussion of "babbling" in Gray's "Elegy" [chap. V]).

16. Hardy did not name the two who had accompanied him and Emma on that summer picnic. This suits well with the poem's general tendency toward isolating the elegist, stripping him here of the brief companionship that has since vanished like an entire age. The two have "wandered far . . . Into urban roar," as though that region were some consuming battleground "where no picnics are." Hardy himself had, in fact, spent much of that summer of 1912 in London, so that the occasion of the picnic might well have been in early June. Of the possible companions, there are in fact two who visited Hardy in June *and* who afterwards returned to the city. Biographers have therefore supposed them to have been the representatives of The Royal Society of Literature, who came out to Max Gate to present Hardy with a gold medal "in recognition of distinguished work on the grand scale."

I am not convinced that these visitors actually went on a picnic with the Hardys. One of them wrote about the visit, making no mention of such an outing and describing instead a rather awkward luncheon at Max Gate. He wrote of their having been inconveniently seated at remote places around the dining table and of feeling that he was "about to play a card game which [he] did not know." While Hardy interrogated him about the architecture of Rome and Venice, Mrs. Hardy fixed her "famous pair of Blue Eyes" on the other guest, giving him "much curious information about two very fine cats, who sat to right and left of her plate on the table itself." This other guest, we are told, looked "like an Eastern Magician overpowered by a Northern witch."

The guest who recorded all this was Sir Henry Newbolt, head of the London School of Economics, as well as editor of the *Tory National Review*, and author of such popular patriotic songs as "Drake's Drum" and "The Fighting Temeraire." "The Eastern Magician" was Yeats. See *The Later Life and Letters of Sir Henry Newbolt*, ed. M. Newbolt (London: Faber & Faber, 1942), 166–68.

Chapter X. Yeats: "In Memory of Major Robert Gregory"

1. Ezra Pound, *Collected Shorter Poems* (London: Faber & Faber, 1952; reprint ed., 1973), 108. The poem at large draws heavily on generic conventions, from its

elegiac epigraph, "Vocat Aestus In Umbram," to its concluding images of Aphrodite (Anadyomene) and in this case reduced or even divided light ("half-watt rays") beneath which "eyes turn topaz." While the poem lacks neither grief nor elegiac anger vengefully directed against corrupt enemies, the poet obviously questions and mocks the elegiac displacement of desire into aesthetic pursuits. At the same time, he protests the passing of true elegiac heroes (Sappho, Dionysus), and seems partly to mourn the loss of an adequate subject ("what gods, man, or hero / Shall I place a tin wreathe upon?"). As with *The Waste Land*, I have chosen not to discuss "Hugh Selwyn Mauberley" because it is not *primarily* occasioned by the death of an individual. Nevertheless, a generic approach would unquestionably shed light on these poems.

2. Cf. Wilfred Owen's "Dulce et Decorum Est," published in the same year as Pound's poem (1920) but written earlier, during the war.

3. As early as 1915, Pound had published the impersonated, frequently elegiac poems in *Cathay*.

4. See most recently, and most comprehensively, James E. Miller, *T. S. Eliot's Personal Waste Land* (University Park: Pennsylvania State University Press, 1977).

5. William Butler Yeats, *The Poems*, ed. Richard J. Finneran (New York: Macmillan, 1983), 155. Subsequent quotations of Yeats's poetry are from this edition, henceforth referred to as *Poems*.

6. William Butler Yeats, *Letters*, ed. Allen Wade (New York: Macmillan, 1955), 600; henceforth referred to as *Letters*.

7. "I do nothing but write verses, and have just finished a long poem in memory of Robert Gregory, which is among my best works" (to J. B. Yeats, 24 June, 1918; *Letters*, 650). Graham Martin calls it "perhaps Yeats's first indisputably great poem" (*"The Wild Swans at Coole,"* in *An Honoured Guest: New Essays on W. B. Yeats*, ed. Denis Donoghue and J. R. Mulryne [New York: St. Martin's Press, 1966], 70). And Peter Ure regards the poem as "Yeats's finest achievement in this particular genre" (*Towards a Mythology* [Liverpool, 1946; New York: Russell & Russell, 1967]). A strong dissenting voice is that of Yvor Winters in *The Poetry of W. B. Yeats* (Denver: A. Swallow, 1960). Other commentaries that I have found particularly helpful include Frank Kermode's outstanding study of the poem in *Romantic Image* (London: Routledge & Kegan Paul, 1957); Marion Witt's scholarly article "The Making of an Elegy: Yeats's 'In Memory of Major Robert Gregory,'" *Modern Philology* 48, no. 2 (November 1950), 112–21; D. J. Gordon, with contributions by Ian Fletcher, Frank Kermode, and Robin Skelton, *W. B. Yeats: Images of a Poet* (Manchester: Manchester University Press, 1961); A. Norman Jeffares, *A Commentary on the Collected Poems of W. B. Yeats* (Stanford: Stanford University Press, 1968); Harold Bloom, *Yeats* (New York: Oxford University Press, 1970); and Thomas Whitaker, *Swan and Shadow: Yeats's Dialogue with History* (Chapel Hill: University of North Carolina Press, 1964). An especially good essay on four other elegies by Yeats is Helen Vendler's "Four Elegies," in *Yeats, Sligo and Ireland: Essays to Mark the 21st. Yeats International Summer School*, ed. A. Norman Jeffares (Totowa, N.J.: Barnes & Noble, 1980). I have chosen not to discuss such poems, since I am con-

centrating, once again, on elegies primarily occasioned by the death of one principal individual.

8. *The Observer,* 17 February 1918; quoted in Kermode, 32–34.

9. See, for example, "Vacillation," "Her Vision in the Wood," "Two Songs for a Play," and "Parnell's Funeral."

10. "The Wild Swans at Coole," "Men Improve with the Years," "The Living Beauty," "A Song," "Lines Written in Dejection."

11. Quoted in Basil Willey, *The Seventeenth-Century Background* (New York: Columbia University Press, 1935; Anchor Books, 1953), 228.

12. Quoted in ibid., 212.

13. Yeats, *Essays and Introductions* (New York: Macmillan, Collier Books, 1968), 521; henceforth referred to in the text as *EI.*

14. Hugh Kenner has instructively compared the stanzas of Yeats and Cowley, in *A Colder Eye: The Modern Irish Writers* (New York: Alfred A. Knopf, 1983), 184–86. One may wonder how Yeats came upon Cowley's poem so opportunely. Perhaps in trying to move beyond the pastoral fictions of "Shepherd and Goatherd" he had recalled Dr. Johnson's attack on "Lycidas," an attack that had included a contrast in favor of Cowley's elegy for Hervey. For comparison with Yeats's stanza, a stanza from Cowley follows:

> Say, for you saw us, ye immortal Lights,
> How oft unweari'd have we spent the Nights?
> Till the Ledaean Stars so fam'd for Love,
> > Wondred at us from above.
> We spent them not in toys, in lusts, or wine;
> > But search of deep Philosophy,
> > Wit, Eloquence, and Poetry,
> Arts which I lov'd, for they, my Friend, were Thine.

(Abraham Cowley, *Poems,* ed. A. R. Waller [Cambridge: Cambridge University Press, 1905], 33).

15. Cf. "The Phases of the Moon," in which Robartes says of the poet in the tower: "He wrote of me in that extravagant style / He had learned from Pater" (*Poems,* 164).

16. "Blood and the Moon," *Poems,* 237.

17. Synge and Pollexfen were both Irish, and both were closely associated for Yeats with his own sense of Irishness. The association with Synge is well known. But Pollexfen, too, was associated for Yeats with "the romance of Ireland" and with the rural imagination—his servant Mary Battle inspired much of Yeats's *Celtic Twilight* ("Much of my *Celtic Twilight* is but her daily speech"). Although not *immediately* of Ireland, Lionel Johnson "belonged to a family that had, he told us, called itself Irish some generations back. . . . He had joined a London Irish Literary Society, attended its committee meetings, and given lectures in London, in Dublin, and in Belfast, on Irish novelists and Irish poetry . . ." (*The Autobiography of William Butler Yeats* [New York: Macmillan, 1938; reprint ed., Collier Books, 1971], 149; henceforth referred to as *A*).

18. "Meditations in Time of Civil War," *Poems*, 201. Cf. also: "The far tower where Milton's Platonist / Sat late, or Shelley's Visionary prince: / The lonely light that Samuel Palmer engraved / An Image of mysterious wisdom won by toil" ("The Phases of the Moon," ibid., 163).
19. *Literary Essays of Ezra Pound*, ed. T. S. Eliot (London: Faber & Faber, 1954), 367.
20. Yeats, *Memoirs: Autobiography—First Draft Journal*, ed. Denis Donoghue (New York: Macmillan, 1973), 35; henceforth referred to as M.
21. The phrase "mirror-resembling dream" is crucial to an understanding of this elegy. It occurs in an illuminating context within Yeats's elegiac "The Tower," where the poet speaks of having "prepared [his] peace / With . . . / All those things whereof / Man makes a superhuman / Mirror-resembling dream" (*Poems*, 199).
22. "To such a tremulous wisp constantly reforming itself on the stream, to a single sharp impression, with a sense in it, a relic more or less fleeting, of such moments gone by, what is real in our life fines itself down. It is with this movement, with the passage and dissolution of impressions, images, sensations, that analysis leaves off—that continual vanishing away, that strange, perpetual weaving and unweaving of ourselves" (Walter Pater, *The Renaissance: Studies in Art and Poetry* [1893], ed. with notes by Donald L. Hill [Berkeley and Los Angeles: University of California Press, 1980], 188).
23. For a good account of Synge's particularly arduous translation of world to text see Kenner, 126–28.
24. Avrom Fleishman has pointed out that this passage serves, too, as an elegiac tribute to Lady Gregory (*Figures of Autobiography: The Language of Self-Writing in Victorian and Modern England* [Berkeley and Los Angeles: University of California Press, 1983], 335–36).
25. Robert Langbaum, *The Mysteries of Identity* (New York: Oxford University Press, 1977), 161. If we think of Socrates' daemon as a form of conscience, we may look ahead to Freud's definition of the superego, which, like Plutarch's daemon, is also made up largely of renounced love-objects, particularly the "illustrious" dead. From this perspective, Yeats's poem performs the elegy's generic task of establishing and submitting to an identification with the totemic, here daemonic, authority of the dead—an authority associated with the elegist's ideal self. Harold Bloom associates the daemon with Freud's imago rather than with the superego; but Freud's account of the latter's genesis and the daemon's antithetically idealized relation to the ego also support the association of daemon with superego (Bloom, 213; Freud, *The Ego and the Id* [1923], trans. Joan Riviere, rev. and ed. James Strachey [New York: Norton, 1960; Norton Library, 1962], chap. 3, "The Ego and the Super-Ego [Ego Ideal]").

   Note: Yeats's own spelling of *daemon* occasionally alters to *daimon*. Apart from actual quotations, I have standardized the spelling as *daemon*.
26. Yeats, *Essays* (London: Macmillan, 1924), 488.
27. "A Prayer for My Daughter," *Poems*, 189.
28. See Witt's article, as well as the commentaries of Kermode, Gordon, Fletcher, and Bloom, all noted in n. 7, above.

29. *Essays*, 486.

30. *Hamlet* 3.1.151.

31. "Sidney is dead, dead is my friend, dead is the world's delight." Fulke-Greville's poem appears under the title "Another of the Same" in the poems following "Astrophel" in Edmund Spenser, *Poetical Works*, ed. E. de Selincourt (Oxford: Oxford University Press, 1912; reprint ed., 1969), 559.

32. Cf. Yeats to Lady Gregory, 4 January 1918: "You will be astonished at the change in my work, at its intricate passion" (*Letters*, 644).

33. "Lapis Lazuli," *Poems*, 294.

34. In "Shepherd and Goatherd" Yeats wrote of Gregory's having "put his heart into some game" (ibid., 144).

35. "Two Songs from a Play" (ibid., 213).

36. Apart from its archaic sources, Yeats's image was perhaps approached by Swinburne in "Cor Cordium," his epitaphic prayer to Shelley: "O heart whose beating blood was living song" (*The Complete Works of Algernon Charles Swinburne*, ed. Sir Edmund Gosse and Thomas James Wise, Bonchurch Edition, 20 vols. [London: William Heinemann, 1925], 2:233).

37. W. H. Auden, "In Memory of W. B. Yeats," *Collected Shorter Poems, 1927–1957* (London: Faber & Faber, 1966; reprint ed., 1969), 141.

Epilogue: The English Elegy after Yeats; a Note on the American Elegy

1. See for example Philippe Ariès, *Western Attitudes to Death: From the Middle Ages to the Present*, trans. Patricia Ranum (Baltimore: Johns Hopkins University Press, 1974); idem, *The Hour of Our Death*, trans. Helen Weaver (New York: Random House, 1982); Geoffrey Gorer, *Death, Grief, and Mourning in Contemporary Britain* (London: Cresset Press, 1965); Elisabeth Kubler-Ross, *On Death and Dying* (New York: Macmillan, 1969); Jessica Mitford, *The American Way of Death* (New York: Simon & Schuster, 1963); Jacques Choron, *Death and Western Philosophy* (New York: Macmillan, Collier Books, 1963); and Herman Feifel, ed., *The Meaning of Death* (New York: McGraw Hill, 1959).

2. Seamus Heaney, *Poems, 1965–1975* (New York: Farrar, Straus, Giroux, 1975), 171.

3. Quoted in Richard Ellmann, *The Identity of Yeats* (London, 1954; reprint ed., London: Faber & Faber, 1964), 231–32.

4. William Butler Yeats, *The Poems*, ed. Richard Finneran (New York: Macmillan, 1983), 326.

5. Ezra Pound, *Pavannes and Divagations* (Norfolk, Conn.: New Directions, 1958), 228.

6. Lawrence I. Lipking, *The Life of the Poet: Beginning and Ending Poetic Careers* (Chicago: University of Chicago Press, 1981), 151–60.

7. This and following quotations from Auden's "In Memory of W. B. Yeats" are taken from W. H. Auden, *Collected Shorter Poems, 1927–1957* (London: Faber &

Faber, 1966; reprint ed., 1969), 141–43. Citations of other poems by Auden will be from this edition, henceforth referred to as *CSP*.

8. "In Memory of Sigmund Freud," *CSP*, 166–70; "In Memory of Ernst Toller," ibid., 144–45; "At the Grave of Henry James," ibid., 197–99.

9. "To T. S. Eliot on His Sixtieth Birthday. (1948)," ibid., 275.

10. Even the more private elegy for Auden's Austrian housekeeper, Emma Eiermann, repeats the image of the reproved child, portrays the dead woman as a protector of the fruit and flowers, coaxes an abiding image of her shyness, protectiveness, and chaste affection, and finally utters a benediction in *her* language, as if to emphasize the elegist's homage to her, as well as his submission to a language not his own (*City Without Walls* [London: Faber & Faber, 1969], 27–29).

11. Wilfred Owen, *Collected Poems*, ed. C. Day Lewis (London: Chatto & Windus, 1964), 44.

12. Edward Thomas, *Collected Poems* (London: Selwyn & Blount, 1920; reprint ed., New York: W. W. Norton, 1974), 23.

13. Edith Sitwell, "Dirge for the New Sunrise," *The Canticle of the Rose: Poems, 1917–1949* (New York: Vanguard, 1949), 270.

14. Dylan Thomas, *The Poems of Dylan Thomas*, ed. Daniel Jones (New York: New Directions Press, 1971), 192.

15. Geoffrey Hill, *Somewhere Is Such a Kingdom: Poems, 1952–1971* (Boston: Houghton Mifflin, 1975), 11; henceforth cited as *Kingdom*.

16. Although Hill substitutes a bird of prey for Milton's "dovelike" power, we recall how that power "mad'st [the abyss] pregnant" and how Milton called on it to "illumine" his own darkness that he might "assert Eternal Providence, / And justify the ways of God to men" (*Paradise Lost* 1.21–25). The precise elements of the allusion are themselves thus extremely appropriate to Hill's elegy, concerned as it is with ongoing creativity and with the justification of mortal loss.

17. Geoffrey Hill, *Tenebrae* (Boston: Houghton Mifflin, 1979), 39.

18. Unfortunately, Hill's long elegiac poem, *The Mystery of the Charity of Charles Péguy*, has appeared too recently for inclusion even in the very cursory observations above. *The Mystery* is a magnificent, deeply generic work—one that pursues several motifs noticed above, even while carrying them to a new amplitude. With a continued but less exclusive bleakness, individual sacrifice and mass slaughter are now situated in a persuasively registered context of pastoral beauty, of strong regional and ancestral piety, and of a religious grace associated with imagery of pilgrimage and medieval sacred sculpture. The entire poem is marked by a passionate reverence in which "sweetness devours sorrow." Hill's title and stanzaic form in themselves pay allusive homage to Péguy, as do his uses of quotation and translation. Emerging from the carnage of history, the figure of Péguy is celebrated as that of an exemplary soul, revealed in "the triumph of his 'defeat'" and praised to the end in a language that is and is not singularly Hill's: "Take that for your example! But still mourn, / being so moved: éloge and elegy / so moving on the scene as if to

cry / 'in memory of those things these words were born.'" Repeating yet revising a line of Marcel Raymond's account of Péguy's poetry and of the poet's pilgrimage to Chartres, Hill closes here with an elegiac image of the memorializing birth of the poet's language itself. (*The Mystery of the Charity of Charles Péguy* [New York: Oxford University Press, 1984], 32.)

Geoffrey Hill's are not the only contemporary English elegies worth studying. J. H. Prynne's "Es Lebe der König" for Paul Celan (in Prynne's collection, *Brass* [London: Ferry Press, 1971], 32–33) is a noteworthy example. George Barker's elegy "To John Berryman," (in *Dialogues Etc* [London: Faber & Faber, 1976], 17–19) is another example—a poem replete with familiar motifs of martyrdom, Jovian rule, rejected surmise, the spirit of preceding voices, the universalizing renaming of the dead, and reference to the surviving powers of the elegist. So, too, are several elegies by the Irish poets John Montague and Seamus Heaney. The latter's "Elegy" (for Robert Lowell) and "In Memoriam Sean O'Riada" are particularly fine examples of poems that both mourn and celebrate an artist, while his "The Strand at Lough Beg" and "Casualty" have the uncommon ability to grieve effectively both for particular individuals and for the political situation surrounding their death (Seamus Heaney, *Field Work* [New York: Farrar, Straus, Giroux, 1979]). In each of these poems, an application of our generic approach would find much of interest.

19. Emily Dickinson, *The Poems of Emily Dickinson*, 3 vols., ed. Thomas H. Johnson (Cambridge, Mass.: Harvard University Press, Belknap Press, 1958), poems numbered 1695 ("polar privacy") and 49 ("Burglar").

20. Robert Lowell, "For the Union Dead," in *Selected Poems*, rev. ed. (New York: Farrar, Straus, Giroux, 1977), 135.

21. I do not mean to suggest that the Puritans were opposed to writing elegies. Indeed, the elegy was one of the dominant genres in Puritan literature. But the attitude toward grief and mourning was one of severe rationalization—both in the sense of justifying bereavement and in the practice of such rigidly formal schemas as those of anagram and acrostic. See, for example, David Stannard, *The Puritan Way of Death* (New York: Oxford University Press, 1977); and Larzer Ziff, *Puritanism in America: New Culture in a New World* (New York: Viking, 1973).

22. William Vaughn Moody, "An Ode in Time of Hesitation," *The Poems and Plays of William Vaughn Moody*, ed. J. M. Manly, 2 vols. (Boston: Houghton Mifflin & Co., 1912), 1: 15–25; Allen Tate, "Ode to the Confederate Dead" and Tate's discussion of the poem in "Narcissus as Narcissus," *The Man of Letters in the Modern World* (New York: Meridian Books, 1955), 332–45; Theodore Roethke, *Collected Poems* (New York: Doubleday, 1966), 102.

23. Walt Whitman, *Collected Poetry and Prose*, ed. Justin Kaplan (New York: Viking, 1982), 671. Subsequent citations of Whitman's poetry will be from this edition, henceforth cited as *CPP*.

24. Sylvia Plath, *The Collected Poems*, ed. Ted Hughes (New York: Harper & Row, 1981), 224; John Berryman, Dream Song 156 in *His Toy, His Dream, His Rest* (London: Faber & Faber, 1969), 85.

25. We have, of course, seen variants of the elegist as child in English elegies, for example, in *In Memoriam* (124). More recently, see Heaney's "Elegy": "you found the child in me / when you took farewells" (*Field Work*, 32).

26. Wallace Stevens, "The Owl in the Sarcophagus," *The Collected Poems of Wallace Stevens* (New York: Knopf, 1954), 436. Subsequent citations of this poem are from this edition.

27. Allen Grossman, *Of the Great House* (New York: New Directions Books, 1982), 27. In addition, at a more literal level the American elegy includes many more poems on the death of actual parents than does the English elegy. From the poem that is surely among its first examples, Anne Bradstreet's elegy for her father, to the more contemporary works by such poets as Plath, Lowell, Berryman, Warren, Bidart, Grossman, and Clampitt, to name only some, American poets have created an almost unique tradition of elegies occasioned by the death of a parent.

28. This and following citations of "When Lilacs Last in the Dooryard Bloom'd" are from *CPP*, 459–67.

29. Cf. "There Was a Child Went Forth" (1855): "There was a child went forth every day, / And the first object he look'd upon, that object he became, / And that object became part of him for the day or a certain part of the day, / Or for many years or stretching cycles of years. / The early lilacs became part of this child" (*CPP*, 491).

30. Citations of the poem will be from *Selected Poems*, 66–71. For readings of the poem see Hugh B. Staples, *Robert Lowell: The First Twenty Years* (London: Faber & Faber, 1962), 77–81; Marjorie G. Perloff, *The Poetic Art of Robert Lowell* (Ithaca: Cornell University Press, 1973), 145–53; and Stephen Yenser, *Circle to Circle: The Poetry of Robert Lowell* (Berkeley and Los Angeles: University of California Press, 1975), 136–45.

31. Elizabeth Bishop's "First Death in Nova Scotia" includes a similar association between royal portraits, stuffed birds, and a father figure: "In the cold, cold parlor / my mother laid out Arthur / beneath the chromographs: / Edward, Prince of Wales, / with Princess Alexandra, / and King George with Queen Mary. / Below them on the table / stood a stuffed loon / shot and stuffed by Uncle / Arthur, Arthur's father" (*The Complete Poems, 1927–1979* [New York: Farrar, Straus, Giroux, 1983], 125. Cf. also Roethke, "My Papa's Waltz," *Collected Poems*, 45; and Robert Penn Warren's elegiac "There's a Grandfather's Clock in the Hall," *Selected Poems, 1923–75* [New York: Random House, 1976], 65–66).

32. *Circle to Circle*, 143.

33. This last description includes a brushed horse, a putty face, a blue jay's tail, and the top of a milk bottle—a further instance of how Lowell revises generic stereotypes even while he preserves this particular compound figure's necessary blend of powerlessness and talismanic, animated force.

34. Citations of "A Procession at Candlemas" are from Amy Clampitt, *The Kingfisher* (New York: Knopf, 1983), 22–28.

35. One may argue that Clampitt is not focusing on the chastening fate of *any* deity or figure of originally sexual power; rather she is pointing to the way in

which an early male culture revised the figure of Athene, superseding a (therefore wizened and recessive) goddess of fertility by the purified goddess of wisdom. The career of Athene would thus seem to bear the mark of a culture's movement from values of motherhood and female sexual power to those of an oppressively purified reason or wisdom. When not located *within* the altering career of Athene, this change is usually regarded as having been reflected in the male culture's substitution of Athene (as wisdom) for a prior figure such as Demeter (as the mother or fertility). Indeed the ceremony described by Clampitt for the obscured figure of Athene resembles those for Demeter. But even before her replacement by Athene, Demeter's power had existed only in relation to her periodically chastening loss of fertility or omnipotence—her loss of Persephone, her suffering of Hades' intervention. As in the recession from Zeus to Cronus to Uranus, it seems that one can never return to an absolute, unchastened figure of sexual power. Clampitt's poem should therefore be seen as seeking to accept only the chastening or wizening that must occur within the logic of figuration (and within the work of mourning) but *not* within the exercised prejudices of a male culture.

36. The earlier description of the journey included a conjuring of natural and cultural ceremonies, a reference to and criticism of a version of the mirror stage ("mirroring / an entity that cannot look into itself and know / what makes it what it is"), and an instance of the evasion and proving of the reality of death.

37. Earlier, Clampitt described Athene as "born—it's declared— / of some man's brain like every other pure idea."

38. Dream Songs 154, 155, *His Toy, His Dream, His Rest,* 83–84.

39. James Merrill, *The Changing Light at Sandover* (New York: Atheneum, 1982), 85; Peter Sacks, "The Divine Translation: Elegiac Aspects of *The Changing Light at Sandover,*" in *James Merrill: Essays in Criticism,* ed. David Lehman and Charles Berger (Ithaca: Cornell University Press, 1983), 159–85.

40. See the commentary by Charles S. Singleton in *Purgatorio: Text and Commentary,* Bollingen Series, 80. (Princeton: Princeton University Press, 1973), 454.

41. Amy Clampitt, "The Dakota," *The Kingfisher,* 29.

42. Jonathan Swift, "Verses on the Death of Dr. Swift," *Poetical Works,* ed. Herbert Davis (London: Oxford University Press, 1967), 506; Sir John Denham, "On Mr. Abraham Cowley: His Death and Burial amongst the Ancient Poets," *The Poetical Works of Sir John Denham,* ed. Theodore H. Banks, Jr. (New Haven: Yale University Press, 1928), 150.

43. Merrill, *The Changing Light at Sandover,* 335, 263.

44. *Collected Poems,* 432–44.

45. *Complete Poems,* 188.

46. *Collected Poems,* 432.

Index

Index

Index

Peter M. Sacks teaches English at the Johns Hopkins University. He is the author of several articles on English and American poetry and of *In These Mountains*, a book of poetry.